SERVICE AND THE ART OF HOSPITALITY

Creating a Dining Experience

JOHNSON & WALES
UNIVERSITY

Johnson & Wales University

Project Manager: Dr. Paul J. McVety

Associate Editor: Debra Bettencourt

Associate Project Manager: John Chiaro

Associate Project Manager: Edward Korry

Associate Project Manager: Dr. Bradley J. Ware

Senior Editor: Dr. Claudette Lévesque Ware

Photographer: Ron Manville

This book was printed and bound by Imago in Singapore

JOHNSON & WALES
U N I V E R S I T Y

10 9 8 7 6 5 4 3 2

ISBN 13: 978-0-9742491-1-7
ISBN 10: 0-9742491-1-4

Contents

This book is dedicated to Chef Robert Nograd, Dean Emeritus and former Corporate Executive Chef for Johnson & Wales University, whose contributions to Johnson & Wales and the culinary profession span the last 50 years.

Chef Nograd is a concentration camp survivor who vowed that he would never know the pain of hunger or thirst again. He dedicated himself to his profession throughout his extraordinary journey – never losing his thirst for knowledge or his hunger to become a world-class master chef.

His commitment to educating others in his art and in his craft as well as his quest to leave a legacy for future culinarians have resulted in a life spent teaching and learning, never content to settle for the status quo. In so doing, he has left an indelible mark on the lives of many past, present, and future chefs.

It is because of his personal generosity and willingness to share his knowledge, his countless contributions to culinary education, and his inspiration to culinarians around the globe that we dedicate this book to Robert Nograd, C.M.C.

WITH PROFOUND RESPECT,

THE FACULTY, STUDENTS, ADMINISTRATION, AND ALUMNI OF JOHNSON & WALES UNIVERSITY

DEAR STUDENT,

The College of Culinary Arts of Johnson & Wales University is committed to your success as a future food service professional. Our revised culinary arts curriculum is a reflection of this commitment. This carefully designed, flexible curriculum provides you with an exciting challenge to learn and to excel in your chosen career.

Johnson & Wales University delivers a multidisciplinary educational experience for driven students who are serious about success and seeking a competitive edge. JWU was the first to offer a four-year Culinary Arts degree in 1993, the first to offer a four-year Baking & Pastry Degree in 1997, and the first to offer a bachelor's degree in Culinary Nutrition in 1999. A JWU education integrates rigorous academics and professional skills, related work experiences, leadership opportunities, career services and our unique experiential education model. Students graduate from our university with the knowledge and skills necessary to achieve success in a global economy. Opportunities for practical and cooperative education complement laboratory and related classroom studies and provide valuable on-the-job experiences.

Your formal education in culinary arts is only the beginning of your lifelong study. However, this education is the foundation upon which your future will be built; a foundation established by *Culinary Fundamentals* and *Service and the Art of Hospitality: Creating a Dining Experience*. From these texts you will learn that food and beverage service is a multifaceted field that is constantly growing and changing to respond to the needs and desires of the customer. In studying the fundamentals, you will learn the facts and theories of preparation and presentation. These fundamentals will prepare you to explore, discover, and create your own food frontiers.

The faculty and staff of the College of Culinary Arts have dedicated countless hours on these texts. They bring their passion for their craft and years of knowledge and experience to the development of this curriculum. I encourage you to take advantage of this combined wisdom. Within the covers of *Culinary Fundamentals* and *Service and the Art of Hospitality: Creating a Dining Experience* you will discover a truly enjoyable learning experience.

JOHN J. BOWEN '77
UNIVERSITY PRESIDENT & C.E.O.

KARL GUGGENMOS
UNIVERSITY DEAN OF CULINARY EDUCATION

Over 40 years ago I selected a career in culinary arts, and to this day, I have never regretted my choice. The numerous opportunities afforded me in this field have been both professionally and personally rewarding. As you embark on your culinary education journey, I ask you to remember that "the choices you make determine the kind of life you lead".

Johnson & Wales' culinary program offers an "education without compromise" that will empower you to achieve in a competitive global market. This broad, hands-on, experientially-based, and globally-minded education will allow you to successfully compete in the 21st century workplace. I encourage you to take full advantage of the resources available so that you might build upon this solid foundation to achieve professional readiness.

Out textbooks, *Culinary Fundamentals* and *Service and the Art of Hospitality: Creating a Dining Experience*, are two of the tools that will provide you with the knowledge necessary in this great profession. It is a valuable collective resource created by talented professionals, faculty and administrators. Whether you pursue employment as an executive chef at a fine dining establishment or at a prestigious hotel, or elect to own a business, you will find that the contents of these texts will be invaluable.

Numerous knowledgeable individuals have collaborated to produce this very current and easy to use resource. They have invested their time in creating books that you will come to appreciate and value. A special thanks to Dr. Paul McVety and his team who spearheaded this project and to all the culinary professionals and writers involved in making these texts a success.

DEAN KARL GUGGENMOS,
M.B.A., A.A.C., WACS GLOBAL MASTER CHEF

Acknowledgements

WEEK OF WELCOME: CHECK – IN CARD

NAME:	**Scheliga**, Thomas	STUDENT ID #:	J01891687
.Major:	CULA	Email Address:	TJS687@students.jwu.edu

Please review this card carefully; it indicates 'holds' you may have on your account. If a 'hold' is indicated in the **hold indicator column** on the left hand side, you will need to visit that office to release the hold. All holds must be released prior to being allowed to move into the residence hall or attend orientation activities.

Admissions   Location: School of Arts & Sciences

Hold Indicator	Type of Hold
	Verify Final Grades Received

Student Academic & Financial Services   Location: Academic Center 1st Level Student Academic & Financial Services

Hold Indicator	Type of Hold	Hold Released
	Perkins Loan MPN (AL)	
	Entrance Interview (EI)	
	Financial Aid (AH) Reason:	
	Financial Planning Hold (F1, F2, F3, F4) Reason:	
	Stafford Loan MPN (MP)	

Health Services Hold   Location: School of Arts & Sciences, 1st Level

Hold Indicator	Type of Hold	Hold Released
	Health Services Hold (HS)	

Work-Study Placement   Location: Academic Center, Ground Level DENACA085

Hold Indicator	Type of Hold	Hold Released
	Work-Study Placement *(eligible students only)*	

Placement Testing – Requirements   Location: Academic Center, Ground Level - Library

Do you need to participate in placement testing for Math and English?	NO REQUIRED	

Additional Task to Complete   Location

Residence Hall Move-In	Assigned Residence Hall
Microfridge Rental	Behind Student Center
Student ID	Student Center: 2nd Floor
Parking Permit	Academic Center: Legacy Hall, Ground Level
Schedule Assistance (Transfer Credit, UCONNECT, Schedule Changes)	Academic Center: Center for Academic Support, 1st Level
Culinary Uniform Distribution *(College of Culinary Arts Only)*	Student Center: Bookstore
E-mail Assistance / Wireless Network Connection	Academic Center: Center for Academic Support, 1st Level
IKON Mailbox Key	Academic Center, Ground Level Atrium
Commuter Meal Plan	Academic Center: Legacy Hall, Ground Level
Student Handbook Review	**Visit the following link:** www.jwu.edu/denver/studentlife

JOHNSON & WALES
U N I V E R S I T Y

DENVER CAMPUS

Memo

To:	**All Resident Students**
From:	**Michael Eaton** **Director of Campus Safety & Security**
Date:	**September 1, 2010**
Re:	**Project ID**

Dear Students:

The Campus Safety Department is offering a crime prevention program this year called "Project ID." This program gives resident students the ability to document personal property information with the Campus Safety Department in the event an item is lost, found, or stolen. This form will be kept on file throughout the academic year to assist Campus Safety with identifying potential owners of found property. This information will also be available to Campus Safety in the event an item is reported missing.

Please document all property on the attached spreadsheet that contains a serial number or is valued at $500.00 or more. Documented property should include items such as laptop computers, televisions, portable electronic devices, and high valued jewelry. Please don't include clothing items, books, and other miscellaneous property. All forms should be turned into the Student Affairs Office located on the 2nd floor of the College of Business.

This program is a crime prevention tool only and does not replace any recommended procedures for property protection. Students are encouraged to always secure personal property and to keep their residence hall room door locked at all times. The university is not liable for lost, stolen, or damaged property on campus.

Thank you for your participation in our Project ID program.

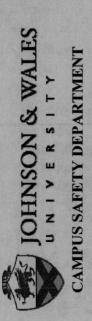

JOHNSON & WALES
U N I V E R S I T Y

CAMPUS SAFETY DEPARTMENT

PROJECT ID WORKSHEET

Description of item (IE: iPod, TV. Xbox etc.)	Serial Number	Value (Actual Purchase Value, not estimated)

Student Name: _____

J# _____

Residence: (Circle One)   Wales Hall   Johnson Hall   Presidents Hall   Triangolo Hall   Gaebe Hall

Room# _____

Acknowledgements

Professionals who truly love educating students have written *Culinary Fundamentals* and *Service and the Art of Hospitality: Creating a Dining Experience.* I wish to thank all the faculty members, administration, students, and friends from the University for their support and participation in this tremendous undertaking.

DR. PAUL McVETY
DEAN CULINARY ACADEMICS
PROJECT MANAGER

A special thanks to Debra Bettencourt, John Chiaro, Edward Korry, Dr. Bradley J. Ware, and Dr. Claudette Lévesque Ware for their tireless efforts and dedication in producing these textbooks.

Educational Task Force

DR. PAUL McVETY
Project Manager

DEBRA BETTENCOURT
Associate Editor

JOHN CHIARO
Associate Project Manager

EDWARD KORRY
Associate Project Manager

DR. ROBERT NOGRAD
Associate Project Manager

DR. BRADLEY J. WARE
Associate Project Manager

DR. CLAUDETTE LÉVESQUE WARE
Senior Editor

Principal Contributing Writer

Edward Korry

Photographs

John Chiaro

Marc DeMarchena

Ciril Hitz

Edward Korry

Photographer

Ron Manville

Alumni and Restaurants

Gracie's – *Chef Joseph Hafner*

Persimmon – *Chef / Owner Champe Speidel*

Siena - *Chef / Owner Anthony Tarro*

Educational Reviewers

Maria Barone	*Reggie Dow*	*Jennifer Pereira*
Thomas Choice	*Marcella Giannasio*	*Linda Pettine*
Michelle Couture	*Katrina Herold*	*Thomas J. Provost*
Elaine Cwynar	*Peter Kelly*	
Marc DeMarchena	*Karin Lucier*	

Student Reviewers

Megan Asselin	*Gayle Hutton*	*Hauke J. Pohl*
Allyson Dwyer	*Sarah Irwin*	*Charles Reed*
Peter Fisher	*Jesse Jackson*	*Santosh Shanbhag*
Michelle Garner	*Jacqueline Keich*	*Peter Spadaro*
Amorette Hinely	*Ji Yea Kim*	
Jalissa Horton	*Michael Paris*	

The College of Culinary Arts Educational Task Force would like to thank the College of Culinary Arts Deans and faculty members for their ongoing support.

Deans

KEVIN DUFFY
Dean Providence Campus

JORGE DE LA TORRE
Dean Denver Campus

PAMELA PETERS
Assistant Dean Providence Campus

MARK ALLISON
Dean Charlotte Campus

BRUCE OZGA
Dean North Miami Campus

WANDA CROPPER
Assistant Dean International Baking & Pastry Institute Charlotte Campus

Faculty

Allison Acquisto	Johannes Busch	Robert Epskamp
Jeff Adel	Michael Calenda	Amy Felder
Michael Angelo	Victor Calise	Jim Flader
Michael Angnardo	Brian Campbell	Gian Flores
Schellie Andrews	Tim Cameron	Paula Figoni
Charles Armstrong	John Chiaro	James Fuchs
Max Ariza	Kimberly Christensen	Jennifer Gallagher
John Aukstolis	Kristen Cofrades	Marcella Giannasio
Adrian Barber	Thomas Choice	Dorothy Gilbert
Ed Batten	Jerry Comar	Armin Gronert
Susan Batten	Cynthia Coston	Frederick Haddad
Joseph Benedetto	Kevin Crawley	Christina Harvey
Alan Bergman	Elaine Cwynar	Mark Harvey
Claudia Berube	David Dawson	James Hensley
Dr. Patricia Blenkiron	Mark DeNittis	Peter Henkel
Dedra Blount	Marc DeMarchena	Katrina Herold
Paul Bolinger	Richard DeMaria	Gilles Hezard
Marina Brancely	Jean-Luc Derron	Rainer Hienerwadel
Drue Brandenburg	Birch DeVault	Ciril Hitz
Robert Brener	Paul DeVries	Helene Houde-Trzcinski
Donald Brizes	John Dion	Jeremy Houghton
Timothy Brown	Kim Dolan	William Idell
Christoph Bruehwiler	Roger Dywer	Steven Johansson
Wayne Bryan	Dr. Mary Ann Eaton	John Kacala
Frances Burnett	Valerie Ellsworth	Peter Kelly

Linda Kender

Kerstin Kleber

Juergen Knorr

Mika Kochi

Kevin Kopsick

Edward Korry

Marcia Kramer

Jean-Louis Lagalle

Lawrence LaCastra

Jerry Lanuzza

Ron Lavallee

Dean Lavornia

Alan Lazar

Carrie Leonard

Alex Leuzzi

Robert Lucier

Michael Makuch

Paul Malcolm

Michael Marra

Dr. Susan Marshall

Deborah Marsella

Theodore McCall

Ray McCue

Kevin Messal

Ashley McGee

Richard Miscovich

Valeria Molinelli

Kim Montello

Dr. Mary Etta Moorachian

Francis Mullaney

Maureen Nixon

James O'Hara

Raymond Olobri

George O'Palenick

Neath Pal

Yves Payraudeau

Shane Pearson

Harry Peemoeller

Ronald Pehoski

Robert Pekar

Jennifer Pereira

David Petrone

Linda Pettine

Craig Piermarini

Maureen Pothier

Thomas J. Provost

CharLee Puckett

Catherine Rabb

Margaret Rauch

Joseph Peter Reinhart

David Ricci

Rolando Robledo

Ronda Robotham

Colin Roche

Joshua Rosenbaum

Robert Ross

Janet Rouslin

Roger Ruch

Adam Sacks

Stephen Scaife

Robin Schmitz

Bernhard Schrag

Louis Serra

Todd Seyfarth

Victor Smurro

Mark Soliday

Mitch Stamm

Gill Stansfield

Carrie Stebbins

Rhonda Stewart

Eric Stein

Heath Stone

Robin Stybe

Marleen Swanson

Frank Terranova

Fred Tiess

Todd Tonova

Lynn Tripp

Peter Vaillancourt

Suzanne Vieira

Alonzo Villarreal

Jean-Michel Vienne

Chris Wagner

Dr. Bradley Ware

Dieter Wenninger

Robert Weill

Gary Welling

Dr. Patricia Wilson

Kenneth Wollenberg

John Woolley

Emmerich Zach

Robert Zielinski

Russ Zito

American Metal Craft, Inc.

Aveleda

Bacardi

Banfi Vintners

Beam Global

Buzzards Bay Brewing Company

Candle Lamp Company

Cardinal International

Carlisle Food Service Products

Castello Banfi

Chateau Ste. Michelle Wine Estates

Cintas Corporation

Classic Wine Imports

Consejo Regulador de los Vinos de Jerez-Xérès-Sherry

Coors Brewing Company

Dinker Ackerlacker

Dogfish Craft Brewing Company

Domaine de Canton

Dudson USA

E&J Gallo Winery

Firestone Walker Brewing Company

Franziskaner

George Howell Coffee Company

Grand Marnier

Hatco Corporation

Homer Laughlin China Company

Illy USA

InterMetro Industries, Inc.

JB Prince Company

Kobrand Corporation

Louis Jadot

Magnuson Group

Maison St-Germain

Moët Hennessy USA

Nestor Wine Imports

Numi Tea

Oneida Ltd.

P.J. Valckenberg

Pasternak Wine Imports

POSitouch

Quady Winery

Robert Mondavi Winery

Rodney Strong Vineyards

Sierra Nevada Brewing Company

Smart Candle Worldwide

Steelite International

Stoelzle USA

Tablecraft Products Company

The Vollrath Company, LLC

Trinchero Family Estates

Vita-Mix Corporation

Waring Products, Inc.

SERVICE *is a critical ingredient in a restaurant's recipe for success. Guests often have different expectations of service, depending on the type of establishment they visit. Cleanliness, consistency, and friendly, competent service may bring customers back to fast food restaurants; but, the expectations of service are much higher for fine dining establishments. In addition to delicious food and elegant décor, guests expect service that enhances the fine dining experience. Service goes far beyond the mechanics or procedures for delivering food and beverage to guests. It reflects an ethos of professionalism; encompasses the highest level of civility; exhibits a passionate respect for the food and beverages served; and is imbued with the spirit of hospitality.*

Service is a term that has been overused and oversold by service oriented industries that advertise the great service they provide, but all too often fail to deliver. It is no wonder that today's consumers frequently view the term "service" cynically. Do most consumers recognize great service when they receive it? Yes. Today's consumer is more sophisticated due to an increased exposure to brands; the media attention given them; and the number and level of experiences they have previously enjoyed. The consumer perceives service as more than a perfunctory greeting such as 'thank you' or 'have a nice day'. Although most consumers cannot list all the elements that contribute to great service; they can certainly identify the feeling and sense of caring that is silently transmitted from server to guest.

In addition to delivering a product in a professional way, service *conveys the feeling to guests that the 'server' is there for them. It also transmits the belief that the server will do whatever it takes to ensure that they receive what was 'promised'; and will work to create an 'experience' that makes them feel special. Such is the Art of Hospitality.*

Quality Service

Although the components of service may seem intangible, poor service can drive away customers, even if the rest of the dining experience is excellent. Conversely, service may bring guests back to an establishment that has otherwise disappointed them.

Servers need to be aware of these service components:

- SMILING
- EYE CONTACT WITH THE GUEST
- REACHING OUT HOSPITABLY TO EVERY GUEST
- VIEWING EVERY GUEST AS SPECIAL
- INVITING GUESTS TO RETURN
- CREATING A WARM ENVIRONMENT
- EXCEEDING GUESTS' EXPECTATIONS

Servers can only understand how to exceed guests' expectations, by first examining what those expectations might be. Servers must have a solid understanding of table manners, civility, and dining etiquette, to provide quality service that exceeds guests' expectations. Since all guests have different expectations, the art of hospitality includes the ability to "read the guest".

Table Manners

Table manners change with the times but are an essential component of civility. Most people are offended by behaviors that are perceived as unwelcome or inappropriate, such as individuals chewing food with the mouth wide open. The sight of food being masticated by someone fails terribly in enhancing the dining experience of other guests.

Table manners are inseparable from civility. They exist out of consideration for the feelings and sensibilities of others, and a respect for their environment and the food they are consuming. Social manners are also essential skills that must be mastered by individuals selecting the hospitality industry as their profession. It is debatable whether these traits are innate or learned, but with proper training and coaching the majority of people do have the potential to become good hosts.

Since early times, civility and manners have been essential in establishing a community of trust in which people might live and peacefully share a meal together. A mastery of table manners also allows individuals to feel more comfortable in a social setting because they are aware of everyone's expectations. The chart that follows includes a list of *table manners;* behavior that is considered acceptable or unacceptable by most in today's society.

While table manners are important for servers to recognize as part of the dining etiquette, it is important to remember that there are considerable differences in acceptable table manners throughout the world. In today's global village, it is necessary to have a knowledge of the table manners of other cultures so as not to be judgmental when eating with, or serving those of these cultures. Eating with the hands, for example, is acceptable in many societies. In much of the world, eating finger foods using the left hand is seen as unacceptable because the left hand is associated with toilet activities. In this country we eat with both hands, which may seem revolting to those where the habit of eating with the left hand is taboo. Belching at the table is not only viewed as acceptable in some Asian countries, but is considered a sign of appreciation for the food just consumed. In the United States, such an act would be perceived as rude. There are also differences in the eating styles and table manners of Western and Eastern cultures.

Appropriate	Inappropriate
Pull out chairs for other guests, in particular for ladies and elders	Sitting down without consideration for others
Put cell phones on vibrate or turned off—never used at the table—in an emergency excuse oneself to take a call	Answering phone calls at the table
Sit straight, with hands on the lap or on the edge of the table. Allow server room to serve and clear	Leaning back in one's seat or slouching on the table
Rest forearms on the table if necessary	Placing arms or elbows on the table
Place and leave the napkin on the lap. Fold and place it to the side when leaving the table	Leaving the napkin on the table while seated
Make eye contact when approached by a server	Failing to address the server and making eye contact
Speak clearly and politely when addressing a server or guest	Mumbling or muttering when responding
Leave the placement of china, flatware, and glassware where it is originally positioned by the server unless in use or if you are left handed	Moving the placement of glassware, china or flatware, especially when finished with the item
Politely ask the person next to you to pass something that is out of reach, such as the salt shaker	Reaching across the table for any reason
Hold stemware by the stem; a base glass by its base	Grabbing a stemmed glass by the bowl or a base glass at the top of the glass
Use the appropriate utensils for each course	Using a knife to put food in the mouth
Use sip sticks, stirrers or straws for stirring or sipping and set aside if not needed on a bread and butter plate	Sticking fingers in a glass or chewing on sip sticks
Hold coffee and tea cups using the handle	Gripping a coffee or tea cup with the whole hand
Sip a beverage	Gulping or slurping a beverage
Offer the person seated next to you bread, butter or a condiment before serving yourself	Serving oneself bread from a bread basket or butter or another condiment without first offering these to others
Wait to eat until all at the table are served	Start eating before everyone has been served
Always taste food before adding seasoning	Add salt and or pepper before tasting the food
Cut or slice foods to an appropriate bite size one mouthful at a time	Placing too much or too large a piece of food on the fork or precutting all food before eating
Scoop food away from you	Scoop food towards you
Let very hot food cool down on its own	Blowing on hot food to cool it off
Remove grape pips, fruit stones, olive pits, fish bones, or gristle using the fork or napkin	Spitting out pips, fruit stones etc., onto a plate
Chew with the mouth closed and only speak when food is not present in the mouth	Chewing with the mouth open or speaking with a mouth full of food
Avoid noisy scraping of the plates or bowls	Noisily scraping china with flatware to get the last bit of soup or sauce
Rest used flatware on edge of plate or underliner while not in use	Placing used flatware on linen
When finished, place the soup spoon on the underliner or the knife and fork in a closed position	Placing dirty/used flatware on the table or cloth/top
Use a napkin to dab the mouth	Wiping the entire face with a napkin or using a sleeve or the back of one's hand to wipe the mouth
Allow servers to crumb the table as part of service	Using the hands to wipe unwanted food particles from the table onto the floor
Politely ask for the check	Getting up before the check is presented
Tooth picks are for use in private	Using a tooth pick for cleaning teeth in a restaurant or in public

Styles of Eating

4

Since the United States is a melting pot of cultures, it has adopted many types of cuisines and dining habits, which include the consumption of finger foods of all shapes and sizes, and the use of chopsticks and flatbreads as utensils for scooping food into the mouth. See Figure 1-1.

Something as simple as eating bread and butter may be a challenge if one is not aware of the 'rules' governing bread and butter etiquette, which varies from one country to another. In the United States, a small piece of butter should be placed on the bread & butter plate using the bread & butter knife. The knife is then returned on the plate in its original position. A small bite-sized piece of bread should be torn off and then it should be buttered before eating. The whole piece of bread should not be buttered prior to breaking off a piece as the fingers would become greasy, and might soil the glassware or other table items. As an added note, the rules may differ if a roll rather than a piece of bread is served. It is perfectly proper to tear a role in half and to use one's knife to place butter inside the center of the roll.

Most rules for proper *table etiquette* are founded on a respect and consideration for other diners, and the property of others. A host or hostess who has spent time polishing crystal glasses would feel less than flattered when the glasses are smudged with grease to detract from the general appearance of the table. Greasy fingers on an item that is being passed to someone else is also less than appealing. The server at a fine dining restaurant who has spent time polishing and cleaning will also question the value of time spent on "making everything perfect."

In France, there are fewer reservations about how bread should be eaten. The use of bread as a sponge for sauce left on a plate is quite proper, while such a practice would not be seen in the same light in this country. The habit may stem from the common use of a *tranche* or *manchette* in the Middle Ages, which was a large piece of old bread that was used as a plate to soak up juices and oils, and was eaten mostly by the poor.

FIGURE 1-1

It is common to see a broad range of eating styles within the food service industry.

Continental and American Styles

There are two basic styles of using flatware when eating: the Continental and the American style (sometimes known as the Zig-Zag style). See Figure 1-2.

The *Continental style* is defined by the diner holding a fork and knife in the left and right hands respectively; cutting a bite-sized piece of food; and then placing the food onto the tines of the fork and into the mouth, while still holding onto the knife in the right hand.

In contrast, the diner who uses the *American style* typically cuts a bite sized piece of food and then pauses to switch the fork from the left hand to the right hand, before placing the knife onto the rim of the plate, and then eating the food from the fork, with the left hand on the lap or on the edge of the table. It has been suggested that the origin of this practice might be attributed to the nonexistence of forks in America during colonial times when only knives and spoons were used. Today's society recognizes either method as a demonstration of proper table manners. See Figure 1-3.

In Chapter 5, "Styles and Sequence of Service," the menu course sequencing, which is part of dining styles, also demonstrates the influence of other cultures, in particular those of France and Italy. In France, for example, it is traditional that salads are served after the entrée because the vinegar-based dressings would overpower the accompanying wine. The salad is also served at this time to re-stimulate the appetite so that a cheese or dessert course might be enjoyed to complete the meal. In contrast, salads or vegetable courses are served before the entrée in Italy and usually without the accompanying vinaigrette. See Figure 1-4.

FIGURE 1-2
The Continental method of using flatware

FIGURE 1-3
The American or "Zig Zag" method of using flatware

FIGURE 1-4
Salad may be served before or after the entrée depending on the menu and the cultural context.

Dining Etiquette and Protocol for Ladies and Gentlemen

In addition to table manners, there are standards of etiquette and protocol of which both the guest and the server should be aware (especially in a more formal setting).

1. Pull out the chairs for ladies and the elderly first.
2. Gentlemen should stand up from their seats when ladies get up from the table.
3. When leaving the table, fold the napkin and place it to the right of the place setting; not on the back of a chair.
4. Serve the guest of honor first, if there is one, and the host last.
5. Serve children, women, and then men (eldest first), in that order.
6. Do not call the server "honey", "dear", "sweetie", "boy", "garçon" or use any other disrespectful term.
7. Do not start eating until everyone has been served, unless another guest's meal has been delayed, and he or she insists that you begin eating (especially if the food is served hot).
8. The plate or bowl does not need to be wiped clean. Garnishes may be left on the plate.
9. When finished with the soup course, place the spoon on the underliner plate.
10. When finished with an appetizer or entrée course, place the fork and knife together on the plate facing 12:00.
11. Use glassware that is placed to the right of the place setting.
12. If you prefer not to be served wine and already have a preset wine glass, just indicate to the server or host that you prefer not to have any. Do not turn the glass upside down.
13. Use the china or plateware that is set to the left of the place setting and the cup and saucer on the right.
14. If the person to your right has taken your bread & butter plate, ask the server for another.
15. If you are uncertain about how to eat something, watch others at the table and imitate them.
16. If in doubt as to whether something should be eaten with the fingers, use a knife and fork.
17. If eating peas or other similarly difficult foods to maneuver, use the knife to push them onto your fork.
18. Do not eat something from another's plate unless dining with just one other individual with whom you are intimate or familiar.
19. Never rush through a meal. It will make others at the table who are taking their time uncomfortable.
20. If coughing, turn away from the table and cough into the napkin to prevent the spread of germs. If the coughing is uncontrollable, politely leave the table and visit the restroom. Clean your hands properly before returning.

Service Protocol and Etiquette

Standards of protocol or precedence of service support guest etiquette. Protocols are rules or sets of procedures that are set by establishments and organizations, including governments.

Server Protocol

The following standards are those that have been adopted as best practices by Johnson & Wales University, based on the premise that a server is there to serve the guest's needs, and that only safety issues should supercede these standards.

1. Always allow guests the right of way when walking through an establishment.
2. Try not to interrupt guests who are engaged in conversation. If the need arises, politely request their attention first.
3. The guest of honor, if there is one, is served first, and the host last.
4. Serve young children, women, and then men. It is also preferable to take age into consideration as an additional sign of respect.
5. Serve all guests at a table at the same time so no one waits for his or her food
6. Serve and clear beverages from the guest's right side, as long as you are "open" to the guest.
7. Wait until everyone at the table has finished a course before clearing.
8. Clear the bread and butter plate from the left side.
9. Carry flatware on a serviette or a *STP (standard transport plate).*
10. Carry glassware on a beverage tray.
11. Do not reuse flatware for a subsequent course.
12. Do not reach across a guest if you can approach from the other side.
13. Do not touch a guest, and do not allow a guest to touch you.

Server Etiquette

Most guests are less concerned with the techniques of service than with the attitude and manner in which they are served. Intrusive service is annoying, regardless of the server's skill level. Considerate service is both efficient and gracious, and it is likely to persuade a guest to return.

General rules:

1. Always address the customer in an appropriate manner. Do not use terms such as "you guys".
2. Carry plates and drinks so that the fingers are well away from the food or rim of a glass.
3. Never rush the guest by bringing the courses to the table too quickly.
4. Position the plate of food in front of the guest as the chef intended it to be presented.
5. Place plates onto the cover carefully and quietly.
6. Try to anticipate guests' requests rather than simply responding after the request is made.
7. Serve each guest without asking what was ordered *(food auctioning)*.
8. Take the time to clean or *groom the table* before serving a course if needed, particularly after the entrée.
9. Serve each guest in a timely manner to prevent repeated requests for service.
10. Take note of any physical limitations or characteristic preferences, such as left-handedness, and make the necessary adjustments.
11. When clearing, don't ask guests "are you done?" Politely ask if you may clear the plates.

As customs and manners have changed over the centuries, the evolution of the restaurant and the role of the food and beverage industry have also evolved. The expectations of guests have also contributed to the enormous variety of restaurant styles, menus, and service needs.

SERVING Children & PEOPLE WITH Disabilities

According to the National Restaurant Association (NRA), families are dining out on average 3.5 times a week. Clearly, these numbers show that servers must address the needs of children.

The following guidelines apply for serving children up to the age of eight.

- *Ask whether a booster seat or high chair is needed.*
- *Ensure that the seats are clean and that the trays on high chairs are clean and sanitized.*
- *Remove any sharp objects from the table.*
- *Remove glassware from the covers of small children. If lidded plastic containers are available for children's beverages, parents generally appreciate their use.*
- *Talk to the children as you serve them.*
- *If the establishment offers children's activities such as paper placemats and crayons, bring these to the table.*
- *If parents approve, help children select an appropriate menu item.*
- *Serve children as quickly as possible, and serve them first.*
- *After the guests depart, make sure that the area beneath the table is thoroughly swept.*

Under the Americans with Disabilities Act (ADA), restaurants are required to provide accommodations for wheelchair users and other disabled guests. Servers should address disabled guests directly, without assuming that they want or need help.

2

Service and The Restaurant Industry

GREAT CIVILIZATIONS

of the past enjoyed elaborate banquets, and travelers throughout history have relied on wayside stations where they could buy food and drink. The actual restaurant concept where anyone could go to enjoy a complete meal that was prepared and served by someone else, however, dates back only to 1765. In that year, A. Boulanger, a soup vendor, opened his business in Paris, offering only a "restorative," or "restaurant," of sheep's feet simmered in white wine. It is from this humble beginning, that the tradition of Paris' luxurious restaurants grew.

The "restaurant" idea spread to the United States in 1827 when Giovanni and Pietro Delmonico opened a café in New York City. Three years later, the first American restaurant "Restaurant Français," opened in an adjacent building.

KEY TERMS

restaurant

servers

tip credit

pool

tips

banquet

fine-dining restaurant

dinner-house restaurants

casual or family restaurants

quick-service restaurants

à la carte

semi-à la carte

prix fixe

table d'hôte

truth-in-menu guidelines

The Restaurant and Banquet Industry Today

According to the National Restaurant Association, the US restaurant industry is a $566 billion industry, which currently employs over 13 million employees or 9% of the work force at over 945,000 locations. It is the largest employer after the federal government. Nearly half of all adults in the United States have worked in the restaurant industry at some point during their lives, and one in four persons got their first job in the restaurant industry. It is expected that this industry will add another 1.8 million jobs over the next decade. According to the Bureau of Labor and Statistics, in 2008, there were approximately 2.3 million servers in the food industry and an additional 500,000 bartenders.

Servers

Servers are most frequently referred to as waiters, waitresses, wait-staff, sales associates, or cast members. The term 'waitron' coined in the 1980s reflects a common view that servers take orders robotically and serve without any social skills. The server's job is also most often perceived as a transitory position that requires little skill or attributes. It is not viewed as a 'profession' because it has traditionally lacked credentialing or certification. More recent developments in certifications by organizations such as the Federation of Dining Room Professionals have elevated the perception of professional servers to one that is challenging and requires skills. The server's qualities are discussed in greater detail in Chapter 4: "The Server". The position of server is considered entrepreneurial in nature because the server controls the potential tip income. The individual also works at a place of business that assumes the costs and provides all the tools necessary to derive an income. The greater the sales a server generates, the larger the tip income. In general, servers earn between 10 % and 15% of their sales. In fine-dining restaurants the percentage increases closer to 20% on average and the server's food and beverage sales are significantly higher as well.

There are also other factors that contribute to a server's income: the number of shifts worked; the type of shift (dinner usually being much more lucrative than lunch); the day or night of the week; holidays; seasons; weather conditions, and staffing shortages. Waitstaff in many states are paid a cash wage of $2.13 per hour and their employers are allowed to apply a *'tip credit'* that makes up the difference between this wage and the federal minimum wage of $7.25 per hour. Restaurant owners do not have to directly pay the minimum wage, but they are responsible for declaring employee tips at a minimum rate of 12% of sales on payroll taxes. Owners are held criminally liable if they fail to carry out this law.

While the system of tipping is predicated on the belief that a tip is a reward for good service, (theoretically the better the service the higher the tip), there are restaurants where employees must *'pool'* tips. All tips are placed into a single 'pool' and are shared equally by waitstaff of the same ranking or level. This system has its critics because it is said to remove the primary incentive for good service. Yet, servers whose main focus is on the tips, tend most commonly not to be the best servers or employees.

There are also some fine-dining establishments that pay their waitstaff salaries and automatically charge a service charge of between 17% to 20% on the bill, including tax. The purpose of this method, which is the European model of how servers are paid, is to provide servers with a steady income; to offer them health and other benefits; and to provide greater parity between the income of the chefs and kitchen personnel, and the income of the front of the house staff. It will be interesting to see if more restaurants eventually adopt this same strategy. When servers are paid salaries their chance of being 'stiffed' is also reduced. This term is applied when a server is not given a sufficient tip. It is up to the restaurant's management to ensure that the waitstaff provides the very best service regardless of the tip potential. When compensation is based on both a salary and benefits, the turn-over rate of the front of the house employees is usually reduced and their jobs are viewed as more professional.

Tips is said to be an acronym for: "To Insure Proper Service," or "To Insure Prompt Service." In reality, the term dates back to the Middle Ages when it was first used to mean to give, to hand, or to pass. The actual practice of tipping dates back to the coffee houses of London, in the 18th century.

Banquet Servers

There are food and beverage servers and bartenders who work in establishments other than restaurants such as hotels and catering operations. The incomes of these individuals is usually determined by higher wages that are supplemented by an 18-20% service charge that is automatically imposed on clients. While the social and technical skills of these individuals are similar to those of restaurant servers, and the service they provide is commensurate, staff need not rely on selling skills. The roles of bartenders and their compensation are be examined in greater detail in Chapter 6, "The Beverage World".

Banquet and Catering

Formal protocol and service etiquette originated with the banquets of ancient times. Banquets and catering continue to be an important aspect of the dining service industry. A *banquet* is defined as a meal or event in which food and beverage has been ordered for a predetermined number of people. A formal legal contract between the host of the event and the establishment is signed, and a deposit is made when the event is first booked. Establishments have various policies regarding the amount they require in advance as a deposit. Most properties request 75% to 100% deposit prior to the event.

Banquets range from very elaborate receptions and dinners, to the off-premise catering of an informal picnic. Restaurants may sometimes have a banquet room or hall to accommodate these functions, or may choose to even close their restaurants to the general public to allow for a catered affair.

Types of Restaurants

There are basically 4 types of commercial restaurants that cater to every occasion, budget, and taste. According to the National Restaurant Association, restaurants provide more than 70 billion "meal and snack occasions," and on a typical day, "more than 130 million individuals are food service patrons".

Fine-Dining Restaurants

A *fine-dining restaurant* offers excellent food, fine wines, and highly skilled and attentive service in an upscale environment. The preparation of more complex food and more obscure and exotic ingredients result in high menu prices. Meals are served in several courses at a relaxed pace, and usually last between one and a half to two hours. Most job opportunities in fine-dining establishments require both training and work experience. Many fine-dining restaurants are independently owned.

Dinner-House Restaurants

Dinner-house restaurants provide moderately priced, easily prepared meals. Some dinner-house restaurants have added ethnic dishes to their menus in response to the growing multicultural market. Most serve alcoholic beverages. Dinner-houses are frequently part of a national chain or a franchise, but may be independently owned and operated.

Casual or Family Restaurants

Casual or family restaurants offer customers a relaxed atmosphere. These operations feature moderate prices, home-style cooking, and child-friendly menus. Some casual or family restaurants serve alcoholic beverages.

Quick-Service Restaurants

Quick-service restaurants provide a limited, fairly consistent selection of food at very reasonable prices. The menu is usually *à la carte,* with items priced either individually or as combination meals. Customers place their orders and pay at the counter or the drive-thru window. These restaurants form the largest segment of the foodservice industry.

The chart below demonstrates a correlation between the type of restaurants and guests' expectations, the type of menu, the ambience and layout of the restaurant, the service provided, and the associated cost.

Correlation of the type of restaurant to guests' expectations, menus, service and cost					
TYPE OF RESTAURANT	GUESTS' EXPECTATIONS	MENU	AMBIENCE TABLE LAYOUT	TYPE OF SERVICE	COST
Fine-Dining Examples: Per Se, No 9 Park, Le Bernardin	Highest	À la carte/ semi- à la carte/ prix fixe/ table d'hôte	Designer driven, luxurious. Free standing Linen covers Banquettes	Highly skilled and knowledgeable brigade/ team tableside/ individualized crafted cocktails and knowledgeable wine service	$$$-$$$$
Dinner-House Examples: Red Lobster, Chili's, TGI Fridays	Moderate +	Semi à la carte	Themed Place mats or table top Booths/ free standing tables	Skilled to moderate skill & knowledge plated/ family style/ waiter/ busser/ limited alcohol beverage knowledge and service	$$-$$$
Family/Casual Examples: Cracker Barrel, Friendly's, Johnny Rockets	Moderate	Semi à la carte	Counter/ Booths/ free standing	Moderate skill and minimal knowledge, very limited to no alcohol beverage service	$-$$
Quick-Service Examples: Mc Donald's, Burger King	Low to moderate	À la carte and semi à la carte fixed menu	Booths/ free standing	Limited skill and knowledge No alcohol beverage service	$

The Menu

The menu impacts every element of a food service operation, including the type of customer the establishment attracts. Numerous factors need to be considered when planning a menu. Both the target market and operational needs, including profitability, must be evaluated. Identification of the target market; an evaluation of its ability to sustain the establishment; and a knowledge of the income level of the market are necessary. Extensive market research must be conducted to determine the feasibility of an operation.

Other factors to consider include:
1. Type of food
2. Price structure
3. Equipment analysis
4. Skill level of employees
5. Geography
6. Social factors such as religion or ethnicity
7. Nutritional concerns
8. Age and Health issues

In addition to considering the needs of the target market and the operational constraints, an establishment must design a menu that offers variety (of ingredients, cooking techniques, textures, taste, and serving temperatures); balance and plate composition; descriptive copy, truth-in-menu, and menu labeling regulations.

Types of Sales Menus

The four most common pricing structures for sales menus include à la carte, semi-à la carte, prix fixe, and table d'hôte. An establishment may combine elements of one or more pricing structures. Additionally, the menu may either be a fixed or a cycle menu. Each system affects the organization of the servers' time management, and ability to build the check.

Carni

Saltimbocca - $19
Veal scaloppine pan-sautéed with Prosciutto di Parma, fresh sage, garlic, white

Scaloppine di Vitello Limone - $19
Veal scaloppine dredged in egg batter and pan-sautéed in a lemon, cape
Prepared with chicken - $17

Scaloppine di Vitello Toscana - $20
Veal scaloppine pan-sautéed with fresh mozzarella, San Marzano
roasted garlic, artichoke hearts and veal sto

Costoletta di Vitello - $29
16oz. Wood-grilled veal chop finished with a Crimin
sherry and veal demi-glaze.

Bistecca Pepperonata - $19
Sirloin skirt steak marinated in Chianti wine, balsamic vinega
grilled over hardwood charcoal and finished with a spic

Manzo di Giuseppe - $29
16oz. Choice Black Angus sirloin finished with sea
hardwood charcoal. Drizzled with extra fine Tuscan oliv
Served with roasted garlic and a side of warm gor
Joey Piccolo (12 oz.) - $24

Pesce

Aragosta Ciopino - $
Native lobster (in shell), shrimp, littlenecks, baby mus
calamari stewed in a spicy (mildly hot) tor
Served over grilled Tuscan crostini and toppe

Pesce Spada alla Grig
Thick center cut domestic swordfish grilled over
with a caper, roasted yellow tomato, le

Branzino - $
Pan-seared Chilean sea bass fillet finished with oce

Gamberi con T
Four jumbo butterflied shrimp sautéed
fresh thyme leaves. Served over a bed of cr

Contorn
All sides are availab

Cime di Rapa - $4/$7
téed tender broccoli rabe.

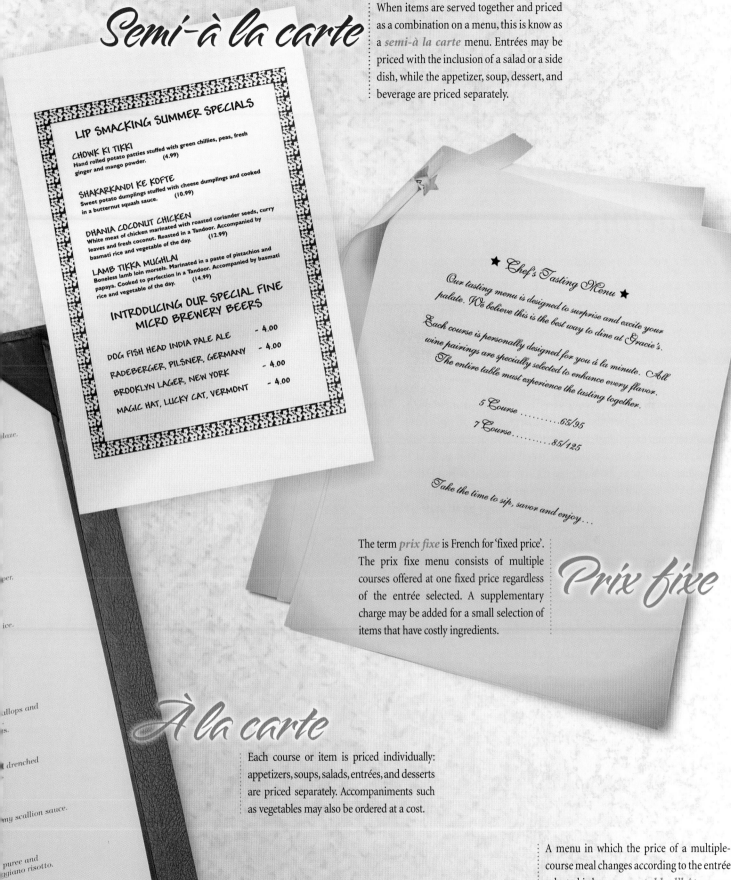

Semí-à la carte

When items are served together and priced as a combination on a menu, this is know as a *semi-à la carte* menu. Entrées may be priced with the inclusion of a salad or a side dish, while the appetizer, soup, dessert, and beverage are priced separately.

LIP SMACKING SUMMER SPECIALS

CHOWK KI TIKKI
Hand rolled potato patties stuffed with green chillies, peas, fresh ginger and mango powder.   (4.99)

SHAKARKANDI KE KOFTE
Sweet potato dumplings stuffed with cheese dumplings and cooked in a butternut squash sauce.   (10.99)

DHANIA COCONUT CHICKEN
White meat of chicken marinated with roasted coriander seeds, curry leaves and fresh coconut. Roasted in a Tandoor. Accompanied by basmati rice and vegetable of the day.   (12.99)

LAMB TIKKA MUGHLAI
Boneless lamb loin morsels. Marinated in a paste of pistachios and papaya. Cooked to perfection in a Tandoor. Accompanied by basmati rice and vegetable of the day.   (14.99)

INTRODUCING OUR SPECIAL FINE MICRO BREWERY BEERS

DOG FISH HEAD INDIA PALE ALE — 4.00

RADEBERGER, PILSNER, GERMANY — 4.00

BROOKLYN LAGER, NEW YORK — 4.00

MAGIC HAT, LUCKY CAT, VERMONT — 4.00

★ Chef's Tasting Menu ★

Our tasting menu is designed to surprise and excite your palate. We believe this is the best way to dine at Gracie's.

Each course is personally designed for you à la minute. All wine pairings are specially selected to enhance every flavor. The entire table must experience the tasting together.

5 Course 65/95

7 Course 85/125

Take the time to sip, savor and enjoy...

Prix fixe

The term *prix fixe* is French for 'fixed price'. The prix fixe menu consists of multiple courses offered at one fixed price regardless of the entrée selected. A supplementary charge may be added for a small selection of items that have costly ingredients.

À la carte

Each course or item is priced individually: appetizers, soups, salads, entrées, and desserts are priced separately. Accompaniments such as vegetables may also be ordered at a cost.

Table d'hôte

A menu in which the price of a multiple-course meal changes according to the entrée selected is known as a *table d'hôte* menu. Steak au poivre at $24.95 might include a soup, salad and dessert, while grilled chicken with the exact same courses sells for $16.95.

Menu Guidelines

To ensure good ethical practices and to accurately represent menu items, it is prudent to adhere to *truth-in-menu guidelines. It is imperative that servers avoid misrepresenting the products they are trying to sell in an effort to make sales. The twelve truth-in-menu guidelines for dining establishments and servers that follow, have been created by the National Restaurant Association:*

1. **Brand names must be accurately represented**—The advertised product must be the one served; for example, another brand of hot sauce cannot be substituted for Tabasco® sauce.

2. **Dietary and nutritional claims must be exact**—To protect consumers from potential health hazards, health claims and nutritional information must be accurate. Low-sodium and fat-free foods must be correctly prepared to ensure the protection of customers. Nutritional claims must be supported with statistical data.

3. **Description of food preservation methods must be accurate**—Food may be preserved as follows: frozen, chilled, dehydrated, dried such as by sun or smoking, bottled, and canned. Terms used must be accurate. For example, fish cannot be listed as "fresh" on the menu if it has been frozen.

4. **Quantity must be correct**—Whenever a menu item indicates that it contains a certain number of items, that number must be served. Weights given for steaks or other cuts of meat should be identified on the menu as weight prior to cooking.

5. **The origin of ingredients must be truthful**—Blue cheese, for example, must not be substituted for Roquefort cheese.

6. **The quality or grade must be exact**—A steak advertised as "charcoal-grilled" must be grilled over charcoal, not merely grilled.

7. **Cooking techniques must be accurately described**—When a cooking technique is given on a menu, i.e. broiled, the chef must prepare the food using the described technique.

8. **Pictures must be precise**—A photo of apple pie with ice cream must be used to represent "apple pie à la mode".

9. **Food product descriptions must be accurate**—A menu that describes shrimp salad made with jumbo shrimp should not consist of medium-sized shrimp.

10. **Pricing structure must be clearly stated**—The menu must indicate whether the price includes a cover charge, gratuity, or service charge. Any supplement charged for side items with more costly ingredients should be listed.

11. **Menus must indicate if substitutions are made**—Substituting one item for another is a common practice because of delivery problems, availability, or price. Examples of substitutions might include maple-flavored syrup for maple syrup, or capon for chicken.

12. **Merchandising terms must be accurate**—Food service establishments may exaggerate in advertising food items as long as they are not misleading customers. Saying "We are the best in town" or "We serve only the finest beef" is acceptable, but implying that the beef is prime when it is not is misleading.

★ *1ˢᵗ Course* ★

Watermelon & Thai Basil Gazpacho
melon salad, prosciutto di Parma, house smoked scallop 12.

Native Corn Soup
crab rangoon agnolotti, piquillo pepper, green onion 12.

Crisp Rhode Island Lobster
tomatoes escebeche, iceberg lettuce, bacon 17.

Organic Greens Salad
red onion, Yukon potato crisp, soy sherry vinaigret

Plum Point Oysters
half shell, sauce mignonette 18.

House-made Gnocchi
local peppers, bacon, Manderone Provolone 15.

Zephyr Farms Slow Poached Egg
Summer vegetable hash, smoked pork 12.

Crisp Veal Sweetbreads
cornmeal crusted, sweet pickle relish, sauc

In addition to the printed menu, which is the primary vehicle for marketing the items an establishment has for sale, selections may be promoted by highlighting items, including clip-ons, using table tents and menu boards, as well as using a website. The Internet has provided innovative and technologically adept restaurateurs with an additional advertising resource. Web site development has become a cost efficient and effective way to disseminate a menu. The Internet may also be used for accepting reservations.

Reservations Systems

The guest's first contact with an establishment may be through its reservation system. Many destination restaurants and those that are more upscale, commonly accept reservations. Other restaurants only accept reservations on special occasions, such as Mother's Day, and for parties of six or more.

Although online services such as "Open Table" are available, manual reservation systems rely on the host or hostess to answer the phone to record the details, and if it is management's policy, to record a credit card number as a guarantee. The host or hostess may also have to answer questions; give accurate directions to the restaurant; and provide clear information about parking.

CHAPTER

3

THE ENVIRONMENT *of an establishment relates to the type of menu and the style of service that is employed. This symbiotic relationship creates a "concept" to which the guest can easily relate. Environment refers to the colors, textures, sounds and smells that create an image and experience for the guest. Fine-dining restaurants have traditionally offered carpeted floors, richly decorated wall and window treatments, full comfortable chairs, and table linens. But today, it is not unusual to find less formality in décor. Fine-dining establishments may have beautifully polished hardwood floors and deliberate design elements that accentuate the volume of noise to make the atmosphere seem more 'alive'.*

When replacing the traditional "environment," it is important to remember that certain creative elements might be rather inappropriate. Harsh lighting would be inimical to creating a soft and romantic mood. The playing of heavy metal music in a fine-dining restaurant would be equally discordant. Unpadded hardwood chairs would also fail to provide a relaxing leisurely fine-dining restaurant experience. The exotic spicy aromas of Indian cuisine would be an anomaly in an Italian restaurant.

side work	waiter's friend
tableware	dollies
serviceware	potage spoons
banquette	service set
statler	pince or pincer
cover	hollowware
fixed or focal point	guéridon
amuse-bouche	réchaud
pre-set menu	blazer pans
service tray	skirting
beverage tray	doily
hand tray	

Restaurant Layout and Flow

The layout of the establishment and the dining room in particular, must accommodate the uninterrupted traffic flow of both guests and servers. The location of the restrooms should not interfere with servers' walkways. Tables should not be positioned to slow down the servers' route to and from the kitchen. The guests should not be caused any discomfort by excessive server traffic. See Figure 3-1.

FIGURE 3-1

Dining room traffic flow impacts the guest experience

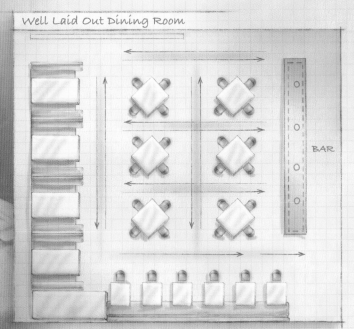

Well Laid Out Dining Room

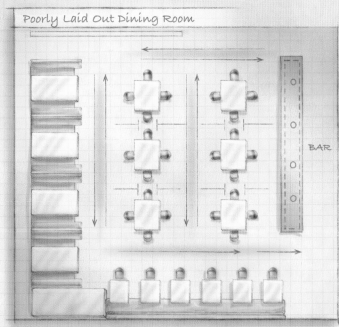

Poorly Laid Out Dining Room

BAR

Opening and Closing Duties

Quality service begins with the availability and proper placement of all the equipment needed to ensure smooth and efficient service. Establishments should have clearly defined duties for each service member to perform prior to the opening or closing of the dining room to the public. Some of these responsibilities may be scheduled daily or by the shift, while others may be required but once a week. These duties are referred to as *"side work."* Though side work varies by establishment, it typically includes:

- Setting tables for service.
- Cleaning and refilling salt and pepper shakers.
- Refilling sugar bowls.
- Cleaning and refilling vinegar and oil cruets.
- Folding napkins for service.
- Polishing flatware and glassware.
- Stocking side stations for service.
- Emptying flower vases and storing flowers under refrigeration.
- Vacuuming, sweeping, and washing any tiled floors.
- Emptying the vacuum after use.
- Ensuring that all light bulbs are in proper working condition.
- Recording refrigeration or glass washer temperatures in log books as necessary.
- Cleaning doors, mirrors, and designated surfaces.
- Cleaning the legs or bases of tables.

Dining Room Equipment and Serviceware

The tableware and serviceware are as significant as the layout. They must reflect the concept that the establishment is trying to create. Tableware and serviceware refer to all utensils, glassware, china and service pieces used in the coverage of a meal. Servers must have an extensive understanding of the inter-relationship of dining room equipment and its proper usage as well as a knowledge of all the related factors to provide quality service.

The Table

Although there are many styles of tables from which to choose, it is important to consider durability, size, and aesthetics when making purchases. There are free standing, booth, banquette, statler, and round tables of different sizes. A **banquette** refers to continuous seating positioned against a wall. A **statler** is a square table that opens into a round. The choice of table surface is largely determined by whether it will be covered with linen. Regardless of choice, servers need to ensure that tables are level, free of wobbling, and are kept in good condition by checking the underside for chewing gum.

A primary concern in selecting tables is size. Both the lay-out of the dining room and the amount of space available for each guest must be considered. The style of menu and service also dictate the type of cover that is used and the amount of space needed for that cover. The *cover* may be as simple as a napkin and a bread-and-butter plate, or as elaborate as a show plate, appetizer fork and knife, soup spoon, salad fork and knife, dinner fork and knife, a dessert fork and teaspoon, a bread and butter plate, a water glass and three wine glasses.

The arrangement of tables in the dining room is also a significant factor when selecting tables. Table placement establishes a sense of uniformity, which is important in creating a positive first impression on the guest. Placement also affects the flow of traffic in the room, which impacts on the guest's comfort. Tables should be numbered in a logical manner to allow for point of sales systems, check writing, and quick identification by all service personnel. See Figure 3-2.

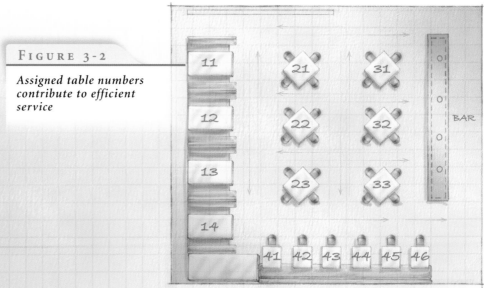

FIGURE 3-2

Assigned table numbers contribute to efficient service

Seats and Seat Numbering

In addition to numbering tables, each seat, and thus each guest, should also have a number, which usually flows clockwise around the table from a *fixed or focal point,* such as the entrance of the restaurant. Using this system, the seat closest to the entrance at each freestanding table is numbered position 1. See Figure 3-3. At a booth or banquette table, the numbering begins at the position where a server stands to take an order. See Figures 3-4 and 3-5. Using this system helps to improve communication among staff members to provide better service. A busy server can easily ask another server to check on the coffee at table 5, for instance, and to make sure that positions 3 and 4 have fresh hot water for their tea.

The type of seat is also important and must fit the concept of the establishment. A comfortable chair lends itself to a more leisurely paced dining experience, and should be selected for fine-dining restaurants rather than quick-service operations.

FIGURE 3-3

Numbering the seats of a freestanding table

FIGURE 3-4

Numbering the seats of a booth table

FIGURE 3-5

Numbering the seats of a banquette table

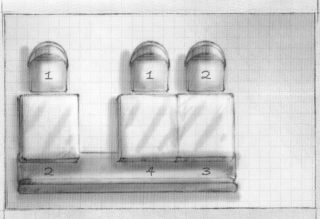

Table Settings

The table setting or cover is determined by the type of menu: à la carte, both traditional and modern or basic, and the banquet/prix fixe.

À la carte

There are two possibilities for presetting the cover for à la carte dining: the traditional and the modern. In a true à la carte set-up, the establishment does not know what or how many courses a guest will select, therefore, the pre-set cover does not include silverware or flatware. If the establishment offers a complimentary *amuse-bouche,* a small, bite-sized sampler, then a cocktail fork might be provided.

The traditional setup includes little but the show plate, napkin, a bread-and-butter plate, and knife. The modern or basic place setting is dictated by aesthetics and the assumption that the guest will order at least an entrée. A less barren place setting might include a show plate, napkin, dinner knife, dinner fork, bread-and-butter plate, butter knife, and water glass. See Figure 3-6.

Prix fixe

A prix fixe menu includes a variety of courses such as a soup/appetizer, salad course, and entrée, therefore the flatware for those courses is included in the pre-set. A wine glass may also be set as a suggestive marketing tool, or as a wine pairing offering that is included in the prix fixe. See Figure 3-7.

Banquet or pre-set

A *pre-set menu* is one that has been determined ahead of time. The table setting depends on what is being served, and includes the utensils and glassware necessary for each course. A bread-and-butter plate, butter knife, salad fork, dinner fork, dinner knife, spoon, coffee cup, wine glass, water glass, dessert spoon, dessert fork, napkin, and show plate may be included. See Figure 3-8.

The Service Tray

A large oval food tray known as a *service tray,* is used to allow servers to carry several dishes to the table at one time. Food trays are usually lined with cork or rubber to prevent slippage. If food trays are not lined, a service napkin is used to prevent slippage. See Figure 3-9.

Tray Stands/Jacks

Tray stands or jacks are collapsible frames on which to rest trays. The frames may be plastic, wood or metal. Some include a low-level shelf that may be used as a small side stand. When not in use, stands should be collapsed and placed out of busy traffic lanes to prevent accidents. Some establishments designate permanent locations in the dining room for tray stands, while others require that service staff carry the stands with them as they transport food trays in and out of the dining room. See Figure 3-9.

FIGURE 3-6

À la Carte "Classic" Place Setting

À la Carte "Modern" Place Setting

FIGURE 3-7

Prix Fixe Place Setting

FIGURE 3-8

Banquet Place Setting

FIGURE 3-9

The service tray and tray stand can increase service efficiency.

FIGURE 3-10

The beverage tray is a formal implement for carrying drinks.

The Beverage Tray

The *beverage tray* is a round (12" to 14" in diameter) hand-held skid-free tray on which to carry beverages. Beverage trays should be clean and dry. See Figure 3-10.

The Hand Tray

The *hand tray* is a small tray used to carry a single small item, such as a drink, a napkin or the check.

Glassware

Glassware available for food service operations includes common glass, fully tempered, and crystal. Restaurateurs are faced with selecting glassware that comes in a variety of types, patterns, costs,

and qualities. Operators are responsible for purchasing the glassware that best suits the particular needs of the establishment. The glass size must also be appropriate to the serving so that a proper pour may be accommodated.

Another important consideration is whether to purchase a glass with a rim that is beaded. The glass will chip less if beaded, although most high end market consumers prefer to drink beverages, especially wine, in an unbeaded rimmed glass.

Caution should also be taken when selecting patterns because patterns are frequently discontinued, and it becomes difficult or expensive to replace glassware. Glassware is available in a variety of sizes and shapes. Standard sizes and shapes are shown in Figure 3-11.

Fully tempered or toughened glassware

Commercial operations commonly use fully tempered or toughened glassware for both practical and safety reasons. This glassware is stronger than other types, and will shatter into small fragments rather than dangerous shards. It is also more scratch, chemical, and shock resistant.

Lead crystal glassware, which is also called 24% lead crystal, is known for its brilliance and clarity, but it is expensive. It is best suited for fine-dining establishments.

FIGURE 3-11   Standard shapes and sized of restaurant glassware.

White Bordeaux   Red Burgundy   Tasting Glass   Champagne Tulip   Carafe

Irish Coffee   Goblet   Water/Soda   Pilsner   Footed Pilsner

Brandy Snifter   Hurricane   Highball   Zombie   Old Fashioned

Martini   Margarita   Sour   Rocks   Cordial

Handling glassware

Glassware must be handled with care at all times.

The following guidelines should be used:

- Glassware should be free of cracks or chips.
- Glassware should be stored upside down in an appropriate glass rack. The height of a glass rack should exceed the length of a glass, and should allow ample room so that the bases of the glasses do not touch.
- Glassware stored on a shelf must be placed upside down on air mats.
- When handling glassware, always hold the glass by the stem or base. See Figure 3-12.
- If polishing a clean glass, use a lint free cloth and do not exert pressure when the bulb of the glass is being turned in one direction and the stem or base being held is turned in another. See Figure 3-13.
- Clean all glassware so that it is immaculate. (Polishing methods will be detailed later under server skills.)
- Use a beverage tray when carrying glasses in the dining room. See Figure 3-14. When carrying clean stemmed glassware by hand, invert the glasses and place their bases between the fingers. Depending on dexterity, hand size, and experience, a server may carry as many as 10 to 16 glasses at once.

Corkscrews

Although the Romans used cork as stoppers, it is not until 1681 that the first known written reference to the use of a corkscrew was made by an Englishman. Today, there are a variety of corkscrew models that range in sophistication, from the first patented design of the Henshall, to the Leverpull of the 1980s. The key to selecting a good corkscrew is to look for one that has a worm that is not too thick and has edges that are sharp enough to cut into the cork, rather than tear it. The most common corkscrew in the food service industry is known as the *"waiter's friend."* See Figure 3-15. This corkscrew usually has a knife blade to cut the capsule of the wine bottle, and its edge should be kept sharpened. This corkscrew should have 5 turns to the screw, and the server should ensure that the worm is not bent, in order to maximize its effectiveness. In the past 10 years the "waiter's friend" has been adapted with a double hinge or two step lever that makes it even easier for the server to open the bottle of wine. Another modification of the original is the substitution of a foil cutter for the small knife blade.

FIGURE 3-12
Correct Glass Handling   *Incorrect Glass Handling*

FIGURE 3-13
Use a clean, lint-free linen to polish glassware.

FIGURE 3-14
Use a beverage tray to carry glassware in the dining room.

FIGURE 3-15
The Waiter's Friend

Pottery

The term pottery applies to clay products made of unrefined clays. As a generic name, pottery includes all fired clayware. More specifically, the term pottery describes low-fired porous clayware, which is generally colored. Ceramic products acquire strength through the application of heat. Along with the heat, the chemical composition of the materials used determines the strength, porosity, and vitrification of the fired product.

There are many types of tableware available to the restaurateur. The final choice is usually determined by how appropriate the tablewares are to the concept and the cost of the products.

Some of the different types of tableware available are:

Earthenware Earthenware is a porous ceramic product that is fired at comparatively low temperatures to produce an opaque body that is not as strong as stoneware or china. The product may be glazed or unglazed.

Stoneware Stoneware is a nonporous ceramic product made of unprocessed clays, or clay and flux additives, which are fired at elevated temperatures. It is quite durable but lacks the translucence and whiteness of china. It is resistant to chipping. Stoneware is available in a variety of colors that are produced by the iron or other impurities in the clay.

Ironstoneware Ironstoneware is the historic term for durable English stoneware. The composition and properties of this product are similar to those of porcelain, although the body of ironstoneware lacks translucency and is off-white in color.

Cookingware Cookingware is the broad term applied to earthenware, stoneware, porcelain, and china designed for cooking, baking, or for serving. It has a smooth, glazed surface and is strong and resistant to thermal shock.

Fine China Fine china refers to a thin, translucent, vitrified product that is generally fired twice at relatively high temperatures: first, to mature the purest of flint, clay, and flux materials; and secondly, to develop the high gloss of the beautiful glaze. It is the highest quality tableware made for the domestic or retail trade.

Porcelain Porcelain is a term that is frequently used for china in Europe. European porcelain, like china, is fired twice. In the Untied States, porcelain may be fired in a one or two fire process. Porcelain has a hard, nonabsorbent, strong body that is white and translucent. European porcelain is made primarily for the retail market, but manufacturers such as Lennox and Rosenthal make commercial grade porcelain that is purchased by upscale hotels and fine-dining establishments.

Bone China Bone china is a specific type of china that was primarily manufactured in England. The body of this china contains a high proportion of bone ash that produces a greater translucency, whiteness, and strength. Like fine china, it is made primarily for the retail trade.

Restaurant China Restaurant china is a uniquely American blend of china and porcelain, which is designed and engineered specifically for commercial operations. Its body was developed in the United States to give it greater impact strength and durability, as well as an extremely low absorption, which is required of china that is used in public establishments. See Figure 3-16. Decorations are applied between the body and the glaze to protect the decoration on the china during commercial use. Most of this tableware is subject to a high temperature during its first firing and a lower temperature during the second. However, some restaurant china is fired in a one-fire operation during which the body and glaze mature at the same time. Like fine china, America restaurant china is vitrified.

FIGURE 3-16

Each china pattern will be available in a range of plate sizes and shapes.

Coffee Cup

Saucer

Demitasse

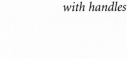
Coffee Mug

Bouillon Cup with handles

Sugar Bowl/ Cover

Fruit/Nappé

Monkey Dish

Coffee Pot

Creamer

Sugar Caddy

Salt and Pepper Shakers

Casserole Dish

Sauce Boat

Dinner 12"

Appetizer/Salad Plate 9 1/2"

Dessert Plate 8"

B&B Plate 6 1/2"

Pasta Plate

Soup Plate/Bowl

Oval Plate

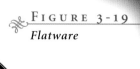

FIGURE 3-17

*Polish clean china
with linen napkins
and hot water.*

The following guidelines should be observed when handling china:

- Check all china for cleanliness prior to service. See Figure 3-17.
- Store all china by category.
- Store china soup and coffee cups in their appropriate racks.
- Handle china plates by the rim. See Figure 3-18.
- Avoid overstacking china cups.
- Do not stack cups with handles.
- Use underliners for china cups and bowls.
- Bleach all coffee cups every two weeks or according to the establishment's policies.
- Do not use china that has chips or clearly visible cracks. (The manager should make the decision on how to dispose of damaged china.)

FIGURE 3-18

Handle hot plates by the rim with a captain's towel	The server's hand should never touch the guest's food

Dollies

Dollies are carts of different shapes and sizes with casters, which are used for storing and transporting glassware. By placing racks onto dollies, the glassware is stored at a minimum of 6 inches above the floor. Plate dollies include standard adaptable partitions that provide enabling the safe and snug placement of stacks of about 50 specific sized plates in each compartment. Glassware dollies (about 21 inches square) hold racks of glasses that should be stacked no higher than one's ability to see over them. They should always be kept clean and sanitized.

Flatware—Cutlery

The term flatware refers to all dining utensils such as forks, spoons, and knives. See Figure 3-19. The origin of the word cutlery is from the Old French word for knife, *coutel.* The term 'silver' is also frequently used because flatware was made from silver until the mid 19th century when a less expensive process using stainless steel was created.

The selection of flatware should be determined by the concept of the establishment. The more elaborate the establishment, the more specialized and varied the pieces of flatware should be. The composition of flatware varies in grade qualities of stainless steel to silver. Many flatware styles are also available.

Some restaurants place the forks with the tines facing down, although most place them facing up. The tradition of placing forks on the table with the tines down stems back to the 16th century when forks were first introduced in the West. The fork would have the family crest engraved on the back of the handle, which the owners would display on the table. When forks became more readily accessible due to mass production, an engraver's mark replaced the crest. By placing the forks with the tines facing up, the potential for damage to table linens is also reduced.

FIGURE 3-19

Flatware

Knives Knives come in different shapes and may have serrated or flat edges. Standard industry knives include: dinner knives, with or without serrated edges; steak knives; fish knives for filleting fish more easily; appetizer knives that are often used for salad and desserts courses; bread and butter knives, which are usually shorter than appetizer knives and may be rounded at the top.

Forks Forks are produced in different sizes and shapes for specific functions. Standard and readily available sizes include: the dinner fork that is used for the entrée; the appetizer fork, which may also be used as a salad or dessert fork; a fish fork that is equal in size to the dinner fork but has a flattened tine to prevent the fish from falling off the fork; and a cocktail fork for foods such as oysters on the half shell.

Spoons Spoons include: teaspoons that are used for hot beverages such as coffee, tea and hot chocolate, and for sorbets and soft desserts; demi-tasse spoons for espresso service; soup spoons, which are also referred to as *potage spoons,* for thick or cream based soups; bouillon spoons, which are shaped so that the diner can sip from the side of the spoon (see Figure 3-20); a sauce spoon that has a slight notch to prevent excess sauce from dripping off onto the diner; and other specialty spoons such as long handled ice tea spoons.

FIGURE 3-21

"Pince Bread Service" utilizes a service set.

Service Set

The *service set* refers to a service spoon and fork that are used to **pince or pincer**: a technique of picking up foods such as rolls, and placing them on a plate. See Figure 3-21.

Holloware

Holloware is a term that originally described service pieces that were hollow. Today, this term includes: chafing dishes, coffee urns, samovars, coffee pitchers, tea pots, creamers, water pitchers, sauce boats, goose necks, sugar bowls or basins, tureens, silver salt and pepper shakers, butter dishes, compotes, silver bowls, oval platters, round platters, rectangular serving trays, plate covers, cloches, torte stands, tiered pastry stands, cake server holders, wine stands, wine buckets and coolers, champagne buckets, candlesticks, and candelabras. See Figure 3-22.

Holloware may be of different quality levels, from grades of stainless steel to sterling silver. Their purpose is to enhance the presentation of a meal, which can only occur if the correctly sized piece of holloware is used and if it is properly maintained and cleaned.

FIGURE 3-20

A potage spoon is used for thick soups while a bouillon spoon is used for thin soups.

FIGURE 3-22

Assorted holloware or service pieces

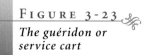

FIGURE 3-23
*The guéridon or
service cart*

FIGURE 3-24
*The copper
réchaud and
blazer pan are
well suited to
tableside cookery.*

The Guéridon

The *guéridon* is a service cart or trolley. It is a portable work station that is used for all tableside preparations including portioning, cooking, finishing, and plating. The *guéridon* is generally 18 inches wide by 30 inches long so that it is narrow enough to be placed between rows of tables. See Figure 3-23.

The *guéridon* generally has three shelves: the top shelf is used for the preparation and plating of the dishes; the middle shelf to store underliners, napkins, condiments and service sets; and the lower shelf for storing the carving board and carving sets.

All the shelves on the *guéridon* should be covered with linen. The linen on each shelf of the *guéridon* should be neatly folded so that it does not drape or hang over the sides of the shelf.

The Réchaud

The *réchaud* is a portable stove designed to cook, flambée, or keep food warm. It is usually made of stainless steel, copper, brass, or silver plate. The base is cylindrical of varying heights with a detachable grate. The pan rests on the grate. See Figure 3-24. The heat sources used are propane gas, alcohol, or solid fuel. It is used in the dining room for the tableside preparation of food items. Some *réchauds* are built into the *guéridon,* while others must be placed on the top of the *guéridon.* Most *réchauds* have been replaced by portable butane gas stoves.

Blazer Pans

Blazer pans may be oval, rectangular, or round. The oval blazer-type pan should be made of copper or stainless steel. Copper, a more efficient conductor of heat, provides an even spread of heat throughout the pan relatively quickly. Copper has a greater aesthetic value and is thus preferred. The shape of the pan is generally designed to suit particular items, although its use is not restricted to those items. For example, Crêpes Suzettes pans are copper plated shallow pans, normally ranging from 9 to 16 inches in diameter. They are primarily used for tableside dessert items, particularly Crêpes Suzettes.

Chauffe-Plats

These heat retaining panels may be stacked in a small battery at a convenient service point inside the dining room, and then brought to the *guéridon* when required. Chauffe-plats are used for keeping foods warm when tableside plating is performed, or when a direct flame is not needed.

Centerpieces

Centerpieces are decorative attention-getters that many establishments use to enhance their table presentations. They may be small and discreet, such as a bud vase with a single flower, or large and flamboyant, such as an ice sculpture on a buffet table. The choice and style of centerpieces depends on the establishment's concept and overall mood. Of the five types of centerpieces—floral and foliage, edible, sculpted, ceramic, and lighting—floral and foliage pieces are the most common.

Floral and Foliage

Floral and foliage centerpieces may be made from fresh flowers and greenery, dried flowers, or silk or synthetic flowers and foliage. When choosing a floral centerpiece, several factors affect the final selection:

- Expense—Fresh arrangements are expensive and need to be frequently replaced. Good-quality dried and artificial arrangements are initially expensive but can last almost indefinitely with good care and storage.
- Proportion—The centerpiece should enhance, not dominate, the table setting. Avoid large arrangements that obstruct conversation or create a visual barrier.
- Scent—Strong scents and perfumes may irritate or trigger allergies in some guests. In addition, strong scents may overpower the aromas of food and beverages.
- Color coordination and seasonality—Fresh and dried flowers, and artificial arrangements should complement the décor and reflect the season.
- Caution—Dried and artificial arrangements may pose a danger if placed too close to candles. Be aware of local fire ordinances that may restrict their use.

Table Accessories

Table accessories include a variety of items that make serving convenient and dining more enjoyable for guests. Ashtrays and matches, salt and pepper shakers, and condiments such as vinegar or ketchup, sugar, and creamers are considered table accessories. In a fine-dining environment, these should be kept to a minimum, but in high-volume restaurants in which servers are under severe time constraints, several accessories may be left on the table.

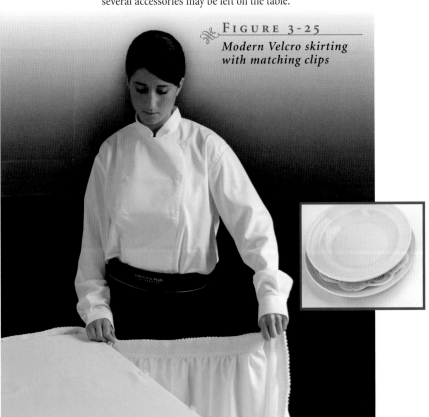

FIGURE 3-25
Modern Velcro skirting with matching clips

Linens

Linen is considered one of the "big four" in the food service industry, along with china, flatware, and glassware. Linen is an expense that must be carefully monitored to control losses and additional costs. The high capital expense for a laundering facility is usually feasible for only those establishments that have a large volume of business and are usually associated with a hotel that can afford this expense. Because of the expense involved, many food service establishments are opting to forego the use of tablecloths and are using placemats, paper, vinyl, and glass table tops.

The style and colors of linens should reflect the environment and the atmosphere of the dining room. Linens may be 100% natural fiber, a 50-50 blend of cotton and polyester, or 100% polyester. Polyester is more easily maintained and colorfast, but cotton or other natural fiber linens are generally more attractive and tend to hold folds better. Creasing is particularly important for folded napkins and formally pleated table skirting and draping.

There are standard guidelines for purchasing tablecloths. The overhang on a square or rectangular table should be a minimum of 7 inches and a maximum of 12 inches. For round tables, the hang of the cloth should be a minimum of 10 inches. It is important to note that it is less expensive to purchase linens that are a standard size. Custom made linens cost considerably more.

Silencers and Napperons

A silencer may include a custom made pad or may simply be a linen or felt cloth that is placed on the table surface underneath the table cloth. Its purpose is to give the linen used a richer texture and to reduce the noise level when plates are placed on the cover. Silencers also help to extend the life of linens. Some tables are manufactured with silencer pads already installed.

A *napperon* is a linen overlay that is placed over a table cloth for both protective and decorative purposes. It is used as a runner on a banquet table, and acts as a seasonal decoration during the holiday season.

Skirting

Skirting refers to the specialized linen used for draping tables. Skirting provides a uniform appearance; is more economical than tablecloths; and requires less labor to maintain. Clips, pins, or tapes are used to attach skirting to a table. See Figure 3-25.

Skirting is available in three types of pleating: sheer, accordion, and box. Sheer pleating is used for lace and other sheer fabrics in overlays. The accordion pleat is a closed pleat; the box pleat is an open pleat that is often used with more substantial fabrics.

Doilies

A *doily* is an intricately patterned lace mat that was traditionally made of cotton or linen thread, and is named after Doily, a seventeenth century London draper. Today, doilies are made of paper and are a standard fixture in most restaurants. They are designed for use in between 2 pieces of china when the base of the upper piece does not fit directly into the well of the piece it is on. They may also be used on trays for hors d'oeuvres or small bite sized pastries to embellish the presentation. Doilies come in a variety of standard sizes such as 4, 6, 8, 10 and 12 inch rounds. A common service mistake is to use a doily under a coffee or soup cup when a saucer is properly sized for it.

FIGURE 3-26

An air pot brewer with a single decanter

Although French presses are more costly to maintain and more labor intensive, many upscale establishments use them to ensure the freshest and most flavorful coffee. French presses come in 10- to 20-ounce (296- to 591-ml) sizes and use medium grind coffee at a rate of 1–1 1/2 ounces (30–44 ml) per 20 ounces (591 ml) of boiling water.

Pour the coffee into the French press pot, and add boiling water. The grounds will float to the top. Then stir the grounds rapidly 2 or 3 times and cover the pot. Wait for 3 minutes before slowly pressing the plunger.

Single pot brewers yield 60 ounces (1.77 l), or 12 5-ounce (148-ml) servings, and may be pour-through or plumbed systems. Each pot requires 3 ounces (89 ml) of ground coffee.

Air pot brewers dispense brewed coffee into an insulated serving decanter that holds the product at 185°F (85°C) for an hour. Because additional heat is not applied, the flavor of the coffee does not deteriorate as it does in single pot brewers. Most air pots hold 75 ounces, (2.22 l) or 15 5-ounce (148-ml) servings, and use 3 1/2 ounces (104 ml) of coffee. See Figure 3-26.

High volume food service operations generally use an automatic urn that yields 60 5-ounce (148-ml) servings of coffee, brewed with 2 1/2 gallons (9.46 l) of water to one pound (.45 kg) of coarse-ground coffee. Unless the urn is equipped with an automatic mixing device, draw the stronger coffee from the bottom of the urn, and pour it back into the brew (but not through the grounds) to ensure uniform strength.

Modular brewers combine a fixed-location brewing module (the heating and volume control) with mobile brewed coffee containers of various capacities (5, 10, and 20 l). Heating systems keep coffee at 185°F (85°C). Most brewers, except the French press, use paper filters that eliminate soluble solids to keep coffee clear. Because paper filters are thrown away after each use, sanitation is easier with these brewers; however, filters can pick up odors that affect the coffee's flavor if stored near aromatic foods.

Coffee Makers

There are many types and brands of coffee makers. There are those machines that make only regular grind coffee, and those that create only espresso and cappuccino. The mechanical features of these makers vary as do the procedures for their usage and maintenance. Most establishments lease coffee makers from the company that is supplying the coffee. The advantage to leasing is a reduction in capital expenditures and free maintenance that is provided by the company in a timely manner.

The most important determinant in the selection of coffee makers is the volume of fresh brewed coffee the machines typically serve. For amounts of less than 3 gallons (11.36 l) of coffee per hour, a French press or a single pot brewer is appropriate. For 3–6 gallons (11.36–22.71 l) per hour, an air pot brewing system gives the best results. An amount of more than 6 gallons (22.71 l) requires either a modular system or an automatic urn system.

Ice Makers and Bins

Ice is a key component of drinks that is often overlooked. An ice machine should be able to produce ice in a quantity that the establishment needs over the course of a day, and should be able to fully recover the maximum quantity for the next business day. Unfortunately, many icemakers produce both thin and hollow or semi-hollow ice that melts too quickly. Ice machines must be properly maintained and kept clean. Ice scoops should be stored in a holster attached to the ice machine, which drains properly.

FIGURE 3-27
Soda dispensed through a soda gun system

Soda Systems

Soda can be dispensed using a dispensing system with a soda gun. See Figure 3-27. There are two types of containers that are currently used on the market: the soda tank and the bag-in-a-box. The tank system is slowly becoming obsolete. The bag-in-a-box system has a single line flowing from a container of syrup to a pump that enables the syrup to travel to the soda dispenser known as a soda gun. A protective cap must first be removed for the line to be properly connected and snapped into place. Some upscale restaurants and bars have recently replaced these systems with high quality bottled mixers that lack convenience and add to the cost.

Bread Warmers

A bread warmer should be turned on ahead of time (approximately 1 hour) so that it is properly heated before use. For soft rolls or breads, place a small cup containing a water-soaked clean napkin in each drawer to keep the rolls moist and to prevent them from becoming dry and hard. This procedure is unnecessary for hard rolls and crusty breads.

At the end of each shift:

- Turn off the warmer.
- Remove the water cups.
- Remove the drawer and empty the contents, and wipe it clean. Return the bread and rolls to the kitchen for use as bread crumbs.
- Replace the drawer.

Note: Refrigerated or frozen rolls need to be re-baked in an oven prior to storing them in the bread warmer.

Toaster

The conveyor toaster is most common in the food service industry. Some toasters use a timer-setting method to ensure proper toasting, while others use a rotisserie cycle span. To clean a toaster:

- Shut the toaster off and unplug.
- Remove the grills and the crumb catch pans from the unit.
- Clean the crumbs and burnt products.
- Reassemble the toaster.

The Server

CHAPTER 4

IN THIS CHAPTER,
we will examine the positions available and the skills that today's professional servers need to be successful. The server's role may vary from establishment to establishment depending on the style of service. As it is a controllable variable cost, management must balance server cost with the needs of guests; the service requirements of the menu; and the cost of training as it relates to food and beverage sales pricing. Most restaurants employ single server systems that are supported by limited assistance. The server is responsible for service that begins with greeting the guest and continues to the farewell. Establishments that use modified team service employ bussers or server assistants. More elaborate and fine dining establishments usually employ a full-service team, which includes a brigade of servers who have different levels of experience and knowledge.

The Brigade

Dining rooms using the brigade system, or full-service team, may be made up of as many as seven positions:

Dining Room Manager/Maître d'

The *dining room manager/maître d'* should be in close contact with every department of the restaurant and should know all aspects of the business. The manager has the ultimate responsibility for the success of the dining room.

Sommelier

The *sommelier* is a wine steward who must have extensive knowledge of wines, spirits, and beverages. This individual is in charge of purchasing, service, sales training, and the control of beverages.

Host/Hostess

The *host* or *hostess'* role may be assumed by the dining room manager, but is frequently filled by another charming and inviting personality who can focus on greeting and seating guests using proper etiquette and protocol. This position also includes the task of ensuring the smooth flow of seating by managing the reservation system so that the seating capacity is maximized with few delays for guests who are waiting to be seated. The host or hostess should not delay seating guests if the entire party has yet to appear. Single diners should also be made to feel welcome and asked if they would prefer dining at the bar.

Captain

The *captain* supervises and organizes every service detail for his or her station or room, including taking orders and synchronizing service for the station.

Waiter or Front Waiter

The *front waiter* assists the captain and should be able to perform all duties in the absence of the captain. The front waiter's primary responsibilities include the service of food and beverages to guests.

Back Waiter

The *back waiter* serves as a bridge between the brigade and the kitchen, and has the primary responsibility of placing and picking up orders from the kitchen. The individual with this title is sometimes referred to as a runner, especially in a banquet department.

Busser

The *busser,* or server assistant position is usually an entry-level position. This person is primarily responsible for clearing and grooming the table. Transitory employees such as high school or college students commonly fill this position.

Server
Attributes

*Quality service cannot be left to chance;
it requires training that is refined through
practice and experience. A professional server
becomes the restaurant's representative and
salesperson, as well as a skilled server.*

Server as Representative

Because the server has more contact with guests
than any other restaurant employee, the server is
the restaurant's ambassador. This individual sets
the mood in the dining room by making guests
feel welcome, relaxed, and secure that their
needs will be met. Courtesy, friendliness, and
superior interpersonal skills are the hallmarks of
a professional server.

FIGURE 4-1
*Effective servers use
suggestive selling
techniques.*

Server as Salesperson

A successful restaurant server is a skilled salesperson who helps guests experience a satisfying dining experience by explaining menu options; describing specials in detail; suggesting
wines or other beverages to complement the food; and helping tailor choices to the diner's
needs and expectations.

Successful selling entails making guests feel pampered, as well as adding to the revenue of
both the restaurant and the server. Effective servers encourage guests to add to their original
orders by guiding them to new, unusual, or premium items. See Figure 4-1. This process,
known as *suggestive selling,* incorporates highlighting, assumptive selling, and upselling.

Highlighting Drawing a guest's attention to particular menu items is called *highlighting.*
By using vivid and enthusiastic descriptions, guests are encouraged to try specials or to order
items that the chef is eager to sell. If the kitchen staff is backed up, a good server may suggest
items that require less preparation and provide guests' service.

Assumptive selling The sales technique known as *assumptive selling* uses open-
ended questions to guide guests in making their choices. The server might ask the guest for
a wine preference, implying that a particular wine would complement the menu selection.
Not only does this technique increase sales, but it also makes guests feel that their needs are
being addressed.

Upselling Sales can be increased by *upselling:* a technique that promotes the sale of items
of a better quality or of a larger size than what was originally contemplated. Taking an order
for scotch, for example, might involve suggesting Dewar's® or Chivas Regal®, which are higher-
quality and priced alternatives to bar scotch. Although the technique is not always successful,
upselling consistently increases the establishment's sales and the server's income.

The Server as a Skilled Professional

The members of a restaurant's service team (busser/runner, server, captain, sommelier, bartender, host, and maître d', or manager) should strive for the following attributes:

1. Positive attitude
2. Good appearance
3. Good communication skills
4. Thorough job knowledge
5. Timeliness.

Positive Attitude

A positive attitude is essential when dealing with the public. Attitudes need to be differentiated from behaviors. Behaviors are the physical expression of a mental process. They may be learned, adjusted, and manipulated by an individual or by management, but the sincerity of the behavior can come into question when the underlying attitude that drives the behavior is absent. When we discuss the behavioral skills associated with the front of the house employees, we must first identify the correct attitude or willingness to please the guest at all times. Without such an attitude or willingness, servers with all the manual skills in the world will not succeed in their responsibilities.

Guests should not be able to read anything into a server's behavior that might detract from a positive dining experience. The server should never be judgmental about a guest or the potential to upsell and build a higher check total. Servers need to be flexible and able to adapt to personalities and circumstances.

Appearance

Servers who make a good appearance present guests with a favorable first impression of an establishment. Good personal hygiene, neat attire, and professional body language are the elements that are most important.

Personal Hygiene:

- Hair that is longer than collar length must be properly restrained.
- Hands must remain clean, which requires frequent washing especially after using the rest room as required by law.
- Fingernails must be kept trimmed and clean.
- Teeth should be clean and the breath should be fresh.
- Servers should pay attention to body odor and use deodorant as needed.
- Colognes and perfumes should not be worn as they detract from the aromas of the food and wine.

Attire (See Figure 4-2):

- Jewelry should be kept to a minimum, e.g., wedding bands.
- Uniforms should be kept clean and well pressed.
- Uniforms should fit properly.
- Shoes should be clean and shined.
- Shirts and blouses should be pressed, free of stains, and not frayed.

FIGURE 4-2

The uniform plays a role in creating both the ambiance and the perceived professionalism of employees in a restaurant.

Body Language:

Servers must be aware of physical mannerisms that might reflect poor sanitary standards or a poor attitude. The following behaviors should be observed:

- Make eye contact with the guest and smile.
- Maintain good posture.
- Do not slouch or lean on walls. "If you have time to lean, you have time to clean."
- Be careful about touching your hair, face, mouth or nose, especially in view of the guests.
- Never curse or use poor language in earshot of a guest.
- Do not chatter with other servers in view of guests.
- Do not stand around with the hands in pockets.
- Smoking, drinking, chewing gum or eating during service, are never permitted.
- Do not wipe the brow or nose with the jacket sleeve.
- Do not sneeze in your bare hands.
- Never produce flatware or a napkin from one of your pockets.
- Stand erect and do not lean on or hold on to the back of a customer's chair. It suggests familiarity with the customer and is unprofessional.
- Maintain a height advantage at the table. It will help you sell.

Communication Skills

It is imperative that management train the front-of-the-house personnel in good communication skills. The people with whom the server must learn to communicate are guests, kitchen and bar personnel, and fellow dining room personnel (servers, bussers, hosts, maîtres d'). The server must recognize that communication takes place in three ways:

❧ FIGURE 4-3
Written checks communicate guest needs to the kitchen.

Written Transmit information that can be read by another person or persons. See Figure 4-3. Computer assisted communication falls into this category. Take care to write orders clearly if the establishment does not use a computerized ordering system. Guest checks should be clear and accurate.

Verbal Communicate directly to the person by speaking. Do not address guests as "you guys," which undermines the guest's perception of the server as a professional. Address guests and fellow staff members professionally. Keep communications with customers friendly, but not familiar.

Non-verbal Non-verbal body language is used to communicate attitudes and feelings knowingly and sometimes unknowingly. Servers should have good eye contact with guests; use facial expressions, such as smiling; but should avoid touching guests.

Job Knowledge

Job knowledge includes a thorough understanding of the workplace: the layout, flow, equipment, communication between departments, familiarity with the food, wine, and beverage menus. It is essential to be able to make recommendations and to answer customers' questions about local events or landmarks, or to deal with customer complaints or problems. A complete understanding of a server's responsibility in serving alcohol is also a key element, and is further discussed in Chapter 9: "Mixology". A thorough knowledge of the manual skills of serving and clearing tables and a familiarity with using a computerized point-of-sale system are equally important.

Timeliness

Typically servers are responsible for the service at more than one table. This group of tables (usually three or four tables) is called a *station* or *section*. See Figure 4-4. The level of service within a station depends on the quality of service as well as the speed with which the server can work accurately and safely. To perform effectively, servers must be well organized and able to prioritize their work load and execute it with an economy of movement; including but not limited to trips to and from the kitchen.

FIGURE 4-4

A three station layout for the dining room

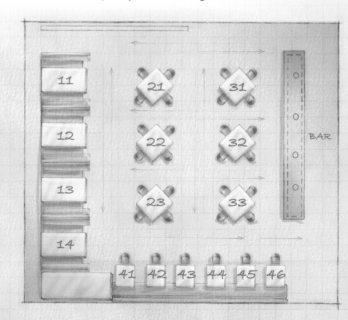

Server Skills

A mastery of equipment use, a food and beverage knowledge, and a demonstration of manual dexterity to provide service seemingly effortlessly, are all hallmarks of a true dining room professional. These server skills are at the heart of the profession.

Setting Tables

Prior to setting a table, the server should check that the table is free of wobbling and correctly positioned so as not to block the flow of traffic. See Figure 4-5. Nothing is more annoying to guests than having servers bump into their chairs or tables as they walk by during service.

Whether setting a table with paper placemats or fine linen, the server must ensure that the tabletop, the chairs, the benches, and the area around each table are clean. Constant inspection of the table should take place during service, particularly when tables are being reset. When using a placemat, whether paper, vinyl or linen, it should be centered on the cover, or at the guest's position, about 1 inch from the edge of the table. A paper or cloth napkin may be placed to the left side of the mat or in the center. Placement of flatware, vases, condiments, salt and pepper shakers, and any other item should be consistent and uniform on all tables.

When using table cloths it is important to remember that the sewn seam should always be on the under side and not visible to the guest. The cloth should be placed so that it falls evenly on all sides, and ideally, should not fall below the surface or cushion of the seats. See Figure 4-6. When setting a round table with four legs, as opposed to a round table with a pedestal, the tablecloth should be laid to allow the corners of the cloth to hide the legs of the table. Cloths that are stained, torn, frayed, or contain burn marks or holes should be sent for repairs or converted into rags. Never attempt to hide stains or holes by placing vases or ashtrays over them. These cloths should be neatly folded and tagged so that they are separated from the inventory. Cloth napkins should be placed in the center of the setting or the center of the show plate or charger. See Figure 4-7. The napkin may also be placed to the side of the place setting, possibly on the B&B plate, or as a decorative fold in the water glass.

Note: The undersides of table tops should always be checked for any chewing gum that may have been placed there by a guest.

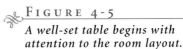

FIGURE 4-5
A well-set table begins with attention to the room layout.

FIGURE 4-6
Table cloths should be placed evenly across the table top.

FIGURE 4-7
A show plate or charger adds to the table décor and the ambiance

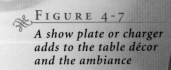

Place Settings

Whether setting flatware for breakfast, lunch, dinner, or banquet service, it is essential to follow certain rules:

- Place the show plate or napkin at the center of each place setting first.
- The place setting should allow adequate space for placing a large service or show plate in the center without requiring the movement of utensils when serving.
- Forks are set on the left side of the cover with tines facing up.
- Knives and spoons are set on the right side of the cover.
- Knives are set with the cutting edge toward the center of the place setting.
- Flatware should be placed so that it does not hang over the edge of the table: one inch from the edge of the table is standard.
- All other flatware is placed parallel to the entrée knife and the fork. The flatware may be staggered or placed with the handles at the same distance from the edge of the table.
- All flatware is set from the outside in, following the sequence of use.
- Do not place flatware to the inside of the entrée knife or fork.
- The dessert fork and spoon are placed at the top of the cover, perpendicular to the other flatware, with the spoon on top of the fork.
- Bread and butter plates are set on the left, next to or above the forks.
- The water glass is set above the tip of the dinner knife, and wine glasses are set from the outside following the sequence of use. All glassware should be polished prior to service.
- If several wine glasses are pre-set in a flight, or row, the water glass may be set directly above the place setting or off to the right. The wine glass furthest to the right would be used for the first wine served, the second glass for the second wine, etc.
- When coffee or tea cups are pre-set, they are placed to the right of the knives and spoons, with the handle at the four o'clock position.
- China, flatware, and glassware should not touch each other.
- On rectangular, square or round tables with an even number of settings, all flatware items on one place setting should be aligned with those on the opposite side, in a straight line.
- If each cover includes an entrée knife and fork, and is set directly across from another cover, the knife is placed directly across from the fork.
- Establishments require different settings that best suit the needs of their menus.
- A decorative centerpiece or 'candlelight' should be placed in the center of the table with a set of filled salt and pepper shakers placed to one side. This should be uniform for all tables so that the salt shaker is, for example, on the left of the pepper shaker at all tables.

Greeting the Guest

Because first impressions are lasting, it is critical that the initial greeting is warm, relaxed, and hospitable. Greeting guests is usually the responsibility of the dining room host or hostess, or maître d', although all front-of-the-house employees should be trained to greet guests properly. Rules for greeting guests include:

- Opening and holding the door open for guests if possible.
- Greeting guests with a warm smile.
- Making good eye contact and using an appropriate welcoming remark.
- Advising guests where they can check or hang their coats.
- Helping to remove coats whenever possible. (Note: Many restaurants dissuade their employees from checking in customers' coats because of liability issues. Any well-managed establishment will have proper controls in place to avoid any potential loss of property.)
- Inquiring if the guests have made a reservation. If so, ask for their name.
- Being honest with guests if there is a waiting period or list. Nothing irritates guests more than to be misled as to how long the wait will be.
- If there is a long delay for a party with a reservation, it is a good restaurant policy to offer a free drink or appetizer.

Seating the Guest and Presenting the Menu

It is usually the responsibility of the maître d' or host /hostess to lead guests to their table and to ensure that they are seated comfortably. According to protocol, the host leads the party to the table and is followed by the men in the party who are then in a position to assist ladies with their chairs. If the aisles are wide enough, gentlemen escort ladies on their right side. Unfortunately there is frequently insufficient space in dining rooms to walk side by side.

The host is responsible for:

- Checking that the menus are presentable and contain all additional inserts.
- Personalizing the way the party is addressed; for example: "Your table is right this way," or "Let me show you to your table."
- Using the guests' surnames whenever possible.
- Leading guests to the table at a pace that does not make them feel rushed.
- Pulling chairs out for the guests, ladies first.
- Presenting menus and wine lists if it is the restaurant's standard operating procedure for the maître d' to do so.
- Presenting the menus to women first and the host of the dining party last from the right side of the guest.
- Relaying any special request concerning the guests to the server.
- Removing any extra place settings.

Note: The host should never rush guests to make them feel unwelcome.

When servers are expected to help with seating, they should be familiar with the interplay between the chair and the floor treatment as it affects the way in which they can assist guests. The server may have to lift the chair slightly and may also need to use a knee to assist with pushing in the chair.

Greeting by the Server

Allow guests to relax and settle into their seats for a few moments before approaching the table. Welcome the guests to the restaurant, and possibly introduce yourself only if it is the establishment's policy to do so. For example, say: "Good evening. My name is Bob, and I'll be your server. Please let me know if there is anything that I can do to make your visit more enjoyable." More formal restaurants choose to create a greater degree of formality by not having servers introduce themselves by name. Servers should remember to:

- Maintain good eye contact with each guest at the table.

- Stand erect at the table rather than bend down.

- Maintain a certain distance between the guest and themselves by creating a buffer that allows one to hear and be heard, while not intruding on the guest's space. The noisier the dining room, the closer one has to stand to the guest.

- Even if in a hurry, never appear rushed at the table.

- Observe the guests' comfort level, their body language and be aware of the type of occasion that has brought them to the restaurant.

Note: The restaurant host or maitre d' should try to determine which guest is the host of the party as well as who the guest of honor might be if there is one, and inform the server.

Napkin Handling

Once guests have been seated, it is the policy of some establishments to have servers assist with guests' napkins. However, it is contrary to guest etiquette to place the napkin on one's lap before everyone is seated as it indicates that the meal has already begun. Other establishments have policies where the server should handle the guest's napkin as little as possible and should only do so when absolutely necessary. If a napkin fold is placed in a glass, the server should request that the guest remove it if it remains in the glass when water service occurs. If the guest leaves the table, the server should either leave the napkin where it is or bring a new napkin and remove the used one. If the guest drops their napkin on the floor, the server should first bring a new one, then pick up the used napkin from the floor and proceed to wash his or her hands.

The Beverage Order

Servers should have a knowledge of popular drinks, and of the brands of liquor, beers, and wines available by the glass. It is essential that beverage service is correctly performed because it is the first point of service. Servers should use appropriate sales techniques to ask guests what they would like to drink. Servers should:

- Take the guest of honor's order first, then those of the women, men, and finally that of the host.

- Use position numbers to ensure that the beverages are served to the appropriate guest.

- Clarify the guests' preferences regarding the preparation of drinks (e.g.: straight up or on the rocks, an olive or a twist of lemon?).

- Repeat the order to each guest if in doubt.

- Serve beverages, whenever possible, from the right side with the right hand, and with the right foot forward.

- Serve the guest of honor first, then the women going in a clockwise direction before serving the men and the host last.

- Avoid reaching in front of guests.

- Handle stemmed glasses by the stem and base glasses by the base.

- Check back for a second round of beverages when the drinks are nearly consumed, using responsible alcohol practices.

- Be sure that it is the intention of all guests to have another drink if a customer orders a second round of beverages.

- Remove the empty glass before serving a fresh drink. Empty glasses should not accumulate on the table.

- Use the same procedure for reordering beverages. Refer to the original order to avoid asking again what each guest is drinking.

- Ask the guest if you may remove a glass, unless it is empty.

Beverage Tray Handling

General rules for the use of a beverage tray follow:

- The tray should be clean and dry before it is used at a table.
- Glasses or cups should be placed as close to the center of gravity as possible and should be repositioned as the service from the tray proceeds.
- The tray should be carried in the left hand and at a level between the chest and the waist. See Figure 4-8.
- Trays should never be held between the server and the guest, or between the server and the table.
- Care should be taken not to tilt the beverage tray at an angle when placing the beverage onto the table. (Note: If you tuck your left elbow into your side, you are less likely to tip the tray.)
- The tray should be held with the left hand under the center of the tray and not held by the edge. See Figure 4-9.
- When removing glassware from a beverage tray, always hold the glasses from the base or by the stem with the fingers away from the rim of the glassware. See Figure 4-10.
- Never allow a guest to remove items from a beverage tray held by a server.

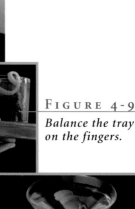

FIGURE 4-8
The beverage tray should be carried in the left hand.

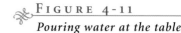 FIGURE 4-11
Pouring water at the table

Cold Beverage Service

Cold beverage service includes the service of water, soft drinks, ready to drink beverages, juices, milk, liquor, beer, and wine. Glasses should be carried on a beverage, cocktail or hand tray during service, though clean stemmed glasses may be safely and most efficiently carried by hand to save time when setting up or resetting a table. This technique prevents contact with the bowl of the glass. Glasses are placed upside down, with the stem between the fingers and the bowls of the glasses touching one another.

Water Service

Many restaurants in the United States automatically serve water to guests. Establishments that do not serve water, often prefer to promote the sale of bottled water or of other beverages. Servers should not say: "bottled or just tap water". Establishments that are becoming more environmentally aware are reducing or eliminating the sale of bottled water unless the water is spring fed, flavored, and a popular request. When serving water,

- pre-set water glasses to the right of the guest's cover, or place setting, usually above and in line with the entrée knife. See Figure 4-11.

FIGURE 4-9
Balance the tray on the fingers.

FIGURE 4-10
Handle glassware by the base or stem.

FIGURE 4-12

An assortment of water pitcher styles.

Mineral Water

Mineral water should be served cold and poured into a glass that is shaped differently from the water goblet for easier identification. Avoid adding ice unless requested by the guest. Guests often order mineral water because they dislike the taste of tap water. Melting ice will add tap water flavors to the mineral water.

Other Cold Beverages

When serving beverages such as soft drinks, milk, and iced tea, use an appropriately sized glass. If using garnishes, ensure that they are appropriate and fresh. Service of some beverages such as iced tea accompanied by a long spoon may be enhanced by placing the glass on a doilied B&B plate. Place the beverage to the right of the guest's cover.

When serving bottled beverages, place the appropriate glass before the guest, and proceed to fill the glass no more than two-thirds of the way to the top. Leave the bottle to the guest's right with the label facing the guest.

Beer Service

There are several factors that determine quality beer service. The first is the correct service temperature of beer. Pilsners and lagers are usually served at 44°F–50°F (7°C–10°C); ales at 50°F–57°F (10°C–14°C); and porters and stouts at 60°F–65°F (16°C–18°C). Secondly, a clear unfrosted glass is the optimal serving choice for beer to display color and clarity. The glass must be thoroughly cleaned and properly rinsed. Any detergent residue will collapse the foam, decrease carbonation, and adversely impact flavor. *"Beer clean"* is a term that refers to the highest standard of cleanliness for serving glasses. The third factor relates to the shape of the glass, which potentially enhances the appearance, flavor, and taste of beer by the way it retains the *head* or foam of the beer. The head helps to retain the aromas. Frosted glasses may have a place in sports bars, but the frosted condensation reduces the 'head'.

When serving bottled or canned beer, allow the glass to remain on a flat surface. Pour the beer so that the stream flows straight into the center of the glass. Do not tilt the glass or pour down its side. Place the bottle to the right of the glass with the label facing the customer.

If drawing from a tap, hold the glass at a 45° angle about 1 inch below the tap and open it fully. As the glass becomes half full, let the beer pour straight down the middle. It may take 2 to 3 minutes to properly serve beer from taps especially stout beers. Close the tap when the beer head has risen slightly above the rim.

Draft beer should remain cold at 40°F–50°F (4°C–10°C), because it is not always pasteurized. Draft beer lines must be cleaned on a frequent and regular basis to avoid bacterial contamination that will negatively impact the flavor of all beer served through the unclean lines. Some states have specific laws governing how frequently draft beer lines are to be cleaned. Carbon dioxide pressure must be monitored and controlled to maintain consistent carbonation and an even distribution rate. A carbon dioxide regulator is usually connected to the tap system to accomplish this.

- bring a pitcher filled with ice water to the table.
- using a neatly folded service towel or STP to catch any drips, pour water into the water glass, being careful not to overfill. The glass should be about three-fourths full.
- refill the glass as needed, never allowing the glass to be less than one-fourth full. Water service in the United States requires constant attention. Don't refill every two minutes.
- if the water pitcher has an insufficiently wide spout or lacks an ice guard (see Figure 4-12), it may be necessary to remove the glass from the table and pour water behind the guest to avoid spills on the table.

Wine Service

A familiarity with an establishment's wine list and the basic principles of pairing wine with food is critical to a server's success. Before suggesting a wine to guests, ask about the kinds of wines they like to avoid making pointless suggestions. Be aware of any wines that may not be available or that may have a different vintage year than the one stated on the wine list. Use the following tips to help guests select wines:

- Take the wine order from the host, either by name or bin number.

- Check the wine label and vintage for accuracy before presenting the bottle to the guest. See Figure 4-13.

- Preset the appropriate wine glasses by handling the stems only, and bring the bucket to the table if serving a white wine. In formal settings, an additional tasting glass may be brought for the host to taste the wine. See Figure 4-14.

- Determine who will be having wine, and ensure that all guests are of legal drinking age.

- Present the wine to the host for verification, and repeat the wine's brand, variety or classification, appellation, and vintage. See Figure 4-15.

- Determine when the guests want their wine poured.

- Pour 1 ounce (30 ml) of wine for the host for tasting purposes. If the wine is refused, determine the reason and find the sommelier or manager. A faulty cork occasionally compromises the flavor of wine. In that event, the manager may replace the wine with another bottle.

- Avoid reaching in front of the guest to pour. Delicately pour wine in a continuous flow for each person from the right side and with the right hand, twisting the bottle at the end of each pour to avoid drips. See Figure 4-16.

- Serve the guest of honor first and moving clockwise serve the ladies first.

- Return the wine to the wine bucket or to the chiller, or on the bread and butter plate/coaster on the table with the label facing the host.

FIGURE 4-16
Pour wine at the guest's right.

Tips to help guests select wines

FIGURE 4-13
Check the wine label to insure accuracy before serving it to the guest.

FIGURE 4-14
Mark the table with glassware before opening the wine.

FIGURE 4-15
Presenting the wine before opening it allows the wine host to verify that the correct wine is being served.

- Avoid overpouring wine.

- Discreetly allow the host to know when the bottle is empty and determine whether another bottle is desired. If the host orders another bottle of wine, bring a clean glass for tasting, even if it is the same wine.

- If guests switch to a different wine, bring clean and appropriate wine glasses.

- When guests have finished the bottle and do not require another, remove it from the table before removing the wine glasses.

Opening Procedures for White, Rosé, and Dessert Wines

Follow these procedures when opening white, rosé, and dessert wines:

- Ask the guest if they prefer the wine in an ice bucket as they may not.

- If using a wine bucket, fill it three-quarters of the way with equal amounts of ice and water. Place it in either a wine bucket stand, or if using a chiller, place it on the table to the right of the host. A chiller is pre-chilled and does not require ice and water. See Figure 4-17.

- Present the wine from the right side with the label facing the host. Read the wine's primary identification: the vintage, the brand, variety, classification, the appellation in that order.

- Then place the wine bottle in the chiller or in the bucket, draping a service napkin in the form of a collar around the neck of the bottle. When opening it, rest the bottle on the side of the bucket for additional support.

- When a table is small and does not allow the server to open the bottle on the table's surface, the server must be adept at opening the bottle in the hands.

- If using the blade of a corkscrew, remove the top of the capsule by cutting it below the lip or bulge of the wine bottle. See Figure 4-18. If using a foil cutter to attain a perfectly neat edge, cut above the lip. If the capsule is torn, remove it from the bottle entirely and put it in your pocket. If the bottle has an exaggerated lip at its top with a small seal affixed to the surface of the cork, perforate the seal with the worm of the corkscrew before proceeding to remove the cork.

- Wipe the top of the bottle with a clean service napkin to remove any mold or debris.

- Insert the worm of the corkscrew into the center of the cork, and twist until four or five turns of the worm are in the cork. See Figure 4-19. Place the corkscrew lever onto the lip of the bottle; and pull the cork straight out, using the lever. If necessary, use a delicate wriggling motion to completely remove the cork. Unscrew the cork from the corkscrew.

- Again, use a clean napkin to wipe any particles from the mouth of the bottle, making sure that your hands do not come in contact with it.

- Present the cork to the host's right side by placing it on a plate with a doily. (The host may wish to examine the condition of the cork to determine the authenticity and storage conditions of the wine.) Remove the plate and cork from the table after the guest has been served the wine.

- Remove the bottle from the chiller or bucket, holding the bottle over the long folded portion of the service towel collar and leave the label exposed to the guests' view.

- Pour about 1 ounce (30 ml) of the wine into a tasting glass for the host's approval. Do not allow the bottle to touch the glass.

- After the wine has been approved, pour wine for the other guests, serving the host last.

- After pouring the wine in 3- or 4-ounce servings (89- or 118-ml), place the bottle back into the ice bucket or chiller, and fold a service towel over the top of the bucket.

- Avoid pouring more than 3 or 4 ounces (89 or 118 ml) of wine at a time to prevent warming that may impair the flavor. Pouring smaller servings is especially important with dessert wines, which are often consumed more slowly as they are either sweeter or higher in alcohol or both.

Note: Today's servers encounter fine wines with a variety of closures. These include glass stoppers, synthetic corks, and stelvin capsules or screw caps. The procedures recommended may be modified, especially for screw caps.

Various opening procedures for white, rosé, and dessert wines

FIGURE 4-17

The mise en place for white wine service.

FIGURE 4-18

Cut below the lip, moving the knife around the neck of the bottle.

FIGURE 4-19

Position the sharp point of the cork screw at the center of the cork.

FIGURE 4-20

A doilied bread-and-butter plate acts as the underliner to the wine bottle.

FIGURE 4-21

Cut below the lip, moving the knife around the neck of the bottle.

44

FIGURE 4-22A

Set the notched end of the lever onto the lip of the bottle.

FIGURE 4-22B

Support the lever while lifting the cork out of the bottle.

FIGURE 4-23

When the bottle is opened the wine host should be offered the cork to inspect it.

Opening Procedures for Red Wine

Red wine is not generally chilled in an ice bucket or chiller, so the procedures for opening red wine differ from those used for chilled wines.

- Bring a wine coaster or doilied bread-and-butter plate to the table along with the bottle of wine. See Figure 4-20.

- Present the wine bottle from the right side, with the label facing the host.

- Place the bottle on the coaster or the doilied bread-and-butter plate, and remove the top portion of the seal as previously described. See Figure 4-21.

- Use the same opening procedures described above, and use the doilied plate to present the cork to the host. See Figures 4-22a, 4-22b, and 4-23.

- After approval, pour 4–6 ounces (118–177 ml) of the wine, depending on the style of glass used, and use standard rules of protocol. See Figure 4-24.

- Place the bottle on the coaster or doilied bread-and-butter plate toward the center of the table, with the label facing the host.

- Remove and pocket the cork.

FIGURE 4-24

Pour the host a taste.

FIGURE 4-25

Carefully open wines to be decanted to avoid disturbing any sediment.

FIGURE 4-26

Pour the wine slowly down the inside neck of the decanter.

FIGURE 4-27

Sediment, or a wine's color and tannin molecules, forms in older red wines.

FIGURE 4-28

A silver wine funnel may be used to decant wine.

Decanting Red Wine

Red wines are decanted for three reasons:

- *Decanting* allows some wines to "breathe" so that the full aromatic bouquet may be revealed.
- Careful decanting removes the wine and leaves any accumulated sediment in the bottle.
- Decanting allows wines from a cellar to reach their proper serving temperatures more rapidly, a process called chambréing.

Do not begin decanting red wine more than a half-hour before it is to be served unless requested by the guest. See Figure 4-25. Pour the wine from the bottle carefully into a glass or crystal decanter (33-ounce, or 1-liter, minimum), in a slow but steady stream along the inside of the glass. See Figure 4-26. If decanting an old wine, pour it slowly and continuously so as not to loosen the sediment. Stop pouring as soon as you see sediment approaching the neck of the bottle.

Young red wines such as a young claret from Bordeaux, may be high in tannins. Aerating such a wine by decanting it allows the hard tannins to seem less astringent and makes the wine more palatable. Avoid decanting more delicate red wines such as a Pinot Noir.

Older red wines (10 years or more), particularly those made from thick skinned grapes such as Cabernet Sauvignon, ideally need to stand upright for 24 to 48 hours prior to serving. If the bottle has just been brought from the cellar, however, place it in a cradle or wine basket and open it with the bottle at a 20-30° angle, taking care not to disturb any sediment. When serving from a wine cradle, a lighted candle on a plate or a flashlight should be placed to the right of the decanter so that the server can clearly observe the flow of wine down the neck of the bottle. Stop pouring as soon as the sediment approaches the neck, and do not interrupt the flow because this will loosen the sediment and allow it to spread through the wine. For very expensive older red wines, the guest might choose to be served the remaining wine, regardless of the sediment. See Figure 4-27. In that case, use a special silver funnel with a strainer to pour this wine into a decanter or separate glass. See Figure 4-28.

White wines may also be decanted, especially those made biodynamically with little or no chemical intervention.

Chambréing Wine

Chambré is a French word meaning "brought to room temperature." Although all wines should be stored in a cool cellar at 50°F (10°C), red wines should be served at warmer temperatures, up to 65°F (18°C). Using a warm decanter is the most effective way of bringing wines to their optimum serving temperature.

Decanting red wine

FIGURE 4-29

Twist the cage tab counter clockwise to loosen it.

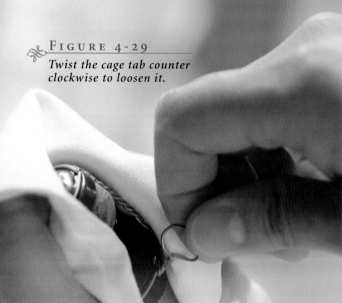

FIGURE 4-30

Holding the cork in a napkin, twist from the bottom of the bottle.

FIGURE 4-31

Present the cork to the wine host.

FIGURE 4-32

Slowly pour a 1 ounce taste in the glass.

FIGURE 4-33

Fill the glasses of all the guests three-fourths full before finishing the host's pour.

Opening Procedures for Sparkling Wines

Sparkling wines should be chilled at 40°F–45°F (4°C–7°C) before opening. The most efficient way to chill sparkling wines is with a sparkling wine bucket, which is taller than a conventional wine bucket. Chilling the wine from storage temperature to serving temperature should take about 20 minutes. Insufficient chilling may cause the cork to exit the bottle explosively; cause the wine to overflow; and force a loss of carbonation. The steps that follow are suggested for the service of sparkling wines.

- At the table, remove the sparkling wine from the ice bucket, and wipe it dry with a service towel.
- Holding the bottle at chest height at a 45° angle, find the perforation or wire loop, and pull it out from under the foil.
- Remove the top part of the foil, and then twist the wire loop counterclockwise about 5 1/2 times until the wire cage can be lifted from the lip of the bottle. Leave the cage (*aggraffe*) on the cork or put it in your pocket. See Figure 4-29.
- While still holding the bottle at a 45° angle, grasp the cork in your left hand, and twist the bottle counterclockwise with your right hand. Do not twist the cork, which may break.
- As the cork is being expelled from the bottle, carefully counterbalance the pressure by gently holding it in and tilting it toward yourself. Allow the slightest amount of gas to escape to help preserve the bubbly character of the wine. The guests should hear a soft hiss rather than a loud pop. See Figure 4-30.
- Continue to hold the bottle at a 45° angle for several seconds to equalize the pressure.
- Present the cork on a doilied plate to the guest. See Figure 4-31.
- Wrap a service towel around the neck of the bottle. Pour a 1-ounce (30-ml) taste for the host's approval. See Figure 4-32.
- After the wine is approved, pour it for each of the guests. Pour the wine down the center of an appropriate fluted or tulip glass, waiting for the foam to subside. Continue to pour until the glass is three-fourths full. See Figure 4-33.
- After pouring, put the bottle back into the bucket with a service towel draped over it.

Service Temperatures of Wine

Serving wine at its appropriate temperature is important. Neglecting this aspect, will at very least, diminish the guest's appreciation of the wine, and at worst, destroy the wine's character and balance.

The senses of taste and smell are important to the appreciation of wine. The volatile compounds of red wine are released at higher temperatures than those of white wine, so the aromas of red wines are easier to detect at 60°F–65°F (16°C–18°C). White wines should be chilled so that their acidity is less pronounced. As a general guideline, the higher the acidity in wine, the lower the serving temperature should be to preserve the balance of the wine on the palate. If red wine is served too warm, the alcohol will become too pronounced and taste less refreshing.

DESSERT AND SPARKLING WINES
40°F–45°F (4°C–7°C)

WHITE WINES, ROSÉS, SHERRIES, BEST CHAMPAGNES
45°F–50°F (7°C–10°C)

BEST QUALITY DRY WHITES, LIGHT REDS (BEAUJOLAIS NOUVEAU, FOR EXAMPLE)
50°F–55°F (10°C–13°C)

LIGHT REDS, ORDINARY BORDEAUX, CHIANTI
55°F–60°F (13°C–16°C)

FULL-BODIED REDS
60°F–65°F (16°C–18°C)

Hot Beverage Service

The quality of hot beverage service is critical because it is often a guest's first or final impression of a dining experience. Coffee or tea may be served as a one-step or two-step procedure, depending on the number of guests at the table, but it is designed so that the server pours at the table. Pouring at the table prevents spilling on the way to the table, and allows guests to see if the cup is clean and the amount of coffee poured is satisfactory.

One-step service means that the warmed cups and saucers, spoons, and condiments are brought to the table on a beverage tray at the same time as the coffee or teapot. The serviceware and condiments are placed appropriately on the table first, and the server proceeds to pour coffee into the cup. A two-step service requires that the server bring and place the preset on the table, and then return with the coffee or teapot to pour it into the cups. Proper coffee or tea service requires that:

- The coffee or teapots and cups are warmed prior to service. See Figure 4-34.
- When using a beverage tray, the lip of the cup and the spoons should not come into direct contact with the tray's surface.
- The cup and saucer are placed at the same time to the right of the cover, with the handle at a 4 o'clock position. The spoon is placed to the right or above the cup on the saucer, or directly on the table to the right of the cup and saucer. See Figure 4-35.
- Cream, half-and-half, or milk are kept refrigerated and poured into a creamer just before service. (In upscale restaurants, the cream or milk might be heated.)
- When unwrapped sugar cubes are used, tongs are provided. The creamer and sugar bowl are placed in front of the guest of honor or the women at the table. See Figure 4-36.

FIGURE 4-34

To quickly warm a hot beverage cup fill it with hot water.

FIGURE 4-35

Mark the course before serving a hot beverage.

FIGURE 4-36

Sugar caddies and creamers are placed nearest the guest of honor or close to the women seated at the table.

Coffee Service

Depending on the style of meal, coffee cups may be preset on the table or brought to the table when the guests order coffee. Breakfast service often requires presetting coffee cups, saucers, spoons, and sugar and sweeteners. Here are the fundamentals of coffee service:

- While pouring, catch drips with a service towel or STP.
- Pour the coffee into each cup at the table, until it is only three-fourths full, unless the guest has specified "black" coffee. See Figure 4-37.
- When using individual pots, place the pot to the right of the guest.
- If a guest orders more coffee after a considerable time has passed, replace the cup with a new one.
- If a French press is offered, ask the guests whether they prefer to press the plunger and serve themselves.

FIGURE 4-37

Pour hot beverages carefully.

Fundamentals for Brewing Coffee

There are five fundamentals for brewing the perfect cup of coffee: proportion, grind, water, freshness, and equipment.

Proportion The proportion of coffee to water must be accurately measured. The recommended formula is 1 ounce (30 ml) of coffee to 20 ounces (591 ml) of fresh, cold water. Prepackaged coffee packs are designed for a specific brewing capacity.

Grind Coffee beans can be ground from coarse to fine, which will determine, along with the roast level and blend, the intensity and balance of taste and flavors. The brew cycle of the coffee machine determines the grind. Fine grind requires 1–4 minutes; drip/medium grind requires 4–6 minutes; and regular/coarse grind requires 6–8 minutes.

Water The quality and temperature of the water helps to determine the flavor and the quality of coffee. Unless the water is hard, purification is usually not necessary.

Freshness Coffee beans lose essential oils and aroma when exposed to air, light, heat, and moisture. To preserve freshness, keep coffee sealed and in a dark cool storage area. Grinding coffee beans immediately before brewing ensures that they are at their best.

Equipment The cleaner the equipment, the better the taste of the coffee. Clean the grinder, dispenser, coffeemaker, filter devices, spray heads, and brewing containers thoroughly at the end of each shift. Coffee is brewed at temperatures between 195°F–205°F (90°C–96°C).

Specialty Coffee Service

Consumers have become much more sophisticated and aware of coffee services that heighten both the flavors and 'the coffee experience.' Today's servers need to master such techniques.

French Presses

Although French presses are more costly to maintain and more labor intensive, many upscale establishments use them to ensure the freshest and most flavorful coffee. French presses come in 10- to 20-ounce sizes (296- to 591-ml) and use medium grind coffee at a rate of 1–1 1/2 ounces (30 ml–44 ml) per 20 ounces (591 ml) of boiling water.

Pour the coffee into the French press pot, and add boiling water. The grounds will float to the top. Stir the grounds rapidly 2 or 3 times and cover the pot. Wait for 3 minutes before slowly pressing the plunger, or allowing the consumer to do so if desired.

Turkish or Arabic Coffee

Coffee drinking was introduced to Europe by the Turks, and the oldest method of coffee preparation was borrowed from the Arabs. Using a long handled narrow necked boiling pot sometimes called an *ibriq*, finely ground coffee and sugar are blended with water and brought to a boil over a low flame. Each time the solution comes to a boil, the pot is removed from heat momentarily and then reheated twice more before being poured into small demitasse cups.

Moka

Moka is a common European form of home coffee preparation that is frequently used in the United States. The moka method for brewing coffee is a steam percolation system. It uses a stove top specialized pot to make an espresso style coffee. Steam is created and forces water to travel from a lower chamber up a funnel that is part of the filter that holds finely ground coffee. The steamed water is then blended with the grounds and forced up to an upper chamber that has a filter that prevents grounds from getting into the final solution and a funnel where the coffee solution ultimately ends up. There is a safety valve on the machine to prevent excess pressure.

Espresso

Espresso is a hot coffee beverage as well as a very specific Italian experience that needs to be authentic to be fully appreciated. It is a very complex beverage that requires the use of excellent quality beans that have been produced and roasted to exacting specifications, and are further prepared with highly skilled service. The perfect espresso is a balance between a rich texture that is created by oils that coat the tongue and prevent a perception of bitterness and acidity, to create a sweet roast of intense coffee flavor. A great espresso should have a lingering taste on the palate that lasts up to a half-hour. Brewed by quickly passing steamed pressurized water at 195° F (91°C) through finely ground coffee, espresso is so named because of the speed at which a 1 ounce (30 ml) espresso can be made from 7 grams of coffee with an espresso machine in 25–30 seconds. Although the process is swift, the flavor captures the essence of the coffee bean.

FIGURE 4-40

Tamp the grounds firmly.

FIGURE 4-38

A demitasse cup and saucer

Traditionally served in a warm *demitasse,* or half cup, espresso is accompanied by a demitasse spoon and sugar. See Figure 4-38. The following steps are used to brew espresso:

- Make sure that the demitasse and portafilter are warm by storing them on the heated surface of the machine. The *portafilter,* also known as the filter holder, is where the espresso grind is held once dispensed.

- Grind the coffee to order, and hold it for no longer than a few minutes before brewing so that it does not oxidize and lose flavor.

- Place the portafilter under the *doser* (See Figure 4-39), which measures out the precise portion, and pull the lever or press the button to release the grounds into the portafilter; then, with the portafilter on the countertop, tamp the grounds firmly, and wipe any excess grounds from the rim. See Figure 4-40.

- Insert the portafilter into the 'group' of the machine, and press the button to pour the shot. (Be sure to use the shot within 30 seconds to a minute, or the espresso will no longer be hot.) See Figure 4-41.

- After the espresso is served, remove the portafilter, knock out the grounds, and brush or rinse the portafilter under hot water. See Figure 4-42.

Espresso uses a specific blend of freshly ground roasted beans to yield a concentrated beverage consisting of a heart, body, and crema. *Crema* is a complex suspension of emulsified coffee oils, carbon dioxide bubbles, and suspended particles that float on the surface of freshly brewed espresso. See Figure 4-43. It should be hazelnut in color. An espresso that is pale in color indicates overextraction and one that is dark brown indicates underextraction. Ideally, the good crema will have a visible pattern of thin lines referred to as *tiger stripes.* Espresso machines usually brew only one or two demitasses at a time. A shot of espresso is critical in drink recipes for caffé latte, café mocha, caffé latte based drinks, and cappuccino. Further discussion of a variety of espresso based recipes is found in Chapter 6, "The Beverage World".

Keeping coffee equipment clean is also key to a well-made espresso or cup of coffee. There should be a daily regimen and weekly schedule for side duties such as: wiping the doser with a brush; cleaning out the espresso machine by using a 'blind' in the portafilter with a cleaning solution; wiping the spray heads of a coffee machine; and presoaking coffee and tea cups in an approved solution to prevent build up of stains.

FIGURE 4-41

The portafilter attaches to the group head for brewing.

FIGURE 4-42

The portafilter is emptied into a knockbox after brewing.

FIGURE 4-43

Crema, the amber foam of a well-made espresso

Steeping time The time needed to steep tea leaves is also based on their level of fermentation or oxidation. Greater levels of oxidation require more steeping time. Teas may be steeped more than once, but later infusion requires more time. Avoid using color as a determining factor when infusing tea because color does not necessarily correspond to flavor.

A wide variety of equipment is appropriate for steeping tea including teapots, teacups, and kettles. Regardless of the kind of equipment, it must be spotless. Constant use of the same equipment leads to a buildup of mineral deposits from the water and tea that may create off-flavors.

Most establishments use commercial-grade bagged tea because it is convenient, although higher-quality loose teas are often preferred in fine dining establishments.

Use the following procedures when serving tea:

- When a guest requests tea, bring a selection of the available teas for the guest's perusal.

- After the guest selects a tea, place the packet on a doilied bread-and-butter plate, or put the loose tea in a tea strainer, or specially designed tea bag.

- Pre-set a warm cup on a saucer, a spoon on the table to the right of the guest, sugar and sweeteners, and lemon wedges or a creamer with milk, depending on the guest's request.

- If using a teabag, the guest may determine how strong or weak the tea should be. Place the teapot with the teabag propped against it on a doilied bread-and-butter plate to the right of the cup.

- For service using loose-leaf tea, place the tea in a warmed teapot, and fill the pot with boiling water. After the tea has steeped for the required time, strain the tea into the cup through a tea strainer. It is also considered proper to bring a second pot of boiling water so that guests may dilute the strength of their tea.

Tea Service

The term "tea" generally refers to a beverage that is made from an infusion of the leaves of *Camellia sinensis* prepared in boiling water. There are, however, a number of herbal blends that also fall into this category. The following fundamentals are essential to steeping the perfect cup of tea:

Proportion The proportion of tea to the volume of water will determine the final taste. Depending on the type and quality of tea leaves, 1 rounded teaspoon of tea is required for 6 ounces (177 ml) of water.

Water Trace chemicals and minerals in tap water may alter the flavors in tea. For that reason, many restaurants use bottled spring water, distilled water, or filtered water for steeping tea.

Freshness Light, temperature, humidity, and oxygen all affect tea leaves, so it is essential to store tea in a sealed container.

Infusion

The two factors to consider when infusing tea in fresh water are temperature and steeping time.

Temperature Tea must be infused in water ranging from 160°F (71°C) to the boiling point temperature in order to release all its aromas and flavors. Generally, the greater the fermentation of the tea, the higher the required temperature of the water.

High Tea Service

Afternoon, or "high" tea is a light, midday meal that bridges the gap between early-morning breakfast and late-evening dinner. It is a Victorian tradition, which has gained a renewed popularity in recent years, and many cosmopolitan hotels and restaurants offer afternoon tea service. It provides an opportunity to sell light foods and beverages when the demand for full-service meals is low. High tea includes a loose tea selection with more detailed service and food accompaniments such as finger sandwiches, tartlets, scones, cookies, or cakes.

Iced Tea

More than 80% of the tea consumed in the United States is iced. Iced tea can be prepared from powdered tea concentrate, a commercial liquid tea concentrate, or a concentrate made on the premises.

To make iced tea from a liquid concentrate, steep the tea for about ten minutes in a quarter of the quantity of boiling water needed for fresh hot tea. Remove the tea bags, or strain loose-leaf tea. If desired, dissolve sugar or other sweetener in the hot concentrate. To serve, blend one part concentrate and two parts fresh water, and serve in a highball glass or tall goblet filled with ice and accompanied by a long handled iced teaspoon.

Selling the Menu and Specials

Describing the menu by providing clear, accurate, and appealing descriptions of menu items not only helps guests to decide on their food orders but also provides an opportunity for additional selling. Begin by offering a confident explanation of any daily specials or other particularly outstanding or appealing selections. Using descriptive adjectives, appropriate hand gestures, and good eye contact with guests, increases their comfort level and helps steer their selections. Food descriptions should include how the item is prepared, the sauce with which it is served, and the accompaniments. Servers should remain neutral about guest selections unless their opinion is asked.

Each type of food may include different descriptive details. For example, soup descriptions generally include the major ingredients, the stock, the texture, and if appropriate, the temperature ("chilled gazpacho" for example). Salad descriptions might identify whether the salad is tossed or arranged, whether cooked ingredients are served warm or cold, and the kind or kinds of dressings available. Entrées, on the other hand, include descriptions of the ingredients, such as the cut of meat; the type of preparation, such as sautéed or braised; and the fashion in which the entrée is served, such as with a specific kind of sauce. If a menu item is sold out, be sure to provide the guest with this information prior to taking the meal order.

After the guest chooses the food items, suggest a range of wines, beer or other beverages to complement the food, and describe any dessert item that must be pre-ordered due to preparation time. Describe the selections with as much appeal as possible, but take care to avoid misrepresentation. When asked a question to which the server does not know the answer, the response should be: "I don't know but I will find out."

Taking the Order

In most restaurants, tables and seats are numbered to simplify taking the order and organizing the workflow. Each server is responsible for a specific group of tables, called a station. Depending on the level of service, a station may be as small as 12 seats or as large as 30 seats. Remember that the numbering of tables and seats in a dining room are critical to the process of taking orders.

The Position of the Server

Carefully gauge when a party is ready to order, although this is not always an easy task. Similarly, evaluate whether the guest has made, or needs assistance in making a selection.

When taking an order at the table, stand to the right of each guest when possible. If there is a guest of honor, take that person's order first, followed by the orders of children, women, men, and finally the host's order. Collect all the specifics necessary from each guest and remove the menu, before moving on to take the next person's order. When appropriate, ask about the cooking temperatures, such as the degree of doneness for a steak or eggs. Repeating the order to the guest helps to avoid mistakes. If a guest has special requests, be sure to check with the chef before the order is taken to see whether the request can be honored. Timing is equally important in determining exactly when to take the order and when to transmit it to the kitchen so as not to overburden the kitchen staff.

The position of the server and the type of service will differ slightly when serving guests at a booth or banquette.

Booth service In establishments with booths—tables that rest against a wall with high-backed and benchlike seats—guests are numbered clockwise around the booth for the purpose of organizing the kitchen order and food service. Service begins with the guest seated farthest away from the server. When clearing the tableware, the service staff starts with the guests seated closest to the server.

Banquette service In a banquette, guests are seated facing the server, with their backs to the wall. As with booth service, the server should number the guests clockwise from the focal point when taking food and beverage orders. Serving should be done as unobtrusively as possible, serving with the hand farthest from the guest.

Writing the Order

In traditional service, a cold item is served before a hot one, and a liquid item precedes the service of one that is solid. In the United States, courses are generally served in the following sequence:

1. Appetizer,
2. Soup,
3. Salad,
4. Intermezzo,
5. Entrée,
6. Cheese,
7. Dessert,
8. Coffee.

The exact sequencing depends somewhat on the order placed by each guest. Assume, for example, that the first guest at a table orders an appetizer, a soup, and a salad, the second guest orders only soup, and the third orders only a salad. Using the system described, bring the first guest an appetizer. After clearing the appetizer, bring soup for the first and second guests. Once the soup has been cleared, bring the salad for the first and third guests.

Orders should be written in the correct sequence on a small order pad or a guest check or entered into a point-of-sale (POS) computer system. See Figure 4-44. Beverage orders are commonly recorded on the back of the check. The seat position of each guest should be written next to the order, and the women's seat numbers should be circled for quick identification. Servers generally use a type of "shorthand" to note information and to communicate with the kitchen staff and among themselves.

Transmitting the Order to the Kitchen

Orders are transmitted to the kitchen verbally, with a written order form, or by a computerized point-of-sale (POS) system. See Figure 4-45. Waitstaff should be familiar with handwritten checks, and able to understand check-writing principles in case a computerized system crashes.

To begin preparing a guest check, fill out the information at the top of each check in the boxes provided for the date, server number or initials, table number, and the number of guests. In the far left column, list the quantity of each item ordered, and in the center column, write the item ordered, and next to it the number of each guest's position.

Prepare the check by transferring the order from the order pad to a guest check. Begin by determining whether there are more items in a single course, such as appetizers, than there are guests. Two people might, for example, order three appetizers. Also check to see whether the same guest number appears twice for one course as when, for example, one guest orders two appetizers while another orders none.

Copy the order pad onto the guest check the way it is written, leaving a space between the courses. For example, if a guest selects an appetizer as an entrée, list the appetizer with the entrées of the other guests.

A verbal ordering system is the least reliable and has very limited application in the industry. A computerized POS (Point of Sale system) is the most widely used as it is the most accurate, accountable, and efficient form of communication. Each server is given an identity code to prevent confusion or any fraudulent use of the computer. The most popular way of entering information into the computer is

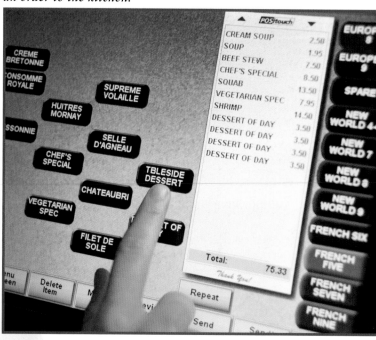

FIGURE 4-45
A computer or POS system can transmit an order to the kitchen.

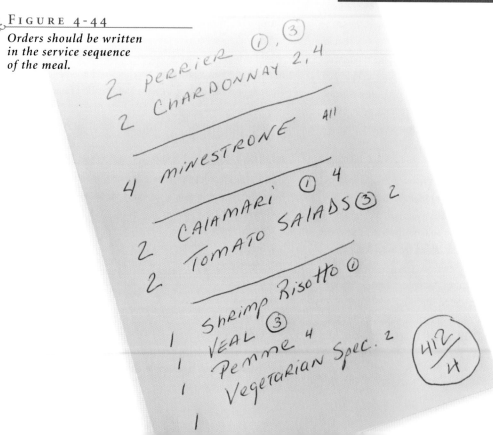

FIGURE 4-44
Orders should be written in the service sequence of the meal.

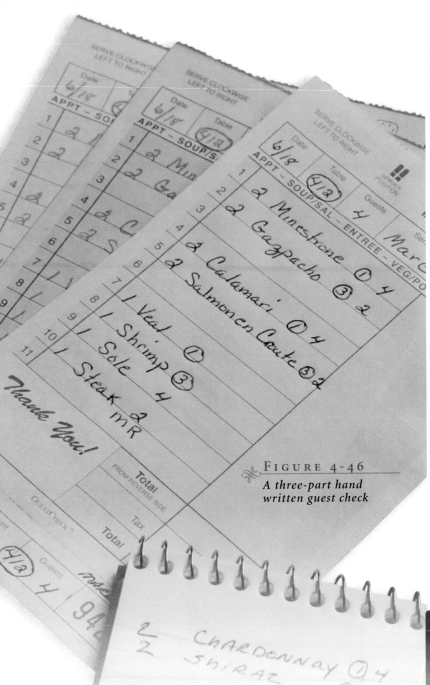

FIGURE 4-46
A three-part hand written guest check

a touch-screen system. The advantage to this system is that it is very easy to master. Many leading restaurant chains employ handheld systems replacing handwriting entirely. It is important to remember these points:

- If handwritten, the top copy or dupe of the check is given to the chef, coordinator or kitchen expediter. See Figure 4-46.

- Servers should be as quiet and unobtrusive as possible in the kitchen.

- Request the course by table number rather than asking for the specific item whenever requesting food from the kitchen ("Chef, may I pick up the soups for table 213?").

- Servers of many establishments may be required to "fire" (instruct the kitchen to begin cooking) the next course they wish to pick up. The process of firing is the server's way of controlling the timing of service. This may be done verbally or transmitted by POS.

- Never serve a course until all the items for that course are ready to be served.

- As a representative of the guest in the kitchen, it is the server's responsibility to ensure that the guests receive exactly what they order. It is at this point of pick-up that servers should verify that the order is correct. See Figure 4-47.

- If the order is not correct and a presentation or temperature problem emerges at this time, it should be resolved in the kitchen. The customer's needs should be the first concern.

- Servers should be aware of where each guest's order is located on the tray. This will ensure that the service of the course is presented in a timely and professional manner. See Figure 4-48.

Communication is essential to the success of an establishment. Taking orders correctly and transmitting them to the kitchen is imperative. Good verbal communication skills facilitate this process as well. See Figures 4-49 and 4-50.

FIGURE 4-47
The server is the last individual who checks the quality before the guest is served.

FIGURE 4-48
Organize the food tray by seat position to insure that the guest receives the correct order.

FIGURE 4-49	Kitchen "Shorthand"
Blkn or B&B	*Black and blue*
R	*Rare*
M/R	*Medium rare*
M	*Medium*
M/W	*Medium well*
86	*Sold out of item*
68	*Item is again available*
SOS	*Sauce on the side*
LOS	*Light on sauce*
Hold	*Chef waits to prepare until server discusses the item*

FIGURE 4-50	Service Slang
deuce	*a party of 2*
4 top	*a party of 4*
fire	*to request to begin cooking an order*
split	*divide item in two*

Handling Flatware

When handling flatware and cutlery in the dining room, the following guidelines should be followed:

- Use a clean side towel to wipe all flatware before placing it on the table. See Figure 4-51.

- Carry flatware through a dining room on a serviette or STP. See Figure 4-52.

- Place flatware on the appropriate side of the guest's cover.

- Forks to the left.

- Knives with blades facing in and spoons to the right except for dessert silverware (on top of the cover), and the bread and butter knife on the butter plate. See Figure 4-53.

- Handle flatware by the "waist" or mid section. Fingers should not come in contact with the end of the utensil that goes into the customer's mouth. Also avoid leaving fingerprints on the handles. See Figures 4-54a and 4-54b.

- Place most flatware parallel one to another and perpendicular to the table. On round tables, the flatware should not follow the contour of the table's edge.

- Pre-set dessert forks and spoons horizontally at the top of the cover with the spoon above the fork.

Cleaning, sanitizing, and storing flatware and cutlery

Flatware and cutlery should be washed and rinsed at high temperatures in the dishwasher and allowed to dry before being stored. The pieces should be organized by type and size in appropriately lined drawers that have washable air mats.

FIGURE 4-51

Properly polishing all service equipment insures quality.

FIGURE 4-52

Carry flatware on a serviette or STP.

FIGURE 4-53

The blade of the knife faces in toward the center of the setting.

FIGURE 4-54A

The CORRECT method of handling flatware.

FIGURE 4-54B

An INCORRECT method of handling flatware.

Proper Use of an Standard Transport Plate (STP) or Serviette

A Standard Transport Plate or serviette is a napkin-lined dinner plate that is used for the purpose of carrying clean flatware to the table. Flatware should not be placed in a napkin pocket fold when using an STP but merely laid on top of a square napkin fold. The flatware should be organized by group or category depending on the size of the party being served. See Figures 4-55 and 4-56.

Marking the Table

"Marking a table" is restaurant jargon for adjusting flatware. A key aspect of service, especially in an à la carte environment, involves adjusting flatware to suit the service order before each course arrives and then clearing it after each course. Flatware should be readjusted after each course is cleared, and missing or used flatware should be replaced. Clean flatware should be carried on a serviette or STP.

If the server notices a utensil on the table from a preceding course, it should be collected and placed in the fingers holding the STP, and treated as a used utensil.

Serving Plated Food

The key to serving plated food is to ensure that the presentation remains as the chef intended: for example, sauces are not flowing onto the rim of the plate; the food arrives at the right temperature; and orders are delivered to the correct guest without being auctioned off.

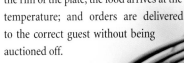

FIGURE 4-55
The grouping method of marking, organized by seat position.

FIGURE 4-56
The categorizing method of marking, organized by the type of flatware.

Hand Service

Hand service refers to carrying and presenting a plated course to the guest in the manner that the chef intended. Carrying multiple plates either from the kitchen or the service tray to the table ensures that the food arrives to the guests quickly and at an appropriate temperature. Generally, a maximum of three plates are held in one hand/arm and a fourth is held in the other hand. See Figure 4-57a. This technique does require practice. There are different techniques that may be used based on the size of the plates as well as the dexterity of the server. See Figure 4-57b. If serving from the left, then use the right hand/arm to hold three plates and hold one in the left hand. Conversely, if serving from the right, hold three plates on the left hand/arm and one in the right hand. It is always most important to serve while being open to the guest. See Figure 4-58.

FIGURE 4-57A
A four-plate carry

FIGURE 4-57B
A two-plate clearing carry

FIGURE 4-58
Serving an entrée while being open to the guest

Serving Plated Food

Tray Service

Most à la carte restaurants and banquet establishments have oval service trays to allow servers to carry either large or heavy loads expeditiously to and from the dining room. Some establishments, especially hotels with room service, have staff transport food on rectangular trays that usually limit how much may be transported at one time. Usually the server will carry the tray by its handles and at waist level. Trays without handles are carried on the shoulder, as are oval trays.

Service Tray Handling

Basic handling of a tray involves these techniques:

- A service tray should be carried in the server's left hand above the shoulder. This is done to enable the server to proceed through a doorway without the door swinging back and hitting the tray. See Figure 4-59.
- The tray should always be placed on a tray stand with the length of the tray crossing the bars of the tray stand.
- Distribute items on the tray so that the tray is as evenly balanced as possible. See Figure 4-60.
- Place tall or heavier items in the center of the tray.
- Never stack plates on top of food when clearing a guest's table.
- Remove all flatware from plates and place off to the side on the tray, separating it by type.
- When setting up the tray, do not place it close to the guest's table. (It is not part of the guest's dining experience.)
- Always carry the food tray over the shoulder, never at the side of the body, even if the tray is empty.
- Signal a server in front of you by saying "behind you" to prevent collisions.
- Be particularly alert when walking behind guests in case they stop suddenly.
- Be careful when carrying glassware on a food tray as there is a propensity to overload the tray and this may result in significant breakage. Glasses should ideally be carried on a beverage tray.
- After clearing a guest's table, cover the tray with a service towel before carrying it from the dining room.
- Never leave unsightly trays in the dining room. As soon as the table is cleared, remove the tray from the dining room.
- Carry the tray on the palm or fingertips, depending on its weight.
- Use the left shoulder to help balance the tray, if need be.
- Carry the tray stand in the collapsed position on your right, when walking in the dining room.
- Extend the right arm, which holds the tray stand and flick the wrist so that the support legs separate, bringing the tray stand to an upright position. The legs should be parallel to the body.
- Turn to the right, bend the knee, and lower the tray in a horizontal position until it sits on the support frame. Slide the tray across the top of the frame so that its weight is evenly distributed.
- When picking up or placing down a loaded tray, keep the back straight and bend and lift with the knees and legs. See Figure 4-61.
- When removing the tray, reverse the process. Collapse the tray stand against the right hip, while holding the tray level.

Stackable Plate Covers

Stackable plate covers are specifically sized to plates so that they remain firmly in place and allow the server to carry as many as 12 to 16 entrées on an oval service tray at one time into the dining room. They also enable the kitchen staff to plate hot entrées in a warming oven immediately prior to service. When removing a plate cover, invert it and stack each of the remaining covers on top of it.

FIGURE 4-59
The food tray is carried on the left hand.

FIGURE 4-60
Food trays should be organized to maximize balance.

FIGURE 4-61
Use the leg muscles when lifting or landing a loaded tray.

FIGURE 4-62A

Classic or Family Bread Service

FIGURE 4-62B

Pince Bread Service

FIGURE 4-62C

Bread Breaking Service

FIGURE 4-62D

Banquet or Pre-set Bread Service

Bread Service

Cloche Service

Cloche is the French word for a bell and refers to the bell-shaped domes that are used as sophisticated and impressive plate covers at fine dining restaurants. In contrast to stackable plate covers, the server would have all guests' entrées served *sous cloches* (under the covers) simultaneously by enlisting the help of other members of the service team. The bell-shaped covers are removed in unison to add drama and to heighten the guests' dining experience.

The Pince Technique

The pince technique is used by a server to transfer appropriately sized and shaped food from a platter, breadbasket, or other serving dish to the guest's plate. The technique requires a large serving spoon and fork, called a serving set. The serving set is held in a single hand (generally the right) with the spoon facing up and is placed under the fork that has its tines pointing upwards. This allows the server to hold the serving platter or basket in one hand, close to the guest's plate, while serving the food using the other hand. This technique is also used for transferring bread from a bread warmer to a bread basket to avoid hand contact.

Bread-and-Butter Service

The sequence of bread service varies from restaurant to restaurant, but typically bread is served as a welcoming gesture after water has been poured or after the food order has been taken. Bread and butter may be served in a number of ways, from the informal breaking off of sections from a loaf to formal Russian or English service using the pincing technique. Figure 4-62 (A through D) shows the 4 bread methods.

The pincing technique involves:

1. Lining a small breadbasket with a clean, folded napkin.
2. Using tongs or a service set to place the bread in the center of the fold, and never handling the bread or rolls with bare hands. See Figure 4-63.
3. Allowing 1 1/2 rolls of bread per guest for the initial serving.
4. Placing the breadbasket in the center of the table and the fresh butter where it is most convenient for the women at the table, when serving family style.
5. Replenishing bread and butter as well.

FIGURE 4-63

The service spoon and fork work together to pince bread.

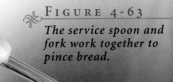

FIGURE 4-64

Simple butter cuts, compound or flavored butter, and seasoned olive oil

Butter service Butter may be served in the form of wrapped patties, chips, curls, balls, florets, or whipped or compounded forms in a ramekin, dish, or specialty butter cup. The butter should be served near room temperature so that it is easy to spread. See Figure 4-64.

Olive oil As Italian-style cuisine dominates much of the restaurant industry, olive oil has become a much more visible alternative accompaniment to bread. It should be served directly from the bottle if the container is elegant and 600 ml or less. Otherwise, it should be served from a cruet or small handled pitcher such as a creamer or monkey dish that is integrated into the décor of the room. A teaspoon and doilied underliner should also accompany the monkey dish.

Appetizer Service

Some fine-dining restaurants provide a complimentary bite-sized hors d'oeuvre at the start of a meal called an 'amuse-bouche' or 'amuse-gueule'. This should serve as both an appetite stimulant and reflect the chef's cuisine. The server should be certain to provide the guest with a list all the ingredients in case a guest has food allergies.

Appetizers are small food presentations that sometimes replace soup or salad, and also present the chef an opportunity to display some creativity. They may be served hot or cold. The general guidelines for serving appetizers follow:

1. When a guest orders both hot and cold appetizers, serve the cold appetizer first, unless the guest requests otherwise.

2. If an appetizer is shared, divide it skillfully, if possible, at the table.

3. Adjust any specialized flatware before serving the appetizer, and remove after clearing the appetizer.

4. Provide fingerbowls if necessary, either before or immediately after clearing the appetizer.

Soup Service

Soups fall into two distinct categories: clear soups (such as consommé), and thick or cream soups (including chowder). Clear soups are served in a warmed soup cup with a bouillon spoon. Thick soups are best served in a warmed bowl or soup plate with a soup or potage spoon. See Figure 4-65. In both cases, an underliner or doilied plate under the cup/bowl helps to prevent accidents. If soups are carried on a food tray into the dining room, assemble the cups and bowls onto the liners in the dining room, not in the kitchen, to avoid soup spills onto the liners. The rim of a soup plate should also be wiped clean, if necessary, before it is placed in front of the guest. When clearing soups, make sure the soup spoon has been placed onto the underliner before removing it.

Tureen Service

When soup is ordered, tureen service may be used for both practical reasons as well as to give the guest the impression of added service. See Figure 4-66. Pre-set warmed soup plates or bowls on underliners in front of the guests. Before it leaves the kitchen, the soup tureen should be placed on a STP/serviette underliner with a ladle in it or beside it. Remove the cover before approaching the table. With the tureen in the left hand, approach and serve guests from the left, drawing the handle of the soup ladle toward yourself, using the right hand to avoid spillage. Return the ladle to the tureen before serving the next guest. Service proceeds counterclockwise around the table. Tureens may also be used for French style service where the server portions the soup onto the cups or bowls on a *guéridon* before presenting them to the guests.

FIGURE 4-65

Thick soup served in a rimmed soup bowl with a doilied underliner.

FIGURE 4-66

The guest is served tableside from a soup tureen.

Salad Service

Salads may be served before or after the entrée. In the United States, the convention is to serve the salad before the entrée, while in France tradition dictates that the salad is served following the entrée.

Cold salads should be served on chilled plates with a salad knife and fork that may also be chilled. If requested, salad oil and vinegar should be presented in clean, filled cruets. When freshly ground pepper is available, it should be offered to the guest when serving the salad. The salad course also provides the waitstaff person a good opportunity to attend to the table for replenishing bread and pouring wine.

Intermezzo Service

An *intermezzo* is a pause or intermission between two courses. Usually a sorbet, sherbet, or granita is served to cleanse the palate between two courses of very different flavors. Serve the intermezzo as quickly as possible. This is a very short course, usually lasting no longer than five minutes.

Entrée Service

Entrée service depends on the establishment's style of service. There are, however, some general guidelines that apply:

- Hot entrées should be served on a hot plate. Use a clean, folded service towel for handling hot plates, and inform the guest that the plate is hot.
- Be aware of the intended presentation, and serve the plate so that the guest can appreciate the full effect of the chef's efforts. See Figure 4-67.
- Whether using a tray or carrying plates by hand, hold them as level as possible to prevent spoiling the presentation.

- Allow about an inch between the plate's edge and the table edge to lessen the risk of spilling food on the guest's clothing.
- If the guest leaves the table after the entrée has been served, keep the food warm by either taking the plate back to the kitchen or covering it with a plate cover until the guest returns.
- Within a couple of minutes of serving entrées, ask the guests if everything has been prepared to their liking. If there is a problem, handle it quickly, efficiently, and apologetically. Inform the manager as soon as possible.
- When clearing the entrée course, remove the empty wine glasses, the salt and pepper shakers, and the bread-and-butter plates and knives, unless guests are opting for a salad or cheese course after the entrée.

Platter Service

When a chef prepares and places food on a platter in the kitchen this is known as *platter service.* Warmed plates are preset in front of the guests before the food is presented.

With platters held on the left forearm and hand, the platter is held parallel to the table to the left of the guest, but without touching the table. Using the pince technique, a portion is placed onto the guest's plate. See Figure 4-68. Each platter requires a clean service set. Sauces are generally served separately, or there is a separate serving spoon for the sauce. The server proceeds to serve counterclockwise.

Casserole Service

In *casserole service,* the dinner plate and any accompaniments are preset on the table from the guest's right side. Holding the casserole dish in the left hand and a service set in the right, the contents of the casserole are served from the left of the guest and as close to the plate as possible. Casserole service can be performed tableside using a *guéridon.* See Figure 4-69.

FIGURE 4-67
Serve all plates as the chef intended.

FIGURE 4-68
Platter entrée service, pinced tableside.

FIGURE 4-69
Tableside casserole service.

Tableside Service

Tableside preparation is generally associated with fine dining, but other dining environments including banquet and catering have also adapted tableside preparation as an enhancement of the dining experience. See Figure 4-70. The four general types of tableside service include assembling, saucing and garnishing, sautéing and flambéing, and carving and deboning.

Assembling Salads and other dishes that involve a quick and simple assembly of ingredients may be completed tableside. Examples include the preparation of Caesar salad and steak tartare.

Saucing and garnishing Servers may put the finishing touches of saucing and garnishing on dishes that have been prepared in the kitchen.

Sautéing and flambéing Both sautéing and flambéing are used for items that can be quickly cooked tableside or hot beverages or desserts that are flamed as part of the preparation.

Carving and deboning Fish, poultry, game, and meats may be carved or deboned at the table. Carving also includes peeling and slicing fruits and cheese to make them more manageable for guests.

Food safety In the dining room, as in every part of an operation, it is critical to follow food safety guidelines and HACCP procedures.

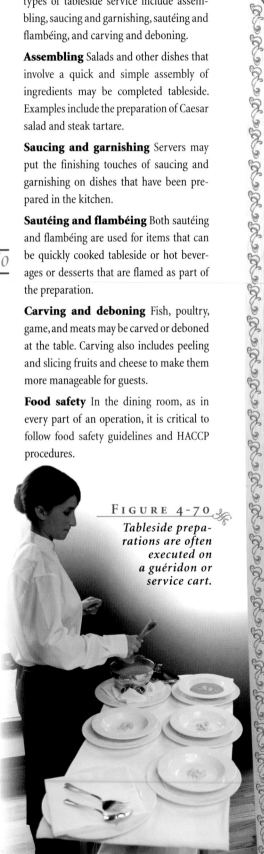

FIGURE 4-70 ❧
Tableside preparations are often executed on a guéridon or service cart.

Preparing Caesar Salad

The best Caesar Salads are prepared tableside not only for dramatic presentation but also because the lettuce remains crisp.

To prepare Caesar Salad tableside, follow these steps:

1 **Attractively arrange mise en place on a guéridon.**

2 **Use the tines of two forks to mash the garlic and to season the bowl. A little kosher salt may also be added if desired.**

3 **Add anchovy and continue to mash using a spoon.**

4 Add pasteurized raw egg yolk and blend with the garlic and anchovy. Add Dijon mustard.

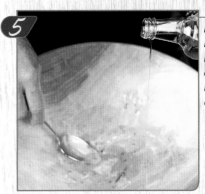

5 Drizzle olive oil into the egg mixture, stirring constantly to maintain an emulsion.

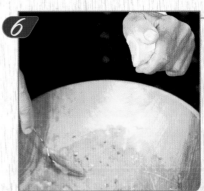

6 Blend in lemon juice, freshly ground black pepper, and wine vinegar if desired.

7 Add romaine lettuce, using a napkin to break it into appropriately sized pieces.

8 Toss the salad with a serving set, and add croutons and grated Parmigiano Reggiano cheese.

9 Plate the salad attractively, using the serving set.

10 Add additional freshly grated cheese, and freshly ground black pepper to the customer's taste.

Preparing Bananas Flambé

Bananas Flambé is a dessert that may be prepared table-side with flair and drama.

To prepare Bananas Flambé, follow these steps:

1

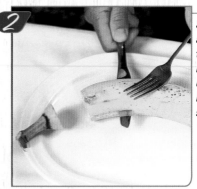

Arrange mise en place attractively on a guéridon.

2

Slice the ends of a banana and cut the banana in half lengthwise using a fork to keep the banana steady.

62

3

Remove the skin using the service set. Cut the banana into quarters.

4

Melt butter and brown sugar in a preheated pan.

5

Use a lemon to stir the mixture. The lemon prevents the caramelized sugar from sticking to the utensil and the juice prevents the sugar caramel from hardening.

6

Place banana quarters in the pan with the sliced side down. Lightly brown the bananas and turn over.

7

Remove the pan from the heat and add liqueur.

8

Place the pan back over the heat and flambé, tilting the pan and drawing it towards you as the sauce gently simmers.

9

Plate the bananas over ice cream in a decorative fashion and nappé with the caramel sauce.

Carving a Duck Tableside

Carving duck, poultry, and other meats requires dexterity and skill particularly in the dining room.

To carve a duck tableside, follow these steps:

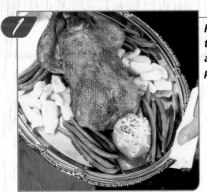
Present the duck to the guests on a decorated platter.

Transfer the whole duck to a carving board without piercing the skin.

Remove the leg section by separating the thigh from the backbone.

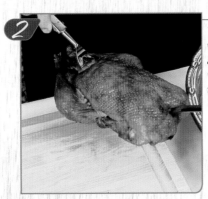
Separate the drumstick from the thigh.

Remove the breast by cutting lengthwise down the keel bone and sliding the knife along the breast bone. Slice the breast into even slices. Repeat the process to remove the other breast.

Place the duck on a warm plate along with accompaniments.

Boning and Serving a Whole Trout

Boning fish tableside also requires dexterity and speed so that guests may enjoy the food without bones while it is still warm.

For an elegant tableside presentation of trout, follow these steps:

1
Present the trout to the guests on a decorated platter.

4
Gently remove the fillets by pushing them away from the bones.

2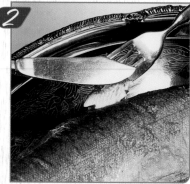
Use a fork and fish knife to remove the fins.

5
Insert the tines of the fork into the backbone and lift the head while separating the bottom fillets.

3
Slide the fish knife under the skin and peel the skin towards the tail.

6
Delicately plate the fillets with the service set.

Caesar Salad

INGREDIENTS	U.S. Standard	Metric
Garlic, *peeled and cut in half*	*l large clove*	*1 large clove*
Salt	*1 teaspoon*	*1 teaspoon*
Anchovy fillet	*1 large*	*1 large*
Dijon mustard	*1 teaspoon*	*1 teaspoon*
Olive oil	*1 ounce*	*30 ml*
White wine vinegar	*1/2 teaspoon*	*1/2 teaspoon*
Lemon juice, *freshly squeezed*	*1 ounce*	*30 ml*
Egg yolk, *pasteurized*	*1 each*	*1 each*
Black pepper, *ground*	*1 teaspoon*	*1 teaspoon*
Romaine lettuce, *washed, dried, torn into pieces*	*4 ounces*	*115 grams*
Croutons	*4 ounces*	*115 grams*
Parmesan cheese, *grated*	*1 tablespoon*	*1 tablespoon*

METHOD OF PREPARATION

1. Gather all the ingredients and equipment.

2. Season the bowl with garlic, using salt as an abrasive, and then discard the garlic pieces.

3. Add anchovy, and mash with a fork. Move the anchovy to one side of the bowl, and add the mustard.

4. Blend oil into the mustard, slowly and steadily.

5. Add the wine vinegar, lemon juice, egg yolk, and pepper. Mix well.

6. Add romaine, and toss lettuce. Toss all the above by rotating service spoon and fork from back to front of bowl until lettuce is fully coated.

7. Add croutons, and toss.

8. Add cheese, and toss. Serve immediately.

Banana Flambé

YEILD *2 serving*   **SERVING SIZE** *7 ounces*

INGREDIENTS

	U.S. Standard	Metric
Sugar, *granulated*	*2 tablespoons*	*2 tablespoons*
Butter	*1 ounce*	*28 grams*
Bananas, *split in half* *lengthwise and crosswise*	*2 each*	*2 each*
Dark rum *(preferably Myers®)*	*1 1/2 ounces*	*45 ml*
Cinnamon-sugar mixture	*1/2 teaspoon*	*1/2 teaspoon*
Banana liqueur	*1 1/2 ounces*	*45 ml*
Vanilla ice cream *(about 2 scoops)*	*4 ounces*	*4 ounces*

METHOD OF PREPARATION

1. Gather all the ingredients and equipment.

2. Heat Suzette pan, and add sugar and butter.

3. Lightly caramelize; then add bananas, and coat with caramel.

4. Remove the pan from the réchaud, and add rum. Return the pan to the réchaud, and flame.

5. While still flaming, sprinkle cinnamon-sugar over the pan.

6. Lower the flame and remove the pan from heat. Add banana liqueur, and return the pan to the réchaud. Allow the sauce to reduce.

7. Arrange four quarters of banana around the ice cream, and nappé with sauce, covering the ice cream.

Crêpes Suzette

YEILD *2 serving*   **SERVING SIZE** *2 crêpes each about 5 oz.*

INGREDIENTS

	U.S. Standard	Metric
Sugar, granulated	2 tablespoons	2 tablespoons
Butter	1 ounce	28 g
Oranges, zest	2 each	2 each
Lemon, zest	1 each	1 each
Grand Marnier®	2 ounces	60 ml
Orange juice	4 ounces	120 ml
Crêpes	4 each	4 each
Cognac	1 ounce	30 ml

METHOD OF PREPARATION

1. Gather all the ingredients and equipment.

2. Heat the Suzette pan, and add sugar. Add butter, and mix until all the sugar is dissolved.

3. While the sugar is dissolving, add the zest of one orange and the lemon.

4. Remove the pan from heat and add Grand Marnier®.

5. Add orange juice. (If sugar caramelizes too quickly, add juice to the pan while zesting.)

6. Return the pan to the heat, but do not flambé. Dip crêpes in the sauce, one at a time; then fold into quarters. Move crêpes to the side of the pan.

7. When all the crêpes are folded, remove the pan from the heat, and add Cognac; return the pan to the heat, and flame.

8. Heat the sauce to a boil. Serve two crêpes on a preheated plate, and nappé with sauce.

9. Garnish with additional orange zest.

Cheese Service

Cheeses are best when served at room temperature. Semi-firm and firm cheeses take an hour to warm to room temperature, while soft and semi-soft cheeses usually need a half hour. Large pieces of cheese need more time.

When serving cheeses, arrange them on a marble or wooden cheese board, trays, or a cheese cart so that they may be easily cut. The cheese should be cut according to its shape so that the rind is evenly distributed. A separate and appropriate cutting knife should be provided with each cheese. Bread or toast should accompany the cheese course, and if fruit is served, ensure that it is washed, dried, and cut into bite-sized portions.

Dessert Service

The dessert course can be both the guests' most anticipated course and the kitchen's last chance to impress the guests. Some restaurants use rolling pastry carts, or display desserts at their entrance to tempt guests. Other upscale, white-tablecloth restaurants offer made-to-order desserts, which require that customers select a dessert at the same time as they place the meal order.

Dessert service procedures may vary with service styles and the type of dessert. However, the fork should always be placed to the left of the cover and the spoon to the right. If the dessert fork and spoon are a part of the place setting, the spoon is placed above the fork on top of the cover with the respective handles pointed toward the appropriate side.

Buffetiering

In addition to the servers, buffets require a *buffetier,* whose responsibilities include a familiarity with, and the ability to describe all the ingredients and methods of preparation for each food item. A detailed description of the buffetier's responsibilities is described in Chapter 5, "Styles and Sequences of Service".

Clearing

There are different philosophies regarding how much a table server should clear at one time. Some fine-dining establishments limit clearing two plates only at one time and do not allow stacking. As time and efficiency are key elements to good service, others including Johnson & Wales University, train servers to clear and stack as need be, as long as guests remain uninterrupted by the scraping sounds or unsightliness. If a guest has a large amount of food left on the plate, the server should inquire if anything was the matter. Once the reason is ascertained, the server should inform the manager and clear that plate first.

When clearing a table, first make sure that all guests have finished a course. See Figure 4-71 The exception is when a guest has moved his/her used plate away from the cover. Clear from the right side, but avoid reaching across the table. Walk around the table clockwise, keeping the cleared plates in the left hand and to the backs of the guests, and avoid overstacking them on your arm. Clearing plates with flatware requires crossing the fork over the knife to prevent utensils from sliding off onto the floor, or worse, the customer. When

FIGURE 4-71

The server INCORRECTLY clears while a guest is still eating.

using food service trays, separate the flatware from the serviceware according to type, and ensure that the tray is properly balanced by placing the heavier items at the center of the tray. See Figure 4-72. Glassware should be cleared separately onto beverage trays to avoid excessive breakage. Clearing the table should be conducted as quietly and unobtrusively as possible.

Crumbing the Table

As the name implies, *crumbing* is the procedure for clearing the table of crumbs and other food particles. See Figure 4-73. It should be done between the entrée and dessert courses as needed, and as quickly, quietly, and unobtrusively as possible.

To clear the table of crumbs and other food particles between courses, follow these steps.

1. Move the glasses or utensils, if necessary, to ensure that the table is clean.
2. Crumb from the center of the table outward, away from the guest, and at a diagonal to an open corner.
3. Use a crumbing utensil such as a special brush, if available, or a folded service towel to sweep the crumbs onto a plate or small pan.

FIGURE 4-72

Organize the food tray when clearing to insure good balance and safe transport.

FIGURE 4-73

Crumb the table onto a bread & butter plate.

Presentation of the Check

Presenting the guest check can be a challenge for servers especially if they do not know which guest in the party is paying or if they are in a hurry to turn the table. In the United States it is perfectly acceptable protocol for a server to present the check before it is requested. One of the greatest failings of a server can be the delay of either presenting or collecting payment of a check. Once a guest has decided that it is time to leave, every minute counts and poor check handling can sour the entire dining experience. There are cues to servers that indicate when guests are ready for the check such as: making eye contact with the server; writing figuratively in the air or against the palms as if signing a check; moving the remaining serviceware away from the cover; folding the napkin and placing it on the table; or placing the wallet or credit card on the table. The server must not only continue to maintain vigilance over the assigned tables, but must also doublecheck the guest check to guarantee that it is accurate.

Servers may also encounter situations when two or more guests at a table ask for the guest check. In most situations, guests indicate to servers upon entering the restaurant that they would like the check. If uncertain, servers can strategically place the check between two guests. If one of the guests is a regular or is known to be the host of the party at the restaurant, the check is presented to that individual. Once the check has been presented, avoid hovering over the guest waiting for payment, but keep a close eye on the check folder for either a credit card or cash payment, and pick it up as soon as possible. Always be discreet, tactful, and gracious.

Handling Payment

Checks are commonly paid either by credit card or cash, although guests may sometimes have a gift certificate or other voucher for the meal. If the guest is paying by credit card, check the card for the cardholder's signature and the expiration date. Process the card appropriately and according to restaurant policy. Return the card with the check and voucher to the guest, along with a pen for signing the voucher.

After the transaction is completed, remove the check to ensure that the credit card voucher has been signed and that the voucher has been left in the check folder. Occasionally, an authorization issue occurs with the credit card. If there is a problem, draw the cardholder aside and explain that there is a problem processing the card. Avoid embarrassing the cardholder in front of guests.

If the guest is paying with cash, ensure that you receive the correct amount, and return any change with a selection of bills to ensure flexibility in leaving a tip. It is inappropriate to ask the guest whether change is needed or to mention the tip unless asked. Some restaurants have a policy of automatically adding a service charge for large parties of 8 or more. Guests should be alerted even though the policy must be stated on the written menu. The check folder should be left on the table until the guests' departure, unless it is handed back to the server.

Farewell

When guests are ready to leave, assist them with their chairs and coats. Check the table to ensure that guests have not left any belongings behind such as a credit card or a purse, and thank them for their patronage. It is not appropriate to ask guests how they enjoyed their experience as it is the job of restaurant personnel to know what kind of experience their guests have had. But, it is most appropriate to thank them for coming and expressing a desire to see them again soon at the establishment.

Re-setting the Table

After the guests have departed, clear the table, and place any accessories such as flowers or candles on a tray, not on a chair. Change the table linens, neatly folding the soiled linens, and taking care not to spill crumbs on the floor. Avoid allowing the surface of the table to be revealed during service.

In re-setting a tablecloth, use the following guidelines:

- The hem of the cloth should be face down.

- The corners of the cloth should line up with the corners of the table.

- If a base cloth is used, the corners of the decorative cloth should line up with the corners of the base cloth.

- The center crease of the cloth should be centered on the table and point upward.

- Use the backs of the hands to smooth the cloth.

- Replace the accessories; place folded napkins at each place setting; and re-set flatware, glassware, and any other serviceware according to the establishment's specifications.

CHAPTER

5

WESTERN STYLES *of service
have evolved and have become formalized over the
last three centuries. They generally reflect social
and gastronomic developments in Europe as well
as in the United States.*

*The terms used to describe the major styles of
service may be confusing, and they are interpreted
differently in the United States and in Europe. The
terms French, Russian, and English services have
very different meanings in Europe than they do in
the United States. The descriptions that follow
are those used in the United States.*

KEY TERMS

entremets
Russian service
plated service
family-style service
French service
sous cloche
wine steward
English service
butler service

Traditional Service Styles

Historically, French service was a ritual of placing elaborate platters of food for each course directly onto a table that was lined with several layers of tablecloths. Guests helped themselves from these platters. In aristocratic society, food presentations were artistic and required enormous resources and skill. These food displays were represented by famous chefs such as Marie-Antoine Carême. Dining in this manner had disadvantages: a diner could only enjoy what was placed within arm's length; and hot food was rarely eaten warm. It was also considered bad form or impolite to reach in front of someone else, just as it is today. After each course was removed from the table along with the top table cloth, the table was reset entirely with the silverware, plates, and the next food course or met. The entremets course was served on the side buffets between each course. The word entremets is French for "between courses," and today refers to a small course, such as a sorbet or a small dessert, which is served between courses. The Italian word intermezzo is a term that is commonly used on menus in the United States.

In the nineteenth century, French service began to incorporate elements of Russian service, or service à la russe. In traditional Russian service, the food was carried from the kitchen, presented, and then finished and served to the guest. This formal protocol was exported to France in the mid-1800s by Prince Alexander Kourakine, where it was incorporated into French service. It was further popularized by English society. This blended service allowed all the guests at the table to enjoy a particular dish that was served. A disadvantage of this service was that guests who did not care for a particular dish, were obliged to partake at the risk of insulting the host. Advantages include simplifying the chef's job and better controlling food cost. A lack of grandiose food showpieces led to the evolution of extremely fancy hollow-ware such as tureens and casseroles, which were made primarily of silver and porcelain.

Today, American, or plated service (known as *"à l'assiette"* service in France), is the most popular service around the world. It is simple and quick, because all the food is plated in the kitchen. It enables a chef to demonstrate and highlight creativity and artistry in the presentation of a dish, and permits serving food at the best possible serving temperature. This style has evolved to accommodate many types of dining establishments, from upscale fine-dining to bistros.

Although most restaurants rely on plated service, many also incorporate elements from other techniques.

Major service techniques include:

- Plated
- Banquet
- Family-style
- French
- Russian/English
- Butler
- Buffet.

Plated Service

Plated service or American Service was at first most widely adopted in America, but is now used internationally. This service is popular as it requires fewer and less extensively trained dining room personnel than other services such as classical *guéridon* service. It is theorized that this service became popular in the United States because Americans consumed more beverages than Europeans during a meal, and by serving food from the left there would be less of a likelihood for interrupting the guest. Today, little emphasis is placed on the side from which food is served as long as the guest is minimally impacted. At Johnson & Wales University students are taught that service and clearing are performed from the right unless the server is left handed or it is intrusive to the guest when these tasks are conducted from the right. *Plated service* is defined as the presentation of food that is completely prepared, plated, and garnished in the kitchen. The servers do not do table side cooking or plating. They carefully and respectfully place dishes in front of the guest. Service is more streamlined and allows for greater speed and efficiency. The server has time to focus on sales and to be more attentive to guests' needs. The net effect is an overall savings in labor cost that is beneficial to both management and the guest. Savings may be passed on to the guest in the form of more reasonable menu prices.

As previously discussed, the sequence of service is predicated on a long evolution. The normal sequence of service in the United States is 1. appetizer, 2. soup, 3. salad, 4. entrée, 5. coffee, and 6. dessert. If the appetizer is hot it follows the soup. If an intermezzo is served, it precedes the entrée.

General Rules of Plated Service

Beverages are always served to the right side of the guest with the server's right hand and right foot forward unless the guest chooses to place the glassware to his/her left. The server should then accommodate the guest. Also, if the guest's glass is unreachable at a booth table or because the guest's positioning makes it inaccessible, the server may then wish to pick up the glass rather than inconvenience the guest.

If serving to the right of a guest, proceed to the next guest in a clockwise direction. When serving to the left of a guest, proceed to the next guest counter-clockwise. Clearing is performed from the right with the right hand and the right foot forward except for items placed to the guest's left, such as the bread-and-butter plate.

Plated Service in a Banquet Setting

A banquet is a predetermined meal for a group of guests. There are basically three types of banquet functions: the first is a private or personal family event such as a wedding reception; the second is a business or corporate event such as a retirement dinner or a breakfast, luncheon or dinner during an annual corporate meeting; and the third is a civic event, which includes proms, rotary club award dinners, political fund raisers and holiday celebrations. A banquet may be for a few guests or for as many as 3000. Events include stand up receptions, cocktail parties, dances and simple breakfasts, to elaborate dinners with white gloved service.

Most banquet meals in this country use plated service. The servers are required to act in unison so that the guests are served each course at approximately the same time. Servers are assigned a station of 20 to 30 guests, depending on the number of courses. For example, a breakfast would usually only require one food course, juice and coffee service. However, a typical dinner would have a soup, an appetizer, a salad, an entrée, coffee, and a dessert.

- Always pay attention to the maître d'/captain who sets the pace of service.

- Serve the guest of honor's table first.

- If there is a split menu that offers a choice of entrées, it is imperative that the proper order is communicated to the kitchen. Note: There are a number of systems that an establishment may employ to assist customers in remembering their orders (such as coded cards which are placed in front of each guest).

- Serve the entire table at the same time for each course.

- Do not carry more than the number of covers at a table, or usually a maximum of 12 entrées on a service tray.

Advantages American service has several advantages. Service is generally quite fast. The service staff needs less training because the service is easier to master. Equipment costs are limited and less space is required between tables, so that more guests can be seated if need be. Chefs also have greater control of costs and presentation under this system.

Disadvantages American service lacks the elegance of French or Russian/English service, and the theatrical presentation that makes the dining experience memorable. Also, guests cannot choose their own portion sizes.

Family-Style Service

In *family-style service,* the chef prepares the dishes in the kitchen, and then servers place platters, casseroles, or tureens in the center of the guests' table with the appropriate serving utensils. Guests serve themselves using plates that servers place in front of them. Table clearing follows the protocol for American service. This service style may also be used for select courses in a banquet setting.

Advantages Family-style service minimizes the costs of dining room labor and helps to create a warm, familial atmosphere. Guests may decide on the portion size they want, and the meal is perceived as a good value for customers.

Disadvantages The lack of portion control can result in considerable food waste, and there is no control over plate presentation. Some guests may miss the personalized service provided by other serving styles.

French Service

French service is usually associated with elegant settings when expense is not a determining factor. Because a key element of *French service* is tableside preparation and plating, servers prepare and plate special dishes tableside in full view of the guest.

In order to deliver such elaborate and labor-intensive service, a restaurant generally requires a team of highly skilled and knowledgeable servers called a brigade, who need to work together closely.

General Rules of French Service

As with plated service, food and beverages are served from the right with the right hand. With the exception of bread-and-butter plates and knives, all dishes are cleared from the right with the right hand, and servers move clockwise around the table whenever possible.

Food is prepared tableside or plated on a *guéridon,* or side stand. See Figure 5-1. Today, as restaurants blend service techniques, some plates are prepared and plated in the kitchen. The serving of these dishes must be coordinated with the tableside items as they are completed so that all plates can be presented to the guests at the same time.

FIGURE 5-1

Proper mise en place is essential when preparing foods tableside.

Because French service is associated with elegant restaurants, specifically designed flatware may be used for particular courses. A fish knife and fish fork might be set in restaurants using this type of service.

Show plates for decorative purposes are preset on the cover, and if removed, may be replaced by service plates after the guest has ordered. If one guest decides not to join others at the table in selecting a course, the guest has a service or show plate placed in front of him or her. Plates that are prepared in the kitchen may be served *sous cloche,* or "under a bell." These large, domed plate covers are removed by servers simultaneously in front of the guests to add to the drama of dining.

Sequence of Service

The generally accepted rule for the sequence of service is that cold food precedes hot food, and liquids are served before solids. If serving a cold soup such as Vichysoisse, the soup is always served first. When the soup is served hot and an appetizer such as smoked salmon is served cold, the soup follows the cold fish. When both the soup and appetizer are hot, the soup is served first. The appetizer may then be followed by a fish course or an intermezzo prior to the entrée. Salads are served after the entrée and may be followed by a cheese course. Desserts are then served prior to coffee service. The meal may end with small petit fours, bonbons, or chocolate truffles.

The Brigade

Elaborate service requires a team or brigade of service personnel who can work together as one. The brigade system is not limited to French Service as its complexity is a reflection of the menu being served. A typical brigade is made up of the following individuals: the dining room manager, captain, front waiter, back waiter, waiter's assistant, and wine steward.

The Dining Room Manager, *Maître d', or Chef de Service, or Chef de Salle* The dining room manager must be in close contact with every department and know all aspects of the business: dining room, banquet facilities, service bar, front bar, kitchen, dishwashing area, and the front office. The responsibilities of this individual include the following:

- Hires and trains the dining room staff.
- Ensures the proper setup of the dining room.
- Inventories all dining room equipment.
- Requisitions the necessary supplies.
- Supervises the reservation system.
- Schedules the dining room staff.
- Opens and closes the dining room each day.
- Seats guests.
- Solves all customer issues or complaints.
- Is responsible for check reconciliations and cash reconciliation at the end of each shift.

The Captain The station captain (chef de rang) has the responsibility of supervising and organizing all the service aspects in an assigned station. Responsibilities include:

- Ensuring that the tables are correctly positioned and set.
- Ensuring that the *guéridon, réchaud,* and all other equipment needed is ready.

- Observing all guests within the station at all times.
- Being attentive to all verbal and non-verbal guest communication.
- Suggestively selling food and beverages.
- Accurately taking all orders.
- Answering all questions regarding ingredients and the preparation of food and beverages.
- Preparing and portioning foods tableside.
- Synchronizing service within the brigade system.
- Overseeing all tables to ensure guest satisfaction.
- Accurately totaling each check and collecting payment.
- Being accountable for all check reconciliations for the assigned station.

The Front Waiter The front waiter *(commis de rang)* assists the captain in serving food, and in the captain's absence must be able to perform all the captain's duties. Responsibilities of the front waiter include:

- Serving food and beverages to the guest.
- Serving beverages immediately upon receiving the order from the captain.
- Serving food once the course is plated by the captain.
- Opening and serving all bottled wine ordered by the captain unless the wine steward or sommelier is performing this service.
- Providing assistance to the back waiter and busser in clearing the guests' table.
- Ensuring that the table is properly marked and flatware is properly adjusted.

(Note: All food items should be taken from the right side of the guéridon with the waiter's right hand and presented to the guest.)

The Back Waiter The back waiter *(commis de suite)* brings all food orders from the kitchen to the service area, and serves as the link between the brigade and the kitchen staff. The back waiter's responsibilities consist of:

- Managing the timing and 'firing' of food orders.
- Placing and picking up all orders, service equipment and utensils from the kitchen and bringing them to the dining room.
- Presenting platters prepared by the kitchen to the guest prior to plating.
- Assisting in the clearing of both the *guéridon* and the guests' table.
- Delivering the necessary ingredients for the preparation of tableside dishes.
- Providing all equipment and utensils for the plating of items (plates, service sets).
- Knowing the ingredients and methods of preparation and garnishes.
- Being aware of the stage of service at each table in the station.
- Coordinating efforts with the captain, the chef in the kitchen, and other members of the brigade.

The Waiter's Assistant or Busser The waiters' assistant or busser *(commis de débarrassage)* is usually an entry level position in an apprentice system. Responsibilities of the waiter's assistant include:

- Serving bread, butter and water, and replenishing these when necessary.

- Clearing the table after each course.
- Cleaning the table after the guests have departed.
- Resetting each table.
- Making sure that a supply of clean linens and flatware is on hand.
- Performing any other duties necessary to keep the dining room in smooth running order.

Note: In some European countries, bread and water are served only if ordered.

The Wine Steward or Sommelier The *wine steward* or sommelier must have extensive knowledge of wines and spirits, and may be in charge of the purchasing and service of wine. In Europe, the sommelier may be wearing the *tastevin* cup; a silver cup hanging on a chain around the neck. This custom evolved in the *caves* or dimly lit tasting cellars of Burgundy. The silver cups refracted the limited light and due to the dimpling of the cup it enhanced the light to enable the cellar master to determine the condition of the wine when it was poured. Today, wearing the *tastevin* is more symbolic and is rarely used as it was originally intended. Responsibilities of the sommelier include:

- Selling and serving bottled wines. Assisting guests in making wine selections based on their selection of food.
- Directing the training of front of the house staff in wine and spirits.
- Developing wine lists.
- Establishing the pricing of wines.
- Developing wine programs to augment sales in the restaurant; for example, wine dinners or the sale of wines by the glass.
- Maintaining the wine inventory.
- Maintaining the correct storage and the cellaring of all wines.

Advantages French service, as a full-service, is elegant, stylish, and highly personalized. It is ideal for presenting certain dishes tableside such as Dover sole or for carving meats. Tableside service allows for the presentation of foods at the best maintained temperatures.

Disadvantages French service takes much longer than American service, reducing the ability to turn tables. Equipment such as *guéridons* and specialty carts require floor space, limiting the number of tables in a restaurant. The cost of equipment needed and the highly skilled servers required push menu prices higher as well.

Russian, English, or Silver Service

In Europe, *English service* refers to a service in which the server spoons or plates portions directly onto a dish that is in front of the guest. In the United States, this type of service is often called Russian service, or sometimes silver service. Regardless of how it is labeled, there are general principles that must be followed. The term English Service is also used when a host or hostess performs the same tasks of carving and plating each guest's portion and having a server serve the accompaniments.

General Rules of Russian/English-Silver Service

When using silver service, all food is prepared, portioned, and garnished before being placed on platters, tureens, or service plates. Unlike French service, silver service can involve a single server or a team of servers. All servers, however, have a clean service towel, usually draped over the left forearm.

Beverages, plates, and bowls on underliners are set in front of the guest from the right side, and food items are served with the right hand from the left side of the guest. Service proceeds counterclockwise around the table. Service sets are used to transfer food from the platter to the guest's plate.

Tureen Service

When soup is ordered, tureen service is a part of Russian service. Warmed soup plates or bowls on underliners are preset in front of the guests. Before leaving the kitchen, the soup tureen is placed on a STP/serviette underliner with a ladle in or beside the tureen. The cover is removed before approaching the table. With the tureen in the left hand, approach and serve guests from the left, drawing the handle of the soup ladle toward yourself, using the right hand to avoid spillage. Return the ladle to the tureen before serving the next guest. If the soup is accompanied by a garnish, the garnish is served from a side dish next to the tureen with an appropriate utensil. Service proceeds counterclockwise around the table.

Platter Service

Another aspect of this service is platter service. The chef prepares and places food on a platter in the kitchen. Warmed plates are preset in front of the guests before the food is presented.

With platters held on the left forearm and hand, position the platter parallel to the table to the left of the guest, without touching the table. Using the pince technique, place the portion onto the guest's plate. Each platter requires a clean service set. Sauces are generally served separately, or there is a separate serving spoon for the sauce. The server proceeds counterclockwise.

Casserole Service

In casserole or *cocotte* service, the dinner plate and any accompaniments are preset on the table from the guest's right side. Hold the casserole dish in the left hand and a service set in the right. The contents of the casserole are served from the left of the guest and as close to the plate as possible. Clearing is done from the guest's right, with the server using the right hand.

Advantages Russian (English, silver) service is faster than French service and requires fewer extensively trained staff. It allows guests to determine their own portion size and gives the chef greater quality control.

Disadvantages Initial costs for equipment used in Russian service are high, and servers need to be skilled in using service sets. More space is needed between guests for server access. Additionally, there can be considerable temperature loss in foods served on a platter. Finally, the last guests served may receive the food from a platter whose appearance is unappetizing.

Butler Service

Butler service is similar to Russian service but allows for the guest to select the food portion from the platter or tureen. This type of service is used most often at receptions, with servers carrying trays of hors d'oeuvres from which guests make a selection. It is important that cocktail napkins are offered to the guest in a convenient manner. There should be trays placed conveniently about the room for guests to dispose of frill picks, used napkins, and any other such items.

Advantages At a full service meal, the handles of the utensils for the platters must be directed toward the guests for their convenience. When the course is presented a second time, new service utensils should be used. The advantages of this type of service are that guests may choose their own portion size, and items can be creatively displayed on trays. Serving guests at stand-up receptions is also cost-efficient.

Disadvantages Butler service has several disadvantages. Portion control is difficult. If guests choose not to serve themselves, the host may be embarrassed. If guests are not dexterous, the presentation of food on their plates may not be appealing. More space is also needed between chairs to allow server access.

Buffet Service

Buffet service can be conducted in an à la carte or banquet environment. It has become a popular dining option because it is relatively efficient and economical. Although the menu may be limited, guests may select from a variety of options and choose the quantity and combinations they prefer.

With the exception of the kitchen staff, buffets often require a limited service staff. A buffet table is used to display both hot and

cold prepared foods. Cold food platters are kept chilled, and hot dishes are kept warm in chafing pans. Hot and cold foods are held at their appropriate temperatures to ensure food safety and appetizing flavors. Today, there are three common types of buffet service: simple, modified deluxe, and deluxe.

Simple Buffet Service

A simple buffet is basically unstaffed. Customers serve themselves, and the server is responsible only for setting tables, replenishing food items, clearing tables, presenting checks, and breaking down the buffet table. The simple buffet is commonly used in conference centers and hotels, where the buffet table can be wheeled into a meeting room so that guests may serve themselves without disrupting the meeting.

Modified Deluxe Buffet Service

Although customers select soups, appetizers, salads, entrées, and possibly desserts from a buffet table using the modified deluxe buffet service, staff members serve beverages and assist at the buffet at various levels, depending on the establishment. In more elaborate environments, the buffet may be partially plated or entirely plated by *buffetiers;* while in casual restaurants, the guests serve themselves. A chef often assists at the carving station. Large parties, such as an office Christmas party or an anniversary celebration, often use this type of service.

Deluxe Buffet

The deluxe buffet provides the most extensive service. With the exception of the entrée, all courses are plated and served. In a buffet service, the server invites guests to the buffet table, or in an à la carte

environment, informs guests of the choices available, and makes recommendations. The server is responsible for serving and clearing beverages and serving any plated course using American service. As needed, the server clears and replaces soiled plates and flatware.

The *buffetiers* supervise the correct positioning of the buffet tables and the organization of the display. Cold items are displayed first, and hot items last. The *buffetier* also estimates the number of guests that a buffet table can accommodate and oversees all the details for the comfort and safety of the guests.

Buffetiers are responsible for the smooth operation of the buffet and the safe handling of the food. They ensure that the food is at the correct temperature. Hot foods are placed in a chafing pan. The insert pan should be at least one-third full of hot water, using at least two heat sources, unless an electric heating element is used. The buffet surface and plates must be checked for cleanliness (including both sides of the plates). Cold buffet foods must be protected by sneeze guards. Chilled plates are available for appetizers and salads. Dinner plates are heated so that they are warm, but not hot to the touch. Service utensils must have clean handles; those with soiled handles are replaced. Chafing pans are kept covered when guests are not using them. Hinged chafers have the hinged side away from the guests.

Any pan with shingled food items has the first piece on top of, rather than under the piece behind it. For two-sided buffets, food is shingled in two opposite lines. Food is reordered when a pan is one-third full and replaced before the pan is empty or when the appearance of the food has diminished because it has been in the pan too long. Food should not be transferred from one pan to another in the dining room. Accompaniments and condiments are placed near the appropriate item with the correct service ware; salad dressing choices, for example, are found near the salads with the appropriate serving utensils.

Plates and bowls are replaced before they are all used but are never stacked more than 30 plates high. Hot pans are removed safely by using two servers, one to remove the used pan and the other to replace a full one. Used pans are not removed until a replacement is ready because the steaming pans pose a risk to guests. Guests are cautioned before the staff approaches the buffet with a hot pan, and chafing pans are changed using service towels. The buffet is broken down safely by discarding leftover food; wiping the table clean; covering chafing pans; extinguishing all canned fuel containers before moving them; and safely discarding the hot water.

Advantages Buffet service minimizes dining room labor costs, and customers have a wider selection of food from which to choose. Guests may also determine their own portions. Buffets can present an impressive display of food, and if properly managed, reduce service time.

Disadvantages Buffets produce a considerable amount of food waste and leftovers. Because of the lag time between when the first table of guests is invited to the buffet table and when the last are summoned, the buffet table may look less attractive for later guests unless it is well maintained. Guests may have to wait in long lines, and individuals with physical disabilities may also be at a disadvantage at buffets. There is also a potential for food contamination and cross-contamination, unless the buffet is carefully managed and supervised.

The Beverage World

THE BEVERAGE WORLD

has never been as exciting as it is today. In every category, there is innovation, diversity, and a renewed focus on quality. Humans have enjoyed beverages and have transformed them into an essential part of social interaction. Professor Patrick McGovern, an archeochemist at the University of Pennsylvania, uncovered the existence of fermented beverages dating back to 7000 B.C. in Jiahu, China, and also concluded that the earliest fermented beverages were derived from fruits and grains, which sometimes included botanicals. Others believe that one of the earliest alcoholic beverages was koumis— fermented mare's milk—that is still enjoyed today by the Mongols. The evolution of non-alcoholic beverages, such as tea, coffee, and other infusions came later. Regardless of the beverage, consumption of both alcoholic and non-alcoholic beverages has become a social ritual in every part of the world and has been perceived as a social 'lubricant'.

The earliest known taverns existed in ancient Sumer in Mesopotamia (modern Iraq) around 3500 B.C. Over thousands of years, various protocols and etiquette for serving beverages evolved into the more modern forms of teahouses, cafés, and taverns, which became prominent in England during the 16th and 17th centuries. These establishments were then brought to these shores by the Puritans and early colonists.

In Asia, early civilizations learned to make tea, while in the Americas, Mayan and Aztec rulers sipped drinks made from chocolate. Coffee growing developed in Ethiopia and was brought to Arabia, Turkey, Central and South America, and the Pacific Islands. Although many beverages have been revered or condemned because they had psychotropic or stimulant properties, beverages today are an important part of restaurant service and a considerable profit center.

The Beverage Industry

Over the past two decades there has been an explosion of beverage choices for consumers. The number of breweries has grown from 60 to over 1,500; the number of wineries in the U.S. alone exceeds 4,500; the availability of bottled waters spans from Iceland to Fiji; there are dozens of single variety coffees served by professional coffee baristas at all kinds of cafés; 2,500 teahouses offer a wide assortment of teas including vintage and flowering teas; and there has been a cocktail renaissance with an emphasis on craft versus volume.

Americans are seeking to replicate experiences they have enjoyed during their travels abroad, and consistent marketing efforts are piquing interests in a variety of brands. Since one in three meals is eaten away from the home, Americans have become more sophisticated in their taste experiences than ever, and are also expecting that servers in the food and beverage industry have a knowledge of new products.

Beverage Profitability

It is important to realize that when analyzing beverage sales in restaurants, non-alcoholic beverages such as bottled water, tea, coffee, juices, and milk are considered part of food sales and food cost. Beverage sales are key to the profitability of most full-service restaurants: overall beverage costs traditionally run between 22% and 28% of beverage sales in a full-service restaurant. All beverages do not have equal cost percentages. For example, wines are usually priced so that they run at a 40% to 45% cost in fine-dining restaurants, while the cost of sales of spirits may run as low as 12% in bars and taverns. In fine-dining restaurants, the sales of beverages may contribute to more than 75% of the establishment's total net profit. In addition to increased sales, research shows that enjoying a great beverage also increases the satisfaction rating of a diner's entire restaurant experience.

The Role of Beverage Personnel

Figure 6-1 shows that there are numerous opportunities for servers to sell all types of beverages. Many studies suggest that up to 62% of drink orders are influenced by servers and bartenders who have visible and innovative programs. Without training, many servers may not realize the opportunities that exist to upsell and to provide their customers the opportunity to experience something new. In Chapter 9, "Mixology" we examine the specific roles of the beverage manager, head bartender, bartender, bar back, and cocktail server as it applies to serving alcoholic beverages. Without proper beverage training for employees, the success of a full-service restaurant is questionable.

Personnel must also be knowledgeable about other beverages that are related to food costs such as coffee. Restaurants rarely expend the energy and resources on non-alcoholic beverage training even though the profit potential is high with the cost of teas, coffees, sodas, and bottled water as low as 8%. But why should servers lack a knowledge of these products when an establishment is attempting to maximize the guest's experience, the restaurant's profitability, and the server's income?

FIGURE 6-1

Beverage Consumption in the US in 2008 in millions of gallons according to The Beverage Group Handbook Advance 2008:	
SOFT DRINKS	15,045
COFFEE	8,000
BOTTLED WATER	7,990
MILK	6,970
BEER	6,588
TEA	2,100
JUICES	1,770
WINE	700
DISTILLED SPIRITS	434
CIDER	10

Coffee

There are over 110 million Americans who enjoy coffee in one form or another. Fifty-two percent of Americans start the day with a cup of coffee, and twenty nine percent drink specialty coffees such as lattes, espressos, or cappuccinos. In fact, coffee is the third most popular beverage in the world after water and tea. There are over 127 million 60 kg bags of coffee produced in 60 countries around the world, with Brazil as the largest producer. Worldwide, more than 25 million acres are devoted to coffee growing. About 20 million people work in the industry, and coffee is the world's second most traded commodity after oil.

The Coffee Plant

Coffee trees produce berries that resemble cherries. The berries, bright red when ripe, usually contain two seeds, or beans, which are processed, roasted, ground, and brewed into liquid coffee. Although more than 25 wild species of coffee trees have been identified, only two, *C. arabica* and *C. robusta* (now reclassified as *C. canephora*), are cultivated for commercial use.

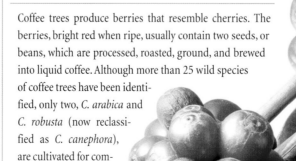

Initially planted from nursery-grown seedlings, the coffee tree begins producing fruit in four to six years and continues to do so for about 40 years. A self-pollinating evergreen, the coffee tree blooms with fragrant white flowers and produces about 2,000 berries—enough to produce a pound and a half of roasted coffee beans. Most growing regions have a single yearly harvest, but regions with two distinct rainy seasons have two harvests.

Coffea arabica About 75% of the world's coffee production comes from *C. arabica* plants. *Arabica,* the highest-quality coffee, grows best in a narrow band on either side of the equator at altitudes ranging from 2,000 to 6,000 feet (610 to 1,829 m). In Central and South America and East Africa, where the majority of coffee grows, year-round temperatures of about 70°F (21°C) and abundant rainfall provide the plants with ideal conditions. Most arabica fruits ripen at different times on the same plant and grow in rugged terrain, so harvesting is labor-intensive. Only ripe berries yield superior coffee, and must generally be picked by hand. Arabica is lower-yielding and more susceptible to disease than robusta. Consumers willingly pay a higher price for arabica's sweet aroma and winy, fresh, and slightly acid taste.

Coffea robusta *Coffea canephora,* or *robusta,* is hardier than Arabica and grows well at lower altitudes in wet valleys and tropical forest climates. It has a significantly higher percentage of caffeine than arabica. Like arabica, a robusta plant begins to mature four to six years after it is transplanted. It is also easier to cultivate, and growers often use machines to harvest it. Large coffee roasters often use these less expensive robusta beans as a supplement in their blends and for use in instant coffees. Robusta's heavy, earthy aroma and flavor provide a heavier body with a characteristically thicker viscosity.

Varietal and specialty coffees About 10% of the world's coffee bean crop is classified as gourmet or specialty quality coffee. A *varietal coffee* is a coffee that comes from a single varietal or *cultivar* from a single growing region. Antigua Guatemalan, Jamaican Blue Mountain, Hawaiian Kona, Costa Rican Tarrazu, Kenyan AA, Ethiopian Yergachev, or Sumatran Gayo Mountain are all examples of varietal coffees. Specialty coffees are often blended by the roaster from two or more varieties of beans that complement one another. Roasters who blend coffees generally do so using their own judgment, and their blends often define the roaster's image.

Certified organic coffee The market for organically grown and processed products has expanded considerably in the last few years. There is however a difference between products that claim to be "organic" and those that are "certified organic." Certified organic coffees have been endorsed by an accredited, independent, third-party inspection. Detailed record keeping must demonstrate that the coffee has at least 95% certified organic ingredients, which are grown without the use of synthetic fertilizers or pesticides. The grower must also practice shade-tree canopy preservation to provide habitats for migratory birds so that the coffee may be designated as "bird friendly." Finally, certified organic coffee must be kept separate from all other coffee throughout its production and processing.

Fair Trade Certified Coffee

Over 100 companies in the U.S. market their coffees as *'Fair Trade Certified'*. Coffee is one of the most price volatile commodities in the world. Coffee prices have been as low as $0.60 per pound, as was the case in 2009. 'Fair Trade' agreements support a livable income of $1.61 per pound for the coffee of small growers' and support organic farming in shade grown areas by offering further premium pricing.

Coffee Production

A number of conditions determine which of three methods growers use to harvest coffee. Where the terrain is too rugged for mechanical harvesting, growers use the most expensive *selective method,* picking only ripe berries from the tree by hand. For varieties that ripen their berries at the same time, one swift movement sweeps the branches clean of berries using the *strip method.* The *mechanical method* of harvesting is most common on coffee plantations, where the trees are planted on relatively flat terrain in even rows. In this method, the harvester straddles the row and agitates the trees to cause the beans to fall onto a conveyor belt.

Processing

As with growing and harvesting techniques, processing methods depend on the kinds of beans and the conditions where the trees grow. Where sufficient water is available, a *wet method* of processing is used; mostly for arabica coffees. Both the kind of bean and the method of processing give the arabica variety its characteristic high quality. In areas where water is not plentiful, processors use the dry method. In the 1990s a third process known as the pulped natural method, which is a hybrid of the two, evolved in Brazil.

The wet method Using the wet method, coffee processors first depulp the berries mechanically. Depulping exposes the parchment-covered beans, which then soak in tanks of water until fermentation softens the mucilage layer for easy removal. Timing is critical because fermentation must not affect the bean itself. The beans are then washed to remove the fermented layer and are spread in the sun on drying patios for 7 to 21 days. More modern drying methods include drum dryers that tumble the beans for two to three days at temperatures from 122°–140°F (50°–60°C). Through the drying process, the moisture content of the beans drops from approximately 70% to about 11%. After a rest period of 20 to 30 days, the parchment and silver skin are peeled off by a hulling machine before the coffee is roasted to fill orders. High-quality beans that are processed by the wet method generally have cleaner flavors, few if any undesirable characteristics, and a more acid taste.

The dry method In areas where water is scarce, processors use the *dry method* of processing to produce sweet, smooth, complex coffee tastes. This method is used primarily in areas such as Yemen or Ethiopia where robusta is the dominant coffee crop. It may also be used for arabicas if water supplies are insufficient.

Processors using this method allow the coffee cherries to dry partially on the tree and then spread them to dry in the sun for 14 to 21 days. Mechanical huskers then remove the dry pulp and parchment. Beans that have been prepared by the dry method have a heavier body but may sometimes develop off flavors.

The pulped natural method Coffee cherries are pulped and the beans are dried without going through a fermentation stage to remove the mucilage in the *pulped natural method.* Excellent coffee can be produced in this way with characteristics of both the dried and wet methods, including a full body.

Sorting and Grading

Dried beans are graded by size, density, and color. Size grading uses screens to separate beans according to their diameter. A number 10 bean, for example, has a diameter of 10/64 inch (4 mm). The beans are sized by passing them through the appropriate screens. Density is determined by subjecting the beans to an air jet that is calibrated to separate heavier beans from lighter ones. Color sorting is usually accomplished by hand, but some processors color-sort electronically. Finally, the beans are packed in burlap or plastic bags and shipped to roasters across the world.

The sorting and grading process varies from country to country. In general though, coffee beans come in six export grades. The top grade is known as SHB, or strictly hard beans. These are grown at a high altitude of at least 4,000 feet (1.2 km) above sea level.

Examples of different grades, classifications, and varieties of coffee beans.

Coffee Classifications

The dried, but still green coffee beans are classified according to botanical variety, processing method, and altitude of growth. The International Coffee Organization has classified green coffee beans, for example as: Colombian milds, other mild arabicas, Brazilian, other arabicas, and robustas. In recent decades the organization has lost its standing, and the above classifications are no longer as readily accepted. They do, however, provide useful descriptions of the wide variability of coffees.

Colombian milds Grown primarily in Colombia, Kenya, and Tanzania, these coffees constitute 16% of the world's production and are graded principally on bean size. These beans produce sweet, highly aromatic brewed coffee with a thick body.

Other mild arabicas This classification encompasses most of the arabicas grown in Central and South America. Accounting for about 26% of the world's production, these beans are graded according to growing altitude, density, color, and the number of defects. Their taste is winy to sour, with moderate aromatics and a smooth body, which is typical of medium-altitude coffee, grown at 2,000–4,000 feet (610–1,220 m).

Brazilian and other arabicas Grown in Brazil and Ethiopia, these beans make up about 37% of the world's coffee production. They are graded by the growing area, which determines the taste characteristics and the number of imperfections. The brewed coffee made from these beans has a winy-to-sour taste, moderate aromatics, and a smooth body.

Robustas Accounting for 21% of global coffee production, robustas are graded on density, size, and the number of defects. These beans produce a brew with a neutral-to-sharp taste, pungent aromatics, and a heavy body. Because robustas are 10% to 40% less expensive than arabicas, they are often used as filler in blended coffees.

FIGURE 6-2   Levels of Roasting

Five common but imprecise levels of roasting give different "roasts" their distinctive flavors and aromas.

CINNAMON ROAST

Cinnamon roast is the lightest commercially available roast. These beans have no visible oils on their surface, and the flavor and body are light.

FULL CITY ROAST

Full City roast is a medium roast.

VIENNA ROAST

Vienna roast describes both a medium roast that is chocolate brown with dark speckles and a particular blend of different roasts.

FRENCH ROAST

Sometimes called New Orleans roast, French roast is heavily roasted to bring out a strong, characteristically bitter flavor and aroma.

ITALIAN ROAST

Italian roast is the darkest stage of roasting. The beans become carbonized and coated with a film of oil. These beans are usually reserved for espressos made by large producers, but great espressos may also be made with beans roasted to a much less carbonized level.

The Roasting Process

Roasting coffee beans brings out their full flavor and aroma. Their flavors depend on the degree to which the beans are caramelized during the roasting process. See Figure 6-2. Many complex chemical changes take place during roasting, which generally takes from 8 to 16 minutes at temperatures of approximately 350°–500°F (180°–260°C). As they reach a temperature of about 400°F (204°C), the beans begin to turn brown, and the oils, called coffee essence, start to emerge. This process, called *pyrolosis,* produces the distinctive flavor and aroma of the coffee.

Espresso and Espresso Beverages

Properly made espresso is thick, dark, and intensely fragrant, with a bittersweet taste. It is topped with creamy golden foam called "crema". A single demitasse, or half-size cup serving contains only 1–1 1/4 ounces (30–37 ml) and is served immediately after brewing. Espresso may be combined with ice, cold milk, steamed milk, whipped cream, mocha, and other flavorings to create a wide range of recipes.

There are several popular espresso-based drinks served in food service operations:

- **Americano**—Americano is a single shot of espresso with 6 to 8 ounces (177 to 237 ml) of hot water added.
- **Caffè latte**—Caffè latte is a single shot of espresso topped with steamed skim milk and a layer of frothed skim milk.
- **Cappuccino**—Cappuccino is a single shot of espresso, topped with 4 1/2 ounces (133 ml) of thick foam of steamed emulsified milk served in a 6- to 8-ounce (177- to 237-ml) cup or glass with sugar on the side.
- **Caffè breve (brief)**—A caffè breve consists of a single shot of espresso and 4 ounces (118 ml) of steamed half-and-half, served in a 6-ounce (177-ml) cup with sugar on the side.
- **Corretto (corrected)**—A corretto is made of a single shot of espresso with a 1-ounce (30 ml) shot of liqueur served in a demitasse.
- **Doppio (double)**—A double shot of espresso served with sugar on the side, makes up a doppio.
- **Espresso macchiato (marked)**—An espresso macchiato is a single or double shot of espresso topped with a heaping teaspoon of steamed milk.
- **Lungo (long)**—A lungo is a single shot of espresso served in a demitasse with sugar on the side.
- **Ristretto (restricted)**—A shot of espresso, served in a demitasse with sugar to the side and a "water-back" composes a ristretto.

THE ORIGINS OF *Espresso*

In 1903 Luigi Bezzera, an Italian manufacturer, was unhappy about the amount of time his workers spent on their coffee breaks. He thought that by shortening the brewing process, which took as long as 20 minutes, he could shorten the breaks.

Bezzera decided to brew the coffee under pressure. He invented a machine he called the "Fast Coffee Machine." Not only did Bezzera's machine reduce the brew time to a mere 20 seconds, but it also made a better cup of coffee than traditional methods made. The quick brewing time extracted the coffee's best qualities while leaving behind the unfavorable qualities, such as bitterness.

Later Achilles Gaggia, a barkeeper, decided to improve on the basic espresso machine by adding a lever and piston that produced more pressure in the brew chamber. Today, Gaggia espresso machines and related equipment are familiar sights behind the counters of the world's coffee bars.

Decaffeinated Coffee

Caffeine, a nitrogen compound found in plants, is a mild stimulant that may increase the heart rate and cause sleeplessness in some people. As little as 10 milligrams may cause discomfort.

The Food and Drug Administration (FDA) guidelines state that coffee labeled *decaffeinated* must have 97% of the caffeine removed from the green coffee bean prior to roasting, so decaffeinated coffee has about two to five milligrams of caffeine per serving. Three main processes are employed to decaffeinate coffee beans. Because caffeine is water-soluble, each process begins with moistened green coffee beans.

The conventional water method In this process, the green beans are treated with steam and water to open their cellular structure. They are then flushed with a decaffeinating agent such as methylene chloride or ethyl acetate. The beans are further treated with steam and water to evaporate all remaining traces of the decaffeinating agent. No traceable amount of the agent is left in the beans.

Swiss water processing Swiss water processing is similar to the water method but uses charcoal filtration rather than chemicals.

Supercritical carbon dioxide decaffeination This method uses carbon dioxide as the solvent agent. The carbon dioxide is passed through the coffee beans under tremendous pressure (250–300 times atmospheric pressure), typically extracting 96%–98% of the caffeine. Although expensive, this method is popular because carbon dioxide is abundant and reusable.

History OF *Coffee*

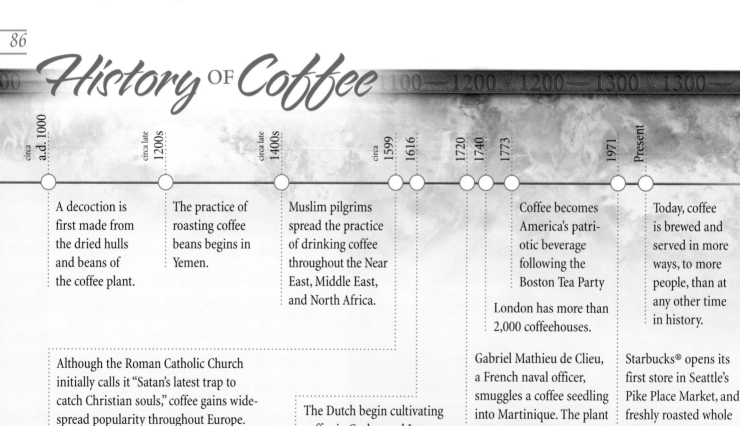

circa a.d. 1000
A decoction is first made from the dried hulls and beans of the coffee plant.

circa late 1200s
The practice of roasting coffee beans begins in Yemen.

Although the Roman Catholic Church initially calls it "Satan's latest trap to catch Christian souls," coffee gains widespread popularity throughout Europe.

circa late 1400s
Muslim pilgrims spread the practice of drinking coffee throughout the Near East, Middle East, and North Africa.

The Dutch begin cultivating coffee in Ceylon and Java.

circa 1599

1616

1720

1740
Gabriel Mathieu de Clieu, a French naval officer, smuggles a coffee seedling into Martinique. The plant is the ancestor of most of the arabica beans cultivated around the world.

1773
Coffee becomes America's patriotic beverage following the Boston Tea Party

London has more than 2,000 coffeehouses.

1971
Starbucks® opens its first store in Seattle's Pike Place Market, and freshly roasted whole beans, gourmet blends, and specialty coffees become trendy.

Present
Today, coffee is brewed and served in more ways, to more people, than at any other time in history.

Degassing and Packaging Coffee

Preserving the maximum flavor, freshness, and aroma of coffee while packaging it for distribution is a complex problem. After coffee beans are roasted, they produce carbon dioxide gas equal to about three times their volume. If the carbon dioxide is not released prior to most commercial packaging, the pressure of the escaping gas will cause the package to burst. Unfortunately, when the carbon dioxide dissipates, the beans can absorb oxygen and become somewhat stale.

Packers have developed ingenious packaging solutions to resolve the gas problem. Greaseproof, moisture-proof, resealable bags are nitrogen-flushed to displace oxygen. A one-way valve allows carbon dioxide to pass out of the bag while preventing air from entering it. After packages have been opened, however, storage conditions have an important effect on the coffee's flavor and quality. One leading producer, Illy, developed another ingenious system that best preserves the aromas of whole beans by packaging the beans in a canister that expands with the CO_2. The container is actually filled with additional carbon dioxide to force the aromatic compounds back into the beans themselves to extend their flavor.

Storing Coffee

To keep coffee's taste and aroma from dissipating, store it away from air, moisture, and heat. See Figure 6-3. Buy smaller quantities of whole beans, and store the coffee in tightly sealed containers. Unopened preportioned nitrogen-flushed coffee packs generally have a "use by" date and can be stored in a cool room. Coffee should not be stored under refrigeration.

Tasting Terms

Humans perceive taste through receptors on taste buds located primarily on the tongue. But taste is also affected by texture and mouthfeel. Although taste is a somewhat subjective sensation, people have generally agreed on the meaning of several taste descriptors: sweet, sour, bitter, mellow, bland, fresh, and sharp, for example. See Figure 6-4. Coffee tasters also have an agreed-upon vocabulary.

Acidity This desirable characteristic refers to the lively, palate-cleansing tartness of coffee. It is a characteristic of arabica from high-altitude growing regions. Acidity should not be confused with bitterness.

Body Body refers to the sense of heaviness or thickness of a coffee. Descriptors for this sensation range from thin, light, and watery to buttery, heavy, and thick. Sumatran can be the heaviest coffee, and Mexican and Ethiopian coffees tend to be the lightest. Several factors, such as the type of grind, the amount of water used, and the brewing method, can also affect the coffee's body.

Flavor Flavor is the most important tasting term, which refers to the overall impression of aromas, flavors, and body. Coffee can often be described as mellow or harsh, grassy or earthy. The terms "chocolaty" or "winy" (winelike) may also be used to describe a coffee's flavor.

Crema Crema is the amber foam that floats on top of a well-made espresso. The amber foam should have 'tiger stripes' created by oils and colloids—suspended coffee particles and carbon dioxide. This mixture not only gives espresso a rich, full mouth feel but coats the tongue to prevent the bitterness of the coffee from being perceived. See Figure 6-5.

Mocha Named for the Yemen port of Moka on the Red Sea, from which coffee was first traded, mocha was a term used to describe coffee in Europe during the sixteenth century. When chocolate was brought from the Americas to Europe, Europeans believed that it had a flavor similar to that of coffee. *Mocha* is a term now used to describe a blend of coffee and chocolate and is not to be confused with Moka brewing, which was discussed in Chapter 3: "The Restaurant Environment."

FIGURE 6-3

Coffee should be stored away from air, moisture, and heat.

FIGURE 6-4

Professional coffee tasters use a technique called "cupping" to evaluate different coffees and to create blends.

FIGURE 6-5

A well-formed crema adds to the enjoyment of a cup of espresso.

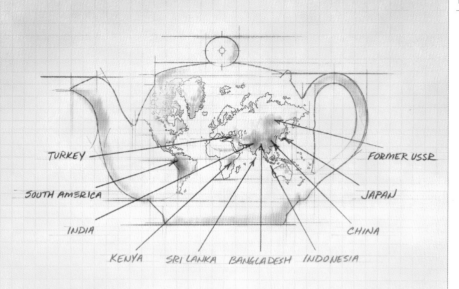

TURKEY

SOUTH AMERICA

INDIA

KENYA   SRI LANKA   BANGLADESH   INDONESIA

FORMER USSR

JAPAN

CHINA

Tea

Legend has it that a Chinese emperor discovered tea in 2737 B.C. when a fragrant leaf or two from a nearby camellia tree blew into some water he was boiling. Tasting the brew, he declared it delectable, and thus was born the cultivation of tea. However, it was not until the Ming dynasty (A.D. 1368–1644) that tea consumption became a part of everyday life in China.

By the 1600s, explorers and traders were importing tea to Europe and then further abroad to America. Tea drinking soon became fashionable among British aristocrats. In the late 1700s, afternoon tea became an everyday ritual among members of English society. Tea among the upper classes included not only the hot beverage but also delicate, crustless sandwiches, and pastries. These offerings soon expanded to include toasted bread with jam, as well as scones and crumpets. The working classes soon developed their own ritual, with "high tea" consisting of meats, cheese, and breads taken as their principal evening meal.

Tea Production

Today, tea is the most popular beverage in the world after water. It is available in a wide variety of forms, ranging from the modest inexpensive tea bag, to extremely rare and proportionately expensive herbs that are gathered by hand in remote regions of the world.

Tea is processed from the leaves of *Camellia sinensis,* a tree or shrub that grows best at higher altitudes under damp, tropical conditions. The leaves are hand-harvested or plucked from the plants' youngest shoots, called the first and second flush. About 4,200 pounds (1,905 kg) of fresh tea leaves produce 1,000 pounds (454 kg) of finished tea.

Although tea grows in many other regions, India, China, Sri Lanka, Indonesia, and Kenya account for most of the world's commercial production and exports. Teas often take their names from the regions in which they are grown.

Tea Classification

Although all tea comes from basically the same plant species, there are approximately 1,500 grades and 2,000 different blends of teas. Four general classifications of tea define the level of enzymatic oxidation that leaves undergo during processing.

White Tea

White tea is unoxidized and silvery in color with the highest concentration of caffeine. It is made from the youngest shoots or buds of specific tea varietal plants. There are several white teas of note particularly in the Fujian province of China. It is also harvested in small quantities in Assam and Darjeeling in India and in Sri Lanka.

Green Tea

Green tea is also unoxidized and yellowish-green with a slightly bitter flavor. Steaming or heating the leaves immediately after picking prevents enzymatic oxidation that turns tea leaves into black tea. After heating, the leaves are rolled and dried. Green teas need to be properly stored and served fresh. Green teas are produced primarily in China, Taiwan, and Japan.

Examples of green tea include:

- **Gyokuro**—the finest grade of exported Japanese tea.
- **Tencha**—the powdered tea used in Japanese tea ceremonies.
- **Sencha**—the most common Japanese tea, which is popular in restaurants and sushi bars.
- **Gunpowder**—the highest Chinese grade, which is rolled into tiny balls.
- **Imperial**—a grade from Sri Lanka, China, or India.
- **Shou Mei**—a Chinese green tea known as "old man's eyebrows."

Oolong Tea

Oolong tea combines the characteristics of black and green teas. The leaves are partially oxidized; the process is interrupted; and the leaves are rolled and dried. Oolong is often flavored with scented agents such as jasmine flowers. It is also graded by leaf size and age.

Examples of oolong tea include:

- **Formosa Oolong**—a delicate, large-leafed oolong tea with a taste reminiscent of ripe peaches. Unique and expensive, it is suited for breakfast or afternoon tea.
- **Black Dragon**—a kind of tea from Taiwan.
- **Pouchong**—a tea grown both in China and Taiwan.

Black Tea

When steeped, *black tea* is strongly flavored and amber or coppery brown. The color and flavor result from plucked leaves that are dried, or withered, and then rolled in special machines to release the enzymes that give the tea its color, specific taste, and aroma. The leaves are then "fired," or heated and compressed to their final shape.

Teas are also sorted by leaf size and according to their brewing time. Larger leaves take longer to brew than smaller leaves. Size classifications include souchong, or large-leaf tea; pekoe, or medium-leaf tea; and orange pekoe, or the smallest whole-leaf tea.

Broken tea leaves are categorized as either fannings or dust and are used for tea bags. Broken orange pekoe is of a high-quality, and generally produces a darker brew of the kind most commonly steeped from tea bags. Black teas are the best known and most popular in the West, but most teas sold in the United States are blends. Even the same tea blend or type of tea will taste different from blender to blender. Some of the most popular types of teas are:

- **Assam**—a rich, black tea from Northern India, valued as a breakfast tea by connoisseurs.

- **Ceylon**—a full-flavored black tea with a delicate fragrance; ideal for iced tea because it does not turn cloudy when cold.
- **Darjeeling**—a full-bodied, black tea with a Muscat flavor, grown in the foothills of the Himalayas.
- **Earl Grey**—a popular choice for afternoon tea, Earl Grey is flavored with oil of bergamot.
- **English Breakfast**—a full-bodied, robust blend of Indian and Sri Lankan teas.
- **Lapsang Souchong**—a tarry, smoky flavor and aroma, best for afternoon tea or as a dinner beverage.

Iced Tea and Tea Bags

Iced tea and the tea bag have "happy accidents" in common. Iced tea was invented at the 1904 World's Fair in St. Louis, Missouri, when the temperature soared and fairgoers were ignoring the hot brew. Tea merchant Richard Blechynden decided to dump a load of ice into the tea and to serve it cold to attract business.

In 1908 New York tea merchant Thomas Sullivan carefully wrapped samples of his product in muslin bags for restaurant managers to test. When he realized that the restaurants were brewing his samples in the bag to avoid the mess of tea leaves, the tea bag was born. It is at about the same time that Thomas Lipton, a British merchant and owner of several tea plantations, began marketing his high-quality tea blend in convenient, inexpensive boxes that were affordable to middle-and-working-class people.

By 2008, according to the Tea Council, tea sales reached $7 billion with only a little more than 1% of the tea brewed in the United States prepared from loose tea. Approximately 80% of tea is served cold. The remaining tea is made from instant tea.

Infusions

Many other "teas" are produced by infusing roots, stems, seeds, berries, flowers, leaves, herbs, and spices in water. Infusion involves steeping flavoring agents in water. The following list contains a summary of different types of infusions:

Scented teas Scented teas are made by blending aromatic petals from flowers such as jasmine, lavender, gardenias, or magnolias with tea leaves.

Flavored teas Flavored teas gain their distinct character by the addition of the essence of citrus fruits, berries, vanilla, or other flavoring components to tea leaves.

Spiced teas Blending flavoring agents such as cinnamon, nutmeg, coriander, and cloves with tea leaves produces spiced teas. The most well known example is *chai* (which is the Hindi word for tea). The *chai* that is most commonly marketed in the U.S. is *masala chai* which is a spiced tea. Most *chais* are traditionally prepared with black teas, spices and hot milk and are sweetened.

Herbal teas Herbal teas, or *tisanes,* are infusions made from herbs such as chamomile, spearmint, ginseng, and lemon balm. One traditional infusion from South America called *yerba mate* is gaining popularity in the US. It is typically infused with hot water and served in a gourd with a silver straw. These beverages do not contain any real tea at all, however, they are prepared in the same way as tea infusions.

Bottled Water

Bottled water consumption has doubled in the last 5 years and has reached sales of 8.6 billion gallons, of which 25% is purified municipal water rather than sourced from springs, lakes, rivers, and aquafers. Bottled water cost between $0.25 and $2.00, while municipal water cost a penny or two to produce. While sales continue to increase, there are critics that point out that bottled water is not regulated to the extent that municipal waters are and may pose some health issues due to the lack of fluoride and a greater concentration of chemicals. Most taste tests demonstrate that consumers cannot differentiate between bottled purified water and municipal water. Sales of bottled waters in restaurants can provide added sales but there are affiliated costs such as storage and disposal costs.

Mineral waters have flavors and tastes that provide consumers with a different experience. They are defined by the U.S. Food and Drug Administration as containing a minimum of 250 per million of total dissolved solids and come from a specific protected source. They are either carbonated or uncarbonated and their characteristics can impact the tastes of accompanying foods or beverages such as wines. The tasting terminology of waters is similar to that of other beverages with the addition of the term "sapidity," which reflects the minerality present in the water. Highly mineralized waters are often described as being hard, while those lacking such intensity are described as soft.

Soft Drinks

Soft drinks are so described due to the absence of (hard) alcohol. Non-carbonated soft drinks were first marketed in France in the 17th century. Joseph Priestly, an English clergyman and scientist first carbonated drinks artificially and may be credited as the forefather of carbonated soda drinks. This novel and refreshing idea was commercialized in the U.S. by Benjamin Silliman, the first professor of chemistry at Yale University.

It was in the U.S., that soda water with additives, whether fruit juices or botanicals such as sarsaparilla, were first commercially marketed and sold. By the mid 19th century, soda fountains had become a fixture. It is no surprise that once the crown cap seal was invented and the bottling of sodas was industrialized, this category of beverage not only became preeminent in the U.S., but also became a fixture in all four corners of the world. The most famous of these beverages came from research done by a John Pemberton who developed a drink called French Wine Coca, which was an alcoholic concoction that included the coca leaf, a known stimulant from South America. He adapted this formula by including a West African kola nut extract that also contained 2% caffeine. He had to change the recipe to conform to prohibition laws that were passed in Georgia in 1886. The drink's name was based on the new recipe's two primary ingredients: coca and kola, and total soft drink sales of this beverage at that time neared $74 billion with continued trends toward diet sugar-free products.

Ready to Drink Market

The ready to drink market includes some of the beverages already discussed as well as flavored iced teas, chais, vitamin waters, and highly caffeinated drinks such as Red Bull™. Establishments need to be aware of the changing market and trends so as to satisfy their guests' needs. At dinner-house and fine dining establishments, bartenders should be able to create unique alcohol free drinks to meet or exceed guests' expectations.

BEER

is the number one category
of alcoholic beverage in
the United States today
in terms of both volume
and dollar amounts. The
majority of those who
consume alcoholic bever-
ages are beer drinkers,
who may also consume
other types of alcohol. A
large proportion of profit
in restaurant alcohol
sales is from beer, with
a gross profit margin of
anywhere between 80%
to 95% in a typical draft
portion.

Today the market for
beer is rapidly expanding,
especially in the craft and
micro brewery segments.
These beers offer a greater
diversity of flavor, higher
prices, and appeal to a
more educated consumer.
A restaurant's alcoholic
beverage program must
have a solid foundation
in its beer offerings to be
competitive today.

The History of Beer

KEY TERMS

Reinheitsgebot
lager
adjuncts
malting
hop
yeast
milling
saccharification/
conversion
wort
lautering
sparging
kettling
trub
dry hopping
green beer
ale yeasts
lager yeasts
wild yeasts
conditioning
lagering
bottle-conditioned
cask-conditioned
priming
kräusen
Bock
head
esters
skunky
oxidized
Sake
Koji
mead
cider
Perry

More than 8,000 years ago, early peoples discovered that wild barley and other grains, when soaked in water, created a type of liquid bread with mysterious intoxicating effects. Ancient civilizations recognized this process as a type of divine transformation, which not only made the beverages more nutritious, but also allowed them to be stored for longer periods of time. The resulting beverage was probably cloudy, brown, and very different from many of today's commercial beers, although its consumption evoked the same feelings of contentment and relaxation that it does today.

According to clay tablets found in Mesopotamia dating back to about 6000 B.C., the earliest known recipe of any kind is one for making beer. The ancient Egyptians were also well-versed in their beer brewing methods. Royal family members were entombed with entire miniature breweries to supply them with this crucial drink in the afterlife. The brewing of beer was also well established, and even regulated throughout the ancient world.

Brewing Develops

By about 4000 B.C., the Babylonians were brewing approximately 16 varieties of beer, and improving its flavor by adding such ingredients as dates and honey. Around 3000 B.C., Egyptians brewed beer from barley bread soaked in water and added their own flavorings, such as herbs and fruits. The Ancient Sumerians, at one time considered the master brewers of the ancient world, boasted over 200 varieties of beer. The Egyptians passed their brewing knowledge on to the Greeks and Romans, and beer became increasingly popular throughout Europe. In climates that were not warm enough for wine growing, beer brewing became an essential part of everyday life, partly because the alcohol eliminated disease-causing bacteria that often contaminated water in early times.

In the tenth century A.D., beer brewing, which was universally done in homes, began to develop along two divergent paths. Commercial beer brewing was done by license from the church, which granted the use of a proprietary blend of herbs and roots (known as Gruit) which acted as a preservative. The Celtic and Anglo-Saxon peoples of Britain continued to brew these spicy ales. Many who brewed at home began using wild hops, even though their inclusion was outlawed by the government at the time. Belgians and Germans however, began regularly using the hops that grew wild as a natural preservative and flavor enhancer.

The Evolution of Lagers

In 1516 the Barvarians passed the beer purity law *(Reinheitsgebot)*, which is still in effect today. This law only allows for the use of four main ingredients in beer: malted grains, water, hops, and (with its discovery by Pasteur) yeast. The law recognized that the hot continental summers of central Europe were not conducive to quality beer brewing, and thus prohibited brewing during these months. This ban necessitated the brewing of an additional supply of beer in the spring and its storage over the summer. Ice-packed caves in Bohemia (today's Czech Republic) and southern Germany's Bavarian Alps allowed brewers to store and preserve beers, and permitted the slow-acting yeast strains to adapt, and to create new beer styles. These Märzen beers (named after the month of March in which they were often brewed), were then released in the early fall during the many festivals that marked the beginning of the brewing season, the most famous of which is Munich's Oktoberfest.

Through this storage of beers, a new strain of yeast that tolerated the cool cave temperatures developed, and thus the *Lager* (German for "storage") style was born. The most famous of lager styles was created in the Czech city of Pilzn, where the Pilsener style was developed. Many lighter American beers were originally modeled upon this type of beer.

IN THE BREWERY.

'BREWER'S DRAY.

The Beginning of American Beer

From the earliest Puritan settlements in the United States, the dominant beer styles were ales, porters, and stouts, until an influx of German immigrants in the mid-1800s introduced lagers. The advent of commercial refrigeration in 1860, pasteurization in 1876, and the subsequent railroad distribution system, all ushered in the modern era of beer brewing. By 1880 about 2,300 breweries were scattered across the United States. The beer industry was all but destroyed by Prohibition, which created the American underground home brewing movement. After Prohibition was repealed in 1933, there were only a handful of small breweries that survived. The grain rationing of World War II led brewers to resort to cheaper ingredients and lighter styles of beer. By the 1950s, only four breweries, Anheuser-Busch®, Miller®, Coors®, and Stroh's®, dominated the market, with a combined 97% share of total sales.

Handcrafted Ancient Ale
with barley, honey,
white muscat grapes & saffron

12 fl. oz.
9% Alc. by Vol.

Craft and Microbreweries

In 1978, President Carter signed a law that legalized the brewing of beer in the home (although today it is still prohibited in certain states.) At the same time, Americans began to develop a taste for imported beers, even though the long voyage of these beers made many of them spoil before they reached the consumer. Nevertheless, the movement towards greater variety and fuller flavors had begun.

The proliferation of local craft and microbreweries in the 1980s and 1990s was a result of this growing American appreciation for diversity, which was created by the growth of the homebrew industry, and the passage of legislation that granted tax advantages to microbreweries. These developments have given Americans an unparalleled choice of beer styles. As of 2009, the United States has more breweries and brewpubs than any other country in the world, with 1,700 breweries and 1,800 brewpubs. See Figure 7-1. As a reaction to this trend towards craft beers, the major brewers have now expanded their portfolios of products, as they see sales of their light-style flagship products softening.

FIGURE 7-1

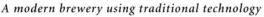

A modern brewery using traditional technology

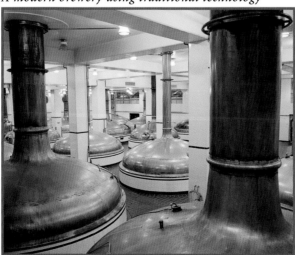

THE
India Pale Ale
STORY

During the time of British colonial rule in India, troops stationed there thirsted for a taste of the Pale Ales of London. Unfortunately, the long tropical sea journey caused the beer to spoil before reaching its intended audience. British brewers in Burton-on-Trent began making a stronger style of Pale Ale with a higher alcohol content to replace the ales of London. Before shipping, abundant amounts of fresh hops were packed into the casks of finished beer to aid in its preservation. Upon its arrival in India, the strong beer was still sound and delicious, and characterized by a heady hop aroma.

Today, IPA is one of the most rapidly growing styles of beer in the U.S., with American versions containing a higher alcohol content, and a more intense hop flavor. Depending on the producer and the variety of the hops used, one can find a dizzying array of these strong aromatic beers.

Belgian Beers

Belgium has long been considered the historic seat of traditional beer brewing techniques. The wide variety of Belgian beers available today internationally shows how these styles have rapidly gained in popularity with beer lovers worldwide. What makes Belgian beers so unique, highly regarded, and widely copied in the U.S. today, is the inclusion of wild yeast strains and time-consuming old-world techniques.

Bière de Garde—Literally, "Beer for Keeping", these are rather strong, intensely flavored beers that improve with bottle age. Many are vintage-dated and highly sought after in the marketplace by collectors.

Lambic—Named after the Belgian town of Lembeek, these beers are fermented with wild yeasts in oak casks, and then bottled for a second fermentation with the addition of fruit purées, which add alcohol, color, and flavor to the finished beers after aging. Many are packaged with a cork and cage, like Champagne. Common flavors are *Framboise* (raspberry), *Kriek* (sour cherry), *Cassis* (black currant) and *Pêche* (peach).

Trappist—Although many beers will call themselves 'Abbey style', only 6 monasteries (5 in Belgium and 1 in Holland) can use the term 'Trappist' to designate the fact that they are brewed by monks to support the monastery. These range in style from producer to producer, but the most famous is St. Sixtus, where hopeful beer lovers line up for days for the chance to purchase a case, with the promise to not resell it. Interestingly enough, St. Sixtus does at times find its way into retail stores.

Geuze—This is a style of Lambic where new beer is added to older beer to increase the acidity and alcohol.

Faro—An unusual style beer, to which brown sugar is added for sweetness.

Wit—A style of Wheat beer that uses adjunct flavorings of coriander, orange peel and other such spices and herbs, which is sometimes known as "Belgian Wheat."

Beer Ingredients

Although the brewing industry offers consumers an expanded list of choices, all beers generally have four essential ingredients: water, malted grain (usually barley), hops, and yeast. Many also have additional ingredients, called adjuncts. *These may be other grain or sugar sources, such as rice or corn, which are added to create lightness and to economize. Adjuncts may also be added for more flavor, with ingredients such as fruits, herbs, spices, coffee, or even chili peppers.*

Water

All beverages are composed mainly of water, but unlike the water used in wine, the water used in brewing is added during the process. Water comprises 90% to 96% of beer's volume, and its quality greatly affects the beverage's quality and style. Brewers are well advised to pay close attention to their water source. Brewers refer to their brewing-quality water as "liquor". The lack of certain minerals may prevent yeasts from fermenting, while the mineral content (hardness or softness) of water directly impacts the brewing process and the beer's ultimate flavor.

Throughout Europe, many of the classic beer styles were developed as a direct result of their water quality. Burton-on-Trent in England produces its famous "Burton" pale ales, which have a distinct taste profile that comes from a particularly high mineral concentration in the water. The famous lagers of Munich and Pilzn, and the dark rich stouts of Dublin, are also examples of beer styles crafted around a local water source. Today's technology allows the brewer to manipulate the mineral composition of the water source to craft a variety of classic beer styles in one location.

Malted Barley

Barley, the most significant solid ingredient in brewing, provides enzymes for starch conversion, nutrients for yeast, and contributes body, flavor, and color to beer. See Figure 7-2. Although other cereal grains (either malted or unmalted)—such as wheat, oats, rye, sorghum and millet – may also be brewed into beer, barley is by far the most popular and practical for malting.

Malting is an essential process with three steps: steeping, germinating, and kilning. In the malting process, the grains are steeped, or soaked by spraying them with water, aerated, and held at 50°F (10°C) and at a 100% humidity over a period of about five days. During this time the barley germinates, or grows, and the sprouting barley forms enzymes (maltase and amylase) that later convert starches to the sugars that are essential for fermentation. After germination, the malt is kilned, or dried. The time, temperature, and moisture level in the kilning process determine the flavor and color characteristics of the malt. Most beers are brewed with anywhere from 50% to 100% of a pale malt, although small amounts of specialty malts may be found in many grain bills (or recipes). These specially kilned malts impart a variety of flavors and colors to beer. Even a small amount of a highly-kilned malt added to a beer will create a very dark beer.

Hops

The cone-shaped flowers of the *hop* vine (humulus lupulus) help preserve beer and impart aromas and bitterness. The bitterness of hops provides structure to the beer as it balances the sweetness of malt. Hops are a perennial vine that grows up to 20 feet tall, mainly in cooler, dry climates. The main hop-growing areas of the world include Belgium, the UK, Germany, the Czech Republic, Poland, Northwestern U.S., and New Zealand. Hops come in dozens of varieties, with the classic European varieties known as "Noble Hops". The aromas of hops vary from herbal or piney to earthy, spicy and tobacco-like, to even citrusy and floral, depending on the variety. In addition to their antiseptic quality, hops also help beer to retain the foam that forms the head when beer is poured. The origin of the hops, the variety of hops, the amount used, and the timing and length they are in contact with the beer, all determine the level of bitterness and the aroma that the hops impart to beer.

FIGURE 7-2

Malted barley is the heart and soul of beer. It determines its color, flavor, and aroma.

Yeast

Yeast is a single-celled fungus that is essential to fermentation. Yeast cells produce alcohol and added natural carbonation to beer. Although the results of yeast growth have long been appreciated in bread making and brewing, it was not until 1876 that Louis Pasteur first described the role of yeast in fermentation. To a great degree, the strain of yeast in brewing determines the type and style of beer. Although there are innumerable variations and strains, beer yeasts are generally classified into three categories: lagers (Saccharomyces carlsbergensis), ales (Saccharomyces cerevisiae, or, as it is now known, S. uvarum), and wild (various strains of Brettanomyces, which are used in many Belgian styles).

Adjuncts

Adjuncts such as rice may be added for economic reasons or to have a lighter bodied and cleaner style beer. Adjuncts are also those flavoring agents mentioned above that give beer added flavors.

The Brewing Process

Milling, mashing, lautering, sparging, kettling, chilling, fermenting, and aging are the essential steps in brewing beer. Although the equipment used has been refined over the ages and the process better understood, the basic method remains the same as that practiced in ancient times. See Figure 7-3.

Milling

After kilning, the malted barley needs to be milled, or ground into a coarse meal called grist, to expose the interior starches to the brewing water. *Milling* is best done just before brewing to preserve freshness and flavor. The grist must be of the proper consistency to allow full extraction of sugars, while keeping the hulls intact to later act as a type of natural filter (See lautering below.)

Mashing

The grist then goes to a large heated and/or insulated container called a mash tun, where it is carefully mixed together with hot liquor (water). At a critical temperature range, the enzymes begin to break down the starches into fermentable and non-fermentable sugars, a process called *saccharification* or *conversion*. The end product is a sweet, sticky liquid known as *wort*.

By adjusting the temperature and length of the mashing process, the brewer can influence the body and alcohol content of the finished beer. If many non-fermentable sugars (called dextrins) are created, then the beer will be full-bodied and even sweet. Step mashing involves slowly bringing the mash up to temperature, thereby converting more starches to fermentable sugars to create a dry high-alcohol beer.

Lautering and Sparging

The process of removing the sticky sweet wort from the spent grains is called *lautering*. This process both rinses all of the sugar from the grain hulls (called *sparging*), and uses those same hulls as a natural filter to clarify the wort. Proper lautering and sparging are essential to ensure that no particles are left in the wort that would later burn in the kettle and impart a burnt flavor to the beer.

During lautering, the wort is pumped and recirculated over the grain bed until it begins to run clear. Then, during sparging, warm water is sprayed over the top of the grains, as the wort is slowly pushed out to the kettle. Since the water is lighter (less dense) than the wort, it does not dilute the wort, but instead slowly replaces the wort in the grains.

FIGURE 7-3

The brewing process

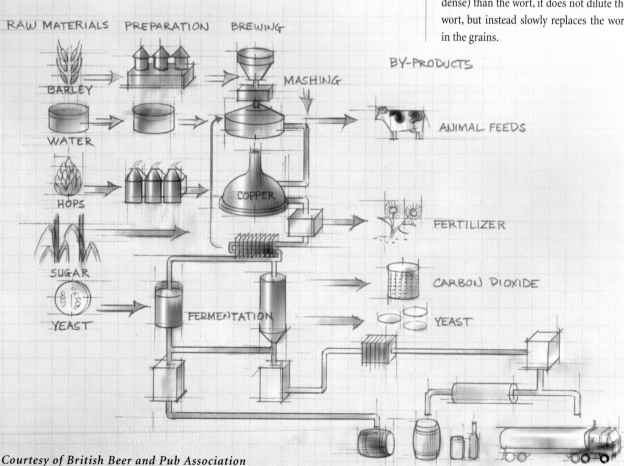

RAW MATERIALS   PREPARATION   BREWING

BARLEY
WATER
HOPS
SUGAR
YEAST

MASHING

COPPER

FERMENTATION

BY-PRODUCTS

ANIMAL FEEDS

FERTILIZER

CARBON DIOXIDE

YEAST

Courtesy of British Beer and Pub Association

Fermenting

The green beer is transferred to a sterile fermenting tank that is temperature controlled. The appropriate yeast is added, or pitched into the green beer. Within 48 hours, fermentation begins and will last anywhere from 7 days to 3 weeks, depending on the fermentation temperatures, the style of beer, and the amount of available sugars for the yeast. See Figure 7-4. *Ale yeasts* (and many wild yeasts) generally collect at the top of the fermentation vessel to create a floating bubbling mass that protects the fermenting wort from oxygen and bacteria. Ale breweries will harvest this yeast from the vessel to use for future batches. Ale yeast prefer to work quickly (7-10 days) at warmer temperatures (60° F/16° C), and will produce fruity esters in the beer. *Lager yeasts,* which ferment at cooler temperatures tend to rest at the bottom of the tanks and ferment slowly. *Wild yeasts,* such as those found in Belgian farmhouse ales, Trappist abbey ales, and the famous Belgian Lambics, give the finished beer an acidic tang that makes it a great partner with foods.

Lagering, Storing, and Conditioning

At the end of fermentation, the beer is chilled, causing the yeast to collect or flocculate, at the bottom of the tank. It is then racked to a clean beer tank, which allows the beer to further clarify and permits its flavors to subtly combine. This is known as *conditioning*— a process that may last from three days to three months. Here the beer may also go through *lagering,* a process by which the beer is stored at cold temperatures and stubborn sugars continue to slowly ferment. This process may last for several weeks, which makes lager beer more expensive and time-consuming to produce for small brewers.

Many beers are *bottle-conditioned* where they undergo a slight secondary fermentation and leave a small yeast sediment visible in the bottle. In the UK, microbrewers produce what are known as Real Ales, which are *cask-conditioned.* Although the wooden casks of yore are long gone, real ales undergo a secondary (final) fermentation in a 9-gallon metal cask (known as a Firkin), and are served without the use of additional CO$_2$ pressure by a siphon system called a beer engine that gently pumps the ale into the traditional 20-ounce 'pint'.

Priming or Kräusening

The process of adding additional sugars to a beer to induce a secondary fermentation is known as *priming.* Mass-produced beers generally do not undergo priming, but instead are artificially carbonated under pressure. The famous Belgian Lambics are produced when fruit purée is added to the bottles for secondary fermentation and the yeast consumes the sugars. The flavors, acidity, and colors of the fruit still remain in the beer.

Some brewers also *kräusen* their beers: a process in which sweet unfermented wort is added to the aging beer to cause a secondary fermentation. This adding of unfermented new wort to previously fermented beer also allows for more consistency from batch to batch for many commercial brewers. Another famous style of Belgian ale is called Geuze (or Gueuze): a beer to which new wort is repeatedly added to fermented beers to create a tart, almost Champagne-like style of beer. Following this stage, if not bottle or cask-conditioned, the beer is put into casks, kegs, bottles, or cans for storage.

Kettling

After sparging, the wort undergoes *kettling.* Since wort is sweet, it is very attractive to bacteria and must therefore be sterilized. During kettling, the wort is brought to a boil, and then simmered for about 1 hour to sterilize it. Kettling further clarifies the wort by coagulating proteins that fall out of the solution and form a deposit on the bottom of the kettle, called *trub.* Kettling also caramelizes sugars to darken the wort, and concentrates the wort through evaporation.

Hops are also added during the kettling process at various times. If added early on in the process, the hops will lose any aromatics, and will merely add bitterness to the beer. Hops used for aromatics are added only toward the end of kettling. (The term *dry hopping* refers to adding hops to beer after fermentation (when it is dry) and allowing the alcohol present to extract the aromatics without as much bitterness.)

Chilling

After the kettling is completed, the wort must be prepared for fermentation. First, the wort undergoes a whirlpool circulation to separate the trub deposits and hop residues. Next it passes through a heat exchanger or chiller to bring the temperature down to a yeast-friendly 70° F (21°C). During this time, the *'green beer'*, as it is referred to, is also oxygenated to allow the yeast to quickly begin fermentation. Oxygen is added using either an in-line injection type or bubbling apparatus in the fermenter.

ALE	LAGER	BELGIAN/WILD
Warm fermentation (60° F–65°F/16°C–18°C)	Cold fermentation (40° F–50°F/4°C–10°C)	Warm Fermentation (60° F–65°F/16°C–18°C)
Fast Fermentation (7–10 days)	Slow fermentation (3–4 wks)	Sometimes a double-fermentation, dep. on style
Usually darker color	Usually lighter color	Varies with style
Generally Served Warm	Generally served cold	Varies with style
Top fermenting yeast	Bottom fermenting yeast	Both, but usually top
Pale Ale, India Pale Ale, Brown Ale, Scotch Ale, Porter, Stout, Barley Wine, Helles Alt, Wheat Ale /Hefeweizen/ Weiss/Wit, Sake	Pilsener, Bock, Doppelbock, Märzen, Vienna, Oktoberfest, Kolsch, Dunkel, Schwarzbier, Rauchbier, American Light Lager Malt Liquor	Lambics, Trappist Ales, Abbey Ales, Geuze, Dubbel, Tripel

Combination Styles of Beer:

Alt Bier—The German word 'Alt' means 'Old' and refers to ales produced before the evolution of lagers. Alt is a lighter, smoother style of ale that lacks many of ale's fruity esters due to cooler fermentation temperatures.

Steam Beer—This is an American invention, made famous by Anchor Brewing Company in San Francisco. It is an ale brewed with a lager yeast that gives it good body, lower maltiness and esters, and emphasizes the fine hop aroma.

"GOT GOAT?"
The Bock Story

Legend has it that a duke from Saxony brought an especially strong beer to Bavaria (southern Germany) from Einbeck. In the local Bavarian accent, this sounded like Einbock, or "one billy goat". The name was eventually shortened to Bock, and these stronger styles of beer usually carry the symbol of the goat on their label.

Monks began brewing this strong Bock style as 'liquid bread' to sustain them during Lent. Double-strength beers were called Doppelbocks and carry two goats on their label. In the city of Munich, the monks in the order of St. Francis of Paula founded the Paulaner brewery in 1634, and named their Bock beer "Salvator" or "The Saviour", in reference to its sustaining qualities. Other brands may now feature the "-ator" ending on their names in reference to this classic beer.

Although a style of Lager beer, Bock is an extra-strong beer (ranging from 8–12% ABV) that features a head that looks like whipped cream, a rich deep amber-brown color, a buttery malty aroma, and a toffee-ish flavor. Doppelbocks' warming effects are meant to cure the winter blues while awaiting the arrival of spring, while Maibocks are generally lighter in color and flavor, and may be dry rather than sweet.

Tasting and Storing Beer

When trying to analyze a beer, beer tasting is as demanding and rigorous an intellectual pursuit as is wine tasting. The primary difference is that professional tasters tend not to expectorate (spit) and therefore taste far fewer beers in one sitting than do wine tasters. (At Johnson & Wales University, students are required to expectorate at tastings).

Tasting Beer

To properly analyze beer, one must first have a clean, appropriate glass. Beer glassware comes in a wide variety of shapes and sizes, each meant to accentuate the particular virtues of a specific style. See Figure 7-5. In the absence of the traditional glass, one may use a standardized tasting glass, such as the tulip-shaped ISO glass commonly found for wine and spirits analysis.

The next step is to ensure that the glass is not only clean from streaks or particles, but that it is "beer clean" or capable of correctly retaining the delicate complex of colloids known as the head. Frosted glasses should not be used for quality beers, as the ice build-up will dilute the beer, and may also distribute unwanted residue.

As with all types of sensory analysis, one must first assess the appearance of a beer. Colors of beers range from pale gold to dark black, and are generally graded according to the Lovibond scale, although other scales are also utilized. The color should correspond to the stated style of beer. Some styles, such as bottle-conditioned or wheat-based beers, have a natural haze, although haziness in other styles may indicate bacterial or other contamination. The quality of the *head* should also be examined as to the color and persistence of the foam. See Figure 7-6. Insufficient head may indicate a flat or stale beer, or unclean glassware. The level of carbonation should also be visible through the glass and will vary according to the style of beer.

The right glass for a beer enhances flavor, aroma, and appearance.

A head of foam is an inviting sight, which also keeps the beer fresher longer.

Next, the aromas are analyzed by a quick sniff. If a sample is very cold, aromas may be difficult to assess (see Serving Beer). The first sniff may have malty or nutty notes from the grains, doughy or toasty notes, floral, citrusy or spicy notes from the hops and/or yeast, and fruity notes (called *esters*) produced by ale yeasts.

Off-aromas are dependent upon the style of beer. A clove or banana aroma is typical of the yeast used for a Bavarian Weiss beer; a slight earthy aroma is common in many British ales; and a slight cannabis like aroma may come from some American hops. A micro-biological, funky taste may be appropriate in many Belgian-style ales, but this wild yeast aroma should not be present in other styles and usually indicates contamination during packaging, or unclean draft lines. (See Serving Beer)

If a beer smells *'skunky'*, it has been light struck and oxidized by exposure to excessive UV or florescent light, which reacts with the hop compounds in the beer. It is for this reason, that most quality beers are packaged in dark brown bottles, although green does offer some protection. Those packaged in clear bottles generally have little to no hop aromas. If a beer is stale or old, it may smell like cardboard or wet paper, a term known as *oxidized,* where dissolved oxygen reacts with the beer and usually darkens the color of lighter-style beers. Vegetal aromas, such as cabbage or broccoli are never desirable and usually indicate the use of stale hops.

Take a small sip and coat the palate to taste beer. When tasting the beer, assess the body or weight of the sample, the effervescence or carbonation level, and look for sweetness, acidity, bitterness, and minerality on the finish. Bitterness may come from the hops, and may be similar to the astringent bite of a grapefruit rind. When dark malts are used, a dark chocolate or coffee taste may be detected. Roasted flavors are from darker malts, and smoky flavors come from smoked malts. A beer should never taste burnt, because this would imply over-sparging or scorching, or excessive residues during the kettling stage. Acidity is more noticeable in wheat-based beers, but in all styles of beers, it adds to the refreshing quality of the beer's finish.

After expectorating, close the mouth and breathe out through the nose, to send aromas up through the nostrils. This process is called the retronasal impression, and will almost always provide additional aromas to those perceived before tasting. The length of time that the tastes of the beer remains in the mouth and nose afterwards is known as the finish or aftertaste. In general, high-quality samples will give a longer finish than lower-quality ones, although the flavors should be pleasant and complex, rather than sickingly sweet (cloying) or excessively bitter.

Final impressions such as trueness to style (if known), potential food pairings, and comparisons to other styles or brands should be noted. The quality level is often difficult for beginners to assess, but with experience, tasters can determine the relative value of samples as well.

Storing Beer

Although it is best consumed as soon as it is packaged, pasteurized beer has a shelf life of about three months. Certain styles, however, such as the highly-hopped India Pale Ales or bottle conditioned beers with yeast sediment can last longer. Higher-alcohol styles - such as Bocks, Barley Wines or Bière de Garde - can actually improve with age for a year or more. Although dark bottles are preferred to minimize the effects of UV light, a dark storage container or environment is even better. High temperatures, or temperature fluctuations will also reduce the beer's shelf life and lead to oxidized or stale beer with a cooked flavor. Ideal temperature ranges are between 50°F–55°F (10°C–13°C). Unpasteurized and draft beers keep only two or three weeks and must be kept refrigerated at all times. Once a keg or cask of beer has been tapped, it should be consumed within a few days. For styles that are less popular, restaurateurs should use smaller kegs, or only serve bottles.

Pairing Beer and Food

Beer can be an ideal companion to a variety of foods. Just as various wines complement different dishes, some beers pair better with particular foods. The right combination can make for an unforgettable dining experience. See Figure 7-7.

Although there are no hard-and-fast rules for which beer is most compatible with which food, here are some general guidelines:

- Higher acid beers, such as Wheat beers, Geuze, or Lambics work well with fatty or fried foods, or most seafood dishes. Acidic beers are best with acidic dishes, such as marinated salads or vinaigrettes. Most "Summer Ales" are variations on wheat beers, and pair with seasonal summer flavors, such as fried clams. These are commonly served with a citrus garnish.

- The flavor of a beer should either complement or contrast nicely with the food with which it is paired. Pale ale, for example, contrasts well with the robust, smoky flavors of barbecue. The same ale would also complement fish or shellfish dishes. A Rauchbier (or smoked beer) or a Scotch Ale, which uses some smoked malt, may also work well with grilled or smoked meats or cheeses.

- If preparing ethnic foods, beer from the same region may pair very well with the food's flavors. A rich, dark lager from Germany is an excellent match for bratwurst and grilled onions, for example.

- Seasonal beers also generally pair well with seasonal foods from the same region. A crisp Mai Bock, for example, is an excellent partner with light spring vegetables or quiche, where as a Märzen or Oktoberfest goes nicely with many pork dishes and fall flavors.

- If the beer style has a dominant taste, then the food may contrast with it—a bitter ale with food that is salty or a little sweet, for example. A classic combination that exemplifies this is stout and oysters.

- There are many styles of beer that can pair well with dessert, depending on their level of sweetness. The beer needs to be sweeter than the dessert. A Framboise Lambic for example, will pair well with fresh fruits, custards or cheesecake due to its high acidity, but any really sweet dessert will make the beer taste too acidic. A chocolate or nut-based dessert, on the other hand, may pair best with a sweet DoppelBock.

FIGURE 7-7 Major Styles of Beer

PILSNER

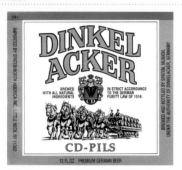

HEFE-WEIZEN/WEISSE

LAGER

AMERICAN PILSNER

PALE ALE

INDIAN PALE ALE

BOCK

AMBER ALE

PORTER

STOUT

Other Naturally Fermented Beverage Categories

There have been, and are, many other fermented beverages that have evolved over the millennia, from tej in Ethiopia to chicha in the Amazon, or pulque in Central America. However, most are rarely seen in the U.S. market with the recent growing exception of sake, which is being featured more prominently in both ethnic and fine-dining establishments.

Sake

Sake is a fermented rice beverage most associated with Japan, although versions are found throughout the Far East. Generally called 'rice wine,' sake is actually a form of beer because it is made from grain. Unlike beers, however, sake does not use barley, only rice. This rice is polished to remove the outer layers. The finest sakes are made from rice that is milled down to less than half of its original size. The rice used for sake is also never malted. To convert the starches to fermentable sugars, a type of mold, *Koji,* is gradually added in batches to the mash of rice, along with more rice. Since a Koji culture does not multiply like yeast, it must be added repeatedly in stages to ensure a healthy population.

Once the mash is ready, it undergoes fermentation, where batches of rice will again be added in stages to gradually build the alcohol naturally up to 16%. Slight variations in the type of rice used, the mashing times and methods, and the type of aging used (if any), create a vast array of high quality styles of sake – from pink sake made from red rice to amber cedar-aged sake.

The grain rationing during WWII also had an effect on the quality of the sake produced in Japan. Cheaper sakes using less rice that were quickly fortified with distilled grain alcohol, began to appear. This cheap sake is the type with which most non-Japanese are most familiar, and it is served warm in restaurants to mask its flavors. Fine sakes are served slightly chilled and make a fine accompaniment to a variety of foods. Unfortunately, the delicate flavors of high-quality sake are quite perishable, so care must be taken to guarantee that the product is fairly fresh when purchased.

Mead

Since the primary fermentable ingredient in mead is neither grain nor fruit, but actually honey, *mead* is neither a beer nor a wine but is in a class of its own. Many meads are made using 100% honey, although many are combined with fermented grain, fruit, or cider. When the majority of fermentable sugar is honey, the product is considered a mead.

Today, meads are quickly being rediscovered by connoisseurs as complex, delicious drinks. Although most popular in northern Europe, meads have been produced around the world, including ancient Egypt, as well as in the United States where many styles are available in the market.

Mead is produced by diluting honey with clean water to the appropriate consistency or sugar content. The origin of the honey is extremely important, as the types of flowers that are used by bees to produce the honey will have a great impact on the flavor of the fermented mead. Water quality is also of the utmost importance, as it is with beer. Depending on the final alcohol content, meads can be quite perishable or have great aging potential. Additional flavors may be added, although strong flavors will overwhelm the delicate flavors of the honey.

Cider

In America, the term *cider* usually refers to unfiltered non-fermented apple juice. In traditional Europe, however, the term cider refers to a fermented apple beverage. (If pears are used, the product may also be called a *Perry.*) Since ciders are made from apples, they are technically a type of wine. Many ciders, however, are relatively low in alcohol, refreshing, and served on draft in pubs and restaurants, which is why they are often compared to beers.

During the early days of colonial America, cider was the principal drink made at the many local orchards and farms throughout the colonies. Once populations began to center in cities, the market for fresh ciders was eventually replaced by beer, which could be freshly brewed in the cities.

Ciders may also be made into higher alcohol beverages, similar to wine. Some actually undergo a double fermentation, producing a Champagne-like texture and effervescence. Some craft breweries are also producing ciders as part of their product line, and these products may be found in most of the New England states, the Pacific Northwest, and Canada. There is also a growing variety of imported ciders available in bottles and on draft. Due to a higher acidity in ciders than beer, ciders can make excellent partners with many foods, especially fall flavors.

SPIRITS AND LIQUEURS

*play a key role in the profitability
of a food and beverage establishment.
They offer both chefs and mixologists the
ingredients to create flavorful food or drink
recipes for the enjoyment of guests.*

spirit

liqueurs

cordials

compounded beverages

congeners

single batch distillation

heart

heads

tails

continuous distillation

column stills

analyser

rectifier

wash

proof

infusion

maceration

percolation

redistillation

generic or value brands

premium brands

high end or super-
premium brands

ultra-premium or
luxury brands

proprietary brand

whiskies

Bourbon whiskey

Scotch whiskies

Highland malts

gin

rum

Rhum Agricole

brandy

cognacs

Armagnac brandy

pomace brandies

Marc

Grappa

Pisco

Tequila

piña

reposado

añejo

bitters

Spirits and Liqueurs Defined

A *spirit* is a highly alcoholic beverage produced by both fermentation and distillation. Alcoholic distillation is the process by which the alcohol from a fermented liquid is evaporated, captured, and cooled to liquid form. Spirits are made from fermented products such as grapes, sugarcane, apples, potatoes, and grains. The fermented liquids are then distilled to create such spirits as whiskey, brandy, tequila, vodka, and rum.

Liqueurs, also known as *cordials*, are highly refined, sweet spirits to which flavorings such as fruits, nuts, herbs, or spices have been added. They are often enjoyed before dining as apéritifs or after dinner as digestifs. They are also essential parts of many cocktails. Most liqueurs contain between 17% and 30% alcohol by volume, and some may contain as much as 50%.

Liquor and Liqueurs in History

It is not known for sure who discovered the method of distillation or exactly when it occurred. Many experts speculate that the Chinese used distillation as early as 3000 B.C. and this technology traveled the Silk Road to India around 2000 B.C. The ancient Sanskrit texts include a variety of terms for high strength alcoholic beverages. The science of distillation was also known to the Ancient Greeks. Aristotle described distilling seawater to capture freshwater in about 400 B.C., but the first recorded distillation of alcoholic beverages in Europe did not occur until circa 900 A.D.

Culinary Relevance

Cocktails and apéritifs traditionally accompany canapés before dinner, and brandies and liqueurs are served with coffee after dinner. Spirits and liqueurs are indispensable parts of dining for many people.

Unlike wine and beer, spirits are not usually prominent features in the preparation of savory foods, though they are sometimes used as an ingredient in marinades or basting sauces. For tableside dessert preparations and for pastry chefs, however, liquors and liqueurs are invaluable flavoring agents.

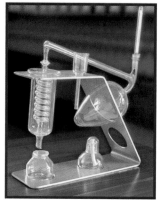

The Distillation Process

Monks and alchemists improved on the process of distillation over the centuries. In 1205, Arnaud de Villeneuve became the first person to distill wine in France. In Great Britain, with the dissolution of the monasteries in the sixteenth century, monks began to share their knowledge with distillers. Over the years, the distillation process has been refined, although the essential process remains basically the same.

Distilling spirits is possible because water and ethyl alcohol, the two primary components of a fermented beverage, have different boiling points. See Figure 8-1. Because alcohol and water boil at different temperatures, a distiller can heat a fermented beverage to the boiling point for ethyl alcohol (173°F/78°C), capture the vapor, and then cool it to condense it into liquid alcohol. Water is left behind because of its higher boiling point of 212°F (100°C). The alcohol is vaporized and then recondensed in an apparatus called a still.

All alcoholic beverages fall into one of three categories:

- Fermented beverages made from products such as grains and fruits with alcoholic strengths ranging from 3.2%–14%.
- Distilled spirits resulting from a distillation of fermented beverages.
- *Compounded beverages* made by combining either a fermented beverage or spirit with a flavoring agent.

Production Processes

There are five necessary steps in the production of distilled spirits: mashing, fermenting, distilling, aging or filtering, and blending. For a flavored spirit or liqueur, there is an additional step of compounding.

Mashing

Corn, barley, and rye are the principal grains used in making beverage-quality alcohol. The process begins with milling the grains to break down the hull and to free the starch that will eventually convert to alcohol. The next step is to turn the grain starch into grain sugar by mixing the grain meal with water to form a mash. Barley malt is then added, and the end result is maltose, or grain sugar.

Fermenting

Fermentation begins when yeast is added to the mash. As the yeast grows, it digests the sugar and releases alcohol and carbon dioxide. The yeast multiplies to create grain alcohol, and the alcohol mixes with congeners, or flavoring agents.

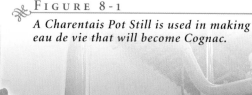

❧ FIGURE 8-1

A Charentais Pot Still is used in making eau de vie that will become Cognac.

108

Distilling

When the fermented liquid is heated to vaporize the alcohol, some water and some *congeners* (flavor and aroma compounds) are left behind. When the alcohol vapor is cooled, it condenses into clear ethyl alcohol. When a pot still is used, a *single batch distillation* is not sufficient enough to concentrate the wash into a desirable and potable spirit. See Figure 8-2. Therefore, the majority of pot still spirits are redistilled multiple times. It is during the second distillation that the *'heart'* of the spirit is separated from the *'heads'* and *'tails'*.

- **Heads**—compounds first released at the lowest boiling point; volatile and harmful
- **Heart**—middle compounds
- **Potable spirit**—ethyl alcohol
- **Tails**—compounds released last

Heads are released at the lowest boiling point (they come off first), while tails release only when the temperatures are at their highest. *Continuous distillation* utilizes a variety of *column stills* fashioned after the Coffey Still invented in 1827. See Figure 8-3. The Coffey Still is comprised of two tall linked columns known as an *analyser* and a *rectifier*. These columns contain a number of perforated plates located at differing heights. The fermented liquid referred to as the *wash* is fed into the rectifier column and flows to the analyser column where it is sprayed out over the top plate. Simultaneously, hot steam pumped from the bottom of the analyser rises and strips the alcohol from the wash. The vapor then passes from the top of the analyser to the bottom of the rectifier where it starts to rise through the perforated plates and is fractioned or separated in a continuous motion. This type of distillation produces high proof, highly rectified spirits. At higher proof levels, fewer flavor components called congeners remain and produce a rather harsh neutral spirit.

Aging or Filtering

To mellow the harshness of this clear spirit, the liquid is either aged or filtered. Aging takes place in charred oak barrels that give color to the spirit, absorb

FIGURE 8-2

The Pot Still

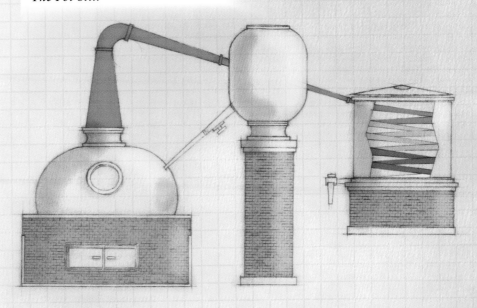

FIGURE 8-3

The Continuous or Column Still

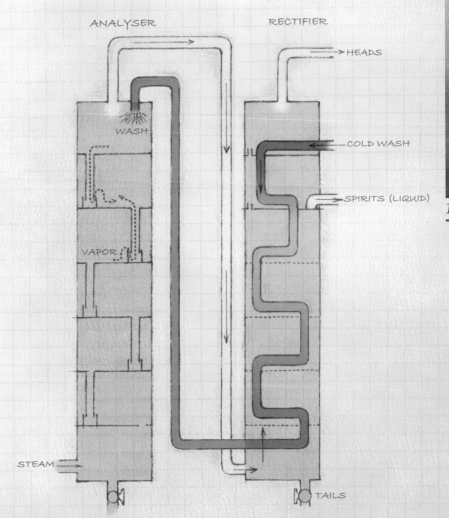

FIGURE 8-5

After aging, whiskeys are blended for uniformity.

impurities, and mellow the flavor. See Figure 8-4. The character of the spirit depends on the aging time—sometimes as long as 18–24 years. Clear spirits, such as vodka, are filtered in activated charcoal systems to mellow them. Higher-quality clear spirits are filtered as many as four or more times.

Blending

After the aging or filtering is completed, the spirits are reduced in *proof,* or percentage of alcohol by volume, to the desired concentration by the addition of demineralized water. In the blending process, spirits of different ages and sometimes from different grains are blended into the final product, which is then bottled and packaged for sale. Once bottled, the product ceases to age or change. See Figure 8-5.

Compounding

The process of compounding blends spirits with other flavorings, including sweeteners. Compounding is achieved through *infusion,* which involves steeping flavoring agents using heat; *maceration,* which steeps them by using a cold method; or *percolation,* which allows the spirit to trickle through a flavoring agent much in the way that water trickles through ground coffee, except that the process is repeated. Compounding may also be achieved by *redistillation,* which involves distilling a spirit with a flavoring agent; gin, for example, is redistilled with juniper berries.

Quality and Branding

There are basically four sales categories of alcohol beverage products: *generic* or *value brands; premium brands; high end* or *super-premium brands;* and *ultra-premium* or *luxury brands.* The price range usually varies by category. For example, Cognacs would fall under the ultra-premium category even though there is great disparity in pricing between a VS Cognac and a XO Cognac. A greater variation by category exists within American whiskies.

Generic or value brands A category such as "coffee brandy" is a general category of coffee liqueur that any number of companies can produce. A *proprietary brand* such as Kahlúa® is a trademarked name that no one else can replicate. When discussing a spirit such as rum, white rum is the generic category while Bacardi® is proprietary. The pricing of this category tends to be the lowest at under $12.00.

Premium brands Premium brands of spirits or liqueurs are proprietary brands, both domestic and imported, which fall into a higher price range based on their perceived quality and brand recognition. The price range is approximately $12.00 to $17.00 per liter bottle.

High end or super-premium brands This alcohol category is based on brand recognition and has a price range that is approximately $17.00 to $24.00 per liter bottle.

Ultra-premium or luxury brands Alcohol brand categories in the $25.00 to $40.00 per liter bottle price range are typically considered the highest quality brands.

American Whiskies

The U.S. government requires that all *whiskies* are made from a grain mash; are distilled at 90% alcohol by volume (ABV) or less; and are reduced to no more than 62.5% ABV (125 proof) before aging in oak barrels. (The exception is corn whiskey, which does not have to be aged in oak.) Whiskies must have the aroma, taste, and characteristics that are generally attributed to whiskey and must be bottled at no less than 40% ABV (80 proof). The eight designations that follow are rigidly defined by law and regulated accordingly.

Straight

Straight whiskey is unblended and contains no neutral spirits. It must be aged at least two years but is generally aged four years in new charred oak. Old Charter® (10 years old) is an example.

Bourbon

Bourbon whiskey must contain a minimum of 51% corn; must be produced in the U.S.; distilled at less than 80% ABV (160 proof); and aged for a minimum of two years in new charred oak barrels, although most are aged longer. This straight whiskey has seen a renaissance with the introduction of single batch and single barrel high-end bourbons. Examples of these include Maker's Mark®, Jim Beam® 80 proof, Early Times®, and Old Grand-Dad® 86 proof. Single batch bourbons include Basil Hayden's®, and Booker's® Knob Creek®.

Corn

Corn whiskey must contain at least 80% corn; be distilled at less than 80% ABV (160 proof); and be aged for a minimum of two years in new or used uncharred barrels. Old Gristmill®, Virginia Lightning®, and Georgia Moon® are examples of corn whiskies.

Sour Mash

Sour mash is the result of the fermentation process, in which the mash is soured with a lactic culture such as that used for sourdough bread. Examples include Jim Beam® Black Label 90 proof and Chester Graves® 90 proof.

Tennessee

Tennessee whiskey differs from bourbon only in that the distillate is leached or filtered through sugar maple charcoal in mellowing vats before it is diluted with demineralized water and aged in charred oak barrels. One of the more popular examples is Jack Daniel's® Black Label 90 proof.

Blended

Blended whiskeys are light bodied with at least a 20% straight whiskey content blended with unaged neutral spirits. Seagram's 7 Crown® 80 proof and Corby's Reserve® 80 proof are examples of blended whiskies.

Bottled in Bond

Bottled in bond is a straight whiskey produced by one distiller. It must be aged at least four years; bottled at 100 proof; and stored in bonded warehouses under government supervision. Examples include Old Forrester® 100 proof, Beam's® 100 proof, and Old Grand-Dad® B/B 100 proof.

Rye

By definition, rye whiskey must be produced from a grain mash containing at least 51% rye grain. It may not be distilled at higher than 160 proof and must be aged in new charred oak barrels. Examples include Jim Beam Rye®, which is 86 proof, Rittenhouse Rye® and Rī®.

Imported Whiskies

A variety of imported whiskies are available in the United States for consumption, including Canadian, Irish, Scotch, and Japanese whiskies.

Canadian

Virtually all Canadian whisky is six years old or older. Anything aged for less time must be labeled as such. All Canadian whisky is aged in oak casks for at least three years, but most are typically aged from six to eight years.

By U.S. law, imported Canadian whisky must be produced in Canada and must contain no distilled spirits fewer than three years old. This whisky is often simply referred to as rye whiskey or rye, even though it contains more corn and other grains. This lighter-tasting whisky is the third most popular spirit category after vodka and liqueurs. Examples include Seagram's VO®, Canadian Club®, and Seagram's Crown Royal®.

Irish Whiskies

Irish whiskey must be produced in Ireland; must be triple-distilled, usually in pot stills, from Irish grain; aged in wooden casks for three years; and bottled at not less than 40% ABV. Its base is barley, with oats and other grains added for additional flavor. The soft mineral content of the water and triple distillation give Irish whiskey a heavier and smoother character than its Scottish counterpart. Examples include Jameson® 80-proof, Bushmills®, Murphy Irish® 86 proof, and Dunphy's Irish®.

Scotch Whiskies

Scotch whiskies include blended Scotch whisky, vatted malt scotch, and single malt whisky. The smoky flavor of Scotch whisky is quite distinctive due to the use of peat smoked sprouted barley in the malting process.

Blended Scotch This whisky consists of a mixture of grain whisky and malt whisky and may contain as many as 40 different malt whiskies. Examples include Cutty Sark®, J&B®, Dewar's®, Johnnie Walker Red®, Johnnie Walker Black® 12 years old, and Chivas Regal® 12 years old.

Vatted malts/blended malts Malted scotches or pure malt scotches are blends from more than one distillery. Vatted malts cannot be made from other grain whiskies. It is also a term that has been discontinued and renamed "blended malts". Examples include Johnnie Walker® Green Label and Hogshead® Vatted Malt.

Single malt Single malt is a whisky brewed from a single batch of wort, also known as a green or mash beer, from one particular Scottish distillery. It is a scotch made from 100% malted barley and is double pot distilled. Scotland has more than 100 distilleries, each of which produces a distinctive single malt whisky.

Highland malts *Highland malts* are generally sweeter and have more body and character than Lowland malts. Examples include The Balvenie® 15 year, The Macallan® 12 year, Dalmore® 12 year Single Highland, Highland Park® 18 year old, and Glenfiddich® 12 year old.

Lowland malts Generally drier than Highland malts, Lowland malts are usually lighter. There are fewer differences among them than there are among malts from other regions. Examples include Glenkinchie® 12 year old and Auchentoshan® 21 year old.

Islay malts Islay malts are the most pungent and heavily peaty of all the malts. They take their characteristics from the peat that is used to dry the barley and from their closeness to the sea. Examples include Bowmore® 12 year old, Laphroaig® Cask Strength 10 year old, Ardbeg® 10 year old, and Lagavulin® 16 year old.

Speyside and Campbeltown single malts These malts have a distinctive, briny taste. The two distilleries in this region produce three single malts, each with its own character. Examples include Cragganmore® 12 year old, The Balvenie® 12 year old Double Wood Speyside, Springbank® 100 proof 10 year old, Hazel bam® 8 years old, and Glen Scotia® 12 years old.

Gin and Genever

Gin is an unaged liquor, made from grains such as barley, corn, or rye and is flavored with juniper berries, coriander, and other herbs and spices. Gin is valued for its ability to blend harmoniously with other mixers. Examples of classic gin recipes include the martini (with dry vermouth), or the gin and tonic.

Most English gins are London Dry gins in style and are similar to American gin. They are generally distilled at a lower proof than Dutch or Genever gin and because they are dry, are conducive to blending with a mixer that is off-dry.

Plymouth Gin and Old Tom Gin are styles that were common in the 19th Century and are today regaining popularity. Plymouth Gin is a Protected Geographic Appellation and is defined by a smooth juniper taste. Old Tom is fuller bodied and sweeter. Genever, the original gin from Holland, is much more highly flavored and fuller-bodied than English gin. Examples of English gins include Beefeater®, Boodles®, Tanqueray®, Bombay®, and Bombay Saphire®.

Vodka

Vodka is produced primarily from grain, potatoes, molasses, or beets. Russian vodkas are typically made from wheat, while Polish vodkas are created from rye or potatoes. In the U.S., domestic vodka is defined as a "neutral spirit," which is refined to be without a distinctive taste, aroma, color, or other characteristics. As a neutral spirit, vodka lends itself well to mixing with other beverages or fortifying other spirits and is preeminent in the U.S. market. The super premium vodkas are triple or quadruple distilled and demand higher prices because they are less harsh and have a lower congener content. Examples of leading brands in the U.S. are: Smirnoff®, Belvedere®, Absolut®, Stolichnaya®, Skye®, Wyborowa® (Vee-ba-rova), Grey Goose®.

Rum

Most **rum** is made from fermented sugar juice, sugarcane syrup, sugarcane molasses, and other sugarcane by-products. Rum is produced wherever sugarcane grows—primarily in the Caribbean on the islands of Puerto Rico, the Virgin Islands, Jamaica, Barbados, Trinidad, Martinique, and Haiti. Rums are classified as white, golden, or dark.

While classifications of rum primarily reflect the length of aging, there are three distinct styles based on colonial experience. The lighter, molasses-based style that is most popular in the U.S. is from Puerto Rico, the Dominican Republic, Cuba, and Central and South America. The second style is reflected by the heavier and darker English styles from Barbados, Bermuda, Jamaica, and Guyana. The third style is the Rhum Agricole from Martinique, Guadaloupe, and Haiti.

White rum White rums are generally highest in alcohol content, and are light-bodied and clear, with a subtle flavor. If they are aged in oak casks they are usually filtered to remove any color. Primarily used as mixers, white rums blend particularly well with fruit flavors. The world's leading brand is Bacardi® Superior but there are many other producers such as Cruzan Estate® Light, and 10 Cane®.

Golden rum Golden, or amber rum is medium bodied, and usually aged for at least three years in oak casks. Its taste is smooth and mellow. Examples include Flor de Cana®, Barcardi® Gold, Appleton Estate®, and Gossling's® Bermuda Gold.

Dark rum Dark rum is the traditional, full-bodied, rich rum, dominated by overtones of caramel. The best are produced in pot stills and are usually aged for a minimum of six years in oak barrels. The best of these rums are consumed straight up. Examples include Bacardi® 8 year, Myer's Dark®, Gossling's® Black Seal, Mount Gay® Extra Old, Flor de Cana® 21 year old, and Zacapa® 23 year old.

Spiced rum Rums infused with spices are known and sold as spiced rums. They are either made with dark rums or colored with caramel and are used in hot drinks and pastry preparations. Examples include Captain Morgan® and Sailor Jerry's Navy®.

Rhum Agricole *Rhum Agricole* is a style of rum produced from sugar cane juice rather than molasses. It is produced primarily in the French-owned islands of Martinique, Guadeloupe, and La Réunion. It has a lighter more vegetal character and is produced by using a continuous still. Examples of producers include Clément® and Depaz®.

Cachaça

Cachaça is the spirit of Brazil. Brazil produces most of the world's sugar cane and cachaça. Like Rhum Agricole, it is produced from sugar cane juice, and shows distinctive vegetal notes. Some traditional distillers use a maize starter in the fermentation that restricts the EU rum designation. Cachaça is the second most widely produced spirit in the world after *shoju* or *soju*, a rice based spirit primarily from China, Korea, and Japan. While there are over 40,000 Cachaça distillers in Brazil, the dominant imported label is Leblon®.

Brandy

The word *brandy* has its roots in the Dutch word *brandewijn*, which means "distilled wine." Dutch traders distilled the highly acidic white wines of the Cognac region to limit taxes (ten barrels of wine produce only one barrel of Cognac). People soon discovered that the longer the distilled beverage aged, the better it tasted. Other brandies are distilled from fruit wines and pulp. Although many countries produce brandies, the best known, such as Cognac and Armagnac, are distilled from grape wine.

Cognac

Cognacs are among the world's elite brandies. Their high quality stems from the kinds of grapes from which they are distilled, the soil and climate of the Cognac region, and the skill of the distillers.

Cognac is distilled twice in pure copper alembic stills soon after the base wine (made from Ugni Blanc, Colombard, and Folle Blanche grapes) has finished fermenting. The first distillation produces a 30% alcoholic liquid called the *brouillis*, which is redistilled to make the *bonne chauffe*. Then the brandy is aged in Limousin and Tronçais oak barrels, in which a slow oxidative reduction gives the cognac its distinctive flavor. The resulting evaporation is called "the angels' share."

The soil's impact is codified into the appellation laws. The more chalk, the better the appellation. The best area, in the heart of Cognac, is Grande Champagne followed by Petite Champagne. The other subdivisions include: Borderie, Fins Bois, Bon Bois, and Bois Ordinaire. Labels with "Fine Champagne" are a blend of 50% Grande and 50% Petite Champagne Cognac.

Like all spirits and brandies, Cognac ages only as long as it remains in wood, but after 25 years, there are diminished returns. The most notable houses for Cognac include Martell®, Hennessy®, Rémy Martin®, Courvoisier®, Otard-Dupuy®, Camus®, Hine®, Delamain®, Salignac®, and Castillon®.

Cognac Labeling Designations

See Figure 8-6.

- **VS**—Very Special is aged no less than 2 1/2 years in oak.
- **VSOP**—Very Special Old Pale cannot be aged less than 4 1/2 years.
- **XO**—Extra Old or Extra Ordinary are house blends that must be aged at least 6 1/2 years, but are usually aged 12 or more years.
- **Vintage**—Vintage Cognacs are allowed since 1988 under special control procedures.

Armagnac

Armagnac brandy is the oldest French brandy. Documented references to the spirit go back to the fifteenth century. Armagnac is mostly produced in the unique alembic armagnaçais, a type of column still, which dates back to the earliest days of brandy production. Although Armagnac shares Cognac's high standards, the two brandies are very different. Armagnac is an Appellation Contrôlée French grape brandy from Gascony, which is produced under strict controls and inspection procedures.

Three growing zones—Bas-Armagnac, Ténarèze, and Haut-Armagnac—are allowed to use the appellation on their label. Like Cognac, Armagnac's unique character comes from a combination of climate, soil, and grape varieties. Also like Cognac, most Armagnacs are blends, although some single vintages or single vineyard varieties are available. Blended Armagnacs generally have a higher proportion of older vintages than Cognac and are frequently a better value. Most Armagnacs shipped to the United States are classified as: 3 Star, which are aged no less than 2 years in oak; V.S.O.P., aged more than 4 years in oak; or Hors d'Age aged more than 10 years in oak. There are also the vintage Armagnacs that are prized as the very best. These must also be aged at least 10 years in wood, although they are frequently aged longer. Armagnacs have a prune, violet, or spice aroma and tend to be drier and more rustic than cognacs. Leading imported brands include Darroze®, Marquis de Montesquieu®, and Clés des Ducs®.

❧ FIGURE 8-6

Distinct labeling terms highlight a Cognac's aging.

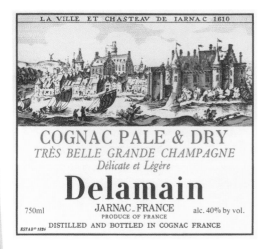

American Brandies

Most brandies produced in the United States may not enjoy the reputation of their French counterparts, but brandies made by artisans such as RMS®, Germain-Robin®, and Jepson® stand up to the very best that France has to offer. For cocktail and culinary use, E & J Gallo Brandy® or Christian Brothers Brandy® are ideal.

Pomace Brandies

Pomace brandies are made from the pressed skin, pulp, seeds, and stems of grapes that remain after wine pressing. They are seldom aged, and are usually harsh and raw, although they may have a fruity aroma that is generally missing from more refined brandies. Many regard pomace brandy as an acquired taste.

Marc *Marc* is the pomace brandy that is produced in all wine-producing regions of France. It is generally consumed locally and very little is exported to the U.S.

Grappa *Grappa,* produced primarily in Italy, has been called the "firewater style" of pomace. In recent years, however, some single variety grappas have been produced with smoother, more elegant results.

Pisco *Pisco* is the specialty brandy of Peru, Chile, and to a lesser degree Bolivia. It was very popular in San Francisco in the nineteenth century and has found renewed interest in the U.S. Chilean Pisco is pot distilled from Moscatél de Alejandria, Torontel, and Pedro Ximénez grape varieties. It is a clear brandy with little or no aging. Peruvian Pisco is made primarily from the black Quebranta grape and the Muscat grape, and is higher proof and tends to be fuller bodied than Chilean Pisco. The best examples of Pisco are aromatic spirits reminiscent of jasmine and orange blossom. Pisco that are primarily imported are Peru's Bar Sol® and Chile's Capel®.

Serving Brandies

Traditionally, brandy is served in a short, squat, tulip-shaped glass called a snifter. The shape of the glass concentrates and emphasizes the brandy's bouquet. The brandy should be at room temperature when it is poured. The glass does not need to be heated because the heat of the hand should be enough to release the aromatic qualities of a good brandy.

Tequila

Tequila is a distillate made from the fermented and distilled juice of the blue agave plant. This cactus-shaped plant that is related to the lily takes nine years to develop a large bulbous core, called a *piña,* which weighs up to 170 pounds (77 kg). The pressure-cooked and shredded *piña* is made into mash, fermented, and then distilled into tequila. Tequila has its own appellation, *Denominación de Origen,* which delineates growing regions and specifies ingredient content. The production of tequila is strictly regulated by the CRT *(Consejo Regulador del Tequila),* whose symbol appears on every label of tequila. Tequila is produced in the Mexican state of Jalisco. There are two types of tequila permitted: 100% Agave and Tequila Mixto. The latter allows up to 49% of other fermentable sugars to be added to the fermentation.

White Tequila—Labeled *blanco* or plata (silver), it is unaged or slightly aged and filtered to remove color.

Gold Tequila—This tequila is the same as blanco but has caramel added for color.

Reposado Tequila—Aged 2 to 11 months, *reposado* must be made from 100% blue agave.

Añejo tequila—This tequila is aged for a minimum of one year, in small barrels less than 600 litres.

Extra Añejo—Extra *añejo* is a new category that signifies that a 100% agave tequila has been aged for three years or more.

Tequila has become extremely popular in the U.S., with 75% of it poured for margaritas, which is the number one called drink. Mescal, an agave based distillate, is made throughout Mexico. Mescal is made from a variety of agaves. The piñas are first roasted in pits or clay ovens, then crushed in a mill and put into fermenters. Mescals are typically unaged and have a distinct smokey character. There are now hundreds of imported brands. Some of the most notable include Herradura®, Sauza®, Don Eduardo®, Patrón®, and José Cuervo®.

Aquavit

Aquavit is a distilled liquor from Scandinavia. It ranges from 42% to 45% ABV. Distilled from a fermented potato or grain mash, it is usually flavored with caraway or cumin seeds but may also be flavored with citrus peel, cardamom, aniseed, or fennel. Aquavit is traditionally served chilled, often straight out of the freezer, in small glasses that are emptied in one shot. It is not typically mixed with any other beverage.

Bitters

As the name suggests, *bitters* are a very bitter, or bittersweet liquids distilled from various herbs and roots. Bitters, though an essential element in many cocktails, are used sparingly in cocktails and cooking to add a dry zest. Because they are both a digestive aid and an appetite stimulant, bitters are used in both before- and after-dinner mixed drinks. Bitters are highly alcoholic and should not be used in non-alcoholic drinks. Most notable producers include Campari®, Fernet Branca, Angostura®, Peychaud's®, and Fee Brothers®.

Liqueurs

Liqueurs still retain the mystique of secret elixirs and potions concocted by monks and alchemists—most often in secret. Benedictine and Chartreuse, for example, are herbal blends developed by ancient religious orders. The Benedictine order first made its famous liqueur in 1510 by mixing herbs, plant parts, and spices into a Cognac base. The recipe for Chartreuse predates the American Revolution and is such a secret that only five monks at a time are permitted to know the 130-ingredient recipe.

Liqueur Production Processes

Production methods of liqueurs vary widely from one liqueur to another. In some cases, the exact manner of production is also a carefully guarded secret. But in general there are five basic methods of production.

Infusion

Infusions are made by steeping flavoring agents in a hot liquid, usually water or fruit juice, much like steeping tea. Because the resulting "tea" must be strong enough to impart flavor to the entire blended liqueur, however, the infusion is generally much stronger than tea.

Maceration

When an aromatic or flavoring agent is immersed in the base spirit until the spirit absorbs the flavoring or aroma, the process is called maceration. A maker might, for example, macerate fresh strawberries in a spirit to avoid losing the aroma, flavor, and color of the berries. Because heating can cause evaporation of both the alcohol and esters, maceration is a cool process that can take up to a year. The final result is called a *tincture* and is the basis of the liqueur.

Percolation

In percolation, the flavoring agents are placed in a container above the base liquor, which is then bubbled up through it. This process can take weeks to absorb the flavors and to form a product called an extract.

Redistillation

Redistillation, which is used mostly for flavoring agents such as seeds, citrus peel, or mint, employs an extraction method. The flavoring agent is steeped in spirits for several days and then placed in a still with other spirits to be distilled. A vacuum is used to permit the distillation to occur at lower temperatures so that more of the flavors are retained.

Cold Compounding

Cold compounding is a simple method of flavoring liqueurs by blending in essences and concentrates to the base spirit. This method is used for the least expensive liqueurs.

Proprietary Brands

There are two general types of liqueurs: generics and proprietaries. Generics are liqueurs such as crème de menthe or crème de cacao that are not proprietary and may therefore be produced by any producer. Proprietaries are trademarked liqueurs that are made according to specific, usually highly secret recipes. Examples include Grand Marnier®, Southern Comfort®, or Benedictine®.

Flavor Classifications

Although liqueurs come in a great variety of flavors, they generally fall into these classifications:

- **Fruit-flavored**—These liqueurs are popular and bear a label that identifies the fruit that flavors the liqueur, such as Midori®, made with melon.
- **Seed-based**—Although one seed predominates in the liqueur, the beverage is usually made from several kinds of seeds.
- **Herbs**—Among the most complex, herbal liqueurs may contain a dozen or a hundred herbs (except for mint or anise seed). Herbal flavors do not usually dominate the liqueur.
- **Crème**—Called crème liqueurs for their creamy texture and sweet taste, crèmes take their name from the dominant flavoring ingredient, such as a fruit (crème de banane).
- **Peels**—The most frequently used peels are those in the citrus family, such as orange or lemon. See Figure 8-7.
- **Fruit brandies**—These fall into three general groups: brandies flavored with apples and pears; those using stone fruits such as plums, peaches, or apricots; and those flavored with berries, such as blackberries or elderberries.
- **Nut liqueurs**—Among these liqueurs there are favorites such as Amaretto (almonds) and Frangelico® (hazelnuts).

Serving Liqueurs

Liqueurs or cordials are sweet, potent, and contain essential oils that may aid in digestion. They are popular as after-dinner drinks. Due to their sweet flavors, they add smoothness, texture, and palatability to many cocktails. In France, certain liqueurs are used in the form of highballs. Crème de cassis, for example, is mixed with wine to make Kir Frappés. A popular way of serving liqueurs is by filling a small stem glass with shaved ice and pouring the liqueur over it.

FIGURE 8-7

Orange peels from Haiti are an essential flavor to the liqueur Grand Marnier®.

ALIZÉ®

From France; a blend of passion fruit, or other flavors and cognac; a variety of colors

AMARETTO

Aromatic liqueur made from apricots and almonds steeped in aquavit (fusion of alcohol); brown color

AMARETTO DI SARONNO®

Brand name of Amaretto; brown color

ANISETTE

Sweet, mild, liqueur with licorice-like flavor; clear

B&B LIQUEUR D.O.M.®

Delicate finesse of Benedictine D.O.M., with drier cognac; amber color

BENEDICTINE D.O.M.®

Classic French herbal liqueur; amber color

BOGGS CRANBERRY LIQUEUR®

Tart, tangy taste of juice of cranberries; red color

CAMPARI®

Italian bittersweet spirit apéritif; infusion of aromatic and bitter herbs; light ruby red color

CHAMBORD LIQUEUR ROYALE DE FRANCE®

From France; rich aroma and taste of framboises (small black raspberries) and other fruits and herbs combined with honey; dark purple color

CHARTREUSE®

Classic herb liqueur with subtle flavor and aroma drawn from 130 wild mountain herbs distilled and blended in brandy; yellow or green color

COINTREAU®

Classic French specialty orange liqueur; fragrant, mellow bouquet, with subtle hint of orange; blends sweet and bitter Mediterranean and tropical orange peels; clear

CREAM LIQUEURS

Bailey's® (dominant brand), Carolans®, Emmets®, Leroux®, Myers®, O'Darby's®

Fresh cream blended with spirits and natural flavorings; Irish whiskey is the most widely used spirit; brandy, cordials, rum, and vodka are also used; creamy brown color

CRÈME DE BANANE

Flavor of fresh, ripe bananas; yellow color

CRÈME DE CACAO (BROWN)

Rich, creamy, deep chocolate flavor drawn from cocoa and vanilla beans, with hint of spices; brown color

CRÈME DE CACAO (WHITE)

Less intense chocolate flavor; clear

CRÈME DE CASSIS

Full, rich, flavor of black currants; very dark purple color

CRÈME DE FRAMBOISE

Raspberry-flavored liqueur; dark purple color

CRÈME DE MENTHE (GREEN)

Refreshing, tangy, natural mint flavor; cool, clean; green color

CRÈME DE MENTHE (WHITE)

Virtually identical to green crème de menthe; lack of color makes it useful in more drink recipes

CURAÇAO

From the the island of Curaçao in the Netherlands Antilles; clear amber color; similar to Triple Sec but sweeter and more subtle; lower proof; clear, orange, or blue color

DOMAINE DE CANTON®

A sweet liqueur made from Vietnamese baby ginger and VSOP Cognac; emerald in color

DRAMBUIE®

Old Scotch whiskey, delicately honeyed and spiced; amber color

FRANGELICO®

Wild hazelnuts (filberts) blended with spirits, berries, and herbs; amber color

FRUIT-FLAVORED BRANDIES

Flavor and aroma of fresh, ripe fruit defined by product name (apricot, blackberry, and so on); higher proof and drier than fruit liqueurs; color varies

FRUIT-FLAVORED LIQUEURS

Flavor and aroma of fresh, ripe fruit, defined by product name (apricot, blackberry, and so on); lower proof and sweeter than fruit brandies; color varies

GOLDWASSER

Flavor blend of herbs, seeds, roots, and citrus peels; tiny flakes of gold imperceptible to the tongue that shimmer in this clear liqueur

GRAND MARNIER®

From France; classic cognac-based orange liqueur; flavor and bouquet from peels of wild bitter oranges; amber color

IRISH MIST®

From Ireland; flavor blend of four whiskeys, honeys from heather, clover; essence of a dozen herbs; amber color

JÄGERMEISTER®

Distinctive flavor blend of 56 roots, herbs, and fruits; dark brown color

KAHLÚA®

Flavor aroma of choicest coffees; dark brown color

KAHLÚA ROYALE®

Blends Kahlúa, fine brandy, a hint of chocolate, and oranges; dark brown color

KÜMMEL

One of the world's oldest liqueurs; fairly dry and usually 70 proof or more; essential flavor is caraway with a hint of cumin seed and anise; clear

116

LIQUORE GALLIANO®

From Italy; natural golden liqueur; distinctive flavor of anise and vanilla; rich, sweet, palatable; natural flavorings of seeds, herbs, and spices; yellow color

LIQUORE STREGA®

From Italy; rich, fragrant, golden liqueur with flavors of more than 70 herbs; yellow color

LOCHAN ORA®

From Scotland; distinctive scotch-based liqueur with subtle flavors drawn from Curaçao and Ceylon; gold color

MALIBU®

From Canada; flavor blend of white rum and coconut; clear

MANDARINE NAPOLÉON®

From Belgium; a tangerine liqueur; flavor and bouquet of ripe Andalusian tangerines and cognac; orange color

MARASCHINO

From Italy; made from cracked Maraschino cherry stones and mixed with elderberries; clear

METAXA®

From Greece; brandy-like liqueur from grape base, slightly sweet, with distinctive flavor; amber in color

MIDORI®

From Japan; light, refreshing taste of fresh honeydew melon; green color

MONTE TECA®

From Mexico; tequila-based liqueur; rich, golden taste; clear in color

OPAL NERA®

From Italy; anise and elderflower flavor with hint of lemon; color of black opal

OUZO

From Greece; sweet, white liqueur; licorice-like anise flavor, slightly drier and stronger proof than anisette; when water or ice is added, it turns milky white

PEAR WILLIAM

From Loire Valley in France; delicate flavor of Anjou pears; clear

PERNOD®

From France; blends select anise seed, special flavorings, and natural herbs with spirits; light pastel green color

PETER HEERING®

From Denmark; famous cherryflavored liqueur produced since 1818; formerly known as Cherry Heering®; dark red color

PIMM'S CUP®

From England; tall "sling" drinks (Pimm's Cup No. one is the gin sling); red color

PRALINE LIQUEUR®

Rich, mellow vanilla- and pecan-based flavor of the original New Orleans praline confection; caramel color

RICARD®

From France; anise and herb liqueur; pastel green color

ROCK AND RYE

Whiskey-based liqueur containing crystals of rock candy, flavored with fruits (sometimes has pieces); amber color

SABRA®

From Israel; flavors of orange and chocolate; dark chocolate color

SAMBUCA ROMANO®

Liqueur flavored with elderberry and anise; clear

SCHNAPPS

Apple Barrel®, Aspen Glacial® (peppermint), Cool Mint®, Cristal® (anise), DeKuyper Peachtree® (peach), Dr. McGillicuddy®, (menthomint), Rumple Minze® (peppermint), Silver Schnapps® (100-proof, peppermint), Steel® (85-proof peppermint)

Predominantly for after-dinner sipping; often too sweet and syrupy for straight drinking; good with many mixers; various colors

SLOE GIN

Bouquet and tangy fruity flavor resembling wild cherries; made from fresh fruit of the sloe berry; red color

SOUTHERN COMFORT®

From America; high-proof, peach-flavored liqueur with a bourbon whiskey base; coppery amber color

ST. GERMAIN®

An artisinal liqueur made with fresh elder flowers from France; light yellow color

TIA MARIA®

From Jamaica; coffee-flavored liqueur; dark brown color

TRIPLE SEC

Crystal-clear orange flavor; like curaçao but drier and higher proof; flavor blends peels of tangy, bittersweet green curaçao and sweet oranges; clear

TRUFFLES®

Combination of spirits and imported chocolate; chocolate color

TUACA®

From Italy; brandy base with a hint of herbs, vanilla, and fruit peels; golden color

VANDERMINT®

From Holland; Dutch chocolate with a hint of mint; chocolate cream color

YUKON JACK®

100-proof blend of sweetened Canadian whiskies; amber color

WILD TURKEY LIQUEUR®

Bourbon base; herbs, spices, and other natural; amber color

'HUMANS HAVE *combined various alcoholic beverages since the earliest of times. In this country, the Puritans and early settlers brought with them "strong waters", a reference most likely to Dutch Gin or Genever. They were also familiar with the social aspects of taverns and mixed drink recipes that were consumed in both England and France as well. These recipes included or evolved into punches, crustas, shrubs, flips, caliboguses, bounces, sangarees, and syllabubs to name but a few.*

The history of social drinking in the U.S. and the art of mixing specific various distilled spirits with a variety of mixtures and ice are said to be uniquely American. The birth of the cocktail is truly an American cultural product. The basic principles, techniques, recipes, and tools may be traced as far back as the early 1800s. Many today salute the immortal Jerry Thomas as the forefather of today's modern mixologist. Mixology is the study of cocktails, mixed drinks, and their ingredients. Those who study mixology—mixologists or bartenders— are highly skilled professionals who must understand complex local, state, and federal laws; possess a working knowledge of psychology and current events; and master hundreds of beverage recipes and techniques. Bartenders generally work in restaurants, bars, hotels, private clubs and resorts, and on cruise lines.

Profits generated from beverage sales may account for 75% of the profit margin in the fine dining segment of the restaurant industry. In the last five years there has been a trend in mixology with a renaissance of crafted cocktails, which are based upon classic recipes that emphasize the use of fresh and top quality ingredients. Most establishments continue to operate cost effective, high volume operations by using less expensive commercially prepared ingredients such as sodas from a bag-in-a-box and generic spirits. Each environment has its own challenges, but all share some basic principles for setting up and managing an efficient and profitable operation.

The Beverage Profession

The beverage profession offers a number of career track job opportunities. In the past, these opportunities depended on an apprenticeship. Today, those interested in climbing the career ladder of beverage opportunities must have a beverage and managerial knowledge, as well as hands-on experience. Internationally recognized education and certifications that validate such knowledge and experience have become crucial to quality job placement.

The Beverage Manager

The beverage manager or beverage director position is often a senior-management position within high-volume establishments, hotels, clubs, casinos, cruise lines and restaurants, which have large wine lists and liquor inventories. A beverage manager must be knowledgeable in, and oversee all aspects of beverages including: beer, wine, spirits, and non-alcoholic offerings. The position involves purchasing, receiving, storing, requisitioning, costing, and inventory control. Responsibilities may include: but are not limited to, interviewing, hiring, training and supervising all beverage personnel, menu development, purchasing equipment, developing and maintaining standards, and ensuring profitability.

Bar Manager or Head Bartender

Multiple and single unit restaurants and even hotels with multiple beverage outlets usually have a manager who is in charge of bar operations. This complex management position requires the expertise of an individual who exercises many qualities to oversee the daily bar business. It is the bar manager's responsibility to achieve the goals established by the owner or upper management and to run an efficient and profitable operation while catering to the needs of the guest. Management responsibilities may include: hiring and firing, training, forecasting and budgeting, scheduling, purchasing, inventory and costing, merchandising and promotional sales, quality control, and implementing standards.

The Bartender

Good *bartenders* share a common set of traits and follow certain guidelines that spell success or failure for the bar operation. They must be friendly, hospitable and customer focused, have expertise in mixology, and must have a thorough knowledge of and adhere to state sanitation and alcohol service laws. Professional bartenders must be knowledgeable about an expansive range of alcoholic and non-alcoholic products and be skillful in marketing and selling to the guest. They should possess good organizational skills and practice effective cost control. The ability to recognize behavioral cues that indicate levels of intoxication is also critical to an establishment's survival in today's society.

The Good Bartender's Guidelines

- Offer a friendly greeting.
- Develop a memory for recognizing regular customers and drink preferences.
- Never hurry the customers.
- Step back after serving the guest.
- Handle complaints courteously.
- Cooperate with and be helpful to other employees: avoid employee conflicts.
- Utilize good telephone etiquette.
- Prepare drinks on the rail or bar in front of the customer.
- Return bottles to their proper places immediately to keep the bar neat and organized.
- Use the appropriate glass and garnish for each drink.
- Handle all glassware according to sanitation guidelines. (See Figure 9-1.)
- Use a fresh sundry for each drink.
- Use a fresh glass for every drink unless the customer specifies otherwise.
- Follow standardized recipes or house recipes.
- Use a consistent measure for drinks. (See Figure 9-2.)
- Avoid overfilling a glass: one-quarter inch from the rim is a good rule of thumb. (See Figure 9-3.)
- When pouring two identical drinks, prepare a double recipe and half-fill each glass. Then pour additional liquid until the glasses are evenly filled.
- Ring drinks on the guest check, and place the check face down in front of the customer.
- Never sit, eat, or smoke at the bar, even when off duty.
- Remain professional at all times.

FIGURE 9-1

The correct procedure for handling stemware and baseware

FIGURE 9-2

A jigger pour

FIGURE 9-3

All drinks should allow for a 1/4 inch margin from the rim.

The Barback

Barbacks assist and support bartenders by performing various tasks during the set up, service, and break down of the bar area. Barbacks support the work of bartenders by cutting fruit, preparing juice and mixers, filling ice bins, setting up sundries, washing and replacing glassware, and stocking product. Barbacks help the bartender in keeping the work area clean during operating hours. Opening and closing duties may vary depending on the bar operation. Typically, a barback relieves the bartender of duties other than preparing drinks and taking care of customers and payment. Many barback positions are apprenticeships for becoming a bartender.

The Cocktail Server

Cocktail servers are usually employed to support service to customers in large establishments such as nightclubs, casinos, and banquet facilities, so that guests need not travel to and from their seats or location. They are responsible for the sales and service of cocktails and beverages to guests. Cocktail servers, generally ring drinks through the POS system and order and pick up drinks from bartenders who may be located at a service bar. Cocktail servers should be familiar with the drink families, appropriate glassware, the sequence of drink orders (call order), and the appropriate garnishes for each drink. Drinks should be delivered and cleared using a beverage tray and cocktail tables should be monitored for cleanliness and sanitation.

Cocktails and Mixed Drinks

The terms cocktail and mixed drink are often used as though they were synonymous. There are, however, several important differences between these two terms. A cocktail is a fairly short drink, made by mixing liquor or wine with fruit juices, eggs, and/or bitters. Cocktails are created by mixing together two or more ingredients to make a new flavor that is both pleasing and palatable. Unless the drink is made to the specifications of a particular customer, no single ingredient should overpower the others. Although cocktails are stirred or shaken with ice in bar glasses or cocktail shakers, they are generally served up, or without ice, in stemmed glasses. If the guest prefers, the cocktail may be served on the rocks, or with ice.

Mixed drinks, on the other hand, are tall drinks, served over ice. Mixed drinks combine liquor with a mixer—one as simple as club soda or as complex as several kinds of fruit juices, various carbonated beverages, and even puréed fruits. Generally served in a base glass, mixed drinks are served with ice.

Cocktails may be distinguished from mixed drinks by the following characteristics:

1. *Presentation: Cocktails are short and served "up" unless called for "on the rocks." Mixed drinks are tall and are served with ice.*

2. *Procedure: Cocktails are stirred or shaken, while mixed drinks are served ice down-pour or speed-shaken.*

3. *Glassware: Cocktails are served in a stemmed glass, and mixed drinks are served in a tall base glass.*

History of Cocktails and Mixed Drinks

Experts differ on the origins of the word *cocktail.* Everyone does agree, however, that the cocktail, like jazz, was born in America. New York Times' restaurant critic William Grimes writes, "other countries can copy the cocktail, but seldom improve it." One of the first uses of the word *cocktail* as a reference to an alcoholic beverage appeared in the 1806 publication of New York's Hudson Valley *The Balance and Columbian Repository.* Here a reference is made to the cocktail as a "stimulating liquor, composed of spirits of any kind, sugar, water, and bitters. It is vulgarly called a bittered sling and is supposed to be an excellent electioneering potion, in as much as it renders the heart stout and bold, at the same time that it fuddles the head" By 1889, the Century Dictionary had formalized the term, defining the cocktail as "an American drink, strong, stimulating, and cold."

Most researchers agree that the origin of the cocktail dates back to the time of the American Revolution, when Americans were unable to import rum and other spirits from Great Britain. Americans began distilling their own whiskey, although some of it was of a dubious quality. Mixing this whiskey with sugar and bitters improved the taste, and the cocktail was born. As the distillers' skills improved, however, distinctive and high-quality whiskies, such as Kentucky Bourbon, began to develop. Eventually whiskey found its way into one of America's earliest classic cocktails, the mint julep.

The first recorded reference to the Julep is in 1787, when the drink was described as a combination of rum, water, and sugar. By the 1830s, however, the julep recipe had acquired mint and ice. Juleps were served ice cold but were created differently depending on social class preferences. The wealthy made them with expensive brandy, while common folk used whiskey.

Key Ingredients

Key ingredients with which bartenders work include the spirit or liqueur, ice and mixers, juices, simple syrups, bitters, and garnishes. Bartenders, like chefs, can only create great cocktails or mixed drinks if all the ingredients are of the highest quality.

Spirits

The quality of the finished drink reflects the quality level of the spirit. Generic spirits generally have more congeners and lack a smooth alcoholic finish. The flavors of each have attributes that allow them to uniquely integrate with different mixers and create countless variations. The general standard alcohol contents of each of the spirit categories are:

- Vodka–40% to 50%
- Gin–40% to 47%
- Blended Whiskies and Bourbon–40% to 45%
- Scotch–40% to 62%
- Rum–40%
- Tequila–40%
- Brandy–40%
- Liqueurs–40% to 45%
- Aperitifs–16% to 30%.

Ice

It was ice that transformed the barkeeper from host and server to juggler, conjuror, and artist. Throughout the 1830s clean ice from New England was available even in the hottest months and ordinary people acquired a taste for it. Crafting drinks with fresh ingredients shaken or stirred over ice was a common practice throughout the 1850s and 60s. Tools and techniques became more elaborate as did the drinks. Ice is the common ingredient in today's cocktails and mixed drinks. Unfortunately, the technology for making ice has focused primarily on speed and volume of production. As a result, inferior ice, such as small hollow cubes, often fails to chill a beverage without over diluting it. Quality ice must be made from quality water, and filtration is recommended. Large, dense cubes may be best when serving spirits on the rocks or in highballs, while cracked ice works best with very sweet drinks, juices and soft drinks.

Garnishes, Juices, Mixers, Simple Syrup, and Bitters

Cocktails created after the 1950s became the victims of artificial ingredients and mass production techniques. Today, many bar operators are able to include fresh, local bounty in syrups, tinctures, bitters, infusions, and even in jams and jellies. With the return of the crafted cocktail, numerous recipes may require fresh juices, culinary ingredients, and an array of garnishes. Only fresh, seasonal, quality fruits, herbs and vegetables should be used at the bar to make the best juices and garnishes.

All fresh juices should be refrigerated with strict rotation and date guidelines, and garnishes should be kept at the appropriate temperature to guarantee freshness and eye appeal. Some fresh juices degrade within hours. Garnishes are intended to add color and flavor to a drink. Refrigeration or temperature control garnish boxes may be used to store ready to use garnish.

The addition of mixers to today's recipes vary from bottled sodas, house charged waters, homemade infusions, and crafted sodas and sours, to prepared mixes and packaged products. See Figure 9-4. For consumers, this means that there are always interesting new cocktails. Many of today's cocktail recipes have replaced the sugars with gum syrup or simple syrup. *Simple syrup* can be prepared in advance by dissolving superfine sugar with equal parts water. Rich simple syrup increases the ratio to 2:1, sugar to water. The infusion of syrups with herbs, spices and natural flavorings can increase the bartender's arsenal of flavor additions.

Cocktail bitters such as Angostura®, Peychaud's®, and Fee Brothers® brands have an alcohol base. See Figure 9-5. When added by the drop they do not affect the alcohol content of a drink but rather enhance the flavor and balance. Prepared or house made bitters can come in a variety of flavors including fruits, herbs, botanicals, and spices.

❧ **F I G U R E   9 - 5**

Cocktail bitters enhance the balance and flavor of a drink.

❧ **F I G U R E   9 - 4**

Mixers can be purchased in a wide range of quality levels to support a bar's concept.

123

Mixology

Bar Glassware

Today's glassware is available in a variety of shapes and sizes. See Figure 9-6. Consider durability, size, and balance when purchasing glassware. One should always use an appropriate glass for each drink. It is recommended to closely match the glass size with the correct proportion of ingredients. When handling glassware, strict sanitary guidelines should be followed. Pick up glasses by the stem or base only; never pick up a glass by the rim or put fingers in the glass; and never scoop ice into a glass by using the glass as the scoop.

Today's glassware is available in a variety of shapes and sizes.

Bar Operations

The layout of a bar must be carefully planned and laid out. A bartender should have almost all tools and ingredients within easy reach to allow for taking no more than a step or two in any direction. The bartender should build drinks on the bar rail within clear view of the guest so that the guest may see the preparation of ingredients and the skill/expertise of the bartender. See Figure 9-7.

Bar Opening Procedures

Follow appropriate procedures for opening the bar to ensure efficiency. Evening bartenders should also adhere to proper bar closing procedures to guarantee a quick and efficient opening the following day. Develop and use checklists to make sure that each task is completed every time the bar is opened. To open a bar, follow these steps:

1. Begin by checking the cash register, and ensure that the previous shift has been closed out properly. Then count the bank, or cash that has been issued in the presence of a manager, and ensure that it is correct. Make sure that there are ample quantities of guest checks or paper for the POS printer.
2. Turn on the glass washer or fill the three-compartment sink: (1) wash, (2) rinse, (3) sanitize. Wash any soiled glasses, and leave them on the drain board until dry. See Figure 9-8.
3. Check bottled drinks: rotate and restock them according to established bar stocks. Restock liquor issued for the day, and turn in empty bottles for inventory control.
4. Clean the soda gun. Check soda levels and the carbon dioxide pressure.

Key Bar Tools

A bartender's tools are a critical component in making drinks accurately and consistently. The following tools are the minimum required tools needed to successfully concoct non-frozen drink recipes.

The 7-piece bar kit: Mixing Glass, Metal Shaker, Speed Shaker, Spring Strainer, Jigger, Long Stirring Spoon, Channel Knife

Muddler, Ice Tongs, Zester, Steel Muddler

Bottle/Can Opener, Fine Mesh Strainer, Flat Bottle Opener, Specialty Bottle Opener, Hand Juicer

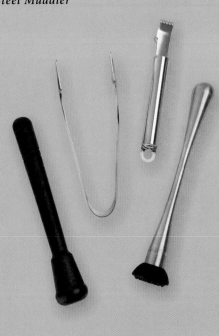

FIGURE 9-7

The bar rail acts as the bartenders stage.

FIGURE 9-8

The three basin sink—wash, rinse, sanitize

FIGURE 9-9

Air mats allow air flow around bar glassware.

5. Check fruit garnishes, fruit juices, cream, and other bar mixes. Wash containers, refill, and refrigerate.

6. Prepare sufficient garnishes for one shift.

7. Check all sundry supplies and bar implements.

8. Wash and polish the bar counter; drain and wash sinks and ice bins; and wipe the neck of each bottle on the back bar. Line up the bottles with labels and pourers facing in the same direction.

9. Visit the rest room to check your appearance.

10. Have a manager watch over your bar should you need to leave.

11. Open the bar on time. All mise en place should be complete and the bar should be fully stocked and ready for business.

Hand-Washing Glasses

It is especially important to keep glasses clean and sanitized. Here is the proper method for hand-washing glasses:

1. Wash glasses in the first compartment of the sink. Use warm water (at least 110°F–120°F/43°C–49°C), a washing compound, and a brush.

2. Use the second compartment to immerse the glasses in clean, warm water of at least 110°F (43°C). Change the rinse water often. Never rinse glasses in dirty water.

3. Sanitize the glasses in the third sink compartment using water containing a chemical sanitizer. The water temperature and immersion time vary depending on the chemical compound used.

4. Drain and air-dry glasses. Store them inverted on shelving lined with air mats. See Figure 9-9.

Use of Chemicals

Several chemical solutions are available for sanitizing hand-washed glasses, including the following:

- A solution of water and at least 50 to 100 parts per million (ppm) of available chlorine.
  Temperature: not less than 55°F (13°C)
  Time: at least 7 seconds

- A solution of water and at least 220 ppm of a quaternary ammonium compound (quats); (or follow manufacturer's instructions).
  Temperature: not less than 75°F (24°C)
  Time: at least 30 seconds

- A solution of water and at least 12.5 to 25 ppm of available iodine in a solution with a pH not less than 5.0.
  Temperature: not less than 75°F (24°C)
  Time: at least 30 seconds

A field test kit should be used to measure the chemical concentration at any time.

Automatic Glass Washer Procedures

In most states, legal requirements call for the use of automatic glass washers in new commercial operations. Properties with automatic washers should have a dump box in which to discard sundries, garnishes, and ice. A *dump box* is a receptacle with a screen over a drain that allows ice or water to drain without allowing garnishes and sundries to clog the plumbing. The temperatures of the glass washer cycle should be checked to ensure that a minimum temperature of 180°F (82°C) for the final rinse is reached.

Bar Closing Procedures

Closing the bar properly helps to ensure efficient operation. To close the bar:

1. Wipe and thoroughly clean the speed rack; wipe bottles and replace.

2. Sanitize empty shelves for clean glasses.

3. Collect all used glassware, and place it on the counter above the sink area. Wash hands.

4. Wash glassware, one type at a time, washing cream-drink glasses last. Replace glasses on the shelf that is covered with air mats.

5. Rinse and wash sinks, and dry them to prevent scaling.

6. Wash and polish the drain board and other parts of the sink.

7. Clean out the ice bin, and wipe dry.

8. Sweep the floor, and remove the trash container.

9. Wrap or store fruit garnishes appropriately, and refrigerate them for the next day.

10. Refrigerate all perishable mixers, label, and date. Wash and store empty containers.

11. Fill in the day's requisition for liquor, wine, and beer.

12. Stock coolers for the next shift, rotating all products (FIFO).

13. Run appropriate closing procedures on the POS system. If using a manual system, count the guest checks and correlate them with the issue register. Note any unused checks. Close out the cash register according to the house policy.

14. Check security, and inform management when ready for inspection.

Bar Set-up

Good bartenders need to ensure that they have properly set up their mise en place of ingredients. Bottles should be enticingly gleaming with labels facing guests. Back up bottles of the most commonly used or near empty products should be stored within easy reach. The bar mats should be placed on the rail with bar tools such as shakers, mixing glasses, and speed shakers inverted and ready for use. *Bar sundries* refer to non-edible supplies such as sip sticks, beverage straws, sword picks, and cocktail napkins that are needed for bartending. Salt and pepper, sugar, commonly used spices and sauces such as Tabasco®, and Lea & Perrins® Worcestershire sauce should also be near at hand.

Fixed versus Portable Bars

Fixed bars are permanently established with running potable water and proper glass washing capabilities. Portable bars may be used in banquet halls and off–premise catering operations to allow for flexibility of location. Portable bars have certain disadvantages that may reduce the number of products, displays, glassware, and the techniques that a bartender may use.

The Speed Rack (The Well)

Bar set-ups vary enormously based on the type, size, and the targeted bar audience. Most bars are set up with *speed racks* that are located in the *well* which is mounted to the sinks and the ice bin. They are designed for bartenders to easily access the most commonly used spirits and mixers. At a high end bar one might find all spirits in the speed rack or well to be "call" or proprietary brands such as Smirnoff® Vodka rather than a generic brand of vodka.

The set-up of the speed rack varies from house to house. At Johnson & Wales University properties the speed rack is set up as follows: from left to right: Rose's® Lime Juice and Grenadine, Vodka, Gin, Blended Whiskey, Scotch, Rum, Brandy, Dry Vermouth, and Sweet Vermouth.

The Back Bar

The *back bar* should be set up to display bottles in an attractive way to promote sales, and to market premium, super-premium, and ultra-premium brands. The arrangement will depend on the type of bar, the space available, and the beverage menu focus. It should also be functional for the bartender.

The following list (although not inclusive), contains the Premium, Super-Premium, and Ultra-Premium brands that are currently significant in the U.S. market:

Irish Whisky
- Bushmills®
- Jameson®

Scotch Whiskies
- Ballantine's®
- Johnnie Walker®
- Glenlivet®
- Chivas Regal®
- Glenfiddich®
- Laphroaig®
- Dewars®

Canadian Whisky
- Canadian Club®
- Seagram's 7®
- Crown Royal®
- Seagram's VO®

Vodka
- Belvedere®
- Ketel One®
- Smirnoff®
- Chopin®
- Stolichnaya®
- Absolut®

Gin
- Beefeater®
- Tanqueray®
- Bols Genever®
- Bombay®
- Grey Goose®
- Plymouth®
- Boodles®

Blended Whiskies and Bourbons
- Jim Beam®
- Wild Turkey®
- Knob Creek®
- Jack Daniel's®
- Baker's®
- Rittenhouse Rye®
- Heaven Hill®
- Basil Hayden®
- Rī®

Rum
- Depaz® Rhum Agricole
- Mount Gay® gold rum
- Bacardi® light rum
- Myer's® dark rum
- Captain Morgan® Spiced Rum

Tequila
- Cabo Wabo®
- Sauza®
- Gran Centenario®
- José Cuervo®
- Herradura®
- Patron®
- Milagro®

Cognacs
- Martell®
- Courvoisier®
- Hine®
- Hennessy®
- Otard-Dupuy®
- Delamain®
- Rémy Martin®
- Camus®

The speed rack

Liqueurs

In addition to premium category spirits, the back bar usually displays liqueurs that may be served as cordials or used in recipes for cocktails and mixed drinks. Liqueurs are also categorized by price and quality. The following list includes both generic and proprietary brands that might be incorporated into a fully stocked bar.

- Apricot-flavored brandy
- Crème de banane
- Crème de cacao (dark)
- Crème de cacao (light)
- Crème de cassis
- Crème de menthe (green)
- Crème de menthe (white)
- Curaçao (blue)
- Curaçao (orange)
- Peach schnapps
- Peppermint schnapps
- Triple sec

Propietary Brands

- Amaretto di Saronno®
- Bailey's Irish Cream®
- Benedictine D.O.M.®
- Campari®
- Chartreuse®
- Cointreau®
- Drambuie®
- Frangelico®
- Galliano®
- Grand Marnier®
- Kahlúa®
- Maraschino®
- Midori®
- Navan®
- Peter Heering®
- Southern Comfort®
- St. Germain®

Bar Terminology

The *jigger,* a legal measure of 1.5 ounces (45 ml), and a *shot,* a measure of liquid (quantity determined by the house) served straight up, are bartending tools of the trade. Other terms include:

- *Back*—A chaser on the side.
- *Float*—The final liquid ingredient added to the drink after the usual procedure is performed; a float finds its own space and should not be incorporated into the drink.
- *Free-pour*—Pouring spirits or liqueurs without using a measuring device, such as a jigger. Less accurate than a measured pour and therefore less professional.
- *Hold/no garbage*—Served without garnishes.
- *Light*—A drink containing a reduced amount of liquor but the normal amount of mixer.
- *On the rocks*—Served on ice, usually in a rocks glass.
- *Straight up or neat*—Served without ice; the drink never comes into contact with ice.
- *Tall/Long*—A drink served in an 8- to 16-ounce (240- to 500-ml) highball or zombie glass; the amount of the mixer is increased, not the amount of liquor.
- *Up*—Prepared with ice to chill, but served strained from the ice in a stemmed glass.

Making Cocktails and Mixed Drinks

Four basic procedures are used in making cocktails and mixed drinks. These are the stir, shake, ice down-pour, or speed-shake methods. Unless otherwise specified, cocktails are usually served up when ordered. See Figures 9-10 and 9-11 for procedures for mixed drinks and the glass planner for the appropriate glasses needed for cocktails and mixed drinks.

For cocktails served up:

- *Stir procedure*—Gently agitate with ice to chill and blend the cocktail ingredients.
- *Shake procedure*—Agitate energetically with ice to disperse or incorporate heavy ingredients.

For mixed drinks or cocktails requested on the rocks:

- *Ice down-pour procedure*—Place ice in a service glass, and then add liquor and the mixer; serve as is.
- *Speed-shake procedure*—In a service glass, agitate with ice to disperse or incorporate heavier ingredients.

VERMOUTH BASE (SERVED UP)

Name of Drink	Procedure	Glass
Gibson	Stir	Cocktail
Manhattan	Stir	Cocktail
Martini	Stir	Cocktail
Negroni	Stir	Cocktail
Rob Roy	Stir	Cocktail

VERMOUTH BASE (SERVED ON THE ROCKS)

Name of Drink	Procedure	Glass
Gibson	Ice down-pour	Rocks
Manhattan	Ice down-pour	Rocks
Martini	Ice down-pour	Rocks
Negroni	Ice down-pour	Rocks
Rob Roy	Ice down-pour	Rocks

SHORT SOURS (SERVED UP)

Name of Drink	Procedure	Glass
All sours (i.e. whiskey)	Shake	Sour
Bacardi® Cocktail	Shake	Cocktail
Between the Sheets	Shake	Cocktail
Cosmopolitan	Shake	Cocktail
Daiquiri	Shake	Cocktail
Gimlet	Shake	Cocktail
Jack Rose	Cocktail Shake	Cocktail
Kamikaze	Shake	Cocktail
Margarita	Shake	Champagne coupe
Pisco Sour	Shake	Cocktail
Sidecar	Shake	Cocktail
Ward 8	Shake	Cocktail

SHORT SOURS (SERVED ON THE ROCKS)

Name of Drink	Procedure	Glass
All sours (whiskey)	Speed-shake	Rocks
Bacardi® Cocktail	Speed-shake	Rocks
Between the Sheets	Speed-shake	Rocks
Cosmopolitan	Speed-shake	Rocks
Daiquiri	Speed-shake	Rocks
Gimlet	Speed-shake	Rocks
Jack Rose Cocktail	Speed-shake	Rocks
Kamikaze	Speed-shake	Rocks
Margarita	Speed-shake	Rocks
Pisco Sour	Speed-shake	Rocks
Side Car	Speed-shake	Rocks

SHORT CREAM BASE (SERVED UP)

Name of Drink	Procedure	Glass
Brandy Alexander	Shake	Champagne coupe
Grasshopper	Shake	Champagne coupe
Pink Squirrel	Shake	Champagne coupe

SHORT CREAM BASE (SERVED ON THE ROCKS)

Name of Drink	Procedure	Glass
Brandy Alexander	Speed-shake	Rocks
Grasshopper	Speed-shake	Rocks
Pink Squirrel	Speed-shake	Rocks

LONG CREAM BASE

Name of Drink	Procedure	Glass
Girl Scout Cookie	Speed-shake	Highball
Orgasm	Speed-shake	Highball
Toasted Almond Bar	Speed-shake	Highball
White Russian	Speed-shake	Highball

LONG SOURS

Name of Drink	Procedure	Glass
Long Island Iced Tea	Speed-shake	Sling/zombie
Sloe Gin Fizz	Speed-shake	Collins
Singapore Sling	Speed-shake	Sling/zombie
(Tom) Collins	Speed-shake	Collins

TROPICAL-POLYNESIAN

Name of Drink	Procedure	Glass
Mai Tai	Speed-shake	Collins
Piña Colada	Speed-shake	Sling/zombie
Planter's Punch	Speed-shake	Collins
Zombie	Speed-shake	Sling/zombie

HIGHBALL

Name of Drink	Procedure	Glass
Juice Highball*	Ice down-pour	Highball
Soda Highball	Ice down-pour	Highball

CORDIALS

Name of Drink	Procedure	Glass
All Cordials	Ice down-pour	Rocks

*Exception to the rule for juice-based drinks: speed-shake juice-based highballs that have a liqueur with a juice mixer.

Performing the Stir Procedure

Drinks prepared using the stir procedure are served cold, but the ice is strained out to prevent diluting the liquor and mixer. Drinks prepared this way are usually served with a garnish.

To perform the stir procedure, follow these steps:

1 Chill a stemmed glass by filling it with ice, and place it on the rail.

2 Put ice into a mixing glass until it is one third full.

3 Pour the base into the mixing glass.

4 Add the liquor.

5 Hold the mixing glass with the fingers closed at the base, and stir. Holding the bar spoon by its helix, roll it back and forth between the thumb and index finger until well chilled. Gently remove the bar spoon.

6 Remove the ice from the chilled serving glass.

7 Using a spring strainer over the mouth of the glass, strain ingredients into the serving glass.

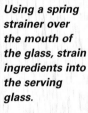

8 Garnish and serve.

Performing the Shake Procedure

Mixologists use the shake procedure to more fully incorporate spirits and mixer ingredients. The ice is strained from the drink before serving it. The key to a well shaken drink is that it is vigorously shaken. This can best be done by holding the shake/mixing glass combination over the right or left shoulder. Shaking too long dilutes the drink. A fifteen second shake adds one-half to three-quarters of an ounce of additional liquid to the drink. This dilution makes a cocktail taste balanced and less alcoholic on the palate. The shake procedure also incorporates air bubbles that change the texture and lighten the drink.

To perform the shake procedure, follow these steps:

1 Put ice into a mixing glass until it is one-third full.

2 Add spirit(s) and/or liqueur(s).

3 Add mixer and/or base ingredient(s).

4 Place a metal cup or base over the top of the mixing glass, making sure that the metal cup is sitting evenly, not at an angle.

5 Give the top (bottom of the metal shaker) a light tap to create a vacuum.

6 Pick up the whole unit from the bar, and flip it over so that the metal is facing down and the glass is near your shoulder.

7 In a quick, even movement, shake vigorously moving the unit back and forth in rapid succession for fifteen seconds.

8  With the metal shaker still on the bottom, hold the unit in the left hand for balance. Press the index finger against the glass mixer. Make a fist with the right hand.

9 Locate the frost line on the metal shaker and strike the side to break the vacuum.

10 Twist off the mixing glass, and strain the liquid through the spring strainer into a glass.

Eight Bases for Alcoholic Beverages

It is important to be familiar with the types of alcohol that are used as the bases for many cocktails and mixed drinks. Note that the base ingredient or mixer for both mixed drinks and cocktails does not change but the liquor changes according to the name of the drink. See Figure 9-12.

FIGURE 9-12

Bases for Alcoholic Beverages

VERMOUTH
Cocktails

SOURS
Short sours–cocktails
Long sours–mixed drinks

CREAMS
Short creams–cocktails
Long creams–mixed drinks

CORDIALS (LIQUEURS)
Two-liquor drinks

CARBONATED HIGHBALLS
Mixed drinks

JUICE-BASED HIGHBALLS
Mixed drinks

POLYNESIAN OR TROPICALS
Mixed drinks

WINES AND PUNCHES SPECIALTIES
Cream- and ice cream-based drinks; coffees mixed with spirits

Performing the Ice Down-Pour Procedure

For mixed drinks and cocktails requested on the rocks, the ice down-pour procedure is used. These drinks are served cold over ice.

To perform the ice down-pour procedure, follow these steps:

1

Fill the base glass with ice, always using an ice scoop.

2

Add measured liquor(s) and/or liqueur(s).

3

Garnish.

4

Add the stirrer or sip stick, and serve.

Performing the Speed-Shake Procedure

The speed-shake procedure is appropriate for mixing spirits and heavier mixers. Drinks that are speed shaken are generally served tall with ice.

To perform the speed-shake procedure, follow these steps:

1
Place a base glass filled to the rim with ice on the bar or rail.

2
Pour liquor(s) and/or liqueur(s).

3
Add the mixer and/or the base ingredient(s).

4
Place the metal speed shaker over the glass.

5
Pick up the unit; flip it, ensuring that the metal speed shaker is on the bottom; and shake the container back and forth in quick, even movements until well incorporated.

6
Pour the drink from the speed shaker into the chilled glass, garnish, and add a sip stick.

Vermouth-Based Drinks

The Martini remains a universally popular cocktail. It is a dry, sharp, appetite-whetting drink that has become progressively drier (less vermouth) over the years. There is no Martini recipe on which all bartenders agree. By the time it came to be called a Martini, the drink had become a mixture of equal parts gin and dry vermouth.

The Manhattan was named for Manhattan, New York, where bartenders in speakeasies cut the harshness of bootlegged liquor with syrups and aromatic flavorings. In addition to whiskey or bourbon, the original Manhattan contained bitters, sugar, and much more vermouth than today's recipe. Although the recipe for a basic Manhattan is sweet vermouth and whiskey, using dry vermouth creates a Dry Manhattan. Using both sweet and dry vermouth makes the drink a Perfect Manhattan.

In Rob Roys, Scotch replaces the whiskey or bourbon used in the Manhattan recipe. Like regular Manhattans, Dry Rob Roys and Perfect Rob Roys vary according to the type of vermouth used in their preparation.

Vermouth-based cocktails are served up in cocktail glasses and are stirred, unless a customer requests the cocktail on the rocks. For an on-the-rocks version, use the ice down-pour method, and serve the drink in a rocks glass.

Garnishes Vermouth-based drinks may be garnished in a variety of ways.

- A Martini may contain either a cocktail olive or lemon zest.

- A Manhattan or a Rob Roy sports a maraschino cherry. When making a Rob Roy with dry vermouth rather than sweet vermouth, use lemon zest. When the drink contains both sweet and dry vermouth, the garnish is optional. Use either a cherry or lemon zest.

- A Negroni, which contains Campari® (a slightly bitter Italian apéritif), is garnished with an orange slice or lemon zest.

- Garnish a Gibson with a cocktail onion.

VERMOUTH-BASE

stir and/or ice down-pour

MARTINI (CLASSIC)

Gin	1 1/2 ounces
Dry vermouth	3/4 ounce
Olive or zest	garnish

DRY MARTINI

Gin	2 ounces
Dry vermouth	1/2 ounce
Olive or zest	garnish

VODKA MARTINI

Vodka	1 1/2 ounces
Dry vermouth	3/4 ounce
Olive or zest	garnish

EXTRA-DRY MARTINI

Gin	2 1/4 ounces
Dry vermouth	1/4 ounce
Olive or zest	garnish

SMOKY MARTINI OR SILVER BULLET

Gin	1 1/2 ounces
Dry vermouth	1/4 ounce
Scotch (float)	1/2 ounce
Olive or zest	garnish

GIBSON

Gin or vodka	1 1/2 ounces
Dry vermouth	3/4 ounce
Cocktail onions	garnish

MANHATTAN

Bourbon or blended whiskey	1 1/2 ounces
Sweet vermouth	3/4 ounce
Cherry	garnish

Classic recipe includes a dash of bitters.

SOUTHERN COMFORT/DELUXE MANHATTAN

Southern Comfort®	1 1/2 ounces
Dry vermouth	3/4 ounce
Cherry or zest	garnish

PERFECT MANHATTAN

Bourbon or blended whiskey	1 1/2 ounces
Dry vermouth and sweet vermouth, combined	3/4 ounce
Cherry or zest	garnish

DRY MANHATTAN

Bourbon or blended whiskey	1 1/2 ounces
Dry vermouth	3/4 ounce
Zest	garnish

ROB ROY

Scotch	1 1/2 ounces
Sweet vermouth	3/4 ounce
Cherry	garnish

Classic recipe includes a dash of bitters.

DRY ROB ROY

Scotch	1 1/2 ounces
Dry vermouth	3/4 ounce
Zest	garnish

PERFECT ROB ROY

Scotch	1 1/2 ounces
Dry vermouth and sweet vermouth, combined	3/4 ounce
Cherry or zest	garnish

NEGRONI

Gin	1 ounce
Sweet vermouth	1 ounce
Campari®	1 ounce
One-half slice of orange	garnish

Build over ice in an old-fashioned glass.

Sours

Sours are drinks that use a sour base, such as lemon or lime juice. The origins of incorporating sours into drinks long predate the invention of the cocktail. They were a standard ingredient of the all popular punches of the seventeenth and eighteenth centuries. Consumption of citrus fruits was recognized by the English to be a valuable source of vitamin C, which also prevented scurvy among their navy's seamen. Limes were often preserved in rum so that they could be consumed on long voyages. Laughlin Rose invented the preservation of lime juice in a non-alcoholic medium in the 1860s that led to including Rose's® Lime Juice as a naval ration. It is considered a staple of any bar.

Sours can be classified as short sours and long sours. Traditionally, bartenders have used simple syrup, lemon or lime juice, and egg whites as a *sour mix.* Today, commercially made sour mixes are commonly used. Short sours are composed of liquor(s) and/or liqueur(s) with sour mix or lime juice. Long sours contain the same ingredients, with the addition of carbonated soda to cut the sour taste. Serve a long sour in a tall glass, garnished with a cherry and an orange slice.

Use cocktail or sour glasses for short sours. The only short sours served with garnishes are sour-type cocktails, such as whiskey sours or apricot sours that are garnished with a cherry. If a customer requests the cocktail on the rocks, however, use the speed-shake procedure, and serve the cocktail in a rocks glass.

Sour Mix

Use fresh lemon and or lime juice mixed with simple syrup to create the perfect balance of sweet and sour. Sour mixes for a whiskey sour should only use lemon. Margaritas are best with only lime. Egg whites may be added to make cocktails slightly foamy and to give the drink a lighter texture.

SHORT SOURS — *shake or speed-shake*

WHISKEY SOUR

Whiskey	*1 1/2 ounces*
Sour mix	*2 ounces*
Cherry	*garnish*

Serve in a sour glass.

DAIQUIRI

Light rum	*1 1/2 ounces*
Sour Mix	*1 ounce*

BACARDI® COCKTAIL

Bacardi® light rum	*1 1/2 ounces*
Sour mix	*1 ounce*
Grenadine	*1/2 ounce*

WARD 8

Whiskey	*1 1/2 ounces*
Sour mix	*1 ounce*
Grenadine	*1/2 ounce*
Cherry or orange slice	*garnish*

Sours

JACK ROSE COCKTAIL

Applejack	1 1/2 ounces
Grenadine	1/2 ounce
Sour mix	1 ounce

MARGARITA

Tequila	1 1/2 ounces
Lime juice or sour mix	1 ounce
Triple sec	3/4 ounce

Rim the champagne coupe with salt. To rim or frost a glass, moisten the rim of the glass with a wedge of citrus fruit, and then dip the glass into a small container of salt or sugar. Set the glass aside. Blend or shake.

PISCO SOUR

Pisco	1 1/2 ounces
Lime juice	1 ounce
Simple syrup	1 ounce
Egg whites	1 each
Angostura® bitters	several drops

BETWEEN THE SHEETS

Brandy	1/2 ounce
Lemon mix	1/2 ounce
Triple sec	1/2 ounce
Rum	1/2 ounce

Using the "BLT on Rye" mnemonic is a handy way to remember the ingredients of this drink, though it does not contain rye whiskey.

SIDECAR

Brandy	1 1/2 ounces
Triple sec	3/4 ounce
Sour mix	1/2 ounce

KAMIKAZE

Gin or vodka	1 1/2 ounces
Rose's® Lime Juice	1/2 ounce
Triple sec	3/4 ounce
Lime wedge (optional)	garnish

STONE SOUR

Apricot brandy	1 1/2 ounces
Orange juice	1 ounce
Sour mix	1 ounce
Cherry	garnish

GIMLET

Gin or vodka	1 1/2 ounces
Rose's® Lime Juice	3/4 ounce
Lime wedge (optional)	garnish

COSMOPOLITAN

Vodka	1 1/2 ounces
Cointreau	1/2 ounce
Lime juice	1/4 ounce
Cranberry juice	1 ounce
Orange	garnish

LONG SOURS *speed-shake*

TOM COLLINS

Gin	1 1/2 ounces
Sour mix	2 ounces
Club soda and 7UP®	to fill
Cherry and one-half orange slice	garnish

Also known as a John Collins

Speed-shake—Collins

Variations

Mike Collins—whiskey

Joe or Ivan Collins—vodka

Pedro Collins—rum

Sandy Collins—scotch

SINGAPORE SLING

Gin	1 1/2 ounces
Sour mix	2 ounces
Club soda and 7UP®	equal parts to fill
Cherry flavored brandy or liqueur (float)	1/2 ounce

Classic recipe includes 1 dash of Angostura® bitters

Speed-shake—Sling/Zombie

SLOE GIN FIZZ

Sloe gin	1 1/2 ounces
Sour mix	2 ounces
Club soda	to fill
Cherry and one-half orange slice	garnish

Speed-shake—Collins

LONG ISLAND ICED TEA

Vodka	1/2 ounce
Gin	1/2 ounce
Rum	1/2 ounce
Tequila	1/2 ounce
Triple sec	1/2 ounce
Sour mix	2 ounces
Coke® (float)	1 ounce
Lemon wheel	garnish

Speed-shake—Sling/Zombie

FROZEN CREAM-BASED DRINKS *blend or shake*

SUMMER RUM FREEZE

Bacardi® rum	1 1/2 ounces
Lime sherbet	2 scoops
Pineapple juice	3 ounces
Cream or milk	3/4 ounce
Pineapple spear or lime wheel	garnish

Place ingredients in the blender. Blend until creamy. Pour into a tall goblet.

SHORT-CREAMS *blend or shake*

BRANDY ALEXANDER

Brandy	1 ounce
Dark crème de cacao	1 ounce
Cream or milk	1 ounce
Nutmeg	garnish

GRASSHOPPER

Light crème de cacao	1 ounce
Green crème de menthe	1 ounce
Cream or milk	1 ounce

PINK SQUIRREL

Light crème de cacao	1 ounce
Crème de Noyaux® or Crème d' Amande	1 ounce
Cream or milk	1 ounce

LONG-CREAMS *speed-shake*

ORGASM

Amaretto	1 ounce
Vodka	1/2 ounce
Kahlúa®	1/2 ounce
Cream or milk	4 ounces

Classic recipe: short cream with Bailey's® Irish Cream instead of milk.

WHITE RUSSIAN

Vodka	1 1/2 ounces
Kahlúa®	1/2 ounce
Cream or milk	4 ounces

Traditionally a layered drink with half-and-half cream set on top of a Black Russian. Today, prepare using speed-shake, serve tall.

GIRL SCOUT COOKIE

Peppermint schnapps	1 ounce
Dark crème de cacao	1 ounce
Milk	4 ounces

TOASTED ALMOND BAR

Amaretto	1 ounce
Dark crème de cacao	1 ounce
Milk	4 ounces

Cream- and Ice Cream-Based Drinks

Cream drinks are usually very sweet, smooth, and pleasing to the palate. They are perfect after-dinner drinks, and many customers order them instead of dessert.

All cream-based drinks may use ice cream instead of cream. Usually, vanilla ice cream is the flavor of choice, but any flavor that blends well with the liqueur's flavor will work, including coffee, strawberry, peach, or chocolate. Sherbets may also be used to make freezes, or frozen drinks. Prepare cream drinks by using either a shake or a blend procedure. The *blend procedure* uses a blender to mix the ingredients more thoroughly and to give the drink a creamier, frothier texture.

The blend procedure is appropriate for any drink that is shaken, but it should always be used when incorporating ice or solids, such as strawberries in a Strawberry Daiquiri. To use the blend procedure:

1. Place the ice in the blender 1/4 full; add the remaining ingredients.
2. The blender container should be one-fourth full; the ice should be covered with the other ingredients.
3. When using a two-speed blender, blend for 3 seconds on low and then 7–10 seconds on high.
4. Using a cocktail spoon to maintain an even flow, pour the blended ingredients into an appropriate glass.

Short cream drinks Serve short cream drinks in a Champagne coupe. The only cream-based drink that has a garnish is the Alexander, which requires a sprinkle of nutmeg.

Long cream drinks Long cream drinks are generally prepared using the speed-shake procedure and are served in a highball glass; they receive no garnish.

Cordials or Two-Liquor Drinks

Cordials are sweet alcoholic beverages in which two-liquor drinks are combined with a distilled spirit or brandy. The spirit helps cut the pronounced sweetness of the cordial. Except for drinks such as the Mud Slide, which requires the speed-shake procedure, two-liquor drinks are served on the rocks in a rocks glass, using the ice down-pour procedure with the spirits poured in first. Cordials that are considered layered drinks must be carefully poured into the glass so that the ingredients do not mix, but rather remain in layers.

The cordial *pousse-café*, French for "coffee-pusher," requires a very steady hand to layer the different colored liqueurs, one on top of the other, in a pony glass. Each layer is created by pouring individual liqueurs into the glass over the back of a cocktail spoon. Generally, the last ingredient is flamed to add drama. As many as 56 different ingredients can be used to make a *pousse-café*. Knowing the specific gravity of each ingredient allows bartenders to pour the densest liqueur first and the least dense last.

CORDIALS
ice down-pour

BLACK RUSSIAN

Vodka	*1 1/2 ounces*
Kahlúa®	*3/4 ounce*

GODFATHER

Scotch	*1 1/2 ounces*
Amaretto	*3/4 ounce*

SICILIAN KISS

Southern Comfort®	*1 1/2 ounces*
Amaretto	*3/4 ounce*

MUD SLIDE

Vodka	*3/4 ounce*
Kahlúa®	*3/4 ounce*
Bailey's Irish Cream®	*3/4 ounce*
Speed-shake	

AFTER 5

Kahlúa®	*1/3 ounce*
Bailey's® Irish Cream	*1/3 ounce*
Peppermint schnapps	*1/3 ounce*
Layered in order	

STINGER

Brandy	*1 1/2 ounces*
White crème de menthe	*3/4 ounce*

GODMOTHER

Vodka	*1 1/2 ounces*
Amaretto	*3/4 ounce*

RUSTY NAIL OR QUEEN ANNE

Scotch	*1 1/2 ounces*
Drambuie®	*3/4 ounce*

B-52

Kahlúa®	*1/3 ounce*
Bailey's® Irish Cream	*1/3 ounce*
Grand Marnier®	*1/3 ounce*

Mixology

Highballs

Highballs consist of carbonated mixers, water or juices, and the appropriate liquor, served tall in highball glasses on ice. Highballs with carbonated mixers or water require only the ice downpour procedure to have their ingredients fully incorporated. Highballs made with liqueurs are speed-shaken to incorporate their ingredients. The basic recipe, however, is the same: 1 1/2 ounces of liquor (or customer preference); and 4 ounces of soda or other mixer. Pour the liquor over ice cubes in a highball glass, top with any flavored soda, and serve.

Highball history Mixed drinks and highballs have origins as fabled as those of the cocktail and the cordial. Many were created by individuals in different occupations and locations, based on practicality or culture.

One of the first mixed drinks was called Gin and Tonic by British troops in the late 1800s. Like many of the original cordials, the drink grew out of the desire to add "a spoon full of sugar" to help the "medicine go down." Required to take daily doses of bitter quinine, a medicine used to ward off malaria, British soldiers in India began adding sugar and water to the dose. Before long, they discovered that adding gin, their favorite liquor, made the medicine go down even better, and so the Gin and Tonic was born.

Highballs were named by railroaders in the 1800s who typically placed a ball on a high pole to indicate to oncoming trains that the track was clear and that they could maintain their speed. When the men had time enough to stop for a fast drink of whiskey and ginger ale, they coined the term "highball" as a name for their drink.

The popular Screwdriver was also named by Americans, who while working in Iran's oil fields where alcohol is forbidden, began using screwdrivers to secretly mix drinks made from vodka and orange juice.

CARBONATED AND JUICE-BASED HIGHBALLS

Today's highball is made of many different combinations of liquors and flavored sodas. Water may also be a base for a highball. Regardless of the combination, the basic recipe is as follows:

Liquor	*1 1/2 ounces*
Soda	*4 ounces*

HIGHBALL

Whiskey	*1 1/2 ounces*
Ginger ale	*4 ounces*

Variations

Presbyterian—whiskey, ginger ale, and club soda
Cuba Libre—Rum and Coke, lime garnish
7 and 7—Seagram's® 7 and 7UP®
Jack and Coke—Jack Daniel's® and Cola

COMFORTABLE SCREW

Southern Comfort®	*1 1/2 ounces*
Orange juice	*4 ounces*
Orange slice	*garnish*
Speed-shake	

BOCCE BALL

Amaretto di Saronno®	*1 1/2 ounces*
Orange juice	*4 ounces*
Club soda *(float)*	
Speed-shake	

CAPE CODDER

Vodka	*1 1/2 ounces*
Cranberry juice	*4 ounces*

HARVEY WALLBANGER

Vodka	*1 1/2 ounces*
Orange juice	*4 ounces*
Galliano® *(float)*	*1/2 ounce*
Orange slice and cherry	*garnish*

TEQUILA SUNRISE

Tequila	*1 1/2 ounces*
Orange juice	*4 ounces*
Grenadine *(float)*	*1/2 ounce*
Orange slice and cherry	*garnish*

MADRAS

Vodka	*1 1/2 ounces*
Cranberry juice	*2 ounces*
Orange juice	*2 ounces*

SALTY DOG

Vodka	*1 1/2 ounces*
Grapefruit juice	*4 ounces*
Rim glass with salt.	

PEARL HARBOR

Midori®	1 ounce
Vodka	1/2 ounce
Pineapple juice	4 ounces

Speed-shake

WOO-WOO

Peachtree® Schnapps	1 ounce
Vodka	1/2 ounce
Cranberry juice	4 oz

Speed-shake

BASIC BLOODY MARY MIX

Vodka	1 1/2 ounces
Tomato juice	4 ounces
Salt and pepper	dash
Lea & Perrins® Worcestershire sauce	dash
Tabasco® sauce	dash
Lemon mix	dash
Horseradish (optional)	1 teaspoon
Celery salt (optional)	dash
Celery stalk or lime wedge	garnish

Speed-shake; serve in a goblet.

Variations

Bloody Maria—tequila

Bloody Jane or Red Snapper—gin

Bloody Caesar—Vodka and Clamato Juice salt & pepper rim

Virgin Mary—non-alcoholic Bloody Mary

ALABAMA SLAMMER

Sloe gin	1/2 ounce
Banana liqueur	1/2 ounce
Orange juice	4 ounces
Southern Comfort® (float)	1/2 ounce

Speed-shake

SEX ON THE BEACH

Peachtree® schnapps	1 ounce
Vodka	1 ounce
Orange juice	2 ounces
Cranberry juice	2 ounces

Speed-shake

SEA BREEZE

Vodka	1 1/2 ounces
Grapefruit juice	2 ounces
Cranberry juice	2 ounces

SCARLET O'HARA

Southern Comfort®	1 1/2 ounces
Cranberry juice	4 ounces

Speed-shake

FUZZY NAVEL

Peachtree® schnapps	1 1/2 ounces
Orange juice	to within 1/2 inch of the rim

Speed-shake

CLASSIC MIXED DRINK

OLD FASHIONED

Sugar	1 package
Bitters	2 or 3 dashes
Club soda	splash
Stemless cherry or orange slice	garnish

Muddle or crush with a muddler, the ingredients to release the oils and juice of the fruit. Then add 2 ounces of blended whiskey or bourbon and a splash of club soda. Serve on the rocks. Garnish with an orange slice and cherry.

MOJITO

Fresh mint	2 sprigs
Simple syrup	1 ounce
Lime juice	3/4 ounce
Bacardi Silver® Rum	1 1/2 ounces
Angostura® bitters (optional)	2 dashes
Club soda	To fill

Muddle mint, simple syrup, and lime juice together in a mixing glass. Add the remaining ingredients and shake with ice. Strain into a highball glass with fresh ice and top with club soda. Garnish with a fresh mint sprig.

SAZERAC

Ricard®	Splash
VS Cognac	1 ounce
Rye Whiskey	1 ounce
Simple syrup	1/2 ounce
Peychaud's® bitters	2 dashes
Angostura® bitters	2 dashes
Lemon peel	garnish

Fill two rocks glasses with ice. Splash the Ricard into one rocks glass, swirl and then pour it out. Add the remaining ingredients into the second rocks glass and stir. Strain the ingredients into the first chilled, seasoned rocks glass, and garnish with the lemon peel.

CAIPARINHA

Cachaça	2 ounces
1/2 lime quartered	
Superfine sugar or (1 oz simple syrup)	2 teaspoons

Fill a rocks glass with ice. In a glass mixer, muddle lime quarters with sugar for 15 seconds. Add cachaça and ice from the rock glass and shake well. Pour contents into a rocks glass and garnish with lime.

Polynesian-Tropicals

The Polynesian or "Tiki" bar culture in the U.S. began in the 1930s with the opening of Don the Beachcomber and Victor Bergeron's Trader Vic. The latter eventually became a worldwide chain with as many as 25 restaurants, which expanded the Polynesian/Tiki culture. Both restaurants claim to have invented the Mai Tai and a number of tropical drinks have since followed.

The Mai Tai, Piña Colada, Zombie, and Planter's Punch, are usually rum-based drinks with tropical fruit flavors such as pineapple, orange, or coconut, which add sweetness to the mix. Polynesian-tropicals are generally prepared using a blender or the speed-shake procedure and are decoratively garnished with combinations of a cherry, orange slice, or pineapple chunk.

POLYNESIAN-TROPICALS

MAI TAI

Sugar or simple syrup	1/2 ounce
Orange curaçao	1/2 ounce
Myer's® rum (dark)	1 ounce
Mount Gay® rum (gold)	1 ounce
Amaretto	1/2 ounce
Lemon mix	3 ounces

PIÑA COLADA

Coco Lopez®	1/2 ounce
Pineapple juice	3 ounces
Mount Gay® rum (gold)	2 ounces

PLANTER'S PUNCH

Grenadine	1/2 ounce
Lemon mix	1 ounce
Orange juice	3 ounces
White rum	1 ounce
Myer's® rum (dark)	1 ounce
Pineapple juice	1 ounce
Sugar or simple syrup	1/2 ounce

ZOMBIE

Grenadine	1/2 ounce
Light rum (bar)	1 ounce
Myer's® rum (dark)	1 ounce
Lemon mix	2 ounces
Orange juice	1 1/2 ounces
Orange curaçao	1 ounce

Non-alcoholic Cocktails and Mixed Drinks

Non-alcoholic cocktails or *"mocktails"* and alcohol-free alternatives are an important aspect of mixology. About 40% of the U.S. adult population does not consume alcohol. Designated drivers, abstainers from alcoholic beverages, and young people may want to take part in social occasions where others are enjoying alcoholic beverages. Diverse, quality, alcohol-free options must be available to them. The ever expanding options of bottled water, crafted soda, tea, juice, energy drinks, alcohol-free beer and crafted mocktails are sales opportunities not to be missed. Possibilities are endless and provide an opportunity for increasing beverage sales. The key is to create recipes and drinks with the same high standards as regular cocktails. Bartenders should use their imaginations and creativity to cater to this market.

NON-ALCOHOLIC COCKTAILS AND MIXED DRINKS

SHIRLEY TEMPLE

Ginger ale	6 ounces
Grenadine	1 ounce
Cherries	garnish

FLORIDA COCKTAIL

Grape juice	2 ounces
Orange juice	1 ounce
Lemon mix	2 ounces
Club soda	fill to 1/4 inch from the rim
Fresh mint leaves	garnish
Speed-shake	

PUSSYFOOT

Lemon mix	2 ounces
Orange juice	2 ounces
Rose's® Lime Juice	1 ounce
Grenadine	1/2 ounce
Pasteurized egg yolk	1 ounce
Orange slice and cherry	garnish
Shake	

Alcohol and the Law

The first liquor-control laws in America's English colonies became effective in 1733, when Georgia's governor prohibited the importation of hard liquor into that colony. Since that time, governments have passed a variety of liquor laws—some to control and deter the consumption of alcohol and others to raise money. Popularly known as "sin taxes," laws taxing such items as alcohol and tobacco are popular with legislators because they are not considered necessities.

Early Alcohol Laws

Shortly after the United States became an independent country, a tax on alcohol prompted the first confrontation between citizens and federal troops. The 1794 Whiskey Rebellion sent Pennsylvania farmers, who found it cheaper to transport alcohol than the grain used to make it, into the streets to protest a tax on spirits. Twenty years later, Indiana prohibited the sale of liquor on Sunday, and by 1833 more than 5,000 temperance groups with more than a million members lobbied for an outright ban on the sale of alcohol. A string of controls across the country, including Maine's 1846 prohibition law, made complete prohibition of the sale of alcoholic beverages an idea whose popularity would continue to grow.

Prohibition

On January 16, 1920, the Eighteenth Amendment, which banned the sale of liquor in the United States, became law.

Prohibition was a failure and turned many ordinary citizens into lawbreakers, paving the way for the development of organized crime, and costing the United States government approximately $1 billion each year in lost revenues and enforcement expenses. Experts estimate that about $36 billion spent for bootlegged and smuggled liquor traveled from the wallets of ordinary citizens into the pockets of criminals.

In the end, Americans opted for regulation over the expensive and largely ineffective Eighteenth Amendment. In 1933, the Twenty-first Amendment repealed Prohibition, setting up a climate for new regulations.

TTB (formerly the ATF)

Federal laws govern trade practices and the issuance of required permits, In 1972, the Bureau of Alcohol, Tobacco, and Firearms (ATF) received its charter to operate under the Department of the Treasury. However, regulatory supervisory changes were made when the *Alcohol and Tobacco Tax and Trade Bureau (TTB)* was established under the Homeland Security Act of 2002 when some of the enforcement functions of the ATF were shifted to the Department of Justice. The TTB's function is to collect taxes owed and to ensure that alcohol beverages are produced, labeled, advertised, and marketed in accordance to Federal law. For example, government regulations require that distilled spirits are bottled in similar containers with affixed Internal Revenue tax stamps. The stamp must span the crevice where the bottle cap ends and the bottle begins so that upon opening the bottle the stamp tears, but a portion of the stamp still remains affixed to the opened bottle. Failure to comply with this regulation may result in a fine of up to $10,000, or imprisonment of not more than five years, or both. Federal law prohibits the use of empty liquor bottles for any reason or the marrying of contents of two or more bottles of the same liquor.

- **Revenue collection**—The bureau collects revenues from all producers of beverage alcohol on the basis of proof gallons.
- **Consumer protection**—Alcoholic beverages must conform to the Standards of Identity and are produced, labeled, advertised, and marketed according to the Federal law.
- **Trade practices**—These practices promote voluntary compliance.

Producers pay excise taxes and retail dealers who sell alcoholic beverages also pay a special federal tax. When the tax is paid in full, the dealer is issued a special tax stamp for the class of business for which the tax is paid.

Legal Definitions

The TTB uses specific definitions to levy taxes on alcoholic beverages:

- **Alcohol**—A volatile, colorless liquid obtained through the fermentation of a liquid containing sugar.
- **Alcoholic beverage**—Any potable liquid containing from 0.5% to 75.5% ethyl alcohol by volume.
- **Spirit**—A potable alcoholic beverage obtained from the distillation of a liquid containing alcohol.
- *Proof* (**American method**)—The strength of a liquor, which was at one time called "gunpowder proof."

To test the strength of liquor, distillers used to pour it on gunpowder and throw a lighted match on it. If the liquor blazed, it was too strong. Liquor at the proper strength, mixed with the powder and slowly burned with a blue flame. The addition of 50% water produced a slow, steady flame. That strength was called "100 proof." Today, regulations apply the same scale on the following basis: Pure 100% alcohol is 200 proof, and 1 degree of proof is equal to 0.5% alcohol. Dividing the proof number by 2 yields the percentage of alcohol by volume. The term proof indicates the strength.

Conversely, the proof number is always twice the percentage of the alcohol in the beverage. The remainder of the content in the beverage includes distilled water, coloring, and flavoring components.

Proof Gallon Taxes

All alcoholic beverages, whether they are produced in the United States or imported, are subject to Internal Revenue taxes. Imported alcoholic beverages are also subject to customs' duties. The alcohol content of the beverage determines the tax rate. The standard one-gallon proof contains 100 proof, or 50%, alcohol. If a gallon contains 150 proof alcohol, it is taxed as 1.5 proof gallons. The trade term for a spirit of more than 100 proof is an overproof spirit.

A tax gallon is the measure used to determine how much tax is paid, according to the rate of taxation and/or duties, times the number of tax gallons of spirits. For beverages containing less than 100 proof alcohol, the tax is paid on the actual gallons.

The federal government taxes wines at different rates, ranging from $1.07 to $3.40 per gallon depending on the alcohol content and the degree and type of carbonation. The beer tax is $18.00 per 31 gallons and $0.05 cents on each 12-ounce can. The tax on distilled spirits is $13.50 per proof gallon. These taxes are paid by on-premise

and off-premise retailers, who must track the sale of each category and maintain written records that are subject to both TTB or local government audit.

Duties

Import duties are imposed in addition to the federal, state, and local excise taxes charged for alcoholic beverages. Imported spirits are therefore often more expensive than domestic varieties. Negotiated trade agreements can alter the amount of duties charged on imported alcoholic beverages. Wines, in particular, are commonly available from countries all over the world, especially Mexico, Canada, the Caribbean nations, European countries, and Australia. Fifty percent of the average retail price of a bottle of spirits consists of federal, state, and local taxes.

State Controls

With the repeal of Prohibition, the federal government turned over most alcoholic beverage sales control to the individual states. This has resulted in enormous differences in controls between states and even within states. State control of the sale of alcoholic beverages falls into two categories: open-license states and control states.

Open-License States

Open-license states grant licenses to private enterprises to operate as wholesalers of alcoholic beverages to both on- and off-premise retailers and to the retailers themselves. Strict rules may govern the manner in which both tiers of the distribution system operate. For example, tied house relationships, whereby the distributor operates or owns part interest in a retailer, may not exist. Most states also have local option laws that leave the decision to allow the sale of alcoholic beverages up to local communities.

In addition to these state controls, some states have "dry" communities to which it is illegal to transport alcoholic beverages from neighboring "wet" communities. Each state and municipality may also enforce the opening and closing hours for establishments that sell liquor. Provisions may be set with respect to the number of licenses permitted in a given area, and restrictions may be enforced concerning the sale of alcohol within a designated proximity from places of worship, schools, or hospitals.

Control States

Eighteen control states operate to varying degrees as the sole distributors of alcoholic beverages to on- and off-premise retailers. In some of these states, the state acts as the only off-premise outlet for liquor sold to consumers. In such cases, beer and certain wines may be sold through private enterprises, such as grocery stores. To prevent consumers or operators of bars and restaurants from purchasing alcoholic beverages across state lines, some control states require a special stamp or mark on each bottle to prove that the item was purchased legally within the state.

State Laws

Those who work in establishments that serve alcohol must be familiar with all the state laws governing the sale of alcoholic beverages. Failure to know the law can have serious consequences for the employer and the employee. Some consequences are legal; others are a matter of conscience, especially if innocent people are injured by someone who should not have been served alcohol.

Dram Shop Laws

For bars and restaurants and their personnel, *dram shop laws* are the most critical issue affecting the sale of alcoholic beverages. Dram shop laws originated in the nineteenth century in England and were first enacted in the United States in 1873. In states with dram shop laws, restaurants, bars, and their employees are held liable for illegal acts committed by patrons under the influence of alcohol served to them in the establishment. These laws are also known as *third-party liability laws.* Lawyers began using these laws in the mid-1980s to litigate civil actions. Many such suits resulted in unprecedented multimillion dollar awards.

Negligence Laws

Even in states that do not have dram shop laws, courts generally apply common law to alcohol-related cases. Basing their decisions on precedents, courts usually favor the victim over the persons who served or sold the liquor. Generally, in non-dram shop states, courts base their decisions on Alcohol Beverage Control (ABC) regulations, either because state laws were violated or because sellers or servers were negligent in serving alcohol to an obviously inebriated person or to a minor.

In addition to facing third-party liability and negligence laws, the operator of a restaurant, tavern, or bar; the employees of such an establishment; or the host of a private party may be subject to criminal liability. If convicted, these persons could receive prison sentences. The establishment and its employees can also face administrative liability, whereby the state or Alcohol Control Board can levy a fine or suspend or revoke a liquor license.

Drunken Driving Laws

The hope of preventing thousands of deaths caused by drunk drivers has encouraged many states to strengthen drunken driving laws. In these states, offenses that are commonly referred to as DWI, driving while intoxicated, or DUI, driving under the influence, are no longer treated lightly. These offenses are punishable under *per se* laws, dictating that a single piece of evidence, such as the results of a Breathalyzer™ test or the refusal to take such a test, is sufficient evidence to presume guilt.

The Impact of Laws on Industry

As we have seen, criminal, administrative, and civil sanctions exist for servers, managers, or owners of establishments who fail to make reasonable efforts to ensure that alcohol consumption occurs in a responsible and moderate fashion.

An establishment and its servers must be acquainted with all pertinent laws and regulations and must undergo alcohol awareness training to demonstrate that negligence has not occurred. Each server should know which persons cannot legally be served. These include anyone

- who is legally intoxicated or who would become intoxicated if served an alcoholic beverage.
- who is a known alcoholic.
- with a propensity toward alcoholism.
- who is legally under age.

All states mandate than only those persons who are 21 years of age or older may purchase or be served alcoholic beverages. Because forging identification has become easier with today's technology, establishments need to stay abreast of publications on identification issues, which are updated yearly.

As a precaution, a server should check the identification of anyone who looks younger than 30 years old. Some national chains have made it a policy to check the identification of all who purchase alcoholic beverages, regardless of age.

Legally acceptable forms of identification include:

- a state-issued driver's license with a photograph
- a state-issued identification card with a photograph
- a military identification card with a photograph
- a United States' passport.

An establishment's employees are not required to accept any identification issued outside the state in which the establishment is located. Some states, such as Rhode Island, require that employees have a "Minors Book" located at the bar. Anyone who presents proper identification but who appears underage or "illegal" for some reason must sign the book before being served. A good guide to follow is that if there is sufficient reason to question the legal age of a patron, politely refuse to serve that person any alcoholic beverage.

The Effects of Alcohol

Alcohol is a food product, but it is classified as an intoxicating drug that depresses the brain and other parts of the central nervous system. Although alcohol is fairly high in calories, it has little nutritional value. An ounce of pure alcohol has 210 calories; one ounce of whiskey (43% alcohol, or 86 proof) has 75 calories. A 12-ounce (355-ml) container of beer has between 120 and 210 calories. Although moderate consumption of alcohol, especially wine, may have some health benefits, long-term abuse will result in permanent damage to the liver, kidneys, and brain, as well as to the central nervous, digestive, and circulatory systems.

Intoxication/Absorption Rate Factors

Because alcohol requires no digestion, it is absorbed and transported by the bloodstream throughout the body in a very short time. A small amount enters the capillaries in the mouth even before the beverage is swallowed. About 20% of the remaining alcohol is quickly absorbed through the stomach lining. However, the presence of food in the stomach slows the absorption of alcohol because alcohol mixes with the stomach's contents and is digested along with the food.

During the initial stage of the digestive process, the "door" between the stomach and the small intestine, called the *pylorus valve,* generally remains closed, trapping food and alcohol in the stomach. Too much alcohol may cause a *pylorospasm,* in which the alcohol-sensitive pylorus valve prevents the food and alcohol from moving through the system.

Pylorospasms trap sufficient alcohol in the stomach to cause irritation and distress. The drinker may elect to stop drinking at this point because he or she feels ill when the stomach lining secretes excess amounts of hydrochloric acid. This process is a self-protective mechanism that can prevent the overconsumption of alcohol, but not all people recognize the symptoms.

When alcohol reaches the small intestine, the remaining 80% is absorbed into the bloodstream. The faster the alcohol is absorbed, the more likely the consumer is to become intoxicated. The higher the alcohol content of the beverage, the more quickly it is absorbed into the bloodstream. Alcohol mixed with carbonated beverages is absorbed faster than alcohol of the same proof mixed with fruit juice. Several other factors also influence the rate of absorption of alcohol, including the following:

- the rate of consumption
- the gender of the consumer
- the height, weight, and physical condition of the consumer
- the mood of the consumer
- the amount of food in the consumer's stomach
- the presence of medications, some of which can speed up the effects of alcohol.

Levels of Intoxication

Learning to recognize and understand the effects of alcohol will help servers determine whether to serve or continue to serve alcoholic beverages to a guest. The brain and other parts of the central nervous system are affected more quickly than are other organs of the body. When blood alcohol content is sufficient to cause intoxication, or drunkenness, it also impairs memory, motor control, and judgment. These behavioral clues can help determine when a patron has become intoxicated:

- **Loss of inhibitions**—An intoxicated person becomes talkative, relaxed, and overfriendly, and exhibits mood swings. Depending on how extreme his or her actions are, the person may fall into a happy category or one of pronounced excitement.

- **Loss of judgment**—An intoxicated person often exhibits erratic behavior. He or she may use foul language, become angry, or act impulsively. The person may be excited to the point of confusion.

- **Loss of reaction**—An intoxicated person may easily lose his or her train of thought. He or she may exhibit unfocused eyes, slurred speech, and unsteady hands.

- **Loss of coordination**—An intoxicated person may suffer loss of balance, drowsiness, and a lack of dexterity. When a drinker reaches this stage, he or she is approaching the fourth stage of intoxication.

Stages of Intoxication

The table below is based on the effects of alcohol consumption on a man weighing 150–160 pounds (68–73 kg). One drink represents 1 ounce (30 ml) of 100 proof distilled spirits, 3 ounces (90 ml) of sherry, 5 ounces (150 ml) of wine, or 12 ounces (355 ml) of beer. Note that a woman who weighs 120–130 pounds (54–60 kg) becomes intoxicated faster than a man of similar weight. This more rapid intoxication takes place because women generally have less water and more body fat than men. The higher rate of water in a man's body dilutes the alcohol, lowering the blood-alcohol level.

Industry Responsibilities

Although the food and beverage industry cannot be responsible for all the problems associated with excess alcohol consumption, servers and establishment operators can ensure that the behavior of staff members promotes responsible consumption of alcoholic beverages by:

- Checking identification as routine in every case in which there is doubt about a patron's age.
- Recognizing the signs of intoxication and refraining from serving anyone who has consumed too many drinks or who exhibits signs of intoxication.
- Declining to serve any customer who appears to have consumed excess alcohol elsewhere.
- Encouraging impaired customers to call for a cab, to contact a friend to get a ride home, or to offer to make the call for the patron, and persuading the customer to surrender the car keys when warranted.
- Observing responsible and reasonable standards in serving and consuming alcohol to set a good example for fellow employees and friends.

Stages of Intoxication

STAGE	DRINKS PER HOUR	BLOOD ALCOHOL	RATE TO METABOLIZE
Happy	1	0.02	Less than 1 hour **Loss of inhibitions:** talkative, relaxed
Excited	2	0.05	Two hours **Loss of judgment:** loud, boisterous, inappropriate remarks and behavior
Confused	4	0.10	Four hours **Loss of reactions:** slurred speech, staggering, mood swings, double vision, some loss of coordination
Stupor	8	0.20	Eight hours **Loss of coordination:** after 6 hours, still legally drunk; emotional, erratic behavior; inability to stand; loss of memory; barely conscious, approaching paralysis
Coma	1 pint	0.40–0.50	**Unable to metabolize:** comatose, and dangerously close to death; brain centers are anesthetized
Death		0.60–0.70	

CHAPTER
10

Enology

ΊT IS LITTLE WONDER *that the ancient Greek god Dionysus was known as the god of wine and ecstasy. Few beverages excite as many senses as does wine. Brilliant colors, inviting aromas, complex bouquets, subtle tastes and textures—the products of the winemaker's art —have made wine an integral part of ceremonies, and social and religious rituals, by enhancing well-prepared meals and cementing friendships. Today, science has also revealed the long-term health benefits of moderate wine consumption.*

Introduction to Wine

The simple definition of wine—the fermented juice of grapes—does little to explain why academics in such diverse fields as archeology, biology, chemistry, microbiology, geography, horticulture, sociology, economics, and medicine have all been fascinated with the study of wine. Perhaps the interest stems from the simple fact that from the vineyard to the table, wine is the perfect blend of art and science, a study of infinite variety and nearly endless permutations.

There are many species of grapes and thousands of varieties within each species. It is the Vitis vinifera species, however, that produces most wines. Of the 10,000 varieties of Vitis vinifera (the name means "wine bearing"), the wine market is concerned primarily with no more than 50 varieties. Because winemaking is both a science and an art form, however, the history of winemaking has been characterized by continual challenges for winemakers and growers alike to produce more complex wines.

The History of Wine

Winemaking is a natural phenomenon: grapes contain sugars that wild yeasts convert to ethyl alcohol. Winemakers today select with infinite care the varieties of grapes and the yeasts that ferment them into wines.

Until the nineteenth century, the history of wine making may be viewed as a struggle against spoilage. Wood inadvertently became an added flavor component in wine when the Romans adopted the same standard medium for transportation and storage used by the ancient Gauls of France for beer. Wood has certain anti-microbiological elements but without proper sanitation wines stored in wood can become both oxidized and affected by microorganisms such as acetobacter, which turn wine into vinegar.

Modern winemakers today, however, have little excuse for making faulty wines. The art and the science of grape growing and winemaking are based on centuries of experimentation and learning about conditions that make for good wines—and sometimes great ones.

Wine and religion Over the centuries, wine has been inextricably linked to religion. From the ancient Greeks and Romans to the Jewish and Christian traditions, wine has been associated with mystical  and religious experiences because of the symbolism of the annual rebirth of the vine as well as the psychological effects of wine.

The earliest years The earliest traces of winemaking may date back to 7500 B.C. in Jiahu, China, although these wines were produced from native Chinese species, while the earliest traces of vinifera date back to approximately 5600 B.C. in the Caucasus region. By 4000 B.C. winemaking had spread to Mesopotamia, Babylon, and Egypt. At that time the Egyptians also began the practice of labeling wines to indicate the place of origin, the grape, the name of the winemaker, and the vintage.

Written references to grapes appear in the Bible, which notes that Noah planted a vineyard after the great flood, which is said to have occurred in about 5600 B.C. When the Phoenicians or Minoans introduced winemaking to Greece circa 2000 B.C., its sale created wealth with which the Greeks built their great civilization. See Figure 10-1. The Greeks spread vineyards and winemaking along the Mediterranean coast including today's Greece, Italy, France, Spain, Turkey, and the islands such as Sicily.

Winemaking technology continued to develop under the Roman Empire. Winemakers began understanding wine production and the relationships between varieties and soil, climate, aging, and storing temperatures. Later, the Romans introduced winemaking to the Gauls (modern-day French). Between 350 A.D. and 1200 A.D., some monastic orders, particularly the Benedictines, Carthusians, and Cistercians, preserved and improved winemaking knowledge in Europe. In the process, they cultivated vineyards to produce wine for sacramental and medicinal purposes, and to generate income.

Trade expands winemaking As world exploration and trade expanded in the 1400s, Europeans looked for ways to preserve wine during long trade voyages. Dutch and English traders learned to fortify wines from France, Portugal, and Spain by adding brandy to stabilize them for sea voyages. The Germans are said to be the first to add sulfur to wine to prevent spoilage. Although this method continues to be widely utilized to this day, it is used more judiciously. Exploration and trade also introduced winemaking to the Americas, Australia, and South Africa when Europeans began to settle in the New World.

FIGURE 10-1
A clay amphora used as a wine vessel.

Technology advances winemaking In the mid-1600s, glass that was strong enough for commercial bottling was developed by the English, although these bottles were not widely used until the 1700s in Europe's wine-making regions. With the increased use of bottles, the use of cork stoppers became more commonplace. See Figure 10-2. These developments contributed considerably to the popularity of dry wines and the need for better quality control and the marketing of brands.

During the 1700s, Dom Pérignon, cellar master at the monastery in Hautvilliers at Épernay, France, made significant advances in the science of winemaking. He began to understand the different characteristics of varieties; the role of *terroir;* the *cuvée,* or blending of different varieties; and the role of temperature in fermentation and cellaring.

In the years following the French Revolution (1789–1815), monastic orders lost their landholdings, and their vineyards were distributed to supporters of the Revolution. The Napoleonic Code of Law granted equal inheritance rights to heirs, resulting in ever-smaller landholdings. *Négociants,* or merchants, took on an increasingly important role of not only distributing, but also "raising" the wines purchased from the owners of these small vineyards.

In 1851, *oidium,* a powdery mildew fungus, devastated many of France's vineyards, particularly in Bordeaux. Growers learned to use sulfur and lime to combat the problem, and this solution is still used today.

By 1855, wine brokers played a pivotal role in creating a list of the best wine producers for the *Paris Exposition Universelle.* The list ultimately became the foundation for the Bordeaux wine "Classification of 1855," which rated the 61 best wines, primarily of the Médoc region, and the 26 best Sauternes dessert wines. The list survives nearly unchanged to this day.

The problem of wine spoilage, however, continued to plague winemakers. In 1862, Napoleon III invited Louis Pasteur, France's premier scientist, to tackle the problem. Pasteur soon discovered that bacteria present in wine, especially *acetobacter* (the organism that turns wine to vinegar), could be controlled if the bacteria were deprived of light and oxygen. He suggested several solutions: fill wine bottles as full as possible; use colored glass to deprive bacteria of light; store wine bottles on their sides so that corks remain moist and swell to keep oxygen from seeping into the bottles; and store wine in a cool environment to retard bacterial growth. Pasteur also developed a pasteurization process for wine, which would later be used primarily to treat milk.

Biological challenges In 1862 the European wine industry faced its biggest challenge when *Phylloxera (now classified as Daktulosphaira vitifoliae),* a microscopic pest, was accidentally introduced to vineyards in France through the importation of American vines by the French merchant Borty to the Rhône Valley. By 1880, *Phylloxera* infestations had become so widespread that the pest was known as the "Blight of Europe." It was not until the 1890s that a solution was found. It is through the efforts of Jules-Emile Planchon and C.V. Riley of Missouri, who grafted the *Vitis vinifera* vines to native American *vitis* species, (particularly *riparia* and the St. George *rupestris* rootstock), that the vines achieved a resistance to this plight. See Figure 10-3. Unfortunately, *Phylloxera* remained a recurring problem, which devastated California vineyards once again in the 1990s. Of the major wine producing regions, only Chile, Cyprus, and Washington State have remained free of the pest and do not graft their vinifera scion onto American rootstock.

FIGURE 10-2
One of the earliest versions of a glass bottle

FIGURE 10-3
Grafting vinifera onto American rootstock protects the vine from Phylloxera.

Hybridizing vitis species to combat *Phylloxera* has proven to be relatively disappointing because of the inferior quality of most hybrids. A *hybrid* is a cross between a vitis vinifera and an American species, for example. Only a few hybrid varieties, notably Seyval Blanc and Vidal Blanc for whites, and Chambourcin and Maréchal Foche for reds, are still grown, particularly in New England and in Mid-Western states due to their hardiness and their ability to survive severe winters.

Interaction between Europe and North America resulted in another imported blight that attacked Europe's vines. When grafting began to enjoy success, huge quantities of American rootstock were imported to Europe. With them came downy mildew, a plague that weakened the vines, reduced the crops, and killed 30% of France's vines outright. It took four years for growers to learn that spraying the vines with copper sulfate could prevent this mold. The spray is still used today.

In 1920 the wine industry was again suppressed in the United States, this time with the enactment of the *Volstead Act,* which made the production for sale of alcoholic beverages illegal or prohibited. *Prohibition* devastated most wineries. Only the limited production of sacramental or medicinal wines was permitted. However, a legal loophole allowed citizens to make up to 200 gallons of wine per year for home consumption. The planting of high-yielding table grape varieties doubled grape production. When Prohibition was repealed in December of 1933, it left a legacy of second-rate wines, which would last for over 30 years. Prohibition also led to the eventual varietal labeling of wines. When U.S. producers first began to market their wines, they were unable to label them by variety as they were for the most part made from inferior blends. Later, most wines were labeled using 14 different *semi-generic labels,* which are still used today: Californian Chablis or Californian Champagne are such examples. See Figure 10-4. In the 1950s, in an attempt to differentiate better wines, producers in California began to label wines varietally.

Improved quality control During the 1930s, France focused on improving the quality of wines after re-establishing its vineyards. The country developed the *Appellation d'Origine Contrôlée (AOC or AC)* system, which was adopted from the regulatory governing system for the production of Roquefort cheese. This system delimited the name of a wine to a region, and determined the varieties best suited to the particular environment of that region. Thus, the concept of *terroir* was born. The system recognized that in addition to the soil, the complete ecosystem of an area, including climate, wind, temperature, rainfall, sunlight, and topographical features, all affected a wine's distinctive quality.

American wines improve Ernest and Julio Gallo preserved American wine consumption from the 1930s to the 1960s by producing well-made "table wine" that was readily accessible to the American table. In the 1950s fine winemaking was again recognized as feasible in California as a result of the action of a few creative vintners.

James Zellerback, for example, who replicated the details of a Burgundian cellar down to the type of oak used for aging, developed a Chardonnay that was reminiscent of Burgundy's best white wine. Inspired by his success, Joseph Heitz and Robert Mondavi visited Europe and came away impressed with the importance of the use of French oak for barrel aging. American winemakers began to focus on planting top-quality vines. Robert Mondavi can certainly be credited with the renaissance of the production of fine wine in California, and for achieving world-wide recognition for Napa as a premier wine growing region. During this same period of time the University of California-Davis School of Oenology became a world leader in the study of viticulture and winemaking.

A blind wine tasting held in Paris, France in 1976, resulted in French judges rating some American wines as superior to some of the best that France had to offer. Consequently, a "grape rush" occurred, especially in Napa Valley. This pivotal event, now known in the wine world as the "Judgment in Paris", also resulted in wine producers from around the world believing that they too could produce world class wines. Tax advantages inspired heavy investments in vineyards, and led to the creation of the more than 400 wineries now operating in Napa Valley alone. Europeans and Australians have made major investments in such American wineries.

Beginning in 1980, certain geographic areas became identified as *American Viticultural Areas (AVA)* as a result of the concept and centrality of place or *terroir*. This designation, however, does not guarantee quality as does an Appellation of Origin. Some AVAs are geographically huge making the centrality of place somewhat meaningless. The first AVA was the Augusta AVA in Missouri, but it was the Napa Wine Growers Association that was actually able to make its appellation a critical marketing tool in the U.S. consumer's mind. Other regions witnessed the marketing advantages of developing their AVAs, and in 2009 there were approximately 200 AVAs in the U.S.

When *Phylloxera* reasserted itself in vines grafted on AxR1 rootstock that offered insufficient resistance to the pest due to its partial vinifera genes, most California vines had to be replanted in the 1990s. This disaster allowed producers to apply recently acquired knowledge to plant more appropriate clones and to realign vineyards to optimize sunlight and spacing more efficiently and more densely—all contributing to improved quality.

Despite the problems that periodically surface, areas around the world have dedicated their resources to viticulture in support of the belief that great wines are first created in the vineyard. New World wines have made great inroads in fine wine markets, offering consumers ever improving quality. Concurrently, there has been a major shift throughout the world from consuming "table" wines to enjoying premium and super-premium wines. One of the primary marketing messages of New World wine producers for the past 30 years has been an emphasis on the fruit intensity of their wines rather than a focus on the "earthy" and more "minerally" characteristics found in Old World wines. This division is not as clear at the premium quality level of wines, because Old World wines blur the lines even further with the creation of their more 'fruit forward' wines. Although consumption in the U.S. remains low at almost 2.5 gallons per adult, in comparison to 15 gallons per adult in France, there is excitement among U.S. consumers who are now discovering wines from around the world.

FIGURE 10-4

Examples of semi-generic California labels

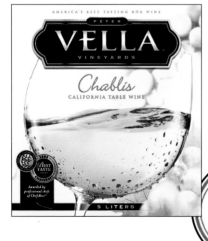

Winemaking

The critical elements in producing good wines are the grapes, the climate, the viticulture or growing conditions, and the vinification or the process of winemaking.

The Grape Variety

The essence of wine is the grape used to produce it. A thorough knowledge of the categories, the composition, and the varieties of grapes is essential to the winemaker's art.

Grape categories Grapes are generally divided into four categories: Native American *Vitis* species such as Labrusca; two subdivisions of *Vitis vinifera;* and a hybrid, or cross between a native American species and a *vinifera.*

- Native American *Vitis* North American wild grapes are overly acidic and typically lack the balance or subtlety of *vinifera.* They commonly have a "foxy" flavor that many associate with Concord grape juice. Wines made from these species do not generally pair well with food, although the Norton variety with its very dark color and lack of 'foxiness' is an exception.

- *Vitis vinifera* grapes, typified by varieties such as the Thompson Seedless, also known as Sultana in Europe, are primarily used as table grapes or for raisins because of their undistinguished quality, which makes them unsuitable for fine wines. Both in Europe and the United States, winemakers blend these grapes into table or jug wines, although this category is declining in importance.

- *Vitis vinifera* grapes that produce fine wines, on the other hand, have a distinct character that makes them the focus of the winemaker's art. These varieties are also highlighted in this chapter.

- French-American hybrid grapes generally produce less satisfactory wines than *vinifera* varieties, though some, such as Seyval Blanc and Vidal Blanc, may be made into palatable, if not distinctive, wines.

Grape composition The well-known adage "fine wine is created in the vineyard" recognizes the pivotal role of grape varieties in creating a fine wine. The grape captures the sun's energy, stores it as sugar, and retains the water and minerals absorbed by the vine's root system. In exceptional growing years, wines are made in which the alcohol, sweetness, acidity, and *tannins* (a chemical compound found in grape skins), stems, and *pips* (seeds), are perfectly balanced and the flavors are fully developed. The key to fine wine is always balance—and balance begins with perfectly balanced grapes. See Figure 10-5.

Grapes consist of 70%–85% water, 15%–30% sugar and extracts, 0.3%–1.8% acids, and 0%–0.2% tannins. By the time grapes are fermented, the resulting wine has developed more than 300 organic compounds, of which many are volatile aromatic compounds with distinct odors.

Aromas refer to fragrances derived from the grape itself, and include compounds found in all fruits. Bouquets refer to those fragrances that result from fermentation and aging. These sometimes take years to develop as the wine slowly evolves and changes in chemical composition.

FIGURE 10-5

Every part of the grape contributes to the flavor and aroma of the wine.

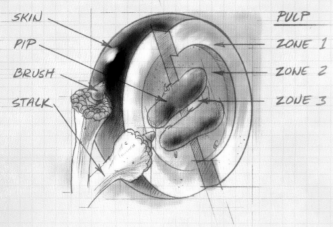

When grapes ferment into wine, the fermentation process creates alcohol from sugar stored in the grape. If the sugars are completely fermented, the wine is dry. If the sugars are not completely fermented, the wine retains varying degrees of sweetness and may be described as off-dry to very sweet. In addition, ethanol, the main form of alcohol produced by fermentation, is perceived by humans as sweet, so that wines high in alcohol but without residual sugars seem to be a little sweet.

In red wines, tannins and phenolics found in the grape's skins, stems, and pips are important to the wine's balance and mouthfeel. Tannins vary in **astringency,** creating a chalky "dried-out" feeling in the mouth to a very spicy and harsh taste. They provide significant textural components and act as a preservative in red wine. In white wines, tannins are generally negligible because the skins, stems, and seeds from which tannins are derived are removed very early in the winemaking process, although wood or oak tannins can be a factor, especially with oak aged Chardonnays. The acid component in wine not only provides balance but also allows wine to age well. Several acids—tartaric, malic, lactic, and succinic—are found in wine, each with unique characteristics.

Although the very acidic tasting tartaric acid is uncommon in most other fruits and vegetables, it is important in grapes, and therefore in wines. Because the salt in tartaric acid (potassium bitartrate), is only partially soluble in alcohol, it may precipitate from the wine. Crystals of potassium bitartrate are sometimes present on the cork or are found floating in the wine. The crystals look like glass, but they are not harmful; in fact, as a by-product of winemaking, they are sold for culinary use as cream of tartar.

The tart or acidic taste of malic acid, which is also found in green apples such as Granny Smiths, may also be detected in wine. Malic acids are partially or fully converted to lactic acid in wines that undergo malolactic fermentation. Almost all red wines undergo this secondary bacterialogical fermentation, which reduces the overall perception of the wine's acidity, making it seem "softer." Citric acid is rare in wine unless it is used for acidifying inexpensive bulk wine. Succinic acid is present in small amounts in grapes and is a byproduct of fermentation. It is mostly significant because it binds to other molecules to form esters to provide a greater concentration of flavors. Acids are, however, important to wine because they give it liveliness, and balance the alcohol and/or sugars.

Grape Varieties

The world of wine owes much of its variety to the genetic instability of *vitis vinifera,* the "wine vine." More than 10,000 identified varieties, and hundreds of different clones of these varieties, have resulted from this instability. Most wine connoisseurs, however, are primarily interested in only 50 or so of these varieties, which are divided into white and black grape varieties. Most wines produced in the New World are sold using varietal names—those that identify the wine by the variety from which the wine is made. Old World wines may be made from essentially the same grape variety, although their names are most often reflective of the geographic region or appellation where they are grown rather than on the grape variety. This is because the characteristics of the soil, moisture, temperature, and orientation have profound effects on the grapes of each region. A wine labeled *Puligny-Montrachet,* for example, is a Chardonnay made in Burgundy, France. In the United States the wine is simply labeled *Chardonnay.* However, due to pressure from the world market, Europeans are more apt to use varietal labeling to support the appellation name.

White Grape Varieties

Applied to grapes, the term *white* has a specialized meaning. White grapes are any light-skinned grapes that range from pale green to gold and even pink. White wines differ from red wines because they lack the anthocyanins or pigmented tannins found in the skins, and the stems and pips of black grapes, in some cases. White wines can also be fermented from black grapes if the juice does not come in extended contact with the skins. There are white and red Zinfandel wines, for example, but both are made from the same black grape.

Chardonnay Growers are particularly fond of the Chardonnay grape because it is so malleable and adaptable to different climates. The classic Old World model of wine making is used for white Burgundies such as Chablis, Montrachet, Meursault, and Pouilly-Fuissé. These wines have a moderate to high acidity, a dryness with apple or melon aromas, and vanilla and buttery notes when aged in oak. They can develop enormous complexity with bottle age.

New World wines made from Chardonnay tend to have higher alcohol levels and flavors with hints of sweetness; more peach and tropical nuances; more oak-derived notes such as coconut; and lower acidity, which may result in their somewhat reduced ability to age.

Sauvignon Blanc The principal white grape of Bordeaux and the eastern Loire Valley, Sauvignon Blanc makes a clean, dry, intense, aromatic white wine with a herbaceous, mineral-like character. In fact, the name *Sauvignon* comes from the French word *sauvage,* or "wild." Sauvignons from South Africa often have characteristics similar to those of Old World grapes. Sauvignon Blancs are frequently blended with Sémillons to mellow the tart, herbal character of Sauvignon Blanc—a practice that is common in Bordeaux, France, as well as in other locations such as California and Australia.

New Zealand Sauvignon Blancs have their grapefruit acidity balanced by the richness of a higher alcohol content, while retaining their intense herbaceous flavors, and tropical guava notes. In California, wine produced from Sauvignon Blanc is often referred to as Fumé Blanc, especially if oak aged, although the wines do not have a smoky character. California Sauvignon Blanc wines are more diverse than in the past: many are aged in oak and often have a more floral and a softer fig or melon character, while others have a more New Zealand clean dry fruit and herbaceous character with a high acidity.

Some Chilean wines labeled *Sauvignon Blanc* were actually made from Sauvignon Vert or Sauvignasse grapes, a variety that is less herbal and unrelated to Sauvignon Blanc. Most of these Chilean vineyards, however have now been replanted with Sauvignon Blanc, and offer both a New World and Old World style as do the wines of South Africa.

Riesling Often identified as the most noble of the white grapes, the Riesling grape can produce wines with a searing acidity that is balanced by a residual sweetness, delicate rose aromas, and notes of peaches, apricots, and melons. These qualities, coupled with a Riesling's often low alcohol content when made into wine, are responsible for this grape's light body, delicacy, and transparency.

Produced in the classic regions of Germany such as Mosel, Riesling can develop mineral or earthy notes balanced by a delicate sweetness. Rieslings from the Alsace region of France are fuller-bodied than those from Germany, northern Austria, New York, and the Clare or Eden Valleys of Australia, which are light-bodied but complex. This is perhaps because Rieslings adapt well to the cooler growing sites that these locations offer. The Rieslings grown in warmer regions in Australia and California, and those from Washington State and Oregon, are generally softer and slightly fuller, sometimes with more diffuse flavors. Riesling is one of the most versatile wines for pairing, complementing foods as diverse as smoked, cured or salty cuisine, as well as spicy Asian dishes.

Chenin Blanc Old World wines made from Chenin Blanc are vibrant, complex, long-lived, and shimmering in their acidity. These wines include the great wines from Vouvray, Savennières, and Saumur. In the Loire Valley of France, these grapes are fermented to varying degrees of sweetness, from bone-dry to lusciously sweet, to balance their high acidity.

In California, Chenin Blanc was once the most widely planted classic grape variety, but it has now been supplanted by Chardonnay. Chenin Blanc is grown for volume in the warm climate of California's Central Valley producing indistinct bulk wines. In South Africa, where it is also known as *Steen,* Chenin Blanc makes up 20% of the country's grape harvest. When compared with Chenin Blancs made from grapes grown in the Loire Valley of France, wine from South Africa reflects a broad spectrum of styles, although generally characterized by less acidity and with a distinct perfumed and honeyed character.

Gewürztraminer A pink-skinned native grape of Germany and Alsace, Gewürztraminer produces particularly aromatic and full-bodied white wines. The name perfectly describes the character of the grape. *Gewürz* in German means "spiced" and the wine made from these grapes has slightly tannic spicy notes. *Traminer* identifies the older grape variety from which the Gewürztraminer mutated. Wine tasters use such words as lychee nuts, gingerbread, honey, and musk to describe the flavors of wines made from these grapes, but it is their scents of jasmine and roses that make them some of the most recognized wines in the world.

The very best Gewürztraminers grow in Alsace, where the region's fine, crisp autumns produce late-picked grapes that make wines of a low acidity and a mouthfilling viscous quality with a hint of bitterness and spicy notes. Germany also produces delicious products. One of only a few white wines with a slightly bitter finish, Gewürztraminer may be dry if produced in Austria, or off-dry when produced in Germany, California, Washington State, and Southeastern New England.

Sémillon A golden grape variety from southwest France, Sémillon is one of the principal varieties produced in Bordeaux's sweet wine-producing communes. This grape plays two roles in winemaking: one as the star and the other as an understudy. For Sauternes—those rich, complex dessert wines counted among the world's most long-lasting unfortified wines—Sémillon is the star. It produces luscious, richly honeyed wines with perfectly balanced sweetness, acidity, and alcohol, partly because its thin skin makes it particularly susceptible to *Botrytis cinerea,* or "noble rot." In its supporting role, Sémillon is blended with Sauvignon Blanc, particularly in Bordeaux and in California. In Australia, Sémillon is blended with Chardonnay, to improve the balance of both the varieties.

Sémillon plays quite another role in Australia, however, especially in the Lower Hunter Valley. Hunter Valley Sémillon wines are light, acidic, dry, and unoaked, but they age very well. After about five years, this variety develops into rich wines with an intensely honeyed bouquet and an almost orange color.

Pinot Gris A natural mutation of Pinot Noir, Pinot Gris grapes come in colors as varied as the strikingly different flavors of the wines made from them. Pinot Gris (gray pinot) grapes can be bluish to silver, mauve-pink, or a gray or ash yellow. Depending on where they are grown, they produce very different wines mainly because of their different levels of alcohol and acidity. In Italy the grapes are called Pinot Grigio, and the wine is generally crisp and light.

By contrast, the Pinot Gris of Alsace, once known as Tokay-Pinot Gris, produces rich, somewhat spicy and fuller-bodied wines. In Germany, the variety is called *Grauburgunder* or *Ruländer,* and the wines have a broader flavor.

The Pinot Gris of the New World, particularly in Oregon, produces wines with flavors that some tasters compare to spice cake and pears. High quality Pinot Gris are also produced in the Russian River Valley, Sonoma Coast, Napa, and Monterey.

Viognier Viognier originated in the Rhône Valley of France, and although close to obscurity until recently, it found its best expression in the appellations of Condrieu and Château Grillet. It is planted in many different AVAs in California and has found impressive expressions in Virginia. Viognier has many characteristics of Chardonnay in that it is somewhat full-bodied, has good acidity, and is malleable. Wines produced from this variety are described as elegant and exotic, with hints of honeysuckle or musky fruit and a smooth texture. Without oak, it has distinctive floral and peach aromas with a nutty almond finish.

Muscat Muscat is the many-hued grape that Pliny the Elder once called "the grape of the bees" for its attractive aroma. With four major clones in its family tree, the variety has grown around the Mediterranean Sea for centuries. Most Muscats thrive in relatively hot climates such as those of Greece, Morocco, Sicily, and Sardinia, where they are made into sweet or semi-sweet wines with generally low alcohol content and a pronounced taste of the grape. In Italy, Muscat is the grape of choice for sparkling Asti.

In Alsace, however, the Muscat Blanc à Petits Grains and Muscat Ottonel branches of the family tree produce fresh and fruity wines that are always fermented to dryness. In Australia, the Muscat Gordo Blanco (most often times called the Muscat of Alexandria) is used to make "liqueur Muscats." Californian Andrew Quady produces a number of Muscat-based dessert wines, particularly in the fortified style of a French V*in Doux Naturel* such as Beaumes-de-Venise.

Palomino Palomino grapes yield a neutral-tasting wine that oxidizes easily because of its low acidity. The variety grows prolifically in hot climates and is the grape used to make sherry in Spain.

Ugni Blanc Ugni Blanc or Trebbiano originated in Italy and is the most widely-planted white grape in both France and Italy. It is the basis for Cognac and Armagnac in France, as well as for traditional balsamic vinegars in Italy.

Muscadet Although the variety is technically called Melon de Bourgogne, it derives its name from the region of the Loire Valley closest to the Atlantic where it thrives—an area called Muscadet de Sèvre-et-Maine. The wine is frequently allowed to remain on the *lees* sediment formed during fermentation until the wine is bottled. Wine made from Muscadet develops a more defined and refreshing character with a lively spritz. Such a wine would be labeled *sur lie* (on the lees) and is particularly suitable to serve with seafood.

Albariño (Alvarinho) is a thick-skinned grape variety that is particularly adapted to damp climates. Some versions of the wines made from Albariño, principally those grown in northwest Spain (Rías Baixas) and Portugal, are characterized by delicate floral aromas and high acidity. In other versions, the wines are fuller bodied and have a greater alcohol content. Albariño is one of the few Spanish wines sold as a varietal.

Grüner Veltliner Grüner Veltliner is Austria's most planted wine grape. The variety has also spread to other areas of Eastern Europe. Although some wines produced from this grape are quite simple, those from the best growing regions are complex with tropical fruit notes and high acidity to balance the high alcohol content.

Pinot Blanc Pinot Blanc is derived from Pinot Noir and has characteristics similar to those of Chardonnay, although the wines made from this variety are generally not as complex in flavor, aroma, or texture. There are notable exceptions from Alsace and Germany.

Black Grape Varieties

Just as "white" grape varieties are not really white, but rather green, or yellow; "black" grape varieties are not really black, and their colors may range from red to purple, to deep blue violet. They do share one important characteristic: black grapes are necessary to produce red wines because these wines derive their color from maceration with the skins.

Pinot Noir Pinot Noir is a difficult grape to grow successfully in the necessary cool growing regions, but it is responsible for France's fine red Burgundies and many Champagne wines. Connoisseurs believe that Pinot Noir produces among the finest red wines in the world. The wines are more delicate and have lower tannins and a higher acidity than varieties such as Cabernet Sauvignon. Burgundies have aromas of cherries, raspberries, mint, and herbs, but New World Pinot Noirs have more baked cherry and floral aromas. With bottle aging, the wines develop distinct earthy bouquets of leather, mushrooms, and game.

While Pinot Noir has long found a home in Germany and Austria where it is known as Spätburgunder, it was generally very light in color and body with a high acidity and a frequently fermented off-dry. Due in no small measure to global warming, some of the world's best Pinot Noirs are now being produced in Germany where they have fuller body and deeper color and might easily be mistaken for a great growth from Burgundy.

The legendary silky quality of Pinot Noir has also made it a world traveler. In the late 1960s and 1970s, Pinot Noir became the wine star of Oregon due to the pioneering efforts of producers such as David Lett. In the 1980s, growers in the Russian River Valley, Carneros, and Santa Barbara, California, took advantage of cool growing areas to produce notable Pinot Noirs. The film 'Sideways' also put Pinot Noir in the spotlight in the U.S. and its sales increased significantly early in the 21st century. By the 1990s, New Zealand growers were also planting Pinot Noir grapes, and by 1997 the variety overtook Cabernet as the region's most-planted black grape. New Zealand Pinot Noirs, especially those from Otago, Marlborough, and Martinborough have won world-wide acclaim.

Cabernet Sauvignon Cabernet Sauvignon, a small dark purple grape that Sotheby's describes as "the noblest variety of Bordeaux," produces satiny, rich, and complex wines with proper barrel and bottle aging. Proper aging is important because the fruit's small size gives Cabernet a high ratio of skin to pulp to potentially produce a very astringent young wine. With aging, however, Cabernet's acidity allows it to mature into complex wines with blackberry, black currant, cassis, plum, mint, violet, roasted bell pepper, eucalyptus, and cedar bouquets. When less fully ripe, Cabernet Sauvignon makes wines with a more vegetable-like character.

The most notable Cabernet Sauvignon-based wines in the Old World come from the Médoc growers of Margaux, St.-Julien, Pauillac, and St.-Estèphe, in Bordeaux. In the New World, California growers, particularly in Rutherford and Oakville AVAs in Napa, and the Alexander Valley in Sonoma County, are producing world-class Cabernets. Today Cabernet Sauvignon is widely grown in Italy, Spain, California, Washington State, Chile, and Australia. In the Médoc region of France, Cabernet is frequently blended with Merlot and Cabernet Franc to achieve mellowing and balance. Similar blends in California are sometimes called Meritage if Cabernet Sauvignon does not represent a legally required minimum percentage of 75%.

Merlot Merlot—the name means "little blackbird"—is a deep blue cousin to Cabernet Sauvignon. Merlot is the predominant variety grown in the Bordeaux region of France, especially in St. Émilion and Pomerol. Merlot, when fully ripe, produces textures that are softer and smoother than Cabernet, with plum and blackberry character. The bouquets are more buttery and creamy, and the wine has cocoa and earthy flavors. Merlot is frequently blended with Cabernet to moderate Cabernet's astringency, particularly in Bordeaux. Because of Merlot's ripe and less tannic profile, it became a fad variety in the 1990s and is frequently offered in restaurants by the glass. Merlot responds well to heavier clay soils and is easier to ripen in cooler climates, so the variety has also become popular in Long Island's North Fork and in the south-eastern part of Washington state, where it produces some exceptional wines. Chile also makes exceptional Merlot, especially with grapes from the Rapel Valley, although much of the wine labeled Merlot in the past was made from a closely related variety called Carmenère, which gives the wine a different profile and an almost licorice taste.

Cabernet Franc Cabernet Franc is a parent plant of both Cabernet Sauvignon and Merlot, and is the most-commonly planted grape in the Anjou-Touraine region of the Loire Valley. It is also found to a lesser extent in Bordeaux, especially on the right bank of the Gironde River. Particularly suited to cooler, inland climates, these grapes ripen about a week earlier than the Cabernet Sauvignon variety.

Cabernet Franc grapes produce wines that are generally lighter in color, lower in tannins, and slightly more aromatic, with hints of violets, blackberries, and licorice. As New World winemakers follow the Bordeaux recipe of blending with Cabernet Sauvignon, Cabernet Franc grapes are being planted in limited numbers in Australia and New Zealand.

Syrah (Shiraz) Syrah (Shiraz) is an old, black variety of grapes, grown in the northern Rhône region of France, which produces rich, tannic fruits. This smaller-berried grape generally contains more phenolics, which along with anthocyanins, makes Syrah a wine that benefits from long aging in oak and in the bottle. The best French Syrah wines are from Northern Rhône appellations such as Côte Rôtie.

Richly aromatic with hints of black pepper, green olive, violets, and black currants, Syrah also forms the basis for Australia's finest red wines and has been Australia's most-planted variety, perhaps because the variety thrives in warmer climates. Recently, Australian winemakers have blended Shiraz with Cabernet Sauvignon.

Because of its recent surge in popularity, many vintners are producing Syrah in the cool Santa Rita Hills of Santa Barbara and in the Napa Valley, as well as in the warmer regions of Mendocino and Sonoma County. Washington state has also developed some of the U.S.' finest Syrah-based wines.

Gamay Gamay is a plump grape with a characteristic cherry and raspberry aroma, which is grown principally in the southern Burgundy region of Beaujolais. For the most part, simple and fruity, wines made from the Gamay grape tend to be light and fresh, especially when vinified using carbonic maceration, which gives the wine fruity, almost bubble gum, banana, and mint aromas. This style of wine is generally at its best when young. Top quality Cru Beaujolais becomes more similar to good Burgundian Pinot Noir when bottle aged.

Grenache (Garnacha) Grenache (Garnacha) is grown primarily in the southern Rhône Valley of France. The basis for many of the renowned Châteauneuf-du-Pape wines, it is also one of the principal varieties used in Spain's Rioja wines.

Grenache earned much of its reputation as the primary grape used in the high alcohol, dry Tavel rosé wines. Grenache has a floral and white pepper profile along with olive and licorice aromas. Grenache is also found in southeastern Australia and in Monterey County, California, where it is frequently blended with other varieties.

Tempranillo Tempranillo is the key variety in many of Spain's wines. It has good color, attractive cherry and strawberry flavors, moderate acidity, and silky tannins. It derives a spicy, leathery and tobacco leaf bouquet from its adaptability to long-term American oak barrel aging. Its expression reflects the *terroir* in which it is grown, which is now in almost all regions of Spain. It is also one of the most widely planted varieties in Portugal, where it is known as Tinto Roriz. There are a few notable plantings in California's Sierra Foothills and in Oregon.

Zinfandel Zinfandel, according to DNA testing, originated from the Croatian Crljenak (pronounced sirl-yen-knock) Kaštelanski, and is the same variety of grape as the Italian *Primitivo*, which may itself have been imported from the United States. In the United States, Zinfandel grapes were first grown on the East Coast and were then brought to California. Wine made from this grape was hailed as California's claret. The variety produces its best fruits if the growing season is warm, not hot, and the vines are not allowed to overproduce. Producing wines from Zinfandel grapes is not easy. The compact bunches ripen unevenly, leaving a narrow window for harvesting. The best red Zinfandels are dry, acidic, alcoholic wines that are balanced by ripe sweet- or dried-fruit character with fresh tobacco and spice notes. They are ideal accompaniments to barbecues and roast turkey. In California, this formerly predominant variety of grape, has been used for making white Zinfandels.

Sangiovese Sangiovese is Italy's most famous grape, and is so ancient that its name translates to "blood of Jove." It is responsible for Italy's noted Tuscan wines—Chianti, Vino Nobile di Montepulciano, and Brunello di Montalcino. Although the variety's quality varies from year to year because of its slow, late ripening and fluctuations in the weather, Sangiovese has good acidity and makes a good food wine.

Italian immigrants brought Sangiovese to the New World, but it wasn't until the 1980s and 1990s that Italy's reputation for high quality wines developed. Italy's wines became a ubiquitous presence on restaurant wine lists in the United States, prompting a sudden increase in the number of acres planted of this variety in California, although it was unsuccessful in challenging Tuscany's dominance.

Nebbiolo Nebbiolo, which is recognized as one of Italy's most noble grapes, grows almost exclusively in the Piedmont region of northwestern Italy. Wines made from this pale purple black grape are tannic, austere, and highly alcoholic, but they mature into remarkably fine, elegant wines. Their aromas are floral, and their bouquets have an earthy, truffle-like character.

Hybridized Grapes

Although many hybridized grapes were developed in response to *Phylloxera*, some hybrids occurred by chance, such as Catawba, which became the basis of Ohio's sparkling wine industry in the mid-1800s. Other hybrids, such as Chancellor and Baco Noir, are used in winemaking in New England, New York, and Canada, where they better withstand the cold winters. For the most part, however, hybrids have not proven to be successful wine grapes as developers had originally hoped.

Climate

Climate depends to a certain degree on latitude, but several other factors are also important in determining a location's general or prevailing weather patterns. Temperature is an important component of climate, which can be modified by proximity to bodies of water, prevailing wind patterns, precipitation, altitude, and the amount of sunshine in a given location. Climates can be described as belonging to 3 broad classifications: Maritime, Mediterranean, and Continental. The climate has a dominant impact on the types of diseases and pests that affect vines.

CLIMATE	CHARACTERISTICS	EXAMPLES
Maritime	Warm long summer, cool winters	Bordeaux, Loire, Long Island, Napa
Mediterranean	Warm long summers and warm winters	Rhône, Tuscany, Santa Barbara
Continental	Hot short summer, long cold winters	Burgundy, Germany, Austria

Latitude Latitude is a significant indicator of a climate's suitability for viticulture. Tropical areas are generally too hot for growing grapes, and the high latitudes are too cold. Most successful vineyards are located between the 30° and 50° north latitude and south latitude. Because latitude affects the length of days and the relative coolness of nights in a region, different varieties of grapes are often suited to particular locations in a relatively small geographic area. In cool climates, low solar exposure associated with higher latitudes or altitudes, produces the compounds that are responsible for the grape's distinctive aromas. See Figure 10-6.

Temperature The amount of sugar and acidity that a grape variety develops as it ripens depends on the growing season of the area where it is planted. Research done by Maynard Amerine and Albert Winkler at the University of California-Davis School of Oenology demonstrated that different grape varieties need to be grown in specific climatic zones to fully ripen. To conduct their research, Amerine and Winkler developed a model using Heat Summation Areas. The method is based on the fact that vines lie dormant when aggregate temperatures remain below 50°F (10°C). For any day that the temperature averaged above 50°F (10°C), Amerine and Winkler assigned degrees based on the difference between the average temperature for that day and 50° F (10°C). For example, if the average temperature is 69°F (21°C) on April 1, that day is a 19-degree day. The Heat Summation (the sum of all the degree days between April 1 and October 31) determines the classification.

Here are the five classifications:

- Region I–Fewer than 2500°F accrued degrees
- Region II–2501°F–3000°F accrued degrees
- Region III–3001°F–3500°F accrued degrees
- Region IV–3501°F–4000°F accrued degrees
- Region V–4001°F–4500°F accrued degrees

In the Northern Hemisphere, the growing season begins around April 1, when the average temperature is high enough (above 50°F/10°C) for new shoots to develop from the dormant buds (bud-break). Flowering

FIGURE 10-6

Wine grapes grow best in temperate climate zones.

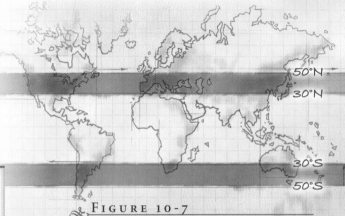

FIGURE 10-7

Veraison—Grapes will complete the color change during the last stages of ripening.

occurs from mid-May to June, and tiny berries appear and develop, but remain green until mid-July. The onset of ripening is called *veraison* (French for "true season"), when the berries develop color and begin to soften. Harvest generally begins in mid-September but varies from region to region based on the weather conditions in the location and the grape variety. See Figure 10-7.

Temperatures are very important to the development of grapes. Higher temperatures elevate the sugar content in the grape and cause acidity to decline more rapidly. This inverse relationship is important to the winemaker, who hopes to balance the alcohol and the acidity in wine. Varietal characteristics are also important in this process. The winemaker and the vineyard manager usually work together to harvest the grapes at their optimum quality. In areas of France, such as Burgundy, the grape may physiologically ripen before sufficient sugars have developed to make a wine with the proper alcohol and acidity balance. Winemakers may then correct an imbalanced condition with sugar prior to fermentation. This process is known as *chaptalization.* In warmer parts of coastal California, on the other hand, grapes may develop sugar ripeness before the grapes are physiologically ripe. Winemakers in these geographic areas are allowing grapes to become physiologically ripe, which explains the higher alcohol levels in their wines. They may also acidify their wines as grapes lose their acidity with longer 'hang time' on the vine.

Early Romans first recognized the correlations between fine wines and cooler climates when they discovered that although grapes grown in cool areas produced smaller quantities, the fruit was of a higher quality. In cooler environments, flavors and colors have a longer time to develop and the grapes retain good acidity. Acidity is the component in wine that makes it refreshing. This is also one of the reasons that the world's best wines are produced from grapes that are grown in cool regions.

FIGURE 10-8

Water helps to moderate or ease the extremes of temperature such as in the Vaud along Lake Geneva, Switzerland.

Bodies of water Bodies of water have a profound influence on climate. Large, deep masses of water, such as oceans, large lakes, or rivers, moderate both summer and winter temperatures. Temperatures become warm later in the spring and fall frosts generally arrive later in the season. See Figure 10-8.

Wind In locations where strong winds cause sudden temperature fluctuations (called wind stress), growers often plant tall shrubs or fast-growing trees to act as windbreaks. Winds can hinder flowering and pollination of ripening vines and decrease their final yields by altering their ability to transpire.

Rainfall and humidity Few crops are as sensitive to rainfall or humidity as grapes. Excessive rain during the growing season can cause rot and fungal diseases in the fruit. During the summer, too much rain leads to excessive plant growth rather than to good fruit development. At harvest time, too much rain can bloat the grapes and dilute their sugar and flavor content. In winter, on the other hand, plentiful rainfall is beneficial because it provides the necessary water table for deep roots of vines to extract needed moisture and trace minerals throughout the summer growing season. Drought can lead to excessive stress and cause the plant to physiologically shut down.

Frost For grape growers, late and early frosts are a disaster. A late spring frost can seriously diminish a vine's production potential, and an early autumn frost can damage the harvest's quality and yield. Frost is one of the primary factors for planting vines on hillsides rather than on valley floors where frost first occurs.

Sunlight The process of *photosynthesis* (the formation of sugars from carbon dioxide and a source of hydrogen—such as water—in the chlorophyll-containing tissues of plants exposed to light) is essential to plant growth and development. The amount of direct sunlight the plants receive, affects not only the health of the vines but also the sweetness of the grapes, and ultimately, the alcohol content of the wines made from them.

Viticulture

Viticulture, or the science of growing grapevines, encompasses all major fruit-growing conditions.

Terroir *Terroir* is a French term that is sometime loosely translated as "territory," but in viticulture, *terroir* encompasses much more than a land location. It includes all the elements that comprise growing conditions—soil, climate, topography, geology, and hydrology.

Soil French wines have long been named according to the region where the grapes are grown because many French winemakers believe that grapes derive flavor and quality from the soil as well as from other regional growing conditions. American and other New World winemakers, have maintained until recently that the soil is merely a support for the vine and a reservoir for water and nutrients. Climate plays the largest part in determining grape flavor and quality. Regardless of their nationality, however, viticulturists agree that grapevines grow best in well-drained soils on bench lands or slopes that encourage deep root growth. Fertility is also important to vine growth, although growers are wary of overly fertile soil that might encourage overgrowth of vines or overproduction of insipid grapes. See Figure 10-9.

Irrigation Irrigation is generally not allowed in the European Union's (EU) quality wine regions after the vine is mature enough to produce yields for appellation designation (usually the fourth year). The reason is due both to the general presence of rainfall during the growing season and the need to stress the vine sufficiently to produce concentrated fruit. Many EU quality wine appellations have suffered near drought conditions in the past few years and have received permission for limited irrigation in such circumstances. In other wine producing regions, where there is little or no rainfall, and no limitations, drip irrigation is common. See Figure 10-10.

FIGURE 10-10

An irrigation system waters a young vine.

Vintage The word vintage comes from the French word *vendange*, which means "harvest," but which also designates the year in which a wine is made. Ideal weather may bring a great vintage year, but early or late frosts, hail, or heavy rains may be disastrous. Until recently, great vintage years have been the exception rather than the rule in the cool wine-growing regions of Europe. Even great growing years require a skilled winemaker to take full advantage of an exceptional grape harvest's flavor development and balance. Some wines may not have a vintage label because they contain blends of grapes of different vintages. Non-vintage champagnes, for example, are such blends and do not necessarily reflect a lower quality.

FIGURE 10-9

Loam and schist from Alsace, France

Beaujolais, France with granite and schist

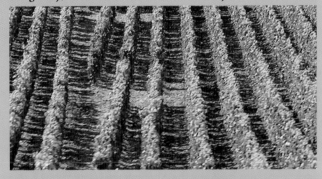

Burgundy, France and its limestone clay

Albariza soils of Jerez, Spain

Gravel of Médoc, France

Viticultural practices Although nature plays a pivotal role in the grape's flavor and composition, nurturing the vines is also critically important. First, the selection of rootstock and clone will affect the grapes, as will the age of the vines. Vines do not provide fruit of high quality in sufficient quantity to make wine until at least their third or fourth year. Some believe that many vines do not attain peak quality until their eighth to tenth year. Although some areas have vines that are 100 years old, most vines are economically productive for 20 to 25 years.

Growers also manipulate the size and shape of the vines by training, trellising, pruning, and using a process called *canopy management.* The canopy is made up of the grape leaves that absorb sunlight for photosynthesis. New World growers, principally those in the United States and Australia, encourage leaf growth to limit yields. They also prune the vines to determine how the vine will grow and the number of buds it will have. The number of buds affects the number of clusters of grapes, or the vines' yields. The correlation between high vine density and good quality is a matter of controversy among growers. In Europe, appellation laws limit vine density, but in New World vineyards, there are no set limits—although grapevines tend to be far less densely planted than in Burgundy, for example.

Yield management The way in which growers manage yields is important to the quality of wine that is produced from grapes. Different varieties yield different quantities of grapes. High-yielding varieties such as French Colombard or Carignan generally produce undistinguished wines, sold formerly as table wines in Europe. The warm areas where they thrive encourage large yields, higher alcohol, lower acidity, and less well-defined flavors.

Growers know that smaller yields and longer *"hang time"* on the vine generally produce harvests with better balance. In the European Union, quality wine regions have specific limits placed on yields. Fine wine varieties are manipulated to reduce yields through pruning and crop thinning, a process called *vendange vert* (green harvest). See Figure 10-11. The resulting wines tend to be much more expensive but are of a considerably higher quality because up to half the crop may be thinned and discarded.

FIGURE 10-11

Green harvesting or crop thinning— Grape clusters are cut from the vine to reduce a vineyards yield while improving the quality.

FIGURE 10-12

The brix or sugar content is measured using a refractometer to help judge ripeness.

Harvesting The point at which to harvest grapes is so important to the quality of wine that the decision is made jointly by the vineyard manager and the winemaker (when the fall weather does not dictate the timing). Growers use a refractometer to determine the Brix measurement, the name given to the scale used to measure sugar density. See Figure 10-12.

The method of harvesting is also significant. Because technology has improved dramatically and the labor shortage of agricultural workers continues to rise, more grapes are mechanically harvested than ever before. Mechanical harvesting does not necessarily have a negative impact on the quality of the juice, though for top quality wines, and some appellations such as Champagne, hand harvesting predominates or is legally required.

Sustainable agriculture Sustainable agriculture is perhaps one of the most important issues facing all agricultural producers. Growers have become increasingly aware of the long-term environmental effects of using chemical pesticides, herbicides, and fungicides. Sprays may drift to neighboring properties, and their residues can contaminate aquifers and impact wildlife habitats. See Figure 10-13. As growers look for alternatives to chemicals, they are adopting more organic methods of sustainable agriculture. By investigating the life cycles and activities of pest species and their predators, growers are finding new ways to control pests. Birds of prey such as owls, or more sophisticated technological solutions such as pheromone strips that disrupt the mating cycles of some pests, are replacing chemical sprays. Vineyard managers are also moving away from the monoculture of the vine. Planting cover crops such as mustard greens between the rows of vines, for example, repels pests from the vines and also helps to reduce soil impaction. Physical barriers such as nets, which do not have a negative impact on the environment, can protect the crops from flocks of migratory birds that might otherwise consume the harvest in minutes. There are vineyards that go far beyond these measures to be certified as organic or biodynamic, which can result in wines that have greater intensity but are more expensive to produce.

Vinification

Among winemakers, there is a frequently repeated adage that states that: "It is easy to make a bad wine from good grapes, but you cannot make a good wine from bad grapes."

Winemakers produce wine on the basis of the quality of grapes that they are able to grow. Over the past decades, science has enhanced traditional viticulture, and grape quality has generally improved with new horticultural methods. Critics charge however, that better science has also been accompanied by a lack of diversity in the international varieties used in winemaking. Although modern wines are clean and generally consistent, they also have fewer individualistic taste profiles. Over the past decade, that concern has sparked a philosophical shift among some winemakers. Minimum treatment or intervention is becoming more common especially in the super-premium category. Although technology has provided winemakers with tools that their predecessors did not have, many have come to believe that the costs exceed the benefits. A strictly scientific approach based on chemistry alone may have led to the homogenization trend that has produced wines with less typicity and fewer subtle differences due to site and *terroir.*

Classification of Wines

Wines are generally organized into five classifications: table wine, dessert wine, sparkling wine, fortified wine, and aromatized wine. Part of the winemaker's art involves deciding on the class of wine that is best suited to the grapes at hand, much as a chef decides on the type and quality of ingredients to use.

Table Wine

The term "table wine" is applied differently in the United States than in the European Union where the equivalent term is "light wine". In the United States, the term is used to distinguish table wines from sparkling or fortified wines. Table wines generally contain from 6.5% to 14.5% alcohol, but the normal range is from 10% to 12% alcohol. Table wines may be fermented to dryness or to off-dryness. Depending on how they are made, the wines may be white or red and range in color from pale white to amber, crimson to tile brick red, or a shade of salmony pink for rosé or blush wines. Beginning in 2011, wine classifications of the European Union will be changing and what has been termed "table wine" will become known merely as "wine".

FIGURE 10-13

A farm worker sprays fungicide in the vineyard.

Making White Wines

The process used to make white wines includes: destemming ➡ crushing ➡ sulfiting ➡ pressing ➡ adjusting ➡ fermentation ➡ racking ➡ [malolactic fermentation]* ➡ blending and aging ➡ fining and adjusting ➡ finishing and bottling.

Note: Only a few white wines, such as Chardonnay, undergo malolactic fermentation.

Making Red Wines

Red wines are processed by destemming and crushing ➡ sulfiting ➡ maceration and skin contact ➡ fermentation ➡ pressing ➡ racking ➡ malolactic fermentation ➡ blending and aging ➡ fining and adjusting ➡ finishing and bottling.

Destemming After grapes are harvested, the stalks and stems are generally removed in the winery by crushing/*destemming.* See Figure 10-14.

Crushing *Crushing* is a misleading term because the process is quite gentle. Its objective is to split the skins of grapes to release free-run juice. Crushing is quite distinct from pressing, during which the juice is squeezed from the pulp that is closer to the skins of the grapes. The juice of white wine may occasionally be kept in skin contact for several hours at low temperatures to extract greater flavor. Grapes for white wines are gently pressed before fermentation, but grapes used for red wines are pressed after fermentation.

Pressing Wines are pressed and strained by various kinds of presses. The extracted juice, with minimal fragments of stems, seeds, or skins, is called the *must.* Some black grapes that are made into red wines may not have all the stems removed from the must if the wine to be made requires the tannins they produce. A key point is that the greater the pressure, the greater the tannin levels in the must. When winemakers make white wines, they try to maximize the amount of must without extracting the tannins and the bitter oils contained in the pips. The first pressing may extract only about 75% of the juice and is used for better-quality wine. Subsequent pressings have more tannin and may be fermented and later blended into the wine or used to produce vinegar or an inexpensive brandy called marc, grappa, or pomace brandy in the United States.

Grapes for red wine are crushed and then fermented before being pressed so that maceration extracts the color and tannins from the grapes' skins and pips. The pressing need not be gentle because the release of tannins is desirable in red wines. See Figures 10-15a and 15b.

Must adjustments Winemakers can make adjustments to the must before it is fermented, including chaptalization or must enrichment, SO2 treatment, settling, and acidification or deacidification.

Chaptalization is the process of adding sugar to the must to increase the potential alcoholic content of a wine. Increasing the alcohol in the wine gives it a rounder, softer texture because alcohol counterbalances acidity. However, must is more commonly enriched using rectified concentrated grape must, a colorless and tasteless concentrate of grape sugars including glucose and fructose. Enrichment of the must is common in the wine regions of northern Europe, especially in parts of France, where it is carefully regulated. This practice is also allowed in Canada and in the northeastern United States where cool climates may prevent grapes from having enough sugar to develop sufficient alcohol to give the wine the necessary balance.

Musts are also commonly treated with sulfur dioxide to prevent oxidation; to control the growth of bacteria; and to eliminate any undesirable wild yeasts that may have been present on the grapes. If winemakers use cultured yeasts to ferment the must, they may be added at this time.

Winemakers may also need to adjust the pH, a measurement of the acidity of the must. In warm climates where grapes fail to develop sufficient acids to ensure good balance in the finished wine, winemakers may acidify the wine by adding tartaric acid. In cooler areas, it is sometimes necessary to deacidify the wine by adding calcium bicarbonate.

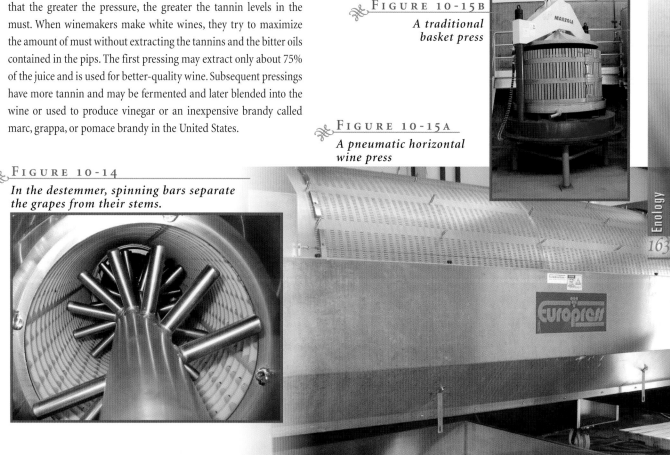

FIGURE 10-15B
A traditional basket press

FIGURE 10-15A
A pneumatic horizontal wine press

FIGURE 10-14
In the destemmer, spinning bars separate the grapes from their stems.

FIGURE 10-16

Stainless steel, temperature controlled fermentation tanks

Maceration By definition, *maceration* involves soaking a material in liquid to separate softened parts of the material from the harder ones. When making red wines, winemakers use this process to extract the phenolics, including tannins, coloring materials, anthocyanins, and other glycosides, which include flavor precursors and compounds from the grape skins and sometimes the pips or stems that are in the must.

Left untreated, the must would normally begin to ferment during maceration because the sugar and yeasts needed for this process are already present in the grapes. To macerate without fermentation, winemakers need to keep the must cold—below 48°F (9°C), the point at which yeast growth is retarded. Cold maceration may last for two or three days. It is not uncommon for high-quality red wines to undergo extended maceration (including fermentation) of up to 36 days to create longer chain tannins that will feel less astringent and taste less bitter. If the winemaker is making a blush or rosé wine, the maceration period is a few hours.

Fermentation During fermentation, yeasts in the must convert sugar to ethyl alcohol and carbon dioxide as part of their metabolic cycle, and further release heat as a by-product. Violent fermentation can raise temperatures to more than 100°F (38°C) if left uncontrolled. At that temperature, the yeast dies. Conversely, if temperatures are allowed to fall below 48°F (9°C), the yeast will stop growing. Northern Europe's fermenting rooms *(cuveries)* are often warmed, while those in parts of California and Australia are sometimes cooled.

Fermenting white wine Although fermentation creates both white wines and red wines, each type of wine requires different fermentation conditions. One important variable in fermenting white wine is temperature. Today's winemakers control temperatures precisely by using stainless steel vats with cooling jackets (see Figure 10-16), although some winemakers still use small oak barrels (Bordeaux barriques which have 59 gallons or 225ltr capacity) for certain wines such as Chardonnay, whose character can be more adapted to oak flavors.

Winemakers ferment white wines between 50°F (10°C) and 65°F (18°C) for 1–3 weeks. At those temperatures and durations, the wine is refreshing, fruity, and faster to mature. At higher temperatures, fermentation is quicker, but for most wines, quality may suffer. Chardonnays can be an exception. They are fermented in oak barrels at 68°F (20°C) and higher to gain complexity and longevity.

Fermenting red wine Black grapes are fermented with their skins and pips in vats. Most vats are made of wood, but there are also concrete, stainless steel, or glass-lined vats. For red wines, fermentation occurs at 68°F (20°C) to 88°F (31°C). At higher temperatures, the wine's fruitiness and delicacy may diminish.

Because the grape skins are left in the must, red wines also require additional attention during fermentation. Carbon dioxide and heat force skins and any remaining stems to the surface of the must to form a *cap.* Winemakers need to submerge this cap to prevent excessive heat buildup beneath it. Punching down the cap also prevents prolonged exposure to oxygen (allowing actobacter to turn the wine into vinegar) and creates a more uniform maceration and fermentation. Modern winemakers use several processes to ensure that the cap is submerged, including punch down for more delicate reds, and pumping over the cap for more hardy reds. Fermentation ends naturally when all the fermentable sugars in the must are converted or when the alcohol level generally reaches 14% (in some cases over 15%). At that level, alcohol is toxic to the yeast, and it causes the yeast to die.

Several other conditions can also cause fermentation to stop prematurely: some of these are accidental, and others are deliberately created by the winemaker.

1. Temperatures above 105°F (41°C) will kill the yeast, and cause a "stuck fermentation" to occur.
2. Adding brandy or a neutral spirit to the wine raises the alcohol level above the maximum that the yeast will tolerate, and fermentation stops. Winemakers add alcohol when they wish to leave residual sugar in the wine for sweetness.
3. Pasteurizing, or flash-heating wine to 185°F (85°C) for one minute, stops fermentation. Although pasteurization also neutralizes harmful bacteria, many believe that it also strips the wine of some flavor components. Pasteurization, therefore, is not suited to wines requiring bottle aging.
4. To stop fermentation before all of the sugar is metabolized, winemakers may also add sulfur compounds.
5. Some winemakers use a centrifuge and filtration to remove yeasts from the wine. A rough filter followed by a sterile filtration prevents harmful bacteria or yeast from remaining in the wine, especially during clarification and the final bottling stages.

Racking After fermentation has occurred and the lees have precipitated to the bottom of the vessel, winemakers generally siphon the wine into a clean vat, cask, or barrel, leaving the lees behind. Each time wine is racked into a new container, 2%–3% of its volume is lost. All fine wines are racked at least twice, and the finest are racked four times the first year and twice in the second year. *Racking,* a process that gives controlled exposure to air so that the limited contact with oxygen can help the wines mature, not only clarifies the wine but also aerates it.

Malolactic fermentation Concurrent with or after the primary (or alcohol) fermentation is complete, almost all red wines, and a few other white wines such as Chardonay, undergo a *malolactic fermentation.* Unlike the original fermentation, malolactic fermentation is not caused by yeasts, but by lactobacteria that converts harsher malic acid in the wine to softer lactic acid. This fermentation has advantages and disadvantages. It can give cool-climate, acidic wines a softer more buttery character, but it can also leach out or mask the wine's fruit flavors.

❧ FIGURE 10-17A

The stirring wand used for bâtonnage

❧ FIGURE 10-17B

The lees or dead yeast cells in the wine resting at the bottom of the barrel

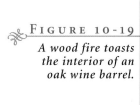

❧ FIGURE 10-18

Aging wine in oak barrels, with bungs/stoppers

Lees and bâtonnage *Lees* is the term for the sediment containing dead yeast and other solids that collect in the bottom of the wine tank or barrel following fermentation. Most wines are racked off the lees as part of the winemaking process. However, some wines that are fermented in barrels are left on the lees and are stirred back into the wine in a process called *bâtonnage.* Bâtonnage also allows for oxygen to be introduced preventing the creation of sulfur compounds. See Figures 10-17a and 17b. This process contributes to *autolysis* (or the breakdown of yeast cells), which releases agents throughout the wine to reduce the bitterness from the wood tannins and to add a creamy quality and complexity to the wine.

Blending and aging Many wines develop greater complexity and better balance if they are blended with other wines. Generally speaking, wines that need blending are fermented separately and then blended before aging. Wine may also develop complexity over time through a process called aging, which generally takes place in wood. Not all wines benefit from oak aging. Winemakers age their wines in oak because the wood is tightly grained enough to store the liquid, and yet sufficiently porous to allow the slow and minute interaction of the content with oxygen. The flavors of oak should support rather than overwhelm the flavors in the wine.

The source of the oak, its treatment, age, and size, all affect how the wood interacts with the wine. Oaks from different regions of France—Limousin, Tronçais, Allier, Nevers, and Vosges—generally have a tighter grain than American oak. The more porous American oak gives wines distinct vanillin, coconut, and tannic flavors. French oaks may cost 3 to 4 times as much as American oak varieties. See Figure 10-18.

Making the oak barrels is complex. Producers called *cooperages* make barrels using carefully controlled processes. The degree to which the oak barrel is toasted affects the amount of toastiness in the

wine's taste. See Figure 10-19. The smaller the barrel, the more contact it has with the wine and the greater its effect on the flavor. Newer oak contributes more oak flavors than older oak. After three years of use, however, old oak barrels contribute little to the wine's flavor.

During the first few months of aging, some of the wine evaporates and some is absorbed by the wood to create an airspace called *ullage,* in the barrel. If the airspace is allowed to remain, the wine will oxidize. Winemakers therefore fill the space with additional wine of the same kind, a process known as topping off. At the point where topping off occurs, wine casks are loosely sealed with bungs (stoppers), which are later replaced with wooden bungs. During aging, impurities sink to the bottom of the cask, so the wine is racked into another cask to leave the accumulated sediment behind.

❧ FIGURE 10-19

A wood fire toasts the interior of an oak wine barrel.

Enology

165

Because many white wines cannot stand up to 100% oak aging, a winemaker may blend different lots of wine from the same vintage and vineyard; for example, the first may be 100% oak aged wine in new casks, the second lot aged in older wood, and yet a third lot aged in stainless steel.

Fining *Fining* is a clarification process used to give wines their brilliance. Although the wine eventually clarifies itself, fining saves time and expense. Fining agents include gelatin, egg whites, casein, isinglass, or bentonite clay. In addition to removing cloudiness, some fining agents may also remove some tannins to achieve a softer wine. Most commercial wines are either fined or filtered.

Finishing and bottling Before bottling, many wines are either centrifuged or filtered twice—the first is a rough filtration used soon after fermentation, and the second is a sterile filtration done immediately before bottling. Although some winemakers centrifuge their wines, the process can dilute the flavors. Consequently, the process is not used for fine wines.

Filtration is used mainly for white wines, especially those with residual sugar or those that do not undergo malolactic fermentation. Fine red wines, however, may not be filtered because the filtration process may also cause the wine to be stripped of some flavor components and complexity. These wines are sold as unfiltered and may not be as brilliant as other red wines. See Figure 10-20.

Winemakers can also correct a wine's balance by adding ascorbic acid to finish or adjust the acidity of wine. Balancing wine with ascorbic acid is most common in warmer climates, where wines often lack acidity.

Cold stabilization Wine is bottled in sterilized bottles. After the bottle has been filled, the neck may be flushed with nitrogen or carbon dioxide to prevent oxidation. The bottle is then corked, and the wine is stored upside down to keep the cork moist. Moisture swells the cork and ensures a tight seal to prevent oxidation of the wine. Wine is not usually shipped for release until it is allowed to rest for several weeks because of the bottle shock that may occur.

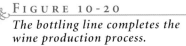

Figure 10-20

The bottling line completes the wine production process.

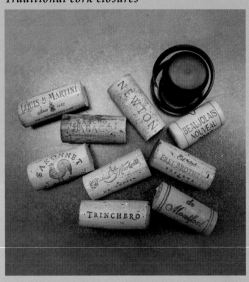

Figure 10-21

Traditional cork closures

A metal screw cap closure

A modern glass cork closure

Cork Cork is the bark taken from a species of oak tree common in southern Portugal and Spain. See Figure 10-21. When the oak reaches 20–25 years of age, the cork bark is stripped manually from the tree. Cork may be reharvested from the same tree every 9–15 years. Cork provides an excellent seal because it is resistant to liquids and provides an efficient barrier to oxygen. However, cork is sometimes tainted by the organic compound TCA (trichloranisole), created during the cleaning process, which gives off a distinctive dank wet basement smell and ruins the potential enjoyment of any fruit in the wine. The problem was recognized and addressed by cork producers within the last five years and is now less common. TCA can also be traced to other sources in the winery such as building materials and pallets. It should be noted that cork is not a perfect seal and trace amounts of oxygen that allow the wine to mature do seep into the wine.

Although the screw cap is a perfect barrier to oxygen it has only recently begun to gain general acceptance because its image has been too closely associated with that of inexpensive jug wines. Because the screw cap can result in a lack of oxygen ingress, wines can become reductive, allowing for the development of skunky sulfur based compounds in the wine. Many screw cap closures have now been adapted to allow for trace amounts of oxygen to enter the bottle. The use of synthetic corks, however, is more controversial because they seem to be less well suited for long term aging.

Cellar and bottle aging Almost all wines are best consumed within 1–3 years and do not improve with age. The tiny minority (less than 1%) that does benefit from bottle aging undergoes revealing changes with time. See Figure 10-22.

Wines mature at different rates on the basis of individual vintage characteristics, their appellation, and vinification. The higher the level of acidity, the greater the potential for aging. Although residual sugar and tannins act as preservatives, they are also key to the evolution of flavors and balance. Without acidity, the wine's balance disintegrates. White wines generally have higher acid levels but few tannins. Fine Riesling and Loire Chenin Blanc wines evolve more slowly than do most Chardonnays. Red wines from Bordeaux that are Cabernet-based have not only the tannins but also the acidity to make them long-lived.

Storage conditions also affect the rate of aging. As a rule, warmer storage conditions accelerate aging, and cooler storage retards it. Longer bottle aging in cool (55°F) and humid (85%) conditions, however, gives the wine greater complexity and a more pleasing bouquet. Bottle size also affects aging times, with wine in smaller bottles aging faster than wine in larger ones.

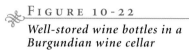

FIGURE 10-22

Well-stored wine bottles in a Burgundian wine cellar

Following the Steps from Grapes to Wine

From first pressing to final racking and finishing, winemaking has not changed essentially for thousands of years, although today's winemakers are rigorously scientific about the process.

Steps in vinification include:

1 The mechanical or hand harvesting that brings the grapes to the winery takes place.

2 White grapes are then pressed before fermentation to extract the must. Black grapes are pressed after fermentation to extract the wine.

3 Fermentation may take place in large open vats.

4 For more delicate red wines, the "punch down" method is preferred.

5 Racking siphons the wine from one vat or container into another, leaving the sediment behind.

6 Wine acquires additional flavors from toasted oak barrels that are used for storage and aging.

7 Fining helps to clarify the wine more quickly than the natural processes.

8 Thieving allows the winemaker to maintain quality control during aging.

Special Winemaking Methods

Various methods for creating distinctive wines have evolved over the centuries.

Carbonic Maceration

Carbonic maceration is a red winemaking method common in, but not limited to, the Beaujolais region of Burgundy, France. Carbonic maceration extracts a fruity, light-bodied, aromatic wine from whole grapes such as Beaujolais Nouveau. In this process, bunches of uncrushed grapes are placed in a carbon dioxide-filled vat. When the grapes are sealed inside, they begin to ferment. The sealed grape bunches undergo an intracellular enzymatic fermentation that produces no more than 2% alcohol. After 1-2 days or up to 1 week, the grapes are crushed, and the must is macerated and fermented in the traditional way. Red wines made using carbonic macerations are ready to drink without long periods of aging because the process results in wine with little tannin and an increased fruity and mentholated aroma. These wines do not age well. This process is generally not suitable for white wines.

Dessert Winemaking

Technically, dessert wines fit into one of two categories that are designated by the Federal Standards of Identity as fortified wines. Not all dessert wines are fortified, however. Some are made using special viticultural or vinification practices. There are five primary methods for making a dessert wine.

Late harvest Late harvest wines are made from grapes that have been allowed to continue ripening for at least one week after the regular harvest. Extended ripening produces intensely sweet grapes, but waiting to harvest them is risky because the grapes are vulnerable to pest infestations or sudden changes in weather.

Botrytis cinerea *Botrytis cinerea* is a mold that causes infected grapes to dehydrate, and proportionately increases their sugar and glycerol content. *Botrytis* is common in sites located near bodies of water where considerable humidity is created in the morning and then burned off by the midday sun. The best-known botrytized wines are: Sauternes, from Bordeaux, France; Trockenbeerenauslese from Germany and the Neusiedlersee in Austria; and Tokay wines from Hungary. These wines are also made in Australia and the United States as Special Select Late Harvest wines. See Figure 10-23.

Raisined grape wines Many famous wines are made from intentionally raisined grapes. These include Vin Santo from Tuscany, Umbria or Pedro Ximénez from Spain, and some of the Muscats from Samos or other Greek isles.

Ice wine *Ice wine,* or eiswein as it is known in Germany (from where it originated), is produced from grapes that have been allowed to freeze naturally on the vine before being harvested and pressed. The result is a high concentration of sugar in the must that produces an intensely sweet wine. Canada's most famous wines are its ice wines, and the best ice wines in the United States are from Washington state and New York's Finger Lakes region. There are also wines called "winter wines" that are made by artificially freezing late-harvest grapes. These can also be of a very good quality. See Figure 10-24.

Mutage Mutage is generally the adding of alcohol or sometimes sulfur dioxide, to prevent the yeast from continuing to convert sugar into alcohol. Wine referred to as *Vin Doux Naturel* from France and Port wines are examples of such wines. (See fortification.)

❧ FIGURE 10-23

Botrytized grapes are used to produce the sweet wines of Sauternes.

❧ FIGURE 10-24

Ice wines are made from grapes harvested when frozen.

Sparkling Wines

Although many people use the term champagne as a synonym for sparkling wine, champagne is only one of many sparkling wines. Champagne takes its name from the region in France where it is produced. Six basic methods are used to create sparkling wines.

- *the classic or traditional method (formally called méthode champenoise)*
- *the transfer method*
- *the méthode ancestrale or rurale*
- *the dioise method*
- *the bulk or charmat method*
- *the carbonation or injection method*

Classic or Traditional Method

True champagne is produced only in the Champagne region of France, though other winemakers may adapt the classic or traditional method. The European Union does not allow using the term *méthode champenoise.* on labeling for non-champagne wines.

Champagnes are made from one, or a blend of up to three, grape varieties: Chardonnay, Pinot Noir, and Pinot Meunier. Other classic method wines may use other varieties. The grapes are hand harvested and carefully pressed to avoid contact with skin and pips. The free run of juice is called the *tête de cuvée* and is reserved for prestige wines such as Dom Pérignon. The juice from the first pressing is called the *cuvée,* and the second pressing is called the *premières tailles,* which may be used by some producers. The total yield of juice is strictly enforced by the *Comité Interprofessionnel du Vin de Champagne* (CIVC) to 2550 liters for each marc or 4000 kg/8800 lbs. of grapes. The must settles and ferments in steel tanks or old oak vats, and then most of the wines undergo malolactic fermentation.

170

The wine is then blended according to the style desired by the winemaker, and 20% is held in reserve for future years. Next, a solution composed of sugar and yeast, known as *liqueur de tirage,* is added to the wine, which is then bottled and capped. The carbon dioxide produced in the bottle during the second fermentation, or *prise de mousse,* causes champagne's characteristic effervescence. The pressure caused by trapped carbon dioxide is between five and six bars or 90 pounds per square inch, which translates to 90 – 100 million bubbles per bottle. After the wine finishes the second fermentation in 3–4 weeks, the bottle is aged on its side for a minimum of one year *en tirage* or on the lees (from January 1 following the vintage) to qualify for non-vintage champagne. (The minimum requirement is nine months in the United States.) The lees or yeast cells are partially absorbed in a process called autolysis, which lends added flavor and complexity to the wine.

The next stage in the classic method is to move the lees stuck to the side of the wine bottle down to the neck. The bottle is angled neck down at 45°, shaken, and turned by hand or by machines (gyropalettes) in a process called *riddling,* or *rémuage,* that may last several weeks. See Figures 10-25a and 25b. After the lees are in the bottle's neck, the bottle may further age upside down *(sur pointe)* or have its lees expelled through a process known as *disgorgement,* or *dégorgement* in which the neck of the bottle is placed upside down in a solution to freeze the top inch or two of wine and trapped lees. When the cap is removed, the gas expels the frozen plug. Then the bottle is topped off with identical wine called a *dosage* or *liqueur d'exposition,* which may have a dose of varying degrees of cane sugar solution dictating the level of sweetness. The levels of sweetness are as follow:

- **Brut Sauvage or Natural**–bone dry: 6 g/l of sugar (extra brut)
- **Brut**–very dry; <15 g/l of sugar; no noticeable sweetness
- **Extra Dry; Extra Sec**–slightly sweet; 12-20 g/l sugar
- **Sec or Dry**–noticeable sweetness; 17-35 g/l sugar
- **Demi-Sec**–quite sweet; 33-50 g/l sugar
- **Doux**–extremely sweet; more than 50 g/l sugar

Transfer Method

Similar to the classic champagne method, the *transfer method* produces a pleasantly carbonated sparkling wine. In this method, the wine is aged on the lees but is neither riddled nor disgorged. It is filtered and dosed in bulk before being rebottled. The wine will tend to have a coarser texture than champagne because of the resulting loss of carbonation.

Méthode Ancestrale or Rurale

This method is the most ancient way of producing sparkling wine. The wine is fermented at cold temperatures and bottled prior to its completion. The resulting wine is less bubbly, sweeter, and may have deposits. This style of wine is found in the Blanquette de Limoux.

FIGURE 10-25A
Hand riddling on a pupître

FIGURE 10-25B
Mechanical riddling through the use of a gyropalette

Champagne Bottle Sizes

CHAMPAGNE AND SPARKLING WINES COME IN A VARIETY OF BOTTLE SIZES

Split
187 milliliters

Half-bottle
375 milliliters

Bottle
750 milliliters

Magnum
1.5 liters (2 bottles)

Jéroboam
3 liters (4 bottles)

Rehoboam
4.5 liters (6 bottles)

Methuselah
6 liters (8 bottles)

Salmanazar
9 liters (12 bottles)

Balthazar
12 liters (16 bottles)

Nebuchadnezzar
15 liters (20 bottles)

Heavy glass bottles have a punt, or indentation, at their bottoms; a mushroom-shaped cork; and a wire cage or muzzle to keep the cork in place.

Enology

171

Dioise Method

The *dioise* method is a variation of the *Méthode Ancestrale* whereby the wine's first slow fermentation in sealed vats is filtered, bottled, and the wine continues to ferment in the bottle until it reaches 7.5% alcohol. The wine is then disgorged and filtered so that it is low in alcohol and has residual sugar. This method is used for Asti and Clairette de Die.

Bulk/Charmat/Cuve Close Method

In the *bulk or Charmat method,* wine is twice fermented in bulk and then bottled. Cheaper and faster than either the transfer or classic champagne method, the bulk method can produce a good wine but one that lacks the complexity of a classic or traditional method sparkling wine.

Carbonation/Injection Method

The least expensive and lowest-quality sparkling wines are made by the carbonation/injection method, in which carbon dioxide is injected into the wine vat and the wine is then bottled under pressure, much in the way that a soft drink is produced. Because the resulting wine is coarser and the effervescence dissipates rapidly, only the least expensive sparkling wines are prepared in this way.

Fortified Wines

Fortified wines are those that have had neutral spirits or brandy added to fermenting or fermented wine to generally raise the level of alcohol from 16% to 22%. When fermentation stops and the wine retains sweetness, the process is called *mutage*. Winemakers also fortify wines to ensure their stability. The most common fortified wines are Port, Sherry, Madeira, Marsala, and Vin Doux Naturel.

Port

Port, which originated in the Douro Valley of northern Portugal, begins its transformation to a fortified wine with grapes that are fermented to the 6%–9% alcohol stage. Then the winemaker mixes in *aguardiente* brandy (77% alcohol) so that the wine is about 20% brandy and 80% grape wine. The Port is then aged in old wooden barrels called *pipes* for varying lengths of time, depending on the type of Port desired.

Two basic types of Port are wood and vintage. *Wood Port* is aged in wood and is ready to be consumed shortly after it is bottled. Of the wood Ports, ruby and tawny are the most significant styles. *Ruby Port* is aged for 2–3 years, and *Tawny Port* is aged for at least six years, up to 40 years. The more Ports age in wood, the more they lose their hard tannins and color. Ruby Ports, named for their deep red color, have a very sweet fruit flavor and are one of very few wines that can stand up to dark chocolate without being overwhelmed. Colheita ports are wood aged ports from a single vintage but are quite distinct from vintage ports. They must be aged in pipes for a minimum of 7 years.

Vintage Port, made from the best available grapes from a single vintage year, are aged 2–3 years in wood and then require at least 10–15 years in the bottle. Some vintage Ports may be aged for 50 or more years. With so much bottle aging, vintage Ports require decanting to separate the wine from its thick sediment. Extensive sediment is so common and prevalent that Port aficionados say that the wine is "throwing a crust."

Recently, a hybrid style of Port has been developed in response to the high cost of vintage Port. Called Late Bottled Vintage (LBV) Port, it is made from a specific vintage, traditionally aged 4–6 years in wood, and then bottle aged. It can continue to improve in the bottle before being consumed. It may also need to be decanted based on the length of the bottle aging.

Sherry

Sherry is produced in the southern region of Spain known as Andalusia. It is made from grapes grown in the chalky soils, called albariza, around the town of Jerez de la Frontera. (Sherry is based on the Arabic name Sheris). Although similar fortified wines have been called sherry, the European Union has now restricted the use of the title sherry to sherries produced in this region, when they are sold in Europe. The Palomino makes up 95% of the grapes grown in that region. Pedro Ximénez, or PX, and Moscatel grapes make a very sweet wine for blending, and are an added component for making sweet cream sherry.

Unlike Port wines, sherry is fortified after fermentation. The Palomino grapes are mostly hand harvested, gently pressed to form must, fermented, and then fortified. Two fundamental processes make sherry unique: biological aging through yeast *flor* development, and fractional blending through the *solera* system. See Figure 10-26. Many sherries also go through an oxidative process of aging to allow the wine to become not only intentionally oxidized, but also more intense because the water content has evaporated and the dry extract is more concentrated.

FIGURE 10-26
The Sherry Solera System in a cathedral-like bodega

There are two basic types of sherries: *fino, amontillado,* and *oloroso. Fino* sherry is light with a very distinctive nose that stems from biological aging and the development of acetaldehyde (a compound the human body produces as it breaks down alcohol). To produce a fino or its lightest style manzanilla, winemakers use the best free run juice. All wines develop a secondary yeast called *flor.* For the flor yeast to develop the wine is fortified to 15.5% alcohol and placed in American oak casks until they are five-sixths full. The flor yeast feed on oxygen, alcohol, and glycerin in the wine. These components need to be replenished by blending new wine into the older wine. This process of fractional blending or "tipping the scales," is called the solera system and continues during its three to six years of aging for fino sherry. True *amontillados* are finos whose flor yeast have died naturally or are wines that have been fortified to 16% ABV or more. Most commercial amontillados are blends that are sweetened. Finos and manzanillas look like white wines and are light bodied, dry, and consumed upon release. Once opened, they deteriorate as quickly as a white still wine.

Oloroso sherry is fortified to 18% alcohol so that the flor cannot develop. The wines undergo aging by oxidation, resulting in mahogany colored, fuller bodied wines that have a different nutty pungency. The wines still go through fractional blending to maintain a consistent style and added complexity. Olorosos are some of the most difficult wines for consumers to appreciate and they need to be paired with intensely flavored or seasoned foods. When blended with PX, Oloroso becomes a sweet cream sherry. A recent development has been the creation of VOS (Vinum Optimum Signatorum but also known as Very Old Sherry) and VORS (Vinum Optimum Rarum Signatorum) made of sherry blends that are a minimum of 20 years and 30 years respectively.

Madeira

Madeira wines, named after the Portuguese island of Madeira, once functioned as ballast in ships that came to this island's revictualing station on voyage from England to the American colonies. It was soon discovered that hot aging in the hold of the ships improved these fortified wines. In fact, Madeira was used by the colonists to toast the signing of the Declaration of Independence.

Madeiras are fortified after fermenting to produce dry styles, but fortified during fermentation for sweeter styles. They undergo a unique baking process called the estufagem system. The best wines are those that are baked naturally in lofts or attics by the heat of the sun. Those of a lesser quality are stored for a minimum of three months at 40°C–50°C in a steampipe heated room (estufa), or are heated directly by heating coils running in the wine vats. This process causes the sugars to caramelize and promote oxidation to make the wines virtually indestructible. A few wines may also go through a sherry-like solera process. The best Madeiras are special reserve, extra reserve, and vintage. Special reserves are blends that are at least ten years old. Extra reserves are at least 15 years old, and vintage Madeiras must be from a single vintage and aged a minimum of 20 years in the barrel and two years in the bottle. Since the formation of the European Union, producers cannot label their wines varietally unless they contain 85% of that variety. Previously, much of the wine sold as Madeira had little of the varieties that originally made

Madeiras famous. There are, however, four varietally and one non-varietally labeled Madeiras:

- **Sercial** Very dry and acidic
- **Verdelho** Dry and smoky
- **Rainwater** Dry but slightly fruity and softer
- **Bual** Medium sweet, aromatic, and reminiscent of nuts and dates
- **Malmsey** An English corruption of Malvasia, the sweetest Madeira, but balanced by high acidity with great, dark, and rich dried-fruit aromas.

Marsala

Originally named for the city of Marsala on the isle of Sicily, Marsala was first produced in 1770 by an English merchant named John Woodhouse. *Marsala* is fortified by alcohol and sweetened by concentrated grape must and has an alcohol content of 17%–19%. These wines may be golden, amber, or ruby-colored, and the sugar level in each color can vary from secco (dry), to semi-secco (semi-dry), to dolce (sweet). Most Marsalas labeled *fine* (pronounced fee-nay) are aged one year, although a number of quality Marsalas that are labeled *Superiore Riserva* (aged four years), *Vergina* (aged five years) and *Stravecchio* (aged ten years) make for delightful sipping.

Vin Doux Naturel

French for "naturally sweet wine," *Vin Doux Naturel* is actually the product of mutage. A majority of these wines are made from Muscat grapes. Especially satisfying as dessert wines, these French sweet wines are best if balanced by acidity. The most famous come from the village of Beaumes-de-Venise in the Rhône Valley. The other famous appellations that use the red Grenache grapes are Rasteau and Banyuls. These Port-like wines are sometimes deliberately exposed to air and topped off with new wine every six months to help develop the quality of *rancio*, a blue cheese bouquet, also found in old Cognacs.

Aromatized Wines

Aromatized, or apéritif wines are best served before a meal because their bitter and aromatic ingredients are appetite stimulants. Any number of aromatic ingredients may be infused into an apéritif, including herbs, spices, flowers, and barks. Aromatized wines such as Vermouth, Dubonnet, and Lillet, are fortified and have an alcohol content of at least 15%. There are wine cocktails that are considered aperitifs when they are blended with a liqueur such as Kir.

Vermouth Vermouth stems from the German term *vermut,* meaning "wormwood," an herb that was once frequently used in beverages. Both dry white and sweet red Vermouth are made in France and in Italy. Dry Vermouth is the result of a white wine fermented to dryness, infused with aromatics, and fortified with brandy to an alcohol content of 19%. After it is bottled, it is aged for 3 1/2–4 years. Dry Vermouth is served chilled and is sometimes substituted for dry white wine in cooking.

Sweet Vermouth uses sweeter white grape varietals fortified to 17% alcohol and infused with aromatics and quinine. After sugar and caramel coloring are added, sweet Vermouth is aged for two years. Sweet Vermouth is usually served on the rocks with soda. Both dry and sweet vermouths are often used in cocktails such as Martinis and Manhattans.

Dubonnet French Dubonnet is available in dry white and sweet red varieties. It is best served chilled or on the rocks with a twist of lemon.

Lillet Infused with citrus flavors, Lillet may be red or white, dry or off-dry. It is best served chilled or on the rocks with a twist of lemon or orange.

Kir Kir is not an aromatized wine per se but is an example of a classic apéritif made by blending the acidic Aligoté white grape wine with Crème de Cassis, a black currant liqueur.

Decoding the Label

AVELEDA
FONTE
VINHO BRANCO · VIN BLANC · WHITE WINE
2008
VINHO VERDE
DOC

TERRA TORO
PINOT GRIGIO
SANTA BARBARA COUNTY

Gallo
FAMILY
VINEYARDS

SONOMA
2008

CHARDONNAY
SONOMA COUNTY

LAMARCA
PROSECCO
SPARKLING WINE
PRODUCT OF ITALY
V.S.A.Q

TWO PRINCES
RIESLING
2006

2006
Riesling Kabinett
RHEINGAU

K'

BARON K'

ESTATE BOTTLED WEINGUT BARON KNYPHAUSEN
ELTVILLE · GERMANY
QUALITÄTSWEIN MIT PRÄDIKAT · A.P.Nr. 33037001407
CONTAINS SULFITE

Alc. 10,5% vol.   750 ml

LOUIS·M·MARTINI
CABERNET SAUVIGNON
ALEXANDER VALLEY
RESERVE
2007

Elysium

California Black Muscat

Dessert Wine
2007

15% alc. / vol.   750ml ~ L0801

RS
RODNEY STRONG
SYMMETRY
2006
MERITAGE
RED WINE
ALEXANDER
VALLEY
ALC. 15.5%
BY VOL.

BELNERO
PROPRIETOR'S RESERVE

TOSCANA
i.g.t.   RED WINE

CASTELLO
BANFI
MONTALCINO

Château Ste Michelle

SYRAH
COLUMBIA VALLEY
WASHINGTON STATE'S FOUNDING WINERY

McWILLIAM'S WINES
ESTABLISHED 1877

McWILLIAM'S
HANWOOD ESTATE

SHIRAZ
South Eastern Australia
2008

California Orange Muscat
sweet dessert wine
Vintage 2007
Produced & Bottled by
Andrew Quady, Madera, California
15% Alc./Vol. ~ 750ml

Kanu
The mythical bird of promise

2008
chenin blanc

STELLENBOSCH
SOUTH AFRICA

BRIDLEWOOD
ESTATE WINERY

SYRAH
CENTRAL COAST
2007

OLDERBOSCH
BLANC
WINE OF ORIGIN WESTERN CAPE
Alc. 12.5% Vol.

IN ADDITION to a knowledge of the various types of wines and how they are made, servers need an overall understanding of the information provided on wine labels. Unfortunately, there is no standardized universal labeling system for all of the wine producing regions of the world. Some wines are labeled by variety, others by appellation, quality standards, brand names, or a combination thereof. Furthermore, wine labels may be in various languages with terms unfamiliar or foreign to both guests and servers. Good servers need an overall understanding and recognition of these terms to help customers decode the wine list.

Wine Purchasing and Tasting

Most restaurants and other beverage establishments, whether on or off-premises, purchase wine from distributors, who in turn, buy from suppliers or importers. This system is known in the U.S. as the three tier system. In most states, it is illegal for an establishment to purchase wine directly from a wine producer unless it is from a small local producer. When food service establishments purchase wines for their wine lists, a number of factors are considered including: the brand name, the place of origin, and the variety; the reputation of the distributor, négoçiant, and/or importer if applicable; the cost of the wine; and finally the wine list's compatibility with the food menu.

Wine Purchasing

Several factors influence the purchasing decisions for wines:

Brand name Wines may be purchased solely on the basis of the brand name and the reputation of the producer. Names such as Château Lafite Rothschild®, Robert Mondavi®, or Opus One® are often the only guarantee of quality a purchaser needs. See Figures 11-1 and 11-2.

FIGURE 11-1

Famous wines of Bordeaux are known by their brand names.

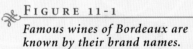

FIGURE 11-2

Some American wines are primarily marketed using their brand names.

Place of origin In the European Union, the appellation or place of origin reflects the most significant differences in the aroma and taste of wines. Generally speaking, the more delimited an area, the better the wine quality. See Figures 11-3 and 11-4. Appellations are becoming increasingly important as the awareness of consumers evolves. Quality wine producers in the United States and the New World are marketing their wines by stressing increasingly recognized appellations such as Napa Valley or Sonoma County. There are now approximately 200 American Viticultural Areas in the United States. See Figure 11-5.

Varietal labeling The marketing of wines by varietal labeling, such as Chardonnay, is a fairly recent phenomenon. In response to the less distinctive wines sold under semi-generic labels such as California Burgundy, producers in the 1940s and 50s, began differentiating their better wines by labeling them with the variety. Many consumers make the varietal the primary factor in their purchasing decision. See Figures 11-6 and 11-7.

Reputation of the *négociant*, importer, and distributor Many *négociants,* who in France are wine merchants, importers, and distributors, have built reputations for their expertise by either

FIGURE 11-3
Beaujolais-Villages is a district of 39 designated villages within the less well ranked Beaujolais region of Burgundy.

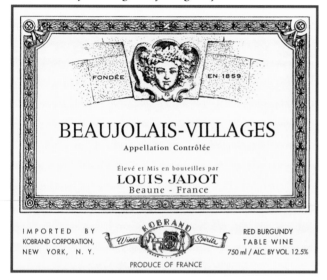

FIGURE 11-4
Moulin-à-Vent is one of the ten more defined Beaujolais Cru Villages.

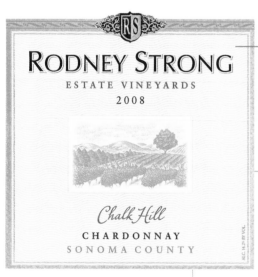

FIGURE 11-5
Chalk Hill AVA is a more narrowly defined appellation within the Sonoma County AVA.

FIGURE 11-6
Most New World fine wines are varietally labeled.

FIGURE 11-7
Unlike other AOC French regions, Alsatian wines are most often varietally labeled.

FIGURE 11-8

Very often the négociant is listed on the back label as with Kobrand's name on this label.

NOZZOLE
CHIANTI CLASSICO
DENOMINAZIONE DI ORIGINE CONTROLLATA E GARANTITA
RISERVA

This fine Chianti Classico Riserva is a special wine that comes from the 13th Century Nozzole Estate located in the heart of the Chianti Classico region. Riserva status for a Chianti Classico mandates extended bottle aging and produces a velvety wine of elegant fruit depth with the aromatic fragrance of the Sangiovese grape. It is superb with robust dishes.

GOVERNMENT WARNING: (1) ACCORDING TO THE SURGEON GENERAL, WOMEN SHOULD NOT DRINK ALCOHOLIC BEVERAGES DURING PREGNANCY BECAUSE OF THE RISK OF BIRTH DEFECTS.(2) CONSUMPTION OF ALCOHOLIC BEVERAGES IMPAIRS YOUR ABILITY TO DRIVE A CAR OR OPERATE MACHINERY, AND MAY CAUSE HEALTH PROBLEMS.

CONTAINS SULFITES

IMPORTED BY KOBRAND CORPORATION
NEW YORK, N.Y.

0 84692 42194 7

Nozzole è una proprietà di

AMBROGIO E GIOVANNI FOLONARI
TENUTE
padre e figli

producing or selecting, storing, and transporting wines, and then delivering them in optimum condition. Their customer service support is important and it is imperative that they keep their restaurant accounts apprised of any wine shortages, and changes or special pricing that may help the establishment's profitability. They may also support additional staff training with seminars and wine tastings, as well as providing point of sale materials such as table tents to augment sales. See Figure 11-8.

Cost Cost is a factor in any purchasing decision. For a food and beverage establishment, the cost of the wine purchased must fall within the budget parameters of the menu. A casual-dining restaurant, for example, would not offer a wine list featuring rare and expensive vintages. See Figure 11-9. It is worth noting that price does not dictate quality, but rather often reflects the marketing, and the wine critic ratings and perceptions. In general, an establishment in the United States looks for a return of 100% or more on the cost of wine. Volume purchases usually result in significant savings.

Compatibility with the food menu Wine lists should not only reflect the restaurant's price compatibility but should also reflect the food menu's theme and tastes. If the restaurant is Tuscan themed, the wines should reflect the style and profile of Tuscan foods even if they are not from that region. If the menu reflects a preponderance of seafood and light sauces, the wines should be lighter in style and have moderately high acidity to pair best with the food.

FIGURE 11-9

Sassicaia—This world renown wine with a proprietary name is also one of the most expensive and would only be found in high end restaurants.

SASSICAIA

MARCHESI INCISA DELLA ROCCHETTA

BOLGHERI SASSICAIA
DENOMINAZIONE DI ORIGINE CONTROLLATA

Imbottigliato all'origine dal produttore
Tenuta San Guido - Bolgheri
ITALIA

L.309 - 02

RED WINE
PRODUCT OF ITALY

ALC. BY VOL. 13.5%
NET CONT. 750 ML

IMPORTED BY KOBRAND CORPORATION, NEW YORK, N.Y.-SOLE U.S. IMPORTERS

Decoding the Label

179

Decoding the Wine Label

Knowing how to read a wine label can provide a wealth of information. Unfortunately, no standard, universal method or legal requirements exist for labeling. Today, however, all European Union wines conform to one set of standards. The information of greatest concern to the purchaser or server is the place of origin, the quality level, the vintage year, and the varietal or proprietary labeling.

Place of Origin

The place of origin is determined and guaranteed by the official state or regulatory agency of each country. The entire appellation system is based on the primacy concept of the place of origin. The wine may be labeled primarily for the location in which the grapes are grown, especially in the case of some quality French, Italian, Spanish, Portuguese, German, Austrian, and Hungarian wines. In Europe, if a label identifies a geographic area, 100% of the grapes must be grown in that area. In Australia and in the U.S., however, the requirement is 85%.

When determining the place of origin, one must examine the geographic level given on the label. In general, the more defined the area, the higher the quality of the wine. The five levels ranging from the broadest to the narrowest geographically defined areas are:

Country

- France
- U.S.A.

Region

- Bordeaux
- California

District

- Médoc
- Napa/Sonoma

Commune/village

- Pauillac
- St. Helena/Dry Creek

Vineyard

- Château Latour
- Mario's Vineyard/Stefani Ranch

See Figure 11-10.

Quality Level

Although much of the world shares similar standards, these are by no means uniform. Members of the European Union must meet hierarchic criteria that vary considerably. Each country has a governmental or regulatory agency to oversee viticultural and winemaking practices. These agencies qualify the level of each wine on the basis of place of origin, which determines viticultural practices and winemaking processes. There are currently three general quality levels: Quality Wines Produced in a Specified Region (QWPSR); Table Wines with a Specified Region; and Table Wines, the lowest category. This is now changing to two overall quality levels with Protected Designation of Origin (POD) and Protected Geographical Indication (PGI) in the first and "Wine" in the second. In countries with less clearly defined appellation-based or hierarchical systems than those of the European Union, there is greater freedom to experiment. The United States also has a federal regulatory agency, the Alcohol and Tobacco Tax and Trade Bureau (TTB), as well as state regulatory agencies to oversee the wine industry.

The brand name or name of a producer may be as significant as the quality rating given by a regulatory agency. For example, Angelo Gaja in Italy produces unconventional wines of the highest quality. His Chardonnay is nontraditional in Piedmont and has not been designated by the Italian regulatory agency as a highest quality wine with a rating of DOCG. In addition, the purchaser should be aware of the reputation of the négociant, wine merchant, or importer (Frederick Wildman and Sons, Neal Rosenthal, or Kobrand Corporations, for examples, are known to be reputable).

Vintage

Vintages reflect the weather for a particular year. Thanks to scientific developments, vintages matter less today than in the past. Although winemakers are able to manipulate wines to extract the greatest amount of flavors possible, there are limits as to what they can achieve. Winemakers can make a good wine, but not a great one, in an "off year". A great vintage increases the potential of a quality wine to develop greater complexity and aging potential than a wine created from a mediocre or poor vintage. In disastrous vintages, the producer may decide not to sell the wine under his primary label in order to protect the label's integrity.

Varietal, Generic, or Proprietary

Wines can be labeled with varietal, generic, or proprietary names. Australian and European varietal wines must contain a minimum of 85% of the grape variety stated on the label. In the United States, varietal wines must contain a minimum of 75% of the stated variety, except in Oregon, where a 90% minimum is required for certain varieties such as Pinot Noir, Chardonnay, and Pinot Gris.

Lower-quality American wines are often *semi-generically labeled*—for example, as California Chablis, Claret, or Madeira. These wines may be composed of any blend of any variety of grapes and typically bear little resemblance to their European namesakes. The United States has 14 acceptable semi-generic labels:

• Burgundy	• Claret	• Moselle	• Sherry
• Chablis	• Hock	• Port	• Tokay
• Champagne	• Madeira	• Rhine	
• Chianti	• Malaga	• Sauterne	

Many wines are also marketed under an exclusive *proprietary or brand name* such as Opus One® from the United States. Those wines do not reflect any single quality. Some proprietary labels, such as Blue Nun® from Germany, represent European table wines, and others, such as Sassicaia® from Italy, represent the best quality.

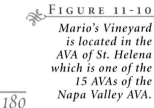

FIGURE 11-10

Mario's Vineyard is located in the AVA of St. Helena which is one of the 15 AVAs of the Napa Valley AVA.

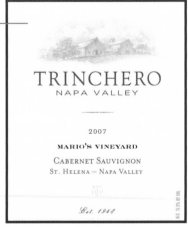

TRINCHERO
NAPA VALLEY

2007

MARIO'S VINEYARD
CABERNET SAUVIGNON
ST. HELENA – NAPA VALLEY

Est. 1948

United States Wine Regions

The United States is currently the world's fourth largest wine producer and is expected to become the world's number one wine consuming nation by 2012. Wine production reached almost 650 million gallons in 2008 with over 5400 wineries located in 50 states. California represents 90% of U.S. production and contributes more than $50 billion to the state's economy. While California has 110 American Viticultural Areas (as of 2009), there are six regional AVAs that encompass most of the others. They are:

- The North Coast AVA, which includes Napa Valley, Sonoma, Mendocino, and the Lake counties. This is the most famous region because it includes Napa Valley and Sonoma County, which produce some of California's finest wines. See Figure 11-11.

- The Central Coast and Santa Cruz Mountain AVAs, which are frequently divided by wine writers into the North Central and South Central Coast divisions, although neither of those exists as AVAs. The Central Coast includes: San Louis Obispo, Paso Robles, and Santa Barbara counties.

- The South Coast area, which primarily includes Temecula County.

- The Sierra Foothills area, which includes six AVAs.

- Klamath Mountains in northern California, which have three AVAs including Trinity Lakes.

- The Central Valley, which is the largest production zone, and includes Lodi AVA and Clarksburg AVA.

California and Oregon's wine growing regions are protected by coastal mountain ranges that keep the inland regions dry. The cold Pacific Ocean and San Pablo Bay effect, drawn inland by the desert heat, forms cooling mists that allow for the successful growth of cool climate grape varietals such as Chardonnay and Pinot Noir in areas closer to the coast. Sunny interior hot weather is equally conducive to warm climate varietals. There are enormous differences in temperatures based on the location of the vineyard as demonstrated by the example of the Carneros AVA at the southern end of Napa where it can be 15 degrees cooler than at the Calistoga AVA in the northern end of Napa just 30 miles away. The same is true of Sonoma County, which is considerably larger in size than Napa, and has the cool climate of the Russian River Valley as opposed to the warm climates of Dry Creek Valley or the Alexander Valley. The top varieties produced in descending order of production are: Chardonnay (W), Cabernet Sauvignon (R), Merlot (R), Zinfandel (R) Pinot Noir (R), Syrah (R), Sauvignon Blanc (W), and Pinot Gris/Pinot Grigio (W).

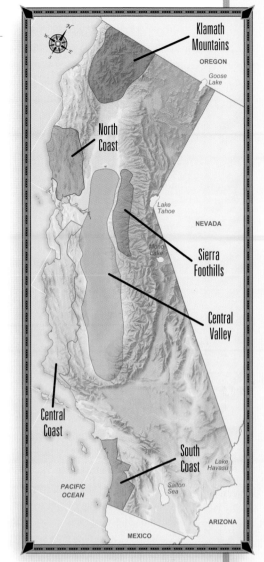

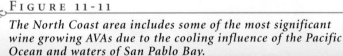

FIGURE 11-11

The North Coast area includes some of the most significant wine growing AVAs due to the cooling influence of the Pacific Ocean and waters of San Pablo Bay.

Oregon

Oregon is less well protected by the Coast Range in the northern half of the state, resulting in a cooler but wetter climate. Oregon produces a small quantity of the U.S.' total production (less than 1%). It is home to 400 small producers who have developed a world renown reputation particularly for Pinot Noir and Pinot Gris wines. There are currently 16 AVAs, six of which are sub-appellations of the most significant region of the Willamette Valley AVA. This area is sandwiched between the coastal mountain range in the west and the Cascade Mountains to the east.

Washington State

Washington State is the second largest producer of vinifera wines in the U.S. Unlike Oregon, most of Washington State's vineyards are located west of the Cascades in the arid Sonoran desert, and are irrigated with water from the Columbia and Yakima Rivers. The desert soils allow growers to plant ungrafted vines to save considerable costs. The climate is continental with short hot summers and cold winters with the ever present danger of frost in the fall. Due to significant diurnal temperature fluctuations and long summer days, many varieties are able to ripen while maintaining high acidity. There are 11 AVAs, the largest of which is the Columbia Valley. This area covers almost 1,000 square miles and includes 9 sub-appellations including Horse Heaven Hills and Wahluke Slopes AVAs. There are now 600 wineries, some of which have developed a deservedly high reputation for producing Chardonnay (W), Cabernet Sauvignon (R), Merlot (R), Riesling (W), Syrah (R), and Sauvignon Blanc (W).

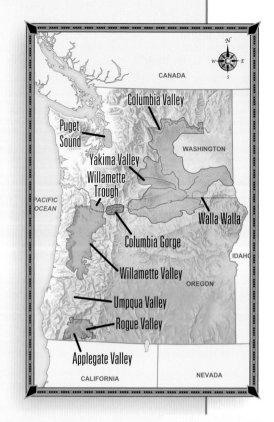

New York and other states

New York is the third largest producer of vinifera wines though it ranks second in total wine production since most wines are made from hybrids such as Vidal Blanc (W), Seyval Blanc (W), Chambourcin (R), and indigenous grape varieties such as Concord (R), Delaware (R), and Catawba (B). Riesling (W) and Gewürztraminer (W) from the Finger Lakes AVA, and Merlot (R) from North Fork AVA in Long Island have developed reputations for quality wines. Humidity and climatic variations in the growing and harvesting seasons create the biggest challenges to growers on the eastern seaboard.

States such as Rhode Island, which is part of the Southeastern New England AVA; North Carolina (especially in the northwest corner of the state) with three AVAs including the Yadkin Valley AVA; and Colorado with its high altitude river valleys (Grand Valley AVA and West Elks AVA), are all producing quality vinifera wines in an industry that is still in its infancy. While all 50 states produce wine, the combined vinifera production total of all states other than that of California, Washington state, Oregon, and New York equals less than 2.5%. Florida ranks 6th in total production, which is derived almost totally from Muscadine native grapes, hybrids, and other fruit wines.

FIGURE 11-12

FIGURE 11-13

Brand Name — Type of Wine — Place of Origin — Alcohol Content — Name and Address of Bottler — Health Warning — Net Contents — Sulfite Statement

RUTHERFORD BENCH RESERVE

RESERVE

SEQUOIA GROVE
CABERNET SAUVIGNON
RUTHERFORD
NAPA VALLEY
ALC. 14.4% BY VOL.

Please visit our small family-owned winery located beneath the giant sequoia trees in Rutherford. Established in 1980. www.sequoiagrove.com

PRODUCED AND BOTTLED BY
SEQUOIA GROVE VINEYARDS
RUTHERFORD, CALIFORNIA

GOVERNMENT WARNING: (1) ACCORDING TO THE SURGEON GENERAL, WOMEN SHOULD NOT DRINK ALCOHOLIC BEVERAGES DURING PREGNANCY BECAUSE OF THE RISK OF BIRTH DEFECTS. (2) CONSUMPTION OF ALCOHOLIC BEVERAGES IMPAIRS YOUR ABILITY TO DRIVE A CAR OR OPERATE MACHINERY, AND MAY CAUSE HEALTH PROBLEMS.

750 ML   CONTAINS SULFITES

United States Labeling Laws

United States law requires that the following information is listed on wine labels:

1. **Brand Name:** Either the name of the producer or the proprietary name
2. **Type of Wine:** Semi-generic, table (red, white or rosé), or sparkling
3. **Country or Place of Origin:** The country or state or appellation must be included
4. **Name and Address of the Bottler**
5. **Alcohol Content:** For table or still wines, a variance of 1.5% is allowed; for sparkling wines < 1%
6. **Net Contents of the Bottle**
7. **Sulfite Statement:** States whether or not the wine contains sulfites (most do)
8. **Health Warning:** To advise pregnant women and heavy machinery operators against consuming alcoholic beverages

See Figures 11-12 and 11-13.

U.S. Labeling Terms

Accepted labeling terms in the United States include:

- Vintage–95% of grapes must be from that vintage year
- Estate Bottled–100% grown, made, and bottled at the winery
- Produced by–75% or more crushed, made, and bottled at the winery
- Cellared and Bottled by–10% or less crushed, made at the winery
- Vineyard Name–95% or more grown at the particular vineyard

Australia

The huge island continent of Australia ranks sixth in the world's wine production and is the second largest producer of imported wine into the U.S. While wine is produced in all of the Australian states, the most important regions lie in the southern third of the country in the 30° latitude (South) where almost all Australian wine is produced. This region includes the states of New South Wales, South Australia, Victoria, the island state of Tasmania, and parts of Queensland; all of which form the super appellation of Southeastern Australia. Bulk wine regions are located in the arid Outback region of New South Wales and Victoria. This area is irrigated by the Murray, Darling, and Murumbidgee Rivers and is similar to California's lush Central Valley. The best growing region for quality wines is along the southern coast along the Tasman Sea where there are cold ocean breezes and moderate temperatures. The famous Barossa Valley, Coonawarra, Eden and Clare Valleys, and the Margaret River appellations are found here.

While Australia's export oriented wine industry may be best known for its inexpensive, easily quaffable, fruity "critter" wines, it does produce high quality white wines primarily from Chardonnay, Sémillon, and Riesling, and reds from Shiraz (a synonym for Syrah), Merlot, and Cabernet Sauvignon. While these wines may be sold varietally, they are frequently blended so that one may find the designations GSM (short for Grenache, Shiraz, and Mourvèdre) on the label.

Australian Labeling Laws

Australia's Wine and Brandy Corporation is the regulatory agency that enforces labeling laws through an annual audit of the Label Integrity Program. The LIP enforces the following regulations:

1. A minimum 85% of the wine must be made from the stated varietal.
2. A minimum of 85% of the wine comes from the stated region.
3. If a wine is composed of more than one variety, the varieties must be named in descending order. For example, a wine labeled Cabernet Shiraz would contain more Cabernet Sauvignon than Shiraz.
4. Semi-generic labels that are named for European appellations, are not allowed.
5. If the term "reserve bin" or "bin number" is listed, the wine must indicate distinctiveness and higher quality.
6. If the term "show reserve" is used, the wine must have won a medal at a winetasting competition, an event that is taken very seriously by wine makers.
7. *Geographic Indications* are an official description of Australian wine zones, regions, and subregions. They are increasingly important, just as American Viticultural Areas are in the United States. There are now 102 Geographic Indications that have been classified (as of 2009). See Figure 11-14.

FIGURE 11-14

CLARENDON HILLS

Minimum 85% (actual 100%) —— GRENACHE
South Australia 85% —— CLARENDON
Vintage —— 2005
Vineyard Name —— *Hickinbotham*

750ML

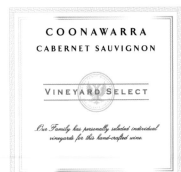

ANGOVE
SINCE 1886
FAMILY WINEMAKERS

COONAWARRA
CABERNET SAUVIGNON

VINEYARD SELECT

Our Family has personally selected individual vineyards for this hand-crafted wine.

New Zealand

New Zealand is a newcomer to the international wine scene since having developed a reputation primarily for two varietals: Sauvignon Blanc and Pinot Noir. Its two islands (North and South Islands) span the wine growing latitudes of 35° to 45° south. The vineyards are almost all located on the eastern side of the islands as they are protected by mountainous ranges that act as a rain shadow. New Zealand's primary appellations include: Marlborough and Central Otago in South Island, and Hawke's Bay and Wellington in the North Island.

New Zealand Wine Laws

New Zealand is still developing its wine laws, but currently the wine's minimum content for the stated variety, appellation, or vintage must be at least 75%. Most wines produced have a minimum of 85% to satisfy the label requirements of major export markets. See Figures 11-15 and 11-16.

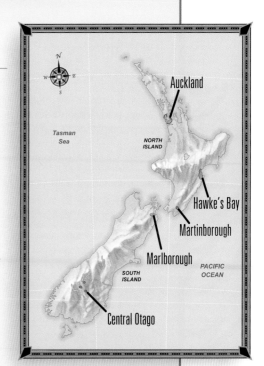

❧ FIGURE 11-15

Sauvignon Blanc is the most popular variety for which New Zealand has become known. Marlborough is a major appellation in South Island.

WHITEHAVEN

Marlborough

SAUVIGNON BLANC

2008

NEW ZEALAND

❧ FIGURE 11-16

Though a recent phenomenon, Pinot Noir has cemented New Zealand's reputation as an up and coming fine wine producer. Some of the best of New Zealand's Pinot Noir comes from the world's most southerly vineyards in Central Otago.

AMISFIELD

PINOT NOIR
2005

CENTRAL OTAGO
WINE OF NEW ZEALAND

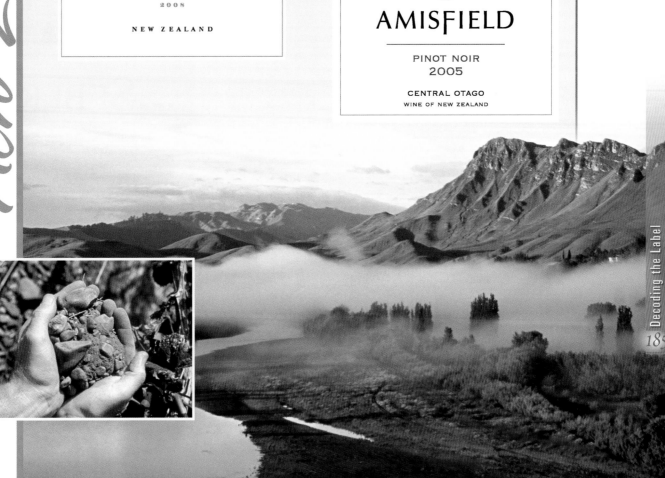

South Africa

Although South Africa is considered a New World wine producer, its production first started in 1659 with the settlement of European colonists who established a revictualing station for European traders travelling to India and the Far East. South Africa's wine growing region is located mostly along the coast especially in the Capetown area where the Atlantic Ocean meets the Indian Ocean, and the cold Benguela current from Antarctica creates winds that cool the hot inland temperatures to produce an ideal Mediterranean wine growing climate. The geographic breakdown of wine areas are super regions, which incorporate regions formed by districts composed of wards. The most significant region is the Western Cape, which encompasses the Coastal Region including the Stellenbosch and Paarl districts.

South Africa had a well-deserved reputable reputation until phylloxera struck in the mid 19th century and its industry became dominated by a single co-op early in the 20th century. Due to the international boycotts created in response to apartheid policies, only 30% of the grapes grown were used for wine production. South Africa's wine industry has since seen a resurgence of quality, which has led it to seek a worldwide export market.

Chenin Blanc, also locally known as Steen, is the most significant variety, although noble international varieties such as Chardonnay (W), Sauvignon Blanc (W), Cabernet Sauvignon (R), Shiraz, and Merlot are also now produced and are earning South Africa a highly regarded reputation. It is also the home of Pinotage, which is a cross between Pinot Noir and Cinsaut that was developed in South Africa almost a century ago.

South African Wine Laws

The wine laws are overseen by the South African Wine and Spirits Board, which supervises the Wine of Origin system certifying that any wine with a stated appellation must be 100% from the region, district, or ward, and that if there is a stated vintage or variety, it must consist of a minimum of 85%. The Board samples all wines for certification and affixes a white paper seal over the cork, but under the capsule to verify its acceptance. See Figure 11-17.

FIGURE 11-17

South African Labels with "Cape Blend" refer to red wines blended with a minimum 20% Pinotage.

Chile and Argentina

Chile is another international newcomer, which has been producing wines since the Spanish settled the Central Valley in the 16th century. Its wine quality was not well considered despite its use of Bordeaux varieties that were planted in the mid 19th century. The dominant varieties were Pais and Muscatel and the wines were mostly insipid. It was only once tariffs and legislative barriers were removed in the 1980s that investments were made so that the number of wineries soared with a focus on the export market.

Due to Chile's long (3000 miles) thin land mass, which is positioned between the Pacific Ocean and the Andes Mountains, Chile enjoys a Mediterranean climate similar to that of California with a wide diurnal temperature range and a lack of rain during the growing season. The traditional location of its vineyards was near the capital, Santiago, in the Central Valley. In the last 15 years there has been an expansion of vineyards to hillsides and bench sites that are more conducive to high quality wine production. Large foreign investments, 'flying winemakers', and improved viticultural knowledge has led Chile to become an important exporter of wines to the U.S. The dominant red varieties are Cabernet Sauvignon, Merlot, and Carmenère (a Bordeaux variety that was misidentified as Merlot until the 1990s), and Sauvignon Blanc and Chardonnay for whites.

Chilean Wine Laws

1. If a wine label has the name of a place, such as a region, sub-region or appellation, 75% of the grapes must come from that place. Chile created a Denominación d'Origen system that recognizes larger regions, which incorporate more distinct *terroirs* forming sub-regions.
2. If a wine label carries the name of a grape variety, the wine must be made from at least 75% of that grape variety, although most are composed of 85% for the export market in the EU.
3. If a wine label carries a vintage, 75% of the wine must come from that vintage. See Figure 11-18.

Argentina

While Argentina is a much larger land mass and produces far more wine than Chile, its wines are made for its domestic rather than export market. Ninety percent of its production is consumed domestically. It is only recently that Argentina has begun exporting quality wines to Europe and the U.S. Argentina's major wine producing region of Mendoza, which is situated east of the Andes and distinguished by its high elevation, has developed a reputation primarily for Malbec, a red wine, and Torrontés, a white wine. The diurnal range helps to keep the wines lively with acidity and the vines benefit from long hang time. One of the greatest challenges is hail storms, which can devastate a crop in minutes.

Argentina's Wine Laws

Argentina has modeled an appellation system on its European counterparts with a DOC at the highest quality ranking. Only two sub-appellations of Mendoza have achieved this designation: Luján de Cuyo and San Rafael. The next level is Indicación Geográfica (IG), which is used for more regional designations; and the third ranking is for Argentina's table wine. For a wine to be varietally labeled it must be 80% of the particular variety. See Figure 11-19.

FIGURE 11-18

The label is representative of the partnerships and the impact of foreign investments in the Chilean wine industry and the dominance of Bordeaux varietals.

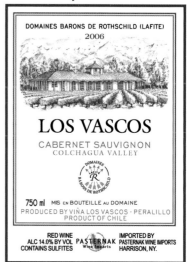

FIGURE 11-19

Malbec grown in high elevations in Mendoza is the varietal that Argentina has become known for.

The European Union

The European Union is now comprised of 27 countries with a combined population of nearly 500 million people, and almost 10 million acres of vineyards that produce 1.8 billion (12liter) cases of wine.

European Union Labeling Requirements and System of Quality

As the new rules for individual members are currently insufficiently clear, this text will reflect only those now used. All European wines must meet the standards established by the European Union Office International du Vin (OIV) and must be labeled accordingly. The label should reflect the primacy of typicity of style from a specific region or *terroir*.

The European Union currently identifies five different categories for still wines. As of January 1, 2011, the new system will include five similar general quality levels, which will be mandatory for all members. There will be two broad types of wines, those with geographic indications, and those without. For those with geographic indications there will be two definitions: *Protected Designation of Origin* (PDO's) and *Protected Geographical Indications* (PGI's). The third category, which was labeled "Table Wine", will now be retired and simply referred to as "Wine". This revised category will allow both the vintage and the variety to be mentioned on the label.

Protected Designation of Origin These regions must be registered with the European Union, and each defined region is governed by regulations established by EU criteria and legislated within the respective member countries. The categories include:

1. Grape varieties recommended or authorized
2. Viticultural practices
3. Maximum yields
4. Winemaking practices
5. Minimum alcoholic content
6. Analysis of the finished wine.

Appellation d'Origine Contrôlée (AOC) for France, Denominazione di Origine Controlata e Garantita (DOCG) and Denominazione di Origine Controlata (DOC) for Italy, are all examples of designations of origin.

Protected Geographical Indication This second level refers to wines produced from a specific European country that has less stringent rules. Whereas 100% of the wine from a PDO must come from that appellation, only 85% need come from the PGI. The wine may also have a vintage and include up to two varieties on the label. This level will include the current French classification of Vin de Pays (VdP) for France, which will change to Indication Géographique Protégée that is similarly used for other agricultural products such as cheese. See Figure 11-20. It is currently unclear as to how the member states will respond to the new regulations when reconfiguring their own label terminology.

Table Wine The third level is the Table Wine category, which will be called "Wine" and can refer only to European-produced wines. Although the current label may not include either the variety or vintage, the new Wine category will.

Non-EU Wine with Geographical Description The fourth level, Wine with Geographical Description, refers to wines produced from specific recognized wine regions outside the European Union such as a wine from Napa.

Non-EU Wine The fifth level is for non-EU wines of lower quality that cannot include either a vintage or a variety on the label. The U.S. health warning requirement is forbidden in the European Union.

FIGURE 11-20

Vin de Pays will be changing to Indication Géographique Protégé.

France

France is viewed by many in the world as a leader in quality wine production and a barometer by which to measure one's own wines. Its historical influence is undeniable as most of the recognized 'international" varieties, such as Chardonnay, Sauvignon Blanc, Pinot Gris, Pinot Noir, Cabernet Sauvignon, Merlot, and Syrah, originated from France. With a vineyard area that is only surpassed by Spain, France is one of the leading wine producers with almost half a billion cases. France's wines are currently the third most imported into the U.S. and also represent about a third of all wines exported in the world. France's climate is ideal for its many varieties because it enjoys the characteristics of all three major climates: Continental, Maritime, and Mediterranean. The primary regions of quality wine production (AOC) are:

- **Champagne**—recognized as the birthplace of the classic or traditional method for sparkling wine. See Figure 11-21.

- **Loire**—famous for Chenin Blanc and Sauvignon Blanc for whites, and Cabernet Franc for reds.

- **Alsace**—home to varietals such as Riesling, Gewürztraminer, Pinot Gris, and Muscat. See Figure 11-22.

- **Rhône**—the white Viognier is the world's model while Syrah and Grenache play a similar role for red wines.

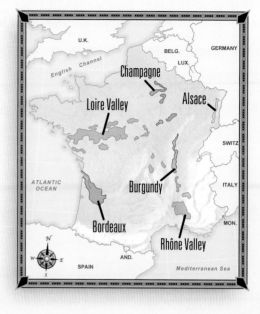

❧ FIGURE 11-21

Hand harvesting in some quality wine producing areas such as Champagne is required by law.

❧ FIGURE 11-22

Specific sites that face southeast and are at higher elevations provide an ideal climate and soil conditions for ripened grapes in Alsace.

FIGURE 11-23

The clay, limestone, and gravelly soils, and the maritime climate provide perfect growing conditions for Merlot and Cabernet Sauvignon based wines.

- **Bordeaux**—produces high quality Sauvignon Blancs generally blended with Sémillon, which is the primary variety used for botrytized Sauternes. Bordeaux also produces the apogee of blended red wines based on Cabernet Sauvignon, Merlot, and Cabernet France. See Figure 11-23.
- **Burgundy**—home to some of the world's greatest Chardonnays and Pinot Noirs. It has become the role model for the rest of the world. Burgundy is also the most important producer of Gamay and a user of the carbonic maceration technique for bright fruity reds. See Figure 11-24.

The Languedoc-Rousillon is equivalent to California Central Valley where the bulk of wine production still takes place. While most of its wine falls under the lowest wine classification it is the most important region for Vin de Pays, and many AOC sub-appellations have developed within its boundaries to produce wines based on Grenache, Carignan, Syrah, and Mourvèdre.

French Wine Laws

The renamed *Institut National de l'Origine et de la Qualité (INAO)* is France's regulatory agency, which governs wine production and labeling. The enforcement arm of this group is called the *Service de Répression des Fraudes,* which enforces the law and punishes fraud. French wines are categorized into three broad classifications:

FIGURE 11-24

This neatly rowed and tidy Pinot Noir site of the AOC Domaine Romanée Conti represents some of the most expensive agricultural land in the world.

Appellation d'Origine Contrôlée (AOC or AC) is the highest classification, representing 57% of all wines produced in France. The wines used to fall under the classification of QWPSR and are governed by the same criteria. Different classifications are unique to each AC region, but most have a tiered system that is defined by the geographic boundaries. In sequence of quality, from highest to lowest, they are as follow:

- *Grand cru classé*—generally a single vineyard site (See Figure 11-25)
- *Premier cru classé*—single vineyard in some regions such as Bordeaux is the highest designation but may not consist of one contiguous vineyard
- **Village**—named after a village or commune but may incorporate the surrounding region
- **District**—a larger geographic designation but one that still shares the same viticultural characteristics
- **Region**—a broader geographic designation where there is less of a defined personality to the wine but one that is still recognizable as coming from a single region

Vin de Pays refers to "country wine", and was created to upgrade wine-growing regions from table wine production. There has been an explosive growth in this category because of the dominance of international varieties (aka French varieties) that are being grown and marketed worldwide. There are over 150 VdPs, which will be labeled Indication Géographique Protégée, and these will represent about a third of France's production. As opposed to AOC wines, which must be made from 100% of grapes grown in the designated appellation, wines with the Vin de Pays designation need only have a minimum of 85% grapes grown in the designated region. *Vin* is ordinary table wine that is equivalent to U.S. bulk wines.

French Labeling Terms

- *Vendange/Récolte*–Vintage/harvest
- *Mis en bouteille au château*–Estate bottled
- *Cru*–"Growth," indicating a specific vineyard of high quality, which is often used as a classification level as well
- *Cuvée*–Blend
- *Clos*–Walled vineyard
- *Brut*–Very dry
- *Sec*–Dry
- *Moelleux*–Sweet

FIGURE 11-25

Bâtard-Montrachet is one of the 31 Grand Cru appellations of Burgundy.

Italy

Although Italy has produced wines for millennia, its modern wine history has been for the most part undistinguished up until the last 40 years. Its mostly Mediterranean climate and perfectly suited volcanic based soils that are blended with limestone and other coil types provide a perfect backdrop for the production of fine quality wines. Italy has the third most planted vineyards in the world and frequently ranks as a top wine producer by volume. Italy is divided into twenty different regions and it is often said that "they are in search of a country." This saying reflects how different each region is from the other culturally, and how varied the wines are as well. There are over 1,000 varieties grown, including Sangiovese, which is the most predominant black grape variety. Other very important red grape varieties include Montepulciano, Merlot, Barbera, Negroamaro, Cabernet Sauvignon, Aglianico, and Nebbiolo. For white wines the most significant are: Trebbiano (which is predominant but not known for making distinctive wines), Malvasia, Chardonnay, Garganega, Pinot Grigio, and Moscato.

The last four decades have seen a wine revolution in Italy, making it one of the most dynamic wine regions of the world with innovative viticultural and vinification techniques. Until Italy developed a sufficiently large urban middle class, wine, for the most part, had been perceived as an essential condiment to a meal, akin to olive oil, which should be well made but not something about which to necessarily contemplate.

Most Americans are less well acquainted with these Italian varieties. Italy's most famous wines are sold under the names of a varietal or an appelation such as Chianti or a combination of grape variety and appellation as in the case of Moscato d'Asti. The most significant regions of Italy include:

Piedmont Piedmont in the northwest, a name that translates as "at the foot of the mountain", is home to many of the highest quality zones including Barolo, Barbaresco, Asti, and Gavi to name but a few. Due to its cooler climate, wines from here have greater acidity and are very food friendly.

The Veneto The Veneto in the Northeast produces the highest volume of DOC/DOCG wine in Italy. It is best known for Soave and Pinot Grigio for whites, and Valpolicella, Amarone della Valpolicella, Bardolino, and Merlot for reds.

Tuscany Tuscany has developed a worldwide reputation for its food and wine. The most famous regions of Tuscany are Chianti Classico, Brunello di Montalcino, and Vino Nobile di Montelpulciano. Tuscany is representative of the Italian wine Renaissance with new DOC's and DOCG's being created and exciting developments taking place on its western coast in the areas of Bolghieri and the former swamplands of Maremma.

Southern Italy and the Islands Southern Italy and the Islands are where the ancient Greeks settled and planted vineyards naming it Oenotria or land of the vine. With a sunny Mediterranean climate on volcanic soils, this region is undergoing a more recent transformation than its northern counterparts. Vineyards here were at one time known mostly for bulk wine production, but now appellations such as Taurasi or Greco di Tufo in Campania and Salice Salentino have helped to transform that impression.

Italy's Wine Laws

The wine laws of 1963 created the *Denominazione di Origine Controllata (DOC)*, which was patterned after France's AOC. These laws spurred the Italian wine industry toward modernization and quality. Approximately 15% of Italy's total wine production is classified DOC or DOCG, and within that category more than 900 types of wines are produced in more than 450 appellations.

Because of the very stringent DOC and DOCG regulations, many producers refused to abide by them and were therefore excluded, even though they were producing some of Italy's finest quality and most expensive wines. This anomaly precipitated changes with the Goria laws of 1992, creating the IGT category. It is no wonder that Italian wine labeling is difficult to understand. Generally, the wines are labeled in four ways:

- **The name of the village, district, or region**–Barolo (See Figure 11-26)
- **The name of the variety**–Pinot Grigio (See Figure 11-27)
- **The name of a variety and the region**–Brunello Di Montalcino (See Figure 11-28)
- **The proprietary names**–such as Summus® or Ornellaia®

Unlike the other EU members, Italy has four wine classifications, though with the new EU laws, it is not clearly understood how DOCG and DOC will be allowed to remain separate PDO classifications.

Denominazione di Origine Controllata e Garantita (DOCG) This most stringent category requires that the producer follows the requirements of the DOC and guarantees what is stated on the label. How this category falls into the new system is anyone's guess. There are currently 48 DOCG wines.

Denominazione di Origine Controllata (DOC) Equivalent to the French AOC designation and governed by the same kinds of regulations; this classification includes more than 320 wines.

Indicazione Geographica Tipica (IGT) This classification is meant to upgrade 40% of Italy's table wines. Producers must apply for this status, and currently more than 118 have done so.

Vino da Tavola (VDT) Table wine, by far the largest category, encompasses 85% of Italy's total wine production. This category will change to "Vino" on the label.

Italian Labeling Terms

- *Vendemmia*–Vintage
- *Azienda agricola, fattoria, tenuta*–Estate (each)
- *Imbottigliato all' castelo*–Estate bottled
- *Imbottigliato all' Origine*–Estate bottled
- *Classico*–From the center of a DOC wine region
- *Riserva*–A DOC(G) wine with additional aging
- *Superiore*–A DOC(G) wine with 0.5% or more alcohol than is required
- *Bianco*–White
- *Rosso*–Red
- *Nero*–Dark red
- *Rosato*–Pink
- *Secco*–Dry
- *Abboccato*–Semi-dry
- *Dolce*–Sweet
- *Spumante*–Sparkling
- *Frizzante*–Sparkling
- *Cantina Sociale*–Vine-growers cooperative
- *Marchio Nazionale*–Appears on a red seal on the neck of a wine bottle, indicating compliance with government controls for wines exported to the United States

FIGURE 11-26

Barolo is a small town for which one of Italy's great wines is named.

FIGURE 11-27

Pinot Grigio, synonymous with Pinot Gris, has become a world favorite in just the last two decades.

FIGURE 11-28

Brunello is a Sangiovese clone that has been named for its dark almost brown color and is most famous around the medieval Tuscan town of Montalcino.

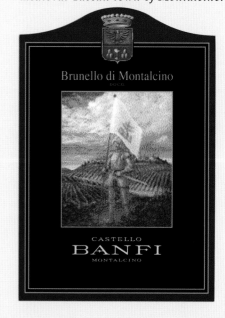

Germany

Because Germany lies in the most northern latitude where the ripening season is shorter, almost all the wine regions are in the southwestern corner of the country. Germany's vineyards cover approximately 250,000 acres, which is about the size of Bordeaux' vineyards alone. Germans consume most of their own wines and provide a significant import market for others. The U.S. is an important import market for Germany's high end wines.

The Romans were the first to plant vineyards in the thirteen wine growing regions of Germany and used the Rhine as a natural defensive border against its opponents. The best wine growing sites are located on the steep slopes of rivers such as the Mosel and the Rhine where warmer waters moderate ambient temperatures and reflect sunlight back onto the vineyards. Eighty percent of Germany's wines are white and Riesling is the most important in terms of quality. *Spätburgunder*, which is German for Pinot Noir, has undergone a transformation because of global warming, and has allowed producers to make wines that are comparable to those produced in Burgundy. Müller-Thurgau, which is the second most planted grape variety and is a cross between Riesling and Silvaner, is still important commercially. It is hardier than Riesling, but it does not have the same attributes.

FIGURE 11-29

Traditional labels are difficult for English speaking people to understand, though they have a great deal of useful information.

FIGURE 11-30

The latest marketing efforts are represented by labels such as this one, which is easy to read and will attract less traditional wine drinkers in their 20s and 30s.

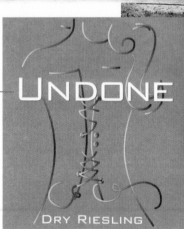

The most important wine growing regions are:

- **Rheingau**—renowned for its Rieslings from south facing slopes and grown in blue and red slate
- **Rheinhessen**—the largest of the 13 wine growing regions with quality Riesling and red wines
- **Pfalz**—produces one quarter of all Riesling grown in Germany
- **Mosel**—incredibly steep slopes on the banks of the twisting and winding Mosel river, and its tributaries producing some of Germany's most distinctive wines

German Wine Labeling

German wine labels are the most detailed but are also, at times, among the most unintelligible. See Figure 11-29. Fortunately for the U.S. consumer, many have become very modern looking and easier to understood. See Figure 11-30. In accordance with the EU standards, German wines are divided into two categories: *Qualitätswein* (quality wine) and *Tafelwein* (table wine). Wines in Germany are officially classified according to the ripeness of the grapes at the time of harvest. *Tafelwein* is divided into three sub-categories of *Tafelwein, Deutscher Tafelwein* and *Deutscher Landwein*. The latter is of a better quality and mirrors IGP. Consumers in the United States are concerned with *Qualitätswein*, the quality wines, which are divided into two sub-classifications:

Qualitätswein bestimmter Anbaugebiete (QbA) This category is the largest and includes quality wines from one of the 13 specified wine regions. These wines tend to be light, fresh, and fruity and are allowed to be enriched with süss reserve, or sweet reserve made of sterile unfermented must.

Qualitätswein mit Prädikat (QmP) This quality wine with special distinction is the best of Germany's wines. These wines are further classified into six categories with special attributes in ascending order of ripeness at harvest. They include: *Kabinett, Spätlese, Auslese, Beerenauslese, Eiswein, and Trockenbeerenauslese.* See Figure 11-31.

- *Kabinett*—Normal harvest time; lightest of *Prädikat* wines
- *Spätlese*—Late harvest with more intensity and richness; not necessarily sweet
- *Auslese*—Hand-selected grapes; intensely flavored, but may have been affected by *botrytis* and are not usually sweet
- *Beerenauslese (BA)*—Overripe berries that are individually selected; a rare sweet wine that is rich and flavorful
- *Eiswein*—Literally means "ice wine;" has the ripeness of BA and is harvested and pressed while frozen; remarkable acidity balancing sweetness
- *Trockenbeerenauslese (TBA)*—Grapes that are affected by *botrytis* and individually picked, making a very rich, sweet, honeylike wine

Consumers also see the term *trocken* and *halbtrocken* on labels, indicating dry or semi-dry styles of wine.

Because the Prädikat system is not based on a sense of place or *terroir*, this has posed a bit of a challenge to the EU system, which is based on the concept of place. There is another concurrent system, which is a wine producer based classification movement based on *terroir*. This system has more stringent viticultural and vinification requirements than the official system, and now extends from Rheingau, where it originated, to include all 13 growing regions. The association is called the **VDP**, which stands for *Verband Deutscher Prädikat und Qualitätsweingüter,* and is symbolized by an eagle holding a cluster of grapes, which is found on the capsule of the wine bottle. The VDP wines can be designated as Erste Lage (First Growth) while dry wines are designated as Grosses Gewächs (Great Growth). Gewächs that are fruity and sweet are classified by the Prädikat system.

In addition to this classification, vintage 2000 marked the beginning of the use of "Classic" and "Selection" terms. "Classic" wines are the equivalent of above-average quality *QbA* wines, made with traditional varieties. "Selection" wines must be hand harvested from a single vineyard, and thus present German wine producers the opportunity to develop a French "cru" system.

Although confusing, the elements for a classification system based on *terroir* are already in place—13 regions *(anbaugebiete)*, 39 districts *(bereiche)*, 165 collective vineyard sites *(grosslagen)*, and 2,643 individual vineyard sites *(einzellagen)*.

Finally, German wine bottles may have seals and awards placed on them, indicating that the wine has qualified as exceeding the standards for a particular classification. A gold seal on the neck indicates a dry wine; a green seal indicates an off-dry wine; and a red seal indicates that the wine is sweet.

German Labeling Terms

- *Rotwein*–Red wine
- *Weissherbst*–Rosé QbA or QmP wine made from a single variety of black grapes
- *Rotling*–Rosé made from a blend
- *Schillerwein*–QbA or QmP rosé wine from Württenberg
- *Perlwein*–A red or white wine with a light sparkle, usually bcarbon dioxide injection
- *Deutscher Sekt*–A quality sparkling wine with less alcohol than champagne
- *Trocken*–Dry
- *Halbtrocken*–Semi-dry
- *Erzeugerabfüllung*–Estate bottled
- *Gutsabfüllung*–Estate bottled
- *Winzergenossenschaft*–Wine growers' cooperative

FIGURE 11-31

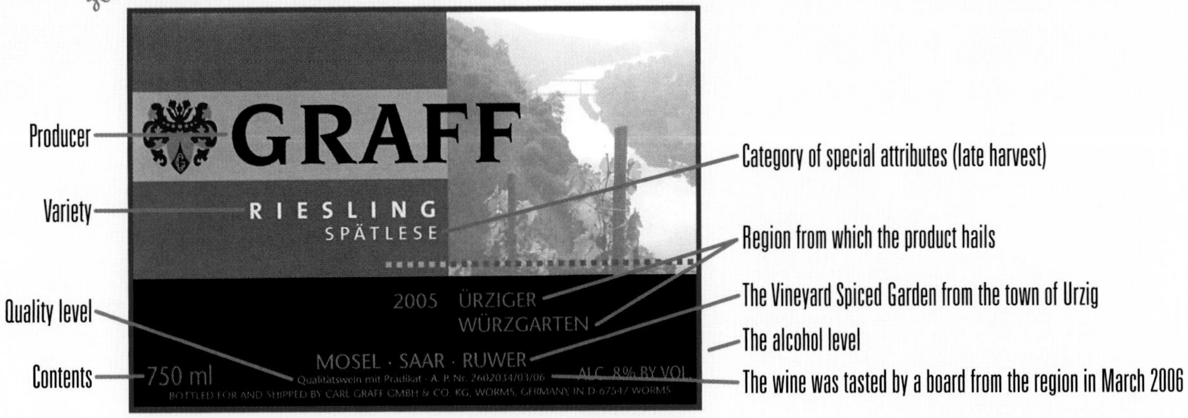

Producer — GRAFF

Variety — RIESLING SPÄTLESE

Quality level —

Contents — 750 ml

2005 ÜRZIGER WÜRZGARTEN

MOSEL · SAAR · RUWER

Qualitätswein mit Prädikat · A. P. Nr. 2602034/01/06

BOTTLED FOR AND SHIPPED BY CARL GRAFF GMBH & CO. KG, WORMS, GERMANY IN D-67547 WORMS

ALC. 8% BY VOL

Category of special attributes (late harvest)

Region from which the product hails

The Vineyard Spiced Garden from the town of Urzig

The alcohol level

The wine was tasted by a board from the region in March 2006

Spain

Spain has a long wine history, yet most of its wines were unknown until recently, with the exception of Rioja and Sherry. Once Spain joined the EU, it was jolted out of its languor by a massive infusion of capital and the creative forces unleashed after decades of fascist rule. Wines of Spain coming from regions unknown even to "wine experts" of a decade ago are now found in every major market of the U.S.

Spain is very mountainous and has distinct regions and climates: the wet fjord region of Ríaz Baixas of Galicia in the northwest; the mountainous northern regions of Rioja and Navarra at the foot of the Pyrenees Mountains; the hot and arid plateau of La Mancha and the Mediterranean coastline of Penedés and Tarragona; to the southern tip of Sherry where the Atlantic meets the Mediterranean. See Figure 11-32.

Spain's most widely planted grape, Airén, is also the world's most planted and is used to produce indistinct bulk wine. The most famous, distinctive, and the most widely spread is the Tempranillo variety, which has many names depending on its location. Garnacha, known as Grenache in France, plays an important role both as a stand alone and a component of blends. Monastrell, also known as Mataro and Mourvèdre in France, is the third most significant black grape. Macabeo, known as Viura in parts of Spain, is the most significant white variety along with Palomino for Sherry, and Pedro Ximénez for sweet solera wines.

Rioja is still one of the most famous regions and is only one of two regions holding the highest labeling designation of Denominación Geográfica de Origen Califcáda (DOCa), the other region is **Priorat** in Catalonia. There are about one thousand growers in Rioja who sell their grapes to three hundred producers, though some may be using their own grapes. The wines are medium bodied with floral and cherry aromas with distinct leathery bouquets and are bottle aged. They have medium high acidity with light to medium tannins and are very food friendly. Roija also produces very good quality whites and rosés.

FIGURE 11-32

Spain's climate, topography and soils are varied from the mountainous regions of Navarre to the chalky plains of Sherry, all resulting in very different wines.

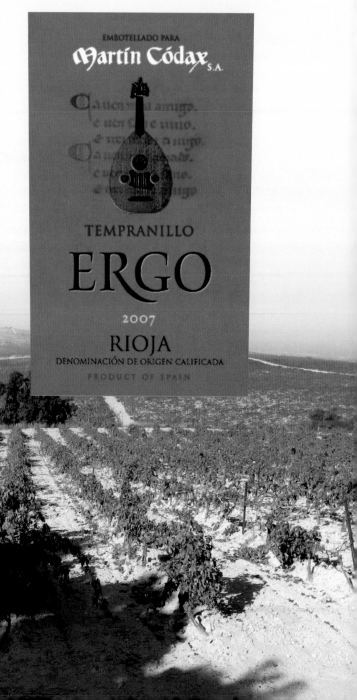

Other regions include:

- **Ribera del Duero**, which is the home of one of the world's most expensive wines, Vega de Sicilia's Unico. This hot region in the Duero River Valley has a wide diurnal range due to its altitude, which allows its Tempranillo based wines (frequently blended with Cabernet Sauvignon, Garnacha and Merlot) to maintain their acidity despite their richness.
- **Toro** and **Cigales** are other appellations in the Duero that make similar wines.
- **Rueda** is strictly a white wine appellation in the Duero, which produces quality acidic food friendly Verdejo based wines.
- **Cava** refers to a classic or traditional method-made sparkling wine produced mainly in Penedés.
- **Rías Baixas** is located in the northwest and produces a fine quality white wine that is sold varietally as Albariño.

There are now as many as 78 DOs in Spain and their island possessions, which represent an exciting new era for wine aficionados.

Spanish Labeling Laws

Although Spain has long been producing wine, it is only as recently as 1972 that it adopted a modern regulatory system with the establishment of the *Instituto de Denominaciónes de Origen (INDO)*. The INDO works in tandem with the local or regional *Consejo Regulador* to maintain and certify that the regulations and standards are applied. Spanish wines are grouped under six classifications:

Vino de Pago This classification is relatively new for "estate wines" that are particularly distinguished whether in official DOs or technically not so. The estates must reach the most stringent standards set for that particular appellation and produce wines that have been evaluated as being distinguished.

Denominación de Origen Calificáda (DOCa) This classification guarantees high standards and is comparable to an Italian DOCG wine. Only Rioja and Priorat are designated DOCa, although several appellations may soon join this rank. See Figure 11-33.

Denominación de Origen (DO) Equivalent to the AC designation of French wines; there are 78 DO appellations. See Figure 11-34.

Vino de la Tierra (VdlT) Equivalent to the French *Vin de Pays*, these wines have a regional character and are striving for DO status.

Vino Comarcal (VC) This classification indicates one of 23 regional appellations for wines that are outside the bounds of a DO.

Vino de Mesa (VdM) This table wine classification is the lowest classification.

In addition to following the EU regulations, Spain's DOCa and DO also follow aging criteria.

Spanish Labeling Terms

- *Vino Joven*–Intended for immediate drinking upon release, in the spring following the vintage
- *Crianza*–Aged a minimum of 6 months in oak and 2 years in the bottle; Rioja and Ribera del Duero wines are aged 1 year in oak
- *Reserva (white)*–Aged 6 months in oak and released after 3 years
- *Reserva (red)*–Aged 1 year in oak and released in the fourth year
- *Gran Reserva*–Only from exceptional vintages; whites are aged 6 months in oak and released in the fourth year; reds are aged 2 years in oak and 3 more in the bottle

Other Spanish Terms

- *Fino*–A light, dry type of sherry
- *Manzanilla*–The lightest sherry, similar to fino
- *Amontillado*–A type of aged fino sherry
- *Oloroso*–A type of oxidized sherry
- *Cava*–Sparkling wine, classic method
- *Cosecha*–Vintage
- *Mistela*–A blend of grape juice and alcohol

 FIGURE 11-33

Rioja's are generally blended from Tempranillo, Garnacha, and Mazuela and come from sub-regions. It is only recently that producers are making Rioja wines from a single vineyard or estate.

 FIGURE 11-34

Catalayud is one of the 72 DOs and Garnacha is one of the most prominent grape varieties in Spain.

Portugal

Portugal has an ancient wine history and has one of the earliest protected appellations, *Oporto,* which dates back to 1756. Until recently, most consumers in the world thought of Port and Madeira wines, and perhaps rosé wines such as Mateus and Lancers as Portugal's only offerings. Portugal's wine industry is one of the most recent to undergo an innovative wine revolution and the results are not only promising but have provided consumers with excellent value wines. Continental Portugal and its islands have 18 regions. The mainland has two very distinct climates with the weather in the northern tier above the Tajo (Tagus) River cooler and wetter (with the exception of its interior), and the southern tier with weather that is hotter and drier. The primary white varieties that are making a name for themselves are Arinto, Loureira, Alvarinho (synonym for Albariño in Spain), and Touriga Nacional, and Tinta Roriz or Aragonez (Spanish Tempranillo) for reds. The primary regions include:

- **Minho**, which produces both white and red Vinho Verde though only the whites are note worthy as they are among the most tart wines of the world. They are a wonderful accompaniment to seafood dishes. See Figure 11-35.

- **Douro** is located along the Douro River and is famous for its Port wines, but is gaining respect for its blended still reds, which are intense but elegant.

- **Dão** is located inland in the northern tier and is known for good quality value driven red wines.

- **Alentejo**, in southeastern Portugal produces excellent red wines with the Trincadeira and Aragonez indigenous varieties. It also produces international varietals such as Syrah.

Portuguese Labeling laws

It is only since joining the European Union that Portugal's regulatory system, through the *Instituto da Vinha e Vinho (IVV)*, has established a comparable tiered system. Portuguese wines are similarly classified as:

Denominaçâo de Origem Controlada (DOC)
This classification is similar to a French AC or Italian DOC wine; there are currently about 27 DOC regions. DOC wines are required to have a paper seal, the *Selo de Origem*, which is placed over the cork but under the capsule.

Indicação de Proveniência Regulamentada (IPR)
This classification compares to the French VDQS, and is phased out as of 2009.

Vinho Regional This classification compares to France's Vin de Pays.

Vinho de Mesa Table wine is the lowest classification. Neither the variety nor the vintage may be mentioned on the label.

Portuguese Labeling Terms

- *Reserva*–Must be from a single vintage and have .5% higher alcohol than *the* minimum for DOC wines

- *Garrafeira*–Aged 2 years in cask and 1 year in bottle for red wine, 6 months in wood and 6 months bottle aging for white wine

- *Colheita*–Vintage

- *Colheita selectionada*–For high quality vintage wines with 1% higher alcohol

- *Engarrafado na origem*–Estate bottled

- *Quinta*–Estate

FIGURE 11-35
Touriga Nacional is an indigenous Portuguese variety that has developed into a hallmark of Portuguese red wine (note the English description on the label).

Storing Wine, Wine Tasting, Food and Wine Pairing

While it is important to have an understanding of wine service, which includes decoding the label, it is also necessary to master how wine is stored. Proper storage preserves wine so that it tastes the way the winemaker intended. It can also allow the best wines to slowly evolve into complex drinkable works of art.

Poor storage will quickly cause wines to degrade and lead to off-flavors and imbalances. A knowledge of the effects of improper wine storage allows servers to better identify and evaluate wines that have deteriorated. An understanding of how wine interacts with food provides servers with an additional tool to enhance the guest's dining experience.

Storing Wine

Because wine is a living entity, it can either suffer or thrive, depending on how it is treated. See Figure 11-36. When storing wine, five important factors must be controlled: temperature, humidity, light, position, and stability. The organization of a wine cellar is also important to food service establishments that purchase wine in volume. Because most wines are made to be consumed within two to three years, it is important to keep track of when the wine was purchased. An efficient inventory system also records the name, vintage, price, amount purchased, distributor, shipper, and the bin numbers.

FIGURE 11-36

Maintaining an organized temperature and humidity controlled storage environment is key to successfully managing an extensive wine list

Temperature Wine should be stored at a constant temperature of 50°F–55°F (10°C–13°C), although temperature stability is more important than the actual temperature level because some bacteria become active as temperature fluctuates. However, the lower the temperature (down to 50°F/10°C), the slower the maturation of the wine. Wines should not be refrigerated for any length of time because refrigeration can cause the cork to dry out and allow oxygen to enter the bottle.

Humidity Wine should be stored in a well-ventilated space with a relative humidity of 70%–85% to prevent the cork from drying out.

Light Avoid storing wine in direct light, whether natural or artificial. Too much light causes heat, and therefore, deterioration.

Position Wine bottles should be stored on their sides to keep the corks moist and to inhibit oxidation.

Vibrations Wine should be stored in a location that is free of agitation or vibration as these conditions can cause rapid deterioration.

FIGURE 11-37

An organized and systematic approach to tasting is a key ingredient to wine knowledge.

Wine Tasting

Wine tasting can be both simple and complex. See Figure 11-37. It is simple to quaff wine and enjoy its attributes without contemplating its subtleties. A fuller appreciation comes with learning to distinguish the subtle characteristics of color, aroma, bouquet, flavor, texture, intensity, balance, and the length of the finish. For a professional wine taster, all of these characteristics must be recognized, identified, and recorded. For the novice and the appreciative amateur, part of the enjoyment of tasting wine comes from exploring and learning about a world of subtle sensations.

Types of Tastings

There are four basic types of wine tastings:

General tastings General tastings are often conducted by retailers or distributors, special event organizers of food and wine expositions, or fund-raisers. Tasters try a variety of wines in an arranged sequence, typically beginning with dry white wines and ending with sweet fortified wines.

Horizontal tastings *Horizontal tastings* are for evaluating wines of a particular region or vintage. Horizontal tastings allow the taster to evaluate the differences among wines produced by several winemakers from the same region, or within the same parameters of varieties and vintage. See Figure 11-38.

FIGURE 11-38

Horizontal tastings are for comparing wines from a region or vintage.

Vertical tastings *Vertical tastings* evaluate wines of different vintages, usually from a limited number of producers. The taster focuses on the wine's maturation and the factors that differentiate the vintages.

Blind tastings *Blind tastings* are the most complex in that the tasters have no prior information about the wines. The wines are generally chosen from the same varietals or vintage. A blind tasting allows tasters to sharpen their skills at differentiating subtleties among wines.

Set-Up and Requirements

An appropriate atmosphere is key to a professional wine-tasting event.

- The room should be well lighted, ideally with natural daylight or nonfluorescent lighting to allow for accurate color evaluation.
- Glassware should be clean and free of any lingering odor of detergent.
- The room should be void of any extraneous scents such as flowers or air freshener.
- Tasters should not wear cologne or other heavy scents that might interfere with accurate sensory evaluation.
- Glasses should be the appropriate size and shape for the wines being tasted. They should be placed on a white background so that tasters can accurately discern a wine's color and intensity.
- Water should be served to cleanse the palate and no foods other than flavorless bread or water biscuits should be served. Spittoons should be provided.
- Each taster should have an evaluation sheet and a pen or pencil for making observations and for evaluating each wine.
- The room should be silent throughout the tasting exercise so that tasters are not distracted.

During wine tastings, wine is served in 1.5- to 2-ounce portions and grouped in *flights*, or groupings of similar vintages, varietals, or other comparable factors. Groupings allow the taster to evaluate the wines against one another and to prevent dissimilar wines from interfering with the subtle tastes of other wines.

When different styles of wine are being evaluated, the sequence in which they are tasted is significant to the taster's ability to discern the subtleties—light-bodied wines before full-bodied wines; dry wines before off-dry or sweet wines; and generally, whites before reds.

The Six S's of Wine Tasting

The six S's of wine tasting are see, swirl, sniff, sip, swallow or spit, and savor.

See Although sight is the least accurate of the senses with which to evaluate wine, it provides clues to, and anticipation of what is to come. First, examine the upper surface of the wine, known as the *disc.* The edge or *rim* of the disc may appear colorless. The variation of color or hue between the rim and the core of the wine will indicate possible aging, origin, and vinification to an experienced taster. Note that the disc is not flat, but rather forms a concave curve, called the *meniscus,* as the wine extends a short way up the sides of the wine glass.

The color or *hue* of the wine is sometimes referred to as the *robe.* The robe gives important clues about the wine. A white wine with little or no color indicates that the fruit was immature, and that the wine will probably lack aroma and flavor. Pale and light-colored wine often comes from cooler climates. Most white wines tend to range from straw green-yellow to light yellow. As white wine barrel or bottle wine ages, it develops more color. Medium yellow and light gold wines tend to be sweet dessert wines. If the wine is brown, it has either been fortified or has oxidized.

A red wine with a blue or purple rim indicates immaturity. Light reds indicate thin-skinned varietals such as a Pinot Noir. The majority of red wines are medium cherry red, but they may develop a red tile or brick hued rim with age. Red wines lose color with age, so examining the color gives clues about the wine's age.

Swirl Swirling the wine lightly coats the upper level of the glass, aerating the wine and allowing it to "breathe" and open. As the wine evaporates off the side of the glass, flavor components are released. The residual wine that clings to the glass is called *legs,* tears, or arches. Legs are caused by alcohol and glycerol levels in the wine. The greater the alcohol content, the denser and more pronounced the legs.

Sniff Smell is the most important sense for wine tasting. The olfactory sense allows tasters to discern hundreds of smells. The taster differentiates between aromas and bouquets. *Aroma* descriptors include such terms as fruity, spicy, floral, or vegetative. *Bouquet* descriptors include nutty, caramelized, woody, earthy, and petroleum. Some wines may have off odors as a result of faulty winemaking or storage. When sniffing wine, the taster should sniff once and then swirl the wine and tilt the glass toward himself or herself, so that the nose is directly in the glass; and then sniff again.

Taking short sniffs without inhaling deeply, the taster notes an initial impression, often called the attack, or first nose. After 30 seconds or so, the wine is sniffed again for second impressions, called the second nose. After a short interval, the sniffing process is repeated to verify or add to the earlier impressions. Sniffing too-frequently will result in palate adaption, in which the taster is unable to discern any differences whatsoever.

Sip Using the mouth alone, humans are able to distinguish only five tastes: sweet, sour, salty, bitter, and umami (the best example to convey its sense is the taste of monosodium glutamate MSG). Research has shown that although most taste buds are concentrated on the tip and sides of the tongue, they are also located on the roof and back of the mouth. This is why it is important to roll the wine on and around the tongue to coat these taste buds. Saltiness is not a typical component of a wine's taste, and bitterness is only slightly less so.

Tasters describe the degree of sweetness in a wine as dry, off-dry or mildly sweet, sweet, and very sweet. Although most wines lack bitterness, wines that are bitter are described as slightly bitter, moderately bitter, and very bitter. Sourness or acidity can be described as "flatness" if the wine is not sufficiently acidic. "Fruitiness" is used when it is normally acidic, and "acidulous" when excessively acidic.

Wine tasting also involves tactility (the texture or *"mouthfeel"* of the wine), which is a function of tannins, glycerol, and alcohol. *Astringency* is the "drying out" effect or rough feeling a taster perceives from tannins. Tannic wines may be described as slightly astringent or chalky, moderately tannic, or astringent.

Alcohol gives the taster a perception of sweetness and a tactile sensation of heat. Glycerol, like alcohol, exhibits a perception of richness and weight on the palate.

Swallow or Spit A taster cannot remain alert and assess a wine accurately if he or she is consuming it. Spitting between tastes is necessary for proper assessment.

Savor Savoring wine involves the taster's appreciation and evaluation of a wine by focusing on the way it lingers in the mouth. The key to tasting wine is to determine the balance between the acidity and the tannins on the one hand and the sweetness and alcohol on the other. The combined sensations of taste, smell, texture, balance, and length, or how quickly or slowly those perceptions remain on the palate, determine the evaluation of the wine's finish.

The best wines have a balanced finish that is integrated into a satisfying whole. If one element dominates, the wine is unbalanced. Wines are described as having a short, medium, or long finish, depending on how long the sensations linger. Wines with short finishes leave lingering flavors for less than 15 seconds. Great wines, on the other hand, have finishes that linger from one to several minutes.

Wine-Tasting Terms

In the past, winetasters tended toward the poetic when they described the taste of wine because it is difficult to communicate abstract and subjective sensations such as taste. To help improve communication among wine tasters, Professor Anne Noble at the University of California-Davis developed the aroma wheel in an attempt to make the adjectives that describe wines more uniform and scientific.

The following terms have become accepted within the wine trade:

- Austere–Unyielding, possibly too young
- Baked–Lacks freshness and acidity
- *Big/Full*–Full-bodied and full-flavored
- Buttery–Soft, round whites with bouquet of malolactic fermentation
- Coarse–Lacking complexity or finesse
- Complex–Multilayered and multifaceted
- Creamy–Denoting richness
- *Crisp*–Good acidity
- Dense–Intensely flavorful and colorful
- Dried-out–Fruit flavors have dissipated
- *Earthy*–Aromas reminiscent of soil or minerals
- Elegant–Great finesse and balance
- Fat–Full-bodied but lacking acidity
- *Firm*–Structure backed by tannins, acid
- Flabby–Lacks acidity; or is "flat"
- Fragrant–Flowery
- Green–A young wine or wine made from unripe grapes
- Hard–Tannic; too young
- Heavy–Overly alcoholic
- Herbaceous–Aromas of grass; herbs
- *Jammy*–Overly ripe fruit
- Lean–Limited flavor; high acidity
- *Long*–A lingering finish
- Mouthfilling–Richly textured
- Pétillant–Spritzy, slight carbonation
- Robust–Full-bodied
- Rough–Coarse; unpolished
- Sharp–High acid
- Short–Lacking finish
- Silky–Smooth; mature tannins
- Simple–Lacking distinction
- Smooth–Mature tannins
- Soft–Mellow flavors
- Sour–Overly acidic; vinegary
- Spritz–Prickly from carbon dioxide
- Stalky/stemmy–Bitter vegetal taste
- Steely–Good acidity
- Supple–Sensuously smooth
- *Thin*–Lacks body
- Vegetal–Vegetable aroma (e.g., bell pepper)
- Velvety–Rich silkiness
- Watery–Weak and thin
- Woody–Odors of old casks
- Zesty–Crisp and fresh

The following terms are used for wines that are spoiled:

- Acetic–Vinegary
- *Corked*–Affected by cork mold TCA
- Maderized–Baked, flat, partly oxidized
- Moldy–Smells of mold
- Oxidized–Cardboardy and papery from air exposure
- Sulfurous–Smells of burnt matches or bad eggs; too much sulfur dioxide

The Six S's of Wine Tasting

Professional wine tasters have trained their senses to make subtle comparisons and judgments.

Use the following steps to fully appreciate wine:

1 SEE–Examine the color of the wine against a white background.

2 SWIRL–Swirl the wine to release its aroma.

3 SNIFF–Sniff the wine to form a first impression; then sniff again to enjoy the wine's subtle aroma and bouquet.

4 SIP–Sip the wine, and roll it around in the mouth so that it touches all the taste buds.

5 SWALLOW (or spit)– Spit the wine into a cup or sink, and cleanse the palate with water or plain crackers or wafers.

6 SAVOR–Savor the finish, or aftertaste, of the wine, and take notes of your impressions before tasting the next sample.

Food and Wine Pairing

Pairing wine with food used to be a straightforward, if not rigid, and a matter of following the French tradition of specific wines with specific dishes. The classic dictum held that red wine was always served with red meats and white wine was served with fish and poultry.

Over the past several decades, however, Western cuisine has expanded and has come to incorporate many cultural ingredients and techniques. As a result, Western society has become much more adventurous with wine pairings. There do remain, however, some common sense guidelines for matching wine with food. See Figure 11-39.

Guidelines

It is important to remember to match the intensity of flavors in both the food and the wine. Use these guidelines to best pair food and wine:

Match or contrast the components of both the food and the wine Having similarities in components (sweet, sour, salty, bitter) may be safe, but not necessarily interesting. For example, sweet food with sweet wines match perfectly as long as the wine is always sweeter than the food; but sweet Sauternes are perhaps more interesting with a salty and creamy rich Roquefort cheese.

Think about the acidity Acidic foods need to be accompanied by acidic wines such as Sauvignon Blanc and cool-climate Chardonnays. Highly acid foods will wash out low-acid wines. Acidic wines also pair well with salty and oily foods. The effect is similar to pairing citrus with fish.

Modify bitterness Bitter food and bitter wine reinforce bitterness, while sweetness or acidity can modify it. A mixed green salad with grilled chicken, for example, might be paired with a white wine such as white Zinfandel or Chenin Blanc.

Match or contrast dominant flavors of both the food and the wine Herbs, spices, seasonings, and cooking techniques can enhance flavors in wine. For example, thyme or basil in a dish will bring out the herbaceous character of a Sauvignon Blanc. Grilled foods such as salmon will match the spiciness and toastiness of Pinot Noir. Contrasting smoky and floral flavors can also be interesting, when serving smoked salmon with a floral Riesling.

Match the intensity of textures To make sure that one does not overpower the other, match the intensity of textures. Lightly textured foods pair well with light-bodied wines, and rich foods with full-bodied wines—a California Cabernet goes well with grilled sirloin steak, for example.

Remember that tannins bind with fat A hard tannic Cabernet Sauvignon will not taste astringent if accompanied by fatty beef, duck, cheese, or rich sauces. Accompany a fine older wine with simpler food that acts as a foil. Use good, drinkable

⅋ **FIGURE 11-39**

Food and wine pairings are based on demonstrable tasting principles of balancing one against the other.

204

quality wine for cooking. Use the same style wine in cooking as will be served with the meal for better harmony. Be aware of interactions between food and wine: artichokes compete with acidity in wine. Foods high in umami, such as anchovies, soy sauce, bonito, or smoked salmon, react badly to tannins and leave a metallic flavor on the palate. Corn is difficult to pair with very dry wine because of its high starch and sugar content.

Remember that mixed green salads, especially those with vinaigrette, will ruin the taste of wine. If possible, avoid using vinegar, and substitute citrus juice; then serve with a slightly off-dry wine with good acidity, such as a Chenin Blanc. Be alert to the difficulty of pairing egg dishes with a wine, especially those without other taste components. Poached eggs, for example, will coat the tongue and palate and limit the perception of the wine. A Western-style omelet, however, has taste and flavor components such as onions, tomatoes, peppers, and cheese—all of which enhance compatibility with wine. Consider the intensity of chocolate; it is difficult to pair if it is very sweet or bitter. It is less of a problem if it is merely a component of a dessert.

If possible, avoid serving wine with very spicy foods, which will not only overwhelm a wine's flavors, but will also enhance the perception of tannins if present. Remember that the best wine is the wine that the taster most enjoys and that many psychological factors are involved in a consumer's wine choice that have little to do with the gustatory senses.

- **Seasonality**—Most people enjoy light and white wines in warm seasons and full-bodied red ones in cold weather.
- **Prestige**—Consumers often want to pair fine quality food with expensive wines, regardless of the wine's suitability.
- **Ethnicity**—Consumers enjoy pairing regional wines with cuisines of the same region.
- **Occasionality**—Some wines, like champagne, are associated with celebrations.
- **The company**—Sharing a bottle of wine may make an experience most memorable.

When serving more than one wine with dinner, here are a few general guidelines:

- Serve dry wine before sweet wine.
- Serve light-bodied wines before full-bodied ones.
- Serve whites before reds.
- Serve young wines before older ones.

As the ancient Greek philosopher Socrates noted, "Wine moistens and tempers the spirit, lulls the cares of the mind to rest; it revives our joys and is oil to the dying flame of life. If we drink temperately and smell drafts at a time, the wine distills into our lungs like the sweetest morning dew. It is then the wine commits no rape upon our reason, but pleasantly invites us to agreeable mirth."

APPENDIX A

Common Measurement Conversions

U.S. Standard	Metric
WEIGHT	
0.035 ounce	1 gram
1 ounce	28.35 grams
16 ounces (or 1 pound)	454 grams
2.2 pounds	1 kilogram
VOLUME (LIQUID)	
0.034 ounce	1 milliliter
1 ounce	29.57 milliliters
8 ounces (or 1 cup)	237 ml
16 ounces (or 1 pint)	474 milliliters (or .47 liter)
2 pints (or 1 quart)	946 milliliters (or .95 liter)
33.8 ounces (or 1.06 quarts)	1,000 milliliters (or 1 liter)
4 quarts (or 1 gallon)	3.79 liters
VOLUME (DRY)	
1 pint	.55 liter
0.91 quart	1 liter
2 pints (or 1 quart)	1.1 liters
8 quarts (or 1 peck)	8.81 liters
4 pecks (or 1 bushel)	35.24 liters
LENGTH	
0.39 inches	1 centimeter
1 inch	2.54 centimeters
39.4 inches	1 meter

Common Conversion Factors

Weight	To convert:	Multiply by:
	ounces to grams	28.35
	grams to ounces	.03527
	kilograms to pounds	2.2046

Volume	To convert:	Multiply by:
	quarts to liters	.946
	pints to liters	.473
	quarts to milliliters	946
	milliliters to ounces	.0338
	liters to quarts	1.05625
	liters to pints	2.1125
	liters to ounces	33.8

Length	To convert:	Multiply by:
	inches to millimeters	25.4
	inches to centimeters	2.54
	millimeters to inches	.03937
	centimeters to inches	.3937
	meters to inches	39.3701

Common Temperature Conversions

Degrees Fahrenheit	Degrees Celsius
32°F	0°C
41°F	5°C
140°F	60°C
150°F	66°C
160°F	71°C
166°F	74°C
180°F	82°C
212°F	100°C
300°F	149°C
325°F	163°C
350°F	177°C
375°F	191°C
400°F	204°C
425°F	218°C
450°F	232°C
475°F	246°C
500°F	260°C

Temperature Conversion Factors

To convert Fahrenheit to Celsius:
Subtract 32, multiply by 5, and then divide by 9.

To convert Celsius to Fahrenheit:
Multiply by 9, divide by 5, and then add 32.

APPENDIX B

Pronunciation Guide

Abboccato	*ahb-bok-KAH-to*
Aglianico	*ah-lyAH-nee-ko*
Alentejo	*ah-len-TEH--zhoo*
Alsace	*ahl sahss*
Amontillado	*ah mohn te YAH doh*
Amuse bouche	*ah mews boo-sh*
Añejo	*ah neeyeh ho*
Arabica	*ah RAH bee kah*
Armagnac	*ar mah nyahk*
Auslese	*aows lah zeh*
Asti	*ahs tee*
Banyul	*ban yul*
Barbera	*bar BEH rah*
Bardolino	*bar doh LEEN oh*
Beaujolais	*boh zhoh lay*
Beaune	*bone*
Beaumes-de-Venise	*bohme duh vuh nees*
Beerenauslese	*bay rehn aows lay zeh*
Bernkastel	*BEHRN kahs tel*
Bianco	*bee AHN ko*
Blanc de Blancs	*blahnk duh blahnk*
Bordeaux	*bohr doh*
Brut	*brewt*
Bual	*boo ahl*
Cabernet Sauvignon	*kah behr nay soh vee nyohn*
Cahaça	*kah SHAH sah*
Calvados	*kahl vah dohs*
Carmenère	*kahr muh nehr*
Catawba	*kuh TAW bah*
Chablis	*shah blee*
Champagne	*shahm PAH nyah*
Château	*shah toh*
Châteauneuf-du -Pape	*shah toh nuf doo pahp*
Chef de rang	*shef duh rahng*
Chenin Blanc	*sheh nahn blahn*
Chianti	*kee AHN tee*
Cloche	*klush*
Clos	*cloh*
Colheita	*ko leeAY tah*
Cosecha	*Koh seh kah*
Crianza	*kree AHN zah*
Cru	*kroo*
Cuvée	*kew vay*
Cynar	*CHEE nar*
Débarrassage	*day BAH rahs sahje*
Denominazione di Origine Controllata	*deh no mee nah tsyo neh dee o reejee neh con trohl LAH tah*
Dolcetto	*dohl CHET toh*
Dão	*DA oo*
Digestif	*dee djehs teev*
Dolce	*DOL cheh*
Doux	*doo*
Dubonnet	*doo boh nay*

Entremets	*ehn treh may*	**Malmsey**	*MALM zee*
Eiswein	*IYS vihn*	**Malvasia**	*mal vAH zyah*
Erzeugerabfüllung	*ehr tsoy geh AHB fool oong*	**Manzanilla**	*mahn thah nEE yah*
Fino	*FEE noh*	**Marchio Nazionale**	*mAHr keeo nAH tsyiohn nAH leh*
Frizzante	*freets SAHN teh*	**Malvasia**	*mahl vAH zyah*
Garganega	*gahr gah NEH gah*	**Marsala**	*mahr SAH lah*
Garrafeira	*gah rah FAY rah*	**Médoc**	*may dohk*
Gewürztraminer	*geh VURTZ tra meen er*	**Minho**	*meen ho*
Graves	*grahv*	**Moelleux**	*mweh luh*
Gutsabfüllung	*goots AHP fool loong*	**Moscato**	*mohs KAH toh*
Gyokuro	*gee oh koo roh*	**Mosel**	*MOH zel*
Haut-Médoc	*oh may dohk*	**Montepulciano**	*mont teh pool chAH no*
Indicazione Feographica Tipica	*in dee kah tsiO neh jeh o grAH fee ha tEE pee kah*	**Moulin-à-Vent**	*MOO lan AH vahn*
Imbottigliato all'Origine	*im bot tee lyAH to al lo rEE jee neh*	**Muscadet**	*moos kah day*
Islay	*eye lay*	**Nebbiolo**	*neb bee OH loh*
Kabinett	*KAH bee neht*	**Negroamaro**	*neh gro ah MAHR ro*
Kräusen	*kroy zen*	**Nero**	*nEH ro*
Liebfraumilch	*LEEB frow milkh*	**Oidium**	*OH id dee yum*
Lillet	*lee lay*	**Oloroso**	*oh loh ROH soh*
Loire	*lwahr*	**Pauillac**	*po yahk*
Madeira	*mah DEER ah*	**Pétillant**	*peh TEE yahnt*
Malaga	*MAH lah gah*	**Pfalz**	*fahltz*

Phylloxera	*fill LOHK suhr rah*	**Sekt**	*zehkt*
Piña	*pee nyah*	**Sémillon**	*seh mee yohn*
Pinot Blanc	*pee noh blahnk*	**Shiraz**	*shEE raas*
Pinot Noir	*pee noh nwahr*	**Spätlese**	*shpAYt lay zeh*
Pouchong	*POO shuhng*	**Superiore**	*soo peh ryOh reh*
Prädikat	*preh dee KAHT*	**Tavel**	*tah vel*
Qualitätswein	*kval ih TAYTS vine*	**Torrontés**	*toh rohn TEHS*
Quinta	*Keen tah*	**Trebbiano**	*trehb byAH no*
Réchaud	*Reh Show*	**Trocken**	*trOH*
Recioto	*reh chee OH toe*	**Ullage**	*uhl ledje*
Rémuage	*reh mew Ahj*	**Valpolicella**	*vahl poh lee CHEH lah*
Rheingau	*RINE gow*	**Vendemmia**	*veh dEHm myah*
Rheinhessen	*RIYN EHs sen*	**Verdelho**	*vehr DEL yo*
Rhum Agricole	*room AHg gree cole*	**Vin de Pays**	*vehn duh payee*
Riesling	*REES ling*	**Vino Comarcal**	*vee no ko mahr kahl*
Rotwein	*ROHT viyn*	**Vino da Tavola**	*vee nO dah tAH vohla*
Saint-Émilion	*sahn tay meel yohn*	**Vouvray**	*voo vreh*
Sake	*SAH keh*	**Weissherbst**	*viys hEH r bst*
Sancerre	*sahn sehr*	**Wit**	*vit*
Sauternes	*soh tehrn*	**Zinfandel**	*TZIN fahn dehl*
Sec	*sehk*		
Secco	*sEHk ko*		

BIBLIOGRAPHY

Books

Anderson, Burton. *Best Italian Wines.* London: Websters International
  Publishers Ltd., 2001.

Anderson, Burton, and Stuart Pigott. *The Wine Atlas of Italy.* UK:
  Antique Collector's Club, 1997.

Axler, Bruce, and Carol Litrides. *Food And Beverage Service.* New York:
  John Wiley & Sons, Inc., 1990.

Bastianich, Joseph, and David Lynch. *Vino Italiano: The Regional Wines
  of Italy.* New York: Clarkson Potter/Publishers, 2002.

Bird, David. *Understanding Wine Technology: The Science of Wine
  Explained.* UK: DBQA Publishing, 2005.

Bird, Owen. *Rheingold: The German Wine Renaissance.* UK: Arima
  Publishing, 2005.

Blom, Philipp. *The Wines of Austria.* New York: Faber and Faber
  Inc., 2000.

Brook, Stephen. *The Complete Bordeaux: The Wines / The Châteaux /
  The People.* UK: Octopus Publishing Group, 2007.

Broom, David, and Jordan Spencer. *The Complete Bartender's Guide.*
  Buffalo, NY: Firefly Books, 2003.

Brostrom, Geralyn, and Jack Brostrom. *The Buisness of Wine: An
  Encyclopedia.* Westport, CT: Greenwood Press, 2009.

Brown, Jared, and Anastatia Miller. *Spiritous Journey: A History of
  Drink.* New York: Jared Brown Publishers, 2008.

Calagione, Sam. *Brewing Up a Business: Adventures in Entrepreneurship
  from the Founder of Dogfish Head Craft Brewery.* Hoboken, NJ: John
  Wiley & Sons, Inc., 2005.

Cass, Bruce, and Jancis Robinson, eds. *Oxford Companion to Wines of
  North America.* New York: Oxford University Press, 2007.

Cecil, Sam A. *The Evolution of the Bourbon Whiskey Industry in
  Kentucky.* Nashville, TN: Turner Publishing Company, 2001.

Cernilli, Daniele, and Marco Sabellico. *The New Italy: A Complete Guide
  to Contemporary Italian Wine.* San Francisco, CA: The Wine
  Appreciation Guild, 2001.

Clarke, Oz. *New Wine Atlas.* London: Websters International Publishers Ltd., 2002.

Clarke, Oz. *Bordeaux: The Wines, The Vineyards, The Winemakers.* London: Websters International Publishers Ltd., 2006.

Cocks, Charles. *Bordeaux and its Wines.* 17th ed. Bordeaux, FR: Éditions Féret, 2004.

Combe, B. G., and P.R. Dry. *Viticulture: Volume 1 Resources.* 2nd ed. South Australia: Winetitles Publishing, 2004.

Combe, B. G., and P. R. Dry. *Viticulture: Volume 2 Practices.* South Australia: Winetitles Publishing, 2006.

Consejo Regulador of Denominations of Origin Jerez- Xérès- Sherry, Manzanilla-Sanlucar de Barameda, and Vinagre de Jerez,ed. *The Big Book of Sherry Wines.* Spain: Regional Ministry of Agriculture and Fisheries, Sub- Ministry: Department of Publications and Dissemination, n.d., 2007.

Cooper, Michael. *Wine Atlas of New Zealand.* 2nd ed. Auckland, New Zealand: Moa Beckett Publishers Ltd., 2002.

Coulombe, Charles A. *Rum: The Epic Story of the Drink that Conquered the World.* New York: Citadel Press, 2004.

Crestin-Billet, *Fédérique. Veuve Clicquot: La Grande Dame de la Champagne.* Translated by Carole Fahy. Grenoble, FR: Editions Glenat, 1992.

Damrosch, Phoebe. *"Service Included: Four-Star Secrets of an Eavesdropping Waiter."* New York: HarperCollins Publishers, 2007.

Daniels, Ray. *Designing Great Beers: The Ultimate Guide to Brewing Classic Beer Styles.* Boulder, CO: Brewers Publications, 2000.

DeGroff, Dale. *The Craft of the Cocktail: Everything You Need to Know to Be a Master Bartender, with 500 Recipes.* New York: Clarkson Potter/ Publishers, 2002.

DeGroff, Dale. *The Essential Cocktail: The Art of Mixing Perfect Drinks.* New York: Clarkson Potter/Publishers, 2008.

Erickson, William. *Noble Rot: A Bordeaux Wine Revolution.* New York: W.W. Norton & Company, Inc., 2004.

Fielden, Christopher. *Exploring the World of Wine & Spirits.* UK: Wine & Spirits Education Trust, 2009.

Fix, George. Principles of Brewing Science: *A Study of Serious Brewing Issues.* 2nd ed. Boulder, CO: Brewers Publications, 1999.

Friedrich, Jacqueline. *A Wine and Food Guide to the Loire.* New York: Owl Books, 2001.

Giglio, Anthony, ed. *Mr. Boston Platinum Edition: 1,500 Recipes, Tools and Techniques for the Master.* Hoboken, NJ: John Wiley & Sons, Inc., 2006.

Goldstein, Evan. *Perfect Pairings: A Master Sommelier's Practical Advice for Partnering Wine with Food.* Berkeley, CA: University of California Press, 2006.

Goode, Jamie. *The Science of Wine: From Vine to Glass.* Berkeley, CA: University of California Press, 2006.

Gregory, Conal R. *The Cognac Companion: A Connoisseur's Guide.* New York: Running Press, 1997.

Grimes, William. *Straight Up or On the Rocks: The Story of the American Cocktail.* New York: North Point Press, 2001.

Hall, Lisa Shara. *Wines of the Pacific Northwest: A Contemporary Guide to the Wines of Washington and Oregon.* UK: Octopus Publishing Group, 2001.

Halliday, James. *Australia and New Zealand Wine Companion.* Australia: HaperCollins Publishers, 2001.

Hanson, Anthony. *Burgundy.* UK: Mitchell Beazley, 2003.

Herbst, Sharon Tyler. *The New Food Lover's Companion: Comprehensive Definitions of Nearly 6,000 Food, Drink, and Culinary Terms.* 3rd ed. Hauppauge, NY: Barron's Educational Series, 2001.

Hindy, Steve, and Tom Potter. *Beer School: Bottling Success at the Brooklyn Brewery.* Hoboken, NJ: John Wiley & Sons, Inc., 2005.

Illy, Andrea, and Rinantonio Viani. *Espresso Coffee: The Chemistry of Quality.* Amherst, NY: Elsier Academic Press, 1995.

Jackson, Michael. *Great Beer Guide: 500 Classic Brews.* New York: Dorling Kindersley, 2000.

Jackson, Michael. *Michael Jackson's Complete Guide to Single Malt Scotch: A Connoisseur's Guide to the Single Malt Whiskies of Scotland.* 5th ed. Philadelphia, PA: Penguin Group, 2004.

Jamieson, Ian. *German Wine.* UK: Faber & Faber, 1991.

Jefford, Andrew. *The New France: A Complete Guide to Contemporary French Wine.* Revised. UK: Mitchell Beazley, 2006.

Jeffs, Julian. *Sherry.* Fully revised and updated. UK: Mitchell Beazley, 2004.

Johnson, Hugh. *The Story of Wine.* UK: Octopus Publishing Group, 1989.

Johnson, Hugh, and Jancis Robinson. *World Atlas of Wine.* 6th ed. UK: Mitchell Beazley, 2007.

Katsigris, Costas, and Chris Thomas. *The Bar & Beverage Book.* 4th ed. Hoboken, NJ: John Wiley & Sons, Inc., 2007.

King, Carol A. *Professional Dining Room Management.* New York: Van Nostrand Reinhold Co., 1988.

Lipinski, Robert, and Kathleen A. Lipinski. *The Complete Beverage Dictionary.* New York: Van Nostrand Reinhold Co., 1992.

Litrides, Carol A., and Bruce H. Axler. *Restaurant Service: Beyond the Basics.* New York: John Wiley & Sons, Inc., 1994.

MacDonogh, Giles. *Portuguese Table Wines: The New Generation of Wines and Wine Makers.* UK: Grub Street Publishing, 2001

MacNeil, Karen. *The Wine Bible.* New York: Workman Publishing, 2001.

Markowski, Phil, with Tomme Arthur, and Yvan De Baets. *Farmhouse Ales: Culture and Craftsmanship in the Belgian Tradition.* Boulder, CO: Brewers Publications, 2004.

Mayson, Richard. *Portugal's Wines & Wine Makers: Port, Madeira & Regional Wines.* New Revised Edition. San Francisco, CA: Wine Appreciation Guild, 1997.

McGovern, Patrick. *Ancient Wine: The Search for the Origins of Viniculture.* Princeton, NJ: Princeton University Press, 2003.

McInerney, Jay. *Bacchus & Me: Adventures in the Wine Cellar.* Guilford, CT: The Lyons Press, 2000.

Myer, Danny. *Setting the Table.* New York: HarperCollins Publishers, 2006.

Norman, Remington. *Rhône Renaissance: The Finest Rhône and Rhône-Style Wines from France and the New World.* San Francisco, CA: Wine Appreciation Guild, 1996.

Paston-Williams, Sara. *The Art of Dining: A History of Cooking & Eating.* London: The National Trust, 1993.

Pendergrast, Mark. *Uncommon Grounds: The History of Coffee and How It Transformed Our World.* New York: Basic Books, 1999.

Plotkin, Robert. *The Original Pocket Guide To American Cocktails and Drinks.* Tucson, AZ: BarMedia, 2004.

Price, Freddie. *Riesling Renaissance.* UK: Mitchell Beazley, 2004.

Radford, John. *The New Spain: A Complete Guide to Contemporary Spanish Wine.* UK: Mitchell Beazley, 2007.

Regan, Gary. *The Joy of Mixology:* The Consumer Guide to the Bartender's Craft. New York: Clarkson Potter/Publishers, 2003.

Robinson, Jancis. *How to Taste: A Guide to Enjoying Wine.* Revised Updated Edition. New York: Simon & Schuster, 2008.

Robinson, Jancis. *The Oxford Companion to Wine.* 3rd.ed. New York: Oxford University Press, 2007.

Saunders, Lucy. *Cooking With Beer: Taste Tempting Recipes and Creative Ideas for Matching Beer & Food.* Canada: Time Life Books, 1996.

Schuster, Michael. *Essential Winetasting: The Complete Practical Winetasting Course.* Revised Edition.UK: Mitchell Beazley, 2009.

Simon, Joanna. *Wine with Food.* New York: Simon & Schuster, 1996.

Smith, Barry C. *Questions of Taste: The Philosophy of Wine.* New York: Oxford University Press, 2007.

Smithsonian Cooper-Hewitt, National Design Museum. *Feeding Desire: Design and the Tools of the Table 1500-2005.* New York: Assouline Publishing Inc., 2006.

Spang, Rebecca. *The Invention of the Restaurant: Paris and Modern Gastronomic Culture.* Cambridge, MA: Harvard University Press, 2001.

Standage, Thomas. *A History of the World in 6 Glasses.* New York: Walker & Company, 2006.

Stevenson, Tom. *The New Sotheby's Wine Encyclopedia: The Classic Reference to the Wines of the World.* 4th ed. New York: Dorling Kindersley, 2007.

Stevenson, Tom. *World Encyclopedia of Champagne and Sparkling Wine.* Revised and Updated Edition. San Francisco, CA: Wine Appreciation Guild, 2003.

Strianese, Anthony J. *Dining Room and Banquet Management.* Delmar, NY: Delmar Publishing, 1990.

Taber, George M. *Judgment in Paris: California vs. France and the Historic 1976 Paris Tasting that Revolutionized Wine.* New York: Scribner, 2005.

Taber, George M. *To Cork or Not to Cork: Tradition, Romance, Science, and the Battle for the Wine Bottle.* New York: Scribner, 2007.

Wagner, Paul, Liz Thach, and Janeen Olsen. *Wine Marketing & Sales: Success Strategies for a Saturated Market.* San Francisco, CA: Wine Appreciation Guild, 2007.

Warner, Jessica. *Craze: Gin and Debauchery in an Age of Reason.* New York: Random House, 2003.

Wilson, James E. *Terroir: The Role of Geology, Climate, and Culture in the Making of French Wines.* Berkeley, CA: University of California Press, 1999.

Wondrich, David. *Imbibe! From Absinthe Cocktail to Whiskey Smash, a Salute in Stories and Drinks to "Professor" Jerry Thomas, Pioneer of the American Bar Featuring the Origina.* New York: Penguin Group, 2007.

Zraly, Kevin. *Windows on the World Complete Wine Course.* 25th Anniversary Edition. New York: Sterling Publishing, 2009.

Web Sources

BeerAdvocate. 1996-2009.
  <http://beeradvocate.com>.

Brewers Association/American Homebrewer's Assocation. N.d.
  <http://www.beertown.org>.

"Coffee Chemistry—Aroma." Coffee Research Institute. March 2002
  <http://www.coffeeresearch.org/science/aromamain.htm>.

Master Brewers Association of the Americas. 2009.
  <http://www.mbaa.com/>

Selected Web Resources

American Culinary Federation <http://www.acfchefs.org >

American Dietetic Association <http://www.eatright.org>

American Disabilities Act Information
   <http://www.usdoj.gov/crt/ada>

American Institute of Wine and Food <www.aiwf.org>

Cook's Thesaurus <http://www.foodsubs.com>

Epicurious <http://www.epicurious.com>

Food Network <http://www.foodtv.com>

Green Restaurant Association <http://www.dinegreen.com>

Hunger Information <http://www.secondharvest.org> and
   <http://www.strength.org>

International Council on Hotel, Restaurant, and Institutional Education
   <www.chrie.org>

Internet Wine Guide <http://www.internetwineguide.com>

The James Beard Foundation <www.jamesbeard.org>

Johnson & Wales University <http://www.jwu.edu >

Les Dames d'Escoffier <www.ldei.org>

National Restaurant Association <http://www.restaurant.org>

Recipe Archives <http://recipes.alastra.com >

U.S. Bureau of Labor Statistics <http://www.bls.gov >

U.S. Department of Agriculture <http://www.ers.usda.gov> and
   <http://www.mypyramid.gov>

U.S. Department of Health and Human Services
   <http://www.hhs.gov>

U.S. Department of Labor <http://www.oalj.dol.gov>

U.S. Environmental Protection Agency <http://www.epa.gov>

U.S. Equal Employment Opportunity Commission
   <http://www.eeoc.gov>

U.S. Food Safety and Inspection Service <http://www.fsis.usda.gov>

U.S. Small Business Administration <http://www.sba.gov>

Glossary

Subject

A

à la carte menus with items priced either individually or as combination meals; customers place their orders and pay at the counter or the drive-thru window

À l'assiette service American service, the most popular service around the world; simple and quick because all the food is plated in the kitchen

abboccato Italian labeling term meaning "semi-dry"

acetaldehyde a compound the human body produces as it breaks down alcohol

acetic wine-tasting term meaning "vinegary"

acetobacter the organism that turns wine to vinegar

adjuncts additional ingredients, such as fruits, herbs, spices, coffee, chili peppers, and other grain or sugar sources like rice or corn, added to beer to create lightness, to economize, and to add more flavor

aging process that takes place in charred oak barrels, which give color to the spirit, absorb impurities, and mellow the flavor

agricola Italian labeling term meaning "estate"

air pot brewer coffee maker that dispenses brewed coffee into an insulated serving decanter and holds the product at 185°F (85°C) for one hour

alcohol a volatile, colorless liquid obtained through the fermentation of a liquid containing sugar

Alcohol and Tobacco Tax and Trade Bureau (TTB) the agency that collects taxes owed and ensures that alcohol beverages are produced, labeled, advertised, and marketed in accordance to federal law

alcoholic beverage any potable liquid containing from 0.5% to 75.5% ethyl alcohol by volume

alcoholic distillation the process by which the alcohol from a fermented liquid is evaporated, captured, and cooled to liquid form

ale yeasts the yeasts that collect at the top of the fermentation vessel to create a floating bubbling mass that protects the fermenting wort from oxygen and bacteria

ales (*Saccharomyces cerevisiae,* or, as it is now known, *S. uvarum*); a classification of beer yeast

alt bier ales produced before the evolution of lagers; a lighter, smoother style of ale that lacks many of ale's fruity esters due to cooler fermentation temperatures

American service also known as plated à l'assiette service; the most popular service around the world; simple and quick because all the food is plated in the kitchen

American style a dining style defined by typically cutting a bite-sized piece of food and then pausing to switch the fork from the left hand to the right hand before placing the knife onto the rim of the plate and then eating the food from the fork, with the left hand on the lap or on the edge of the table

americano a single shot of espresso with 6 to 8 ounces (177 to 237 ml) of hot water added

amontillados finos whose flor yeast have died naturally or wines that have been fortified to 16% ABV or more

amuse-bouche a small bite-sized sampler

analyser two tall linked columns that make up the Coffey Still

añejo tequila tequila aged for a minimum of one year in small barrels less than 600 liters

apéritifs drinks served before dinner

Appellation d'Origine Contrôlée (AOC or AC) system that delimited the name of a wine to a region and determined the varieties best suited to the particular environment of that region; also represents the highest classification, representing 57% of all wines produced in France

aquavit a liquor from Scandinavia distilled from a fermented potato or grain mash and flavored with caraway, cumin seeds, citrus peel, cardamom, aniseed, or fennel

Arabica the highest-quality coffee; grows best in a narrow band on either side of the equator at altitudes ranging from 2,000 to 6,000 feet (610 to 1,829 m)

Armagnac brandy the oldest French brandy mostly produced in the unique alembic armagnaçais, a type of column still, which dates back to the earliest days of brandy production

aroma how a wine smells; descriptors include terms like *fruity, spicy, floral,* or *vegetative*

aromatized wines wines that are best served before a meal because their bitter and aromatic ingredients are appetite stimulants

Assam a rich, black tea from northern India, valued as a breakfast tea by connoisseurs

assumptive selling a sales technique that uses open-ended questions to guide guests in making their choices

astringency the "drying out" effect or rough feeling a taster perceives from tannins

auslese hand-selected grapes; intensely flavored, but may have been affected by botrytis and are not usually sweet

austere wine-tasting term meaning "unyielding, possibly too young"

autolysis the breakdown of yeast cells

automatic urn coffee maker that yields 60 5-ounce (148-ml) servings of coffee, brewed with 2 1/2 gallons (9.46 l) of water to one pound (.45 kg) of coarse-ground coffee

azienda Italian labeling term meaning "estate"

B

back a chaser on the side

back bar displays bottles in an attractive way to promote sales and market premium, super-premium, and ultra-premium brands

back waiter this position serves as a bridge between the brigade and the kitchen; has the primary responsibility of placing and picking up orders from the kitchen

bag-in-a-box system soda system that uses a single line flowing from a container of syrup to a pump that enables the syrup to travel to the soda dispenser known as a soda gun

baked wine-tasting term meaning "lacks freshness and acidity"

banquet a meal or event in which food and beverage has been ordered for a predetermined number of people

banquette refers to the continuous seating positioned against a wall

banquette service in a banquette, guests are seated facing the server, with their backs to the wall; the server should number the guests clockwise from the focal point when taking food and beverage orders

bar sundries non-edible supplies, such as sip sticks, beverage straws, sword picks, and cocktail napkins, needed for bartending

barback this position assists and supports the bartender by performing various tasks during the set up, service, and break down of the bar area

bartender also known as a mixologist; must be knowledgeable about an expansive range of alcoholic and non-alcoholic products and be skillful in marketing and selling to the guest

bâtonnage a process where some wines that are fermented in barrels are left on the lees and are stirred back into the wine

beer clean the highest standard of cleanliness for serving glasses

Beerenauslese (BA) overripe berries that are individually selected; a rare sweet wine that is rich and flavorful

beverage manager also known as the beverage director; a senior-management position within high-volume establishments that have large wine lists and liquor inventories; knowledgeable in all aspects of beverages including beer, wine, spirits, and non-alcoholic offerings

beverage tray a round, 12" to 14" in diameter, hand-held skid-free tray on which to carry beverages

bianco Italian labeling term meaning "white"

bière de garde rather strong, intensely flavored beers that improve with bottle age

big/full wine-tasting term meaning "full-bodied and full-flavored"

bitters very bitter or bittersweet liquids distilled from various herbs and roots

black dragon a type of oolong tea from Taiwan

black grapes this fruit is not really black; its colors range from red to purple, to deep blue violet

black tea tea that, when steeped, is strongly flavored and amber or coppery brown

blazer pans oval, rectangular, or round pans made of copper or stainless steel

blend procedure using a blender to mix a drink's ingredients thoroughly to develop a creamier, frothier texture

blended scotch a mixture of grain whisky and malt whisky; may contain as many as 40 different malt whiskies

blended whiskeys are light bodied with at least a 20% straight whiskey content blended with unaged neutral spirits

blind tastings the most complex type of wine tasting in that the tasters have no prior information about the wines; the wines are generally chosen from the same varietals or vintage

Bock stronger styles of beer that usually carry the symbol of the goat on their label

bone china a specific type of china that was primarily manufactured in England; contains a high proportion of bone ash that produces a greater translucency, whiteness, and strength

booth service in establishments with booths, guests are numbered clockwise around the booth for the purpose of organizing the kitchen order and food service; service begins with the guest seated farthest away from the server

bottle-conditioned a slight secondary fermentation that leaves a small yeast sediment visible in the bottle

bouquet how a wine smells; descriptors include *nutty, caramelized, woody, earthy,* and *petroleum*

Bourbon whiskey whiskey that contains a minimum of 51% corn; must be produced in the United States

brandy distilled wine

bread-and-butter service sequence service that varies from restaurant to restaurant, but typically serves bread as a welcoming gesture after the water has been poured or after the food order has been taken

brigade system a full-service team made up of as many as seven positions

brut French labeling term meaning "very dry"

bual madeiras that are medium sweet, aromatic, and reminiscent of nuts and dates

buffet service this service can be conducted in an à la carte or banquet environment; can be simple and unstaffed, modified deluxe with staff members serving beverages and assisting at the buffet, or deluxe with the most extensive service

buffetier this position supervises the correct positioning of the buffet tables and the organization of the display

bulk or charmat method the process by which wine is twice fermented in bulk and then bottled

busser also known as a server assistant, usually an entry-level position; primarily responsible for clearing and grooming the table

butler service similar to Russian service, but this style allows for the guest to select the food portion from the platter or tureen

butter service may be served in the form of wrapped patties, chips, curls, balls, florets, or whipped or compounded forms in a ramekin, dish, or specialty butter cup

buttery wine-tasting term meaning "soft, round whites with a bouquet of malolactic fermentation"

C

cachaça the spirit of Brazil; it is produced from sugar cane juice and shows distinctive vegetal notes

caffè breve a single shot of espresso and 4 ounces (118 ml) of steamed half-and-half, served in a 6-ounce (177-ml) cup with sugar on the side

caffè latte a single shot of espresso topped with steamed skim milk and a layer of frothed skim milk

caffeine a nitrogen compound found in plants; a mild stimulant that may increase the heart rate and cause sleeplessness in some people

Camellia sinensis a tree or shrub that grows best at higher altitudes under damp, tropical conditions; produces tea leaves

Campbeltown single malts have a distinctive, briny taste

Canadian whisky whisky that is six years old or older

canopy management a manipulation technique whereby the canopy is made up of the grape leaves that absorb sunlight for photosynthesis

cantina sociale Italian labeling term meaning "vine-growers cooperative"

cap the remaining grape stems and skin forced to the surface by carbon dioxide and heat

cappuccino a single shot of espresso, topped with 4 1/2 ounces (133 ml) of thick foam of steamed emulsified milk served in a 6- to 8-ounce (177- to 237-ml) cup or glass with sugar on the side

captain the position that supervises and organizes every service detail for his or her station or room, including the taking of orders and synchronizing the service for the station

carbonation/injection method the process by which carbon dioxide is injected into the wine vat and the wine is then bottled under pressure, much in the way that a soft drink is produced

carbonic maceration a red winemaking method common in, but not limited to, the Beaujolais region of Burgundy, France

cask-conditioned a secondary (final) fermentation that occurs in a 9-gallon metal cask (known as a Firkin), served without the use of additional CO2 pressure by a siphon system called a beer engine that gently pumps the ale into the traditional 20-ounce "pint"

casserole service service where the dinner plate and any accompaniments are preset on the table from the guest's right side

casual, family restaurants establishments that offer customers a relaxed atmosphere; feature moderate prices, home-style cooking, and child-friendly menus

cava Spanish labeling term meaning "sparkling wine, classic method"

cellared and bottled U.S. label meaning "10% or less of grapes crushed, made at the winery"

centerpieces decorative attention-getters used to enhance table presentations; five types—floral and foliage, edible, sculpted, ceramic, and lighting

certified organic coffees coffees that have been endorsed by an accredited, independent, third-party inspection

ceylon a full-flavored black tea with a delicate fragrance; ideal for iced tea because it does not turn cloudy when cold

chambré brought to room temperature

chaptalization a process where winemakers can correct an imbalanced condition with sugar prior to fermentation

chauffe-plats heat-retaining panels that may be stacked in a small battery at a convenient service point inside the dining room and then brought to the guéridon when required; used for keeping foods warm when tableside plating is performed

chef de rang the station captain

chef de service/chef de salle dining room manager or maître d'

cider traditionally, a fermented apple beverage; in the United States, the term usually refers to unfiltered non-fermented apple juice

cinnamon roast the lightest commercially available roast; these coffee beans have no visible oils on their surface, and the flavor and body are light

classic or traditional method method used to make champagne in the Champagne region of France

classico Italian labeling term meaning "from the center of a DOC wine region"

clip-on printed menu piece that attaches to the menu to highlight special selections

cloche service the French word for "bell;" refers to the bell-shaped domes that are used as sophisticated and impressive plate covers at fine dining restaurants

clos French labeling term meaning "walled vineyard"

coarse wine-tasting term meaning "lacking complexity or finesse"

cocktail a fairly short drink, made by mixing liquor or wine with fruit juices, eggs, and/or bitters

cocktail servers responsible for the sales and service of cocktails and beverages to guests

cognacs the world's elite brandies, stemming from the kinds of grapes from which they are distilled, the soil and climate of the Cognac region, and the skill of the distillers

cold compounding a simple method of flavoring liqueurs by blending in essences and concentrates to the base spirit

colheita Portuguese labeling term meaning "vintage"

colheita selecionada Portuguese labeling term meaning "high quality vintage wines with 1% higher alcohol"

Colombian milds grown primarily in Colombia, Kenya, and Tanzania, these coffees constitute 16% of the world's production and are graded principally on bean size

commis de débarrassage the waiter's assistant or busser

commis de rang the front waiter

commis de suite the back waiter

complex wine-tasting term meaning "multilayered and multifaceted"

compounded beverages drinks made by combining either a fermented beverage or spirit with a flavoring agent

compounding the process of blending spirits with other flavorings, including sweeteners. Conditioning process at the end of fermentation where the beer is chilled, causing the yeast to collect or flocculate at the bottom of the tank where it is then racked to a clean beer tank; allows the beer to further clarify and permits its flavors to subtly combine

congeners flavor and aroma compounds that get left behind

consumer protection providing that alcoholic beverages conform to the Standards of Identity and are produced, labeled, advertised, and marketed according to federal law

Continental style dining style defined by holding a fork and knife in the left and right hands respectively, cutting a bite-sized piece of food and then placing the food onto the tines of the fork and into the mouth, while still holding onto the knife in the right hand

continuous distillation method that utilizes a variety of column stills fashioned after the Coffey Still invented in 1827

conventional water method in this process, green coffee beans are treated with steam and water to open their cellular structure then flushed with a decaffeinating agent, such as methylene chloride or ethyl acetate

conversion also known as saccharification; at a critical temperature range, enzymes begin to break down the starches into fermentable and non-fermentable sugars; end product is a sweet, sticky liquid known as wort

cookingware broad term applied to earthenware, stoneware, porcelain, and china designed for cooking, baking, or serving; has a smooth, glazed surface and is strong and resistant to thermal shock

cooperages producers who make barrels using carefully controlled processes

cordials also known as liqueurs; highly refined, sweet spirits to which flavorings, such as fruits, nuts, herbs, or spices, have been added

corked wine-tasting term meaning "affected by cork mold TCA"

corretto a single shot of espresso with a 1-ounce (30 ml) shot of liqueur, served in a demitasse

cosecha Spanish labeling term meaning "vintage"

cover setting; may be as simple as a napkin and a bread-and-butter plate or as elaborate as a show plate, appetizer fork and knife, soup spoon, salad fork and knife, dinner fork and knife, a dessert fork and teaspoon, a bread and butter plate, a water glass and three wine glasses

creamy wine-tasting term meaning "denoting richness"

crema the amber foam that floats on top of a well-made espresso; a complex suspension of emulsified coffee oils, carbon dioxide bubbles, and suspended particles that float on the surface of freshly brewed espresso

crème called crème liqueurs for their creamy texture and sweet taste, crèmes take their name from the dominant flavoring ingredient, such as a fruit (crème de banana)

crianza Spanish labeling term meaning "aged a minimum of six months in oak and two years in the bottle"; Rioja and Ribera del Duero wines are aged one year in oak

crisp wine-tasting term meaning "good acidity"

cru French labeling term meaning "growth," indicating a specific vineyard of high quality; often used as a classification level as well

crumbing procedure used for clearing the table of crumbs and other food particles

crushing splitting the skins of grapes to release free-run juice

cultivar from a single growing region

cutlery originates from the old French word for "knife," *coutel;* the term *silver* is also frequently used because flatware was made from silver until the mid 19th century

cuvée juice from the first pressing of grapes; French labeling term meaning "blend"

D

darjeeling a full-bodied, black tea with a Muscat flavor, grown in the foothills of the Himalayas

dark rum traditional, full-bodied, rich rum, dominated by overtones of caramel

decanting allowing some wines to "breathe" so the full aromatic bouquet may be revealed

demitasse a half cup

Denominaçâo de Origem Controlada (DOC) classification similar to a French AC or Italian DOC wine; there are currently about 27 DOC regions. DOC wines are required to have a paper seal, the Selo de Origem, which is placed over the cork but under the capsule

Denominación de Origen (DO) equivalent to the AC designation of French wines; there are 78 DO appellations

Denominación de Origen Calificáda (DOCa) a classification that guarantees high standards and is comparable to an Italian DOCG wine

Denominazione di Origine Controllata (DOC) equivalent to the French AOC designation and governed by the same kinds of regulations; approximately 15% of Italy's total wine production is classified DOC or DOCG

Denominazione di Origine Controllata e Garantita (DOCG) this most stringent category requires that the producer follows the requirements of the DOC and guarantees what is stated on the label

dense wine-tasting term meaning "intensely flavorful and colorful"

destemming a process where the stalks and stems are generally removed in the winery after the grapes are harvested

deutscher sekt German labeling term meaning "quality sparkling wine with less alcohol than Champagne"

digestifs drinks served after dinner

dining room manager/maître d' position with close contact with every department of the restaurant; knows all aspects of the business

dinner-house restaurants establishments that provide moderately priced, easily prepared meals

dioise method a variation of the Méthode Ancestrale whereby the wine's first slow fermentation in sealed vats is filtered and bottled; the wine continues to ferment in the bottle until it reaches 7.5% alcohol

disc the upper surface of the wine

disgorgement also known as dégorgement; after the lees are in the bottle's neck, the bottle may further age upside down (sur pointe) or have its lees expelled when the neck of the bottle is placed upside down in a solution to freeze the top inch or two of wine and trapped lees

distilled spirits spirits born from the distillation of fermented beverages

district a larger geographic designation but one that still shares the same viticultural characteristics

dolce Italian labeling term meaning "sweet"

dollies carts of different shapes and sizes with casters, which are used for storing and transporting glassware

doppelbocks double-strength bock beers; carry two goats on the label

doppio a double shot of espresso served with sugar on the side

dosage also known as liqueur d'exposition; when the cap is removed, the gas expels the frozen plug and then the bottle is topped off with identical wine

doser to measure out the precise portion

dram shop laws also known as third-party liability laws; these regulations hold restaurants, bars, and their employees liable for illegal acts committed by patrons under the influence of alcohol served to them in the establishment

dried-out wine-tasting term meaning "the fruit flavors have dissipated"

dry hopping adding hops to beer after fermentation, when it is dry, and allowing the alcohol present to extract the aromatics without as much bitterness

dry method produces a sweet, smooth, complex coffee taste; this method is used primarily in areas such as Yemen or Ethiopia where robusta is the dominant coffee crop

DUI driving under the influence

dump box a receptacle with a screen over a drain that allows ice or water to drain without allowing garnishes and sundries to clog the plumbing

DWI driving while intoxicated

E

Earl Grey a popular choice for afternoon tea; Earl Grey is flavored with oil of bergamot

earthenware a porous ceramic product that is fired at comparatively low temperatures to produce an opaque body that is not as strong as stoneware or china; may be glazed or unglazed

earthy wine-tasting term meaning "aromas reminiscent of soil or minerals"

eiswein literally means "ice wine"; has the ripeness of BA and is harvested and pressed while frozen; remarkable acidity balancing sweetness

elegant wine-tasting term meaning "great finesse and balance"

engarrafado na origem Portuguese labeling term meaning "estate bottled"

English breakfast a full-bodied black tea; a robust blend of Indian and Sri Lankan teas

English service service in which the server spoons or plates portions directly onto a dish that is in front of the guest; in the United States, it is often called Russian service or silver service

entremets a small course, such as a sorbet or small dessert, served between courses

erzeugerabfüllung German labeling term meaning "estate bottled"

espresso a hot coffee beverage; a very complex beverage that requires the use of excellent quality beans produced and roasted to exacting specifications

espresso macchiato a single or double shot of espresso topped with a heaping teaspoon of steamed milk

estate bottled U.S. label meaning "100% grown, made, and bottled at the winery"

esters fruity notes

extra añejo a new category that signifies a 100% agave tequila has been aged for three years or more

F

Fair Trade Certified marketing label that states that the coffee was purchased in a fair trade agreement, supporting a livable income of $1.61 per pound for the coffee of small growers' and supporting organic farming in shade grown areas by offering further premium pricing

family-style service service where the chef prepares the dishes in the kitchen, and then servers place platters, casseroles, or tureens in the center of the guests' table with the appropriate serving utensils

faro an unusual style beer, to which rock candy is added for priming and to add sweetness.

fat wine-tasting term meaning "full-bodied but lacking acidity"

fattoria Italian labeling term meaning "estate"

fermented beverages beverages made from products like grains and fruits with alcoholic strengths ranging from 3.2%–14%

fine china a thin, translucent, vitrified product that is generally fired twice at relatively high temperatures; the highest quality tableware made for the domestic or retail trade

fine-dining restaurant an establishment that offers excellent food, fine wines, and highly skilled and attentive service

fining a clarification process used to give wines their brilliance

fino a sherry that is light with a very distinctive nose that stems from biological aging and the development of acetaldehyde (a compound the human body produces as it breaks down alcohol)

firm wine-tasting term meaning "structure backed by tannins, acid"

fixed, or focal, point the entrance of the restaurant; used to number tables, each seat, and thus each guest

flabby wine-tasting term meaning "lacks acidity or flat"

flatware all dining utensils, such as forks, spoons, and knives

flavored teas these teas gain their distinct character by the addition of the essence of citrus fruits, berries, vanilla, or other flavoring components to tea leaves

float the final liquid ingredient added to a drink after the usual procedure is performed; a float finds its own space and should not be incorporated into the drink

flor secondary yeast developed by all wines

food auctioning serving guests by asking what was ordered

fork a utensil produced in different sizes and shapes for specific functions; standard sizes include: dinner fork; appetizer fork; fish fork; and cocktail fork

formosa oolong a delicate, large-leafed oolong tea, with a taste reminiscent of ripe peaches

fortified wines wines that have had neutral spirits or brandy added to fermenting or a fermented wine to generally raise the level of alcohol from 16% to 22%

fragrant wine-tasting term meaning "flowery"

free-pour pouring spirits or liqueurs without using a measuring device, such as a jigger. Less accurate than a measured pour and therefore less professional

French press coffee maker that comes in 10- to 20-ounce (296- to 591-ml) sizes and uses medium grind coffee at a rate of 1–1 1/2 ounces (30–44 ml) per 20 ounces (591 ml) of boiling water

French roast heavily roasted coffee beans, bringing out a strong, characteristically bitter flavor and aroma

French service a key element of this service is tableside preparation and plating; servers prepare and plate special dishes tableside in full view of the guest

frizzante Italian labeling term meaning "sparkling"

front waiter assistant to the captain; performs all duties in the absence of the captain

fruit brandies brandies flavored with apples and pears; stone fruits, such as plums, peaches, or apricots; or berries, such as blackberries or elderberries

fruit-flavored liqueurs bearing a label that identifies the fruit that flavors the liqueur, such as Midori®, made with melon

Full City roast a medium coffee bean roast

G

garrafeira Portuguese labeling term meaning "aged two years in cask and one year in bottle for red wine, six months in wood and six months bottle aging for white wine"

generic or value brand a category, such as coffee brandy, that is a general category that any number of companies can produce

geuze a style of Lambic where new beer is added to older beer to increase the acidity and alcohol

gin an unaged liquor, made from grains, such as barley, corn, or rye, and flavored with juniper berries, coriander, and other herbs and spices

glassware used for serving beverages, includes common glass, fully tempered, and crystal

gold tequila the same as blanco tequila but with caramel added for color

golden rum also called amber rum, a medium-bodied liquor usually aged for at least three years in oak casks

gran reserva Spanish labeling term meaning "only from exceptional vintages;" whites are aged six months in oak and released in the fourth year; reds are aged two years in oak and three more in the bottle

grand cru classé a single vineyard site

grappa "firewater style" of pomace brandy produced primarily in Italy

green wine-tasting term meaning "a young wine or wine made from unripe grapes"

green beer the result when wort is oxygenated to allow the yeast to quickly begin fermentation

green tea tea that is unoxidized and yellowish green with a slightly bitter flavor; steaming or heating the leaves immediately after picking prevents enzymatic oxidation that turns tea leaves into black tea

grind describes how coffee beans are ground, from coarse to fine

groom the table clean the table before serving a course if needed, particularly after the entrée

guéridon a service cart or trolley; a portable work station used for all tableside preparations, including portioning, cooking, finishing, and plating

gunpowder the highest Chinese grade green tea; it is rolled into tiny balls

gutsabfüllung German labeling term meaning "estate bottled"

gyokuro the finest grade of exported Japanese green tea

H

halbtrocken German labeling term meaning "semi-dry"

hand tray a small tray used to carry a single small item, such as a drink, a napkin, or the check

hang time time spent on the vine

hard wine-tasting term meaning "tannic, too young"

head foam of the beer

heads compounds first released at the lowest boiling point during distillation; volatile and harmful

heart middle compounds released during distillation

heavy wine-tasting term meaning "overly alcoholic"

herbaceous wine-tasting term meaning "aromas of grass or herbs"

herbal teas also called tisanes; infusions made from herbs like chamomile, spearmint, ginseng, and lemon balm

high end or super premium brands alcohol based on brand recognition with a price range that is approximately $17.00 to $24.00 per liter bottle

high tea service also called afternoon tea; a light, midday meal that bridges the gap between early-morning breakfast and late-evening dinner

highballs beverages that consist of carbonated mixers, water or juices, and the appropriate liquor, served tall in highball glasses on ice

Highland malts whiskies that are generally sweeter and have more body and character than Lowland malts

highlighting drawing a guest's attention to particular menu items by using vivid and enthusiastic descriptions

hold/no garbage served without garnishes

holloware service pieces, examples include: chafing dishes, coffee urns, samovars, coffee pitchers, tea pots, creamers, and water pitchers

hops grain that helps preserve beer and impart aromas and bitterness

horizontal tastings type of tasting used to evaluate wines of a particular region or vintage

host/hostess a charming and inviting personality focused on greeting and seating guests using proper etiquette and protocol

hue the color of a wine

hybrids a cross between two species of grape, such as a *vitis vinifera* and an American species

I

ice frozen water; a key component of drinks

ice down-pour procedure to place ice in a service glass and then add liquor and the mixer; serve as is

ice machine machine that produces ice in a quantity that the establishment needs over the course of a day; should be able to fully recover the maximum quantity for the next business day

ice wine or eiswein as it is known in Germany (from where it originated); wine produced from grapes that have been allowed to freeze naturally on the vine before being harvested and pressed

imbottigliato all' castelo Italian labeling term meaning "estate bottled"

imbottigliato all' origine Italian labeling term meaning "estate bottled"

imperial a green tea grade from Sri Lanka, China, or India

Indicação de Proveniência Regulamentada (IPR) classification comparable to the French VDQS, phased out as of 2009

Indicazione Geographica Tipica (IGT) classification meant to upgrade 40% of Italy's table wines

infusion steeping flavoring agents through the use of heat

intermezzo a pause or intermission between two courses; usually a sorbet, sherbet, or granita is served to cleanse the palate between two courses of very different flavors

Irish whiskey a whiskey that must be produced in Ireland; must be triple distilled, usually in pot stills, from Irish grain; aged in wooden casks for three years

ironstoneware historic term for durable English stoneware; composition and properties are similar to those of porcelain, but lacks translucency and is off-white in color

Islay malt the most pungent and heavily peaty of all the malts; takes characteristics from the peat that is used to dry the barley and from the closeness to the sea

Italian roast the darkest stage of roasting; the coffee beans become carbonized and coated with a film of oil; usually reserved for espressos

J

jammy wine-tasting term meaning "overly ripe fruit"

jigger a legal measure of 1.5 ounces (45 ml)

job knowledge a thorough understanding of the workplace, including the layout, flow, equipment, communication between departments, and familiarity with the food, wine, and beverage menus

K

kabinett normal harvest time; lightest of Prädikat wines

kettling process in which the wort is brought to a boil and then simmered for about one hour to sterilize it

knife utensil mainly used for cutting food; comes in different shapes and may have a serrated or a flat edge; standard industry knives include: dinner knives, with or without serrated edges; steak knives; fish knives; appetizer knives; and bread-and-butter knives

Koji a type of mold that converts starches to fermentable sugars

koumis fermented mare's milk; one of the earliest alcoholic beverages

kräusen a process in which sweet unfermented wort is added to the aging beer to cause a secondary fermentation

L

lager German for "storage;" a style of beers that tolerate cooler temperatures

lager yeasts yeasts that ferment at cooler temperatures and rest at the bottom of the tanks and ferment slowly

lagering a process by which the beer is stored at cold temperatures and stubborn sugars continue to slowly ferment

lagers *Saccharomyces carlsbergensis;* a classification of beer yeast

lambic beers fermented with wild yeasts in oak casks and then bottled for a second fermentation with the addition of fruit purées, which add alcohol, color, and flavor to the finished beers after aging

lapsang souchong a black tea with a tarry, smoky flavor and aroma, best for afternoon tea or as a dinner beverage

lautering the process of removing the sticky sweet wort from the spent grains

lees the sediment containing dead yeast and other solids that collect in the bottom of the wine tank or barrel following fermentation

legs the residual wine that clings to the glass when swirled

light a drink containing a reduced amount of liquor but the normal amount of mixer

linen tablecloths; may be 100% natural fiber, a 50-50 blend of cotton and polyester, or 100% polyester

liqueurs also known as cordials; highly refined sweet spirits to which flavorings, such as fruits, nuts, herbs, or spices, have been added

long wine-tasting term meaning "a lingering finish"

lowland malts whiskies that are drier than Highland malts; usually lighter

lungo a single shot of espresso served in a demitasse with sugar on the side

M

maceration soaking a material in liquid to separate softened parts of the material from the harder ones; occurs when an aromatic or flavoring agent is immersed in the base spirit until the spirit absorbs the flavoring or aroma

Madeiras wine that is fortified after fermenting to produce dry styles or fortified during fermentation for sweeter styles

maderized wine-tasting term meaning "baked, flat, partly oxidized"

malmsey an English corruption of Malvasi; the sweetest Madeira, but balanced by high acidity with great, dark, and rich dried-fruit aromas

malolactic fermentation process caused by lactobacteria that converts harsher malic acid in the wine to softer lactic acid

malting an essential process in beer making with three steps: steeping, germinating, and kilning

manzanilla Spanish labeling term meaning "the lightest sherry;" similar to fino

marc pomace brandy that is produced in all wine-producing regions of France

marchio nazionale Italian labeling term meaning "indicating compliance with government controls for wines exported to the United States;" appears on a red seal on the neck of a wine bottle

marking a table restaurant jargon for adjusting flatware

Marsala wine that is fortified by alcohol and sweetened by concentrated grape must; has an alcohol content of 17%–19%

Märzen beers named after the month of March in which they were often brewed

mead fermented beverage made from honey; many use 100% honey, although some are combined with fermented grain, fruit, or cider

mechanical method coffee bean harvesting method used when the trees are planted on relatively flat terrain in even rows; the harvester straddles the row and agitates the trees to cause the beans to fall onto a conveyor belt

meniscus the concave curve that the disc forms

menu board used to highlight daily specials, usually handwritten

mescal an agave-based distillate

méthode ancestrale or rurale the most ancient way of producing sparkling wine; the wine is fermented at cold temperatures and bottled prior to its completion

milling grinding the barley into a coarse meal; performed before brewing to preserve freshness and flavor

mineral waters waters with flavors and tastes that provide consumers with a different experience

mis en bouteille au château French labeling term meaning "estate bottled"

mistela Spanish labeling term meaning "blend of grape juice and alcohol"

mixed drinks tall drinks, combined with liquor, and served over ice

mixology the study of cocktails, mixed drinks, and their ingredients

mixologists also known as bartenders; those who study mixology; highly skilled professionals who must master hundreds of beverage recipes and techniques

mocha a blend of coffee and chocolate; not to be confused with Moka brewing

mocktails nonalcoholic cocktails and alcohol-free beverage alternatives

modular brewer coffee maker that combines a fixed-location brewing module (the heating and volume control) with mobile brewed coffee containers of various capacities (5, 10, and 20 liters)

moelleux French labeling term meaning "sweet"

moka a common European form of home coffee frequently used in the United States

moldy wine-tasting term meaning "smells of mold"

mouthfeel the texture of a wine

mouthfilling wine-tasting term meaning "richly textured"

must the extracted juice, with minimal fragments of stems, seeds, or skins

mutage the point when fermentation stops and the wine retains sweetness

N

napperon a linen overlay placed over a tablecloth for both protective and decorative purposes

négociants merchants who not only distribute but also "raise" the wines purchased from the owners of small vineyards

nero Italian labeling term meaning "dark red"

noble hops classic European variety of hops

Non-EU wine the fifth level; for non-EU wines of lower quality that cannot include either a vintage or a variety on the label

Non-EU wine with Geographical Description the fourth level; refers to wines produced from specific recognized wine regions outside the European Union, such as a wine from Napa

non-verbal body language communication of attitudes and feelings, knowingly and sometimes unknowingly

O

oidium a powdery mildew fungus that devastated many of France's vineyards, particularly in Bordeaux

oloroso sherry that is fortified to 18% alcohol so that the flor cannot develop

on the rocks when a beverage is served on ice, usually in a rocks glass

oolong tea a type of tea that combines the characteristics of black and green teas; the leaves are partially oxidized, the process is interrupted, and the leaves are rolled and dried

oxidized when dissolved oxygen reacts with beer and darkens the color of lighter style beers

P

percolation process that allows the spirit to trickle through a flavoring agent much in the way that water trickles through ground coffee, except that the process is repeated

perlwein German labeling term meaning "a red or white wine with a light sparkle," usually by carbon dioxide injection

Perry cider made from pears

pétillant wine-tasting term meaning "spritzy, slight carbonation"

photosynthesis the process that allows the formation of sugars from carbon dioxide and a source of hydrogen–such as water–in the chlorophyll-containing tissues of plants exposed to light

phylloxera a microscopic pest accidentally introduced to vineyards in France through the importation of American vines by the French merchant Borty to the Rhône Valley

piña a large bulbous core which weighs up to 170 pounds (77 kg)

pince/pincer a technique used to pick up foods, such as rolls, and place them on a plate

pince technique used by a server to transfer appropriately sized and shaped food from a platter, breadbasket, or other serving dish to the guest's plate; requires a large serving spoon and fork, called a serving set

pips grape seeds

Pisco a specialty brandy of Peru and Chile

platter service when a chef prepares and places food on a platter in the kitchen

pomace brandies made from the pressed skin, pulp, seeds, and stems of grapes that remain after wine pressing. They are seldom aged and are usually harsh and raw

pool when all tips are placed together and shared equally by waitstaff of the same ranking or level

porcelain a term frequently used for china in Europe

portafilter filter holder where the espresso grind is held once dispensed

POS point-of-sale system

potable spirit ethyl alcohol

potage spoons soup spoons

pottery clay products made of unrefined clays; includes all fired clayware, but more specifically, it describes low-fired porous clayware

pouchong an oolong tea grown both in China and Taiwan

premier cru classé a single vineyard; in some regions, such as Bordeaux, it is the highest designation but may not consist of one contiguous vineyard

premières tailles second pressing of grapes

premium brand a proprietary brand, both domestic and imported, that falls into a higher price range based on its perceived quality and brand recognition

priming adding additional sugars to a beer to induce a secondary fermentation

prix fixe French for "fixed price;" the prix fixe menu consists of multiple courses offered at one fixed price regardless of the entrée selected

produced by U.S. label meaning "75% or more crushed, made, and bottled at the winery"

prohibition time in 20th century U.S. history when the sale and alcoholic beverages was prohibited and the production of sacramental or medicinal wines was limited

proof percentage of alcohol by volume; **(American method)** the strength of a liquor, which was at one time called "gunpowder proof"

proprietaries trademarked liqueurs that are made according to specific, usually highly secret recipes

proprietary brand a trademarked brand, such as Kahlúa, that no one else can replicate

Protected Designation of Origin (PDOs) regions registered with the European Union; each defined region is governed by regulations established by EU criteria and legislated within the respective member countries

Protected Geographical Indications (PGIs) second-level wines produced from a specific European country with less stringent rules

pulped natural method cherries are pulped and the beans are dried without going through a fermentation stage to remove the mucilage

pyrolosis as coffee beans reach a temperature of about 400°F (204°C), they begin to turn brown, and the oils, called coffee essence, start to emerge; this process produces the distinctive flavor and aroma of a coffee

Q

Qualitätswein bestimmter Anbaugebiete (QbA) largest German category, includes quality wines from one of the 13 specified wine regions; these wines tend to be light, fresh, and fruity and are allowed to be enriched with sweet reserve made of sterile unfermented must

Qualitätswein mit Prädikat (QmP) quality German wine with special distinction; further classified into six categories with special attributes in ascending order of ripeness at harvest: Kabinett, Spätlese, Auslese, Beerenauslese, Eiswein, and Trockenbeerenauslese

quick-service restaurants establishments that provide a limited, fairly consistent selection of food at very reasonable prices

quinta Portuguese labeling term meaning "estate"

R

racking process that gives controlled exposure to air; the limited contact with oxygen can help wines mature

rainwater Dry but slightly fruity and softer madeiras

réchaud a portable stove designed to cook, flambée, or keep food warm; usually made of stainless steel, copper, brass, or silver plate

redistillation distilling a spirit with a flavoring agent; used mostly for flavoring agents like seeds, citrus peel, or mint; employs an extraction method

region a broader geographic designation where there is less of a defined personality to the wine but one that is still recognizable as coming from a single region

Reinheitsgebot German laws, passed in the 1500s and still in effect today, to ensure the purity of beer; allows for the use of four main ingredients in beer: malted grains, water, hops, and (with its discovery by Pasteur) yeast

rémuage also known as riddling; process where the wine bottle is angled neck down at 45°, shaken, and turned by hand or by machines (gyropalettes); may last several weeks

reposado Tequila tequila that is aged 2 to 11 months; made from 100% blue agave

reserva Portuguese labeling term meaning "must be from a single vintage and have .5% higher alcohol than the minimum for DOC wines"

reserva (red) Spanish labeling term meaning "aged one year in oak and released in the fourth year"

reserva (white) Spanish labeling term meaning "aged six months in oak and released after three years"

restaurant a place where anyone can go to enjoy a complete meal prepared and served by someone else; the first restaurant was opened in Paris by A. Boulanger, a soup vendor, offering sheep's feet simmered in white wine

restaurant china a uniquely American blend of china and porcelain designed and engineered specifically for commercial operations

revenue collection the bureau that collects revenues from all producers of beverage alcohol on the basis of proof gallons

Rhum Agricole a style of rum produced from sugar cane juice rather than molasses

riddling also known as rémuage; process where the wine bottle is angled neck down at 45°, shaken, and turned by hand or by machines (gyropalettes); may last several weeks

rim the edge of the disc

riserva Italian labeling term meaning "DOC(G) wine with additional aging"

ristretto a shot of espresso, served in a demitasse with sugar to the side and a "water-back"

robe the color of a wine

robust wine-tasting term meaning "full-bodied"

robusta also called *coffea canephora;* hardier than Arabica with a significantly higher percentage of caffeine; grows well at lower altitudes in wet valleys and tropical forest climates

rosato Italian labeling term meaning "pink"

rosso Italian labeling term meaning "red"

rotling German labeling term meaning "rosé made from a blend"

rotwein German labeling term meaning "red wine"

rough wine-tasting term meaning "coarse, unpolished"

Ruby port port that is aged for two to three years

rum spirit made from fermented sugar juice, sugarcane syrup, sugarcane molasses, and other sugarcane by-products

Russian service when the food is carried from the kitchen, presented, and then finished and served to the guest

rye whiskey spirit produced from a grain mash containing at least 51% rye grain; it may not be distilled at higher than 160 proof and must be aged in new, charred oak barrels

S

saccharification also known as conversion; at a critical temperature range, enzymes begin to break down the starches into fermentable and non-fermentable sugars; the end product is a sweet, sticky liquid known as wort

Sake a fermented rice beverage most associated with Japan; a form of beer because it is made from grain

sapidity reflects the minerality present in water

schillerwein German labeling term meaning "QbA or QmP rosé wine from Württenberg"

Scotch whiskies blended Scotch whisky, vatted malt scotch, and single malt whisky

sec French labeling term meaning "dry"

secco Italian labeling term meaning "dry"

section also called a station; group of tables (usually three or four) for which a server is responsible

seed-based liqueur which, although one seed predominates, is usually made from several kinds of seeds

selective method picking only ripe berries from the tree by hand

semi-à la carte menu items are served together and priced as a combination on a menu; entrées may be priced with the inclusion of a salad or a side dish, while the appetizer, soup, dessert, and beverage are priced separately

semi-generic labels 14 different labels that are still used today from when U.S. producers first began to market their wines and were unable to label them by variety as they were for the most part made from inferior blends

semi-generically labeled lower-quality U.S. wines

sencha the most common Japanese green tea; popular in restaurants and sushi bars

sercial very dry and acidic madeiras

servers waiters, waitresses, wait-staff, sales associates, or cast members

service actions that enhance a guest's dining experience; goes beyond the mechanics or procedures for delivering food; a critical ingredient in a restaurant's recipe for success; conveys the feeling to guests that the server is there for them

service à la russe French service that incorporates elements of Russian service

service set a service spoon and fork that are used to pince or pincer

service tray a large, oval food tray that allows servers to carry several dishes to the table at one time; usually lined with cork or rubber to prevent slippage

serviceware all utensils, glassware, china, and service pieces used in the coverage of a meal

serviette a napkin-lined dinner plate used for to carry clean flatware to the table

scented tea a beverage made by blending aromatic petals from flowers, such as jasmine, lavender, gardenias, or magnolias with tea leaves

shake procedure agitating energetically with ice to disperse or incorporate heavy ingredients

sharp wine-tasting term meaning "high acid"

short wine-tasting term meaning "lacking finish"

shot a measure of liquid (quantity determined by the house) served straight up

shou mei a Chinese green tea known as "old man's eyebrows"

side work varies by establishment, but typically includes: setting tables for service; cleaning and refilling salt and pepper shakers; refilling sugar bowls; folding napkins for service; polishing flatware and glassware; vacuuming, sweeping, and washing floors; and cleaning doors, mirrors, and designated surfaces

silencer a custom-made pad or a linen or felt cloth that is placed on a table underneath the tablecloth; gives the linen a richer texture and reduces the noise level when plates are placed on the table

silky wine-tasting term meaning "smooth, mature tannins"

simple wine-tasting term meaning "lacking distinction"

simple syrup a solution created by dissolving superfine sugar with equal parts water

single batch distillation process that is not sufficient to concentrate the wash into a desirable and potable spirit

single malt a whisky brewed from a single batch of wort, also known as a green or mash beer, from one particular Scottish distillery

single-pot brewer coffee maker that yields 60 ounces (1.77 l), or 12 5-ounce (148-ml) servings and may be pour-through or plumbed systems

skirting specialized linen used for draping tables; available in three types of pleating: sheer, accordion, and box

skunky beer that has been exposed to light and oxidized by exposure to excessive UV or florescent light, which reacts with the hop compounds in the beer

smooth wine-tasting term meaning "mature tannins"

soft wine-tasting term meaning "mellow flavors"

sommelier wine steward; must have extensive knowledge of wines, spirits, and beverages.

sour wine-tasting term meaning "overly acidic, vinegary"

sour mash the result of the fermentation process, in which the mash is soured with a lactic culture such as that used for sourdough bread

sour mix the combination of simple syrup, lemon or lime juice, or egg whites used in preparing beverages

sours drinks that use a sour base, such as lemon or lime juice

sous cloche large, domed plate covers placed over the food and then removed by servers simultaneously in front of the guests to add to the drama of dining

sparging the process of rinsing all of the sugar from the grain hulls and using those same hulls as a natural filter to clarify the wort

spätlese late harvest wine with more intensity and richness; not necessarily sweet

specialty coffees beverages made with coffee; includes lattes, espressos, and cappuccinos

speed racks equipment designed for bartenders to easily access the most commonly used spirits and mixers; located in the well which is mounted to the sinks and the ice bin

speed-shake procedure agitating with ice in a service glass to disperse or incorporate heavier ingredients

speyside single malts whiskies with a distinctive, briny taste

spiced rum rum infused with spices

spiced teas a blending of flavorings, such as cinnamon, nutmeg, coriander, and cloves with tea leaves

spirit a highly alcoholic beverage produced by both fermentation and distillation

spoons type of utensil, includes: teaspoons; demitasse spoons; soup spoons; bouillon spoons; a sauce spoons; and other specialty spoons, such as long handled ice tea spoons.

spritz wine-tasting term meaning "prickly from carbon dioxide"

spumante Italian labeling term meaning "sparkling"

stackable plate covers covers specifically sized to plates so they remain firmly in place, allowing the server to carry as many as 12 to 16 entrées on an oval service tray

stalky/stemmy wine-tasting term meaning "bitter vegetal taste"

station also called a section; group of tables (usually three or four) for which a server is responsible

statler a square table that opens into a round

steam beer an American invention, made famous by Anchor Brewing Company in San Francisco; an ale brewed with a lager yeast that gives it good body, lower maltiness and esters, and emphasizes the fine hop aroma

still an apparatus in which alcohol is vaporized and then recondensed

stir procedure gently agitating with ice to chill and blend cocktail ingredients

stoneware a nonporous ceramic product made of unprocessed clays, or clay and flux additives, which are fired at elevated temperatures; quite durable and resistant to chipping but lacks the translucence and whiteness of china

STP standard transport plate used to carry flatware

straight up or neat served without ice; the drink never comes into contact with ice

straight whiskey whiskey produced by one distiller, aged at least four years, bottled at 100 proof, and stored in bonded warehouses under government supervision

strip method harvesting method used for coffee varieties that ripen their berries at the same time; one swift movement sweeps the branches clean of berries

suggestive selling sales technique that incorporates highlighting, assumptive selling, and upselling

sulfurous wine-tasting term meaning "smells of burnt matches or bad eggs, too much sulfur dioxide"

supercritical carbon dioxide decaffeination method that uses carbon dioxide as the solvent agent extracting 96%–98% of the caffeine

superiore Italian labeling term "DOC(G) wine with 0.5% or more alcohol than is required"

supple wine-tasting term meaning "sensuously smooth"

swiss water processing method similar to the conventional water method but uses charcoal filtration rather than chemicals to remove caffeine

T

table accessories a variety of items that make serving convenient and dining more enjoyable for guests: ashtrays and matches, salt and pepper shakers, and condiments, such as vinegar, ketchup, sugar, and creamers

table d'hôte a menu in which the price of a multiple-course meal changes according to the entrée selected

table etiquette rules founded on respect and consideration for other diners, and the property of others

table manners behaviors considered acceptable or unacceptable by most in today's society

table tent printed menu piece that sits on the table; highlights special selections

table wine a third level, referring only to European-produced wines

tableside service type of service that includes assembling, saucing and garnishing, sautéing and flambéing, and carving and deboning

tableware all utensils, glassware, china, and service pieces used in the coverage of a meal

tails compounds released last during distillation

tall/long a drink served in an 8- to 16-ounce (240- to 500-ml) highball or zombie glass; the amount of the mixer is increased, not the amount of liquor

tannin a chemical compound found in grape skins

Tawny port port that has aged for at least 6 but up to 40 years

tea a beverage made from an infusion of the leaves of *Camellia sinensis* prepared in boiling water

tencha powdered green tea used in Japanese tea ceremonies

Tennessee whiskey whiskey that is leached or filtered through sugar maple charcoal in mellowing vats before it is diluted with demineralized water and aged in charred oak barrels

tenuta Italian labeling term meaning "estate"

Tequila a distillate made from the fermented and distilled juice of the blue agave plant

terroir French term loosely translated as "territory"; in viticulture, terroir encompasses all the elements that comprise growing conditions–soil, climate, topography, geology, and hydrology

tête de cuvée free run of juice, reserved for prestige wines, such as Dom Pérignon

thin wine-tasting term meaning "lacks body"

third-party liability laws also known as dram shop laws; regulations that hold restaurants, bars, and their employees liable for illegal acts committed by patrons under the influence of alcohol served to them in the establishment

three-tier system system where most restaurants and other beverage establishments, whether on or off-premises, purchase wine from distributors, who in turn, buy from suppliers or importers

tiger stripes a visible pattern of thin lines on good crema

tip credit monies that make up the difference between the hourly wage paid to servers and the federal minimum wage

tips said to be an acronym for "To Insure Proper Service" or "To Insure Prompt Service"

tisanes also called herbal teas; infusions made from herbs, such as chamomile, spearmint, ginseng, and lemon balm

trade practices practices that promote voluntary compliance

transfer method when wine is aged on the lees but is neither riddled nor disgorged but filtered and dosed in bulk before being rebottled

trappist beers brewed by monks to support the monastery; only six monasteries (five in Belgium and one in Holland) can use the term *Trappist*

tray stands also known as jacks; collapsible frames on which to rest trays; frames may be plastic, wood, or metal

trocken German labeling term meaning "dry"

Trockenbeerenauslese (TBA) grapes that are affected by botrytis and individually picked, making a very rich, sweet, honeylike wine

trub a deposit that forms on the bottom of the kettle

truth-in-menu guidelines twelve guidelines used to help servers avoid misrepresenting the products they are selling

tureen service a part of Russian service used when soup is ordered; with the tureen in the left hand, approach and serve guests from the left, drawing the handle of the soup ladle toward yourself. Service proceeds counterclockwise around the table

U

ullage airspace in a barrel

ultra-premium or luxury brands alcohol brand categories in the $25.00 to $40.00 per liter bottle price range; typically considered the highest quality brands

up when a beverage is prepared with ice to chill, but served strained from the ice in a stemmed glass

upselling a technique that promotes the sale of items of a better quality or of a larger size than what was originally contemplated by the consumer

V

varietal coffee a coffee that comes from a single varietal region

vatted malt also called blended malt; malted scotches or pure malt scotches are blends from more than one distillery

VDP Verband Deutscher Prädikat und Qualitätsweingüter; association symbolized by an eagle holding a cluster of grapes

vegetal wine-tasting term meaning "vegetable aroma" (e.g., bell pepper)

velvety wine-tasting term meaning "rich silkiness"

vendange/récolte French labeling term meaning "vintage/harvest"

vendange vert also known as green harvest; technique used to reduce yields through pruning and crop thinning

vendemmia Italian labeling term meaning "vintage"

veraison the onset of ripening when the berries develop color and begin to soften

verdelho Dry and smoky madeiras

vertical tastings wine tastings used to evaluate wines of different vintages, usually from a limited number of producers

Vienna roast describes both a medium coffee roast that is chocolate brown with dark speckles and a particular blend of different roasts

village named after a village or commune but may incorporate the surrounding region

Vin de Pays refers to "country wine;" created to upgrade wine-growing regions from table wine production

vin doux naturel naturally sweet wine; the product of mutage

vineyard name U.S. label meaning "95% or more grown at the particular vineyard"

Vinho de Mesa table wine; the lowest classification

Vinho Regional classification comparable to France's Vin de Pays

Vino Comarcal (VC) indicates one of 23 regional appellations for wines that are outside the bounds of a DO

Vino da Tavola (VDT) table wine; encompasses 85% of Italy's total wine production

Vino de la Tierra (VdlT) equivalent to the French Vin de Pays; these wines have a regional character and are striving for DO status

Vino de Mesa (VdM) table wine classification; the lowest classification

vino de pago classification for "estate wines" that are particularly distinguished whether in official DOs or technically not so

vino joven Spanish labeling term meaning "intended for immediate drinking upon release," in the spring following the vintage

vintage from the French word *vendange* meaning "harvest;" U.S. label meaning "95% of grapes must be from that vintage year;" a vintage reflects the weather for a particular year

Vintage Port port made from the best available grapes from a single vintage year; aged 2–3 years in wood and then require at least 10–15 years in the bottle

viticulture the science of growing grapevines

Vitis vinifera species of grapes that produces most wines

vodka spirit produced primarily from grain, potatoes, molasses, or beets; a neutral spirit that mixes well with other beverages

Volstead Act U.S. law that made the production and sale of alcoholic beverages illegal or prohibitive

W

waiter's friend a corkscrew that has a knife blade to cut the capsule of the wine bottle and sharpened edge; it should have five turns to the screw, and the server should ensure that the worm is not bent, in order to maximize its effectiveness

waitron a term coined in the 1980s; reflects a common view that servers take orders robotically and serve without any social skills

wash fermented liquid

watery wine-tasting term meaning "weak and thin"

weissherbst German labeling term meaning "rosé QbA or QmP wine made from a single variety of black grape"

well a shelf mounted to the sinks and the ice bin; houses the speed rack

wet method the process by which coffee processors first depulp the berries mechanically then soak them in tanks of water until fermentation softens the mucilage layer for easy removal

whiskey spirit made from a grain mash, distilled at 90% alcohol by volume (ABV) or less

white grapes any light-skinned grape that ranges from pale green to gold

white rum this rum is generally the highest in alcohol content and is light-bodied and clear, with a subtle flavor

white tea a tea that is unoxidized and silvery in color with the highest concentration of caffeine; made from the youngest shoots or buds of specific tea varietal plants

white tequila tequila labeled blanco or plata (silver); it is unaged or slightly aged and filtered to remove color

wild yeasts yeasts that give the finished beer an acidic tang

wine steward position with extensive knowledge of wines and spirits and who may be in charge of the purchasing and service of wine

winzergenossenschaft German labeling term meaning "wine growers' cooperative"

wit a style of wheat beer that uses adjunct flavorings of coriander, orange peel, and other such spices and herbs; sometimes known as "Belgian Wheat"

Wood Port port aged in wood and that is ready to be consumed shortly after it is bottled

woody wine-tasting term meaning "odors of old casks"

wort the end product produced through conversion; a sweet, sticky liquid

Y

yeast a single-celled fungus that is essential to fermentation

Z

zesty wine-tasting term meaning "crisp and fresh"

INDEX

Subject

CREDITS

Adam Woolfitt/CORBIS, **99**

Aveleda, **176**(b), **198**(a, b)

Barry Wiss of Trinchero Family Estates, **186**(b)

Boyd's Coffee Company, **30**

Buzzards Bay Brewery, **104**(e)

Cardinal International, **23**(a-t), **100**

Castello Banfi, **172**(a), **176**(j), **187**(a), **192**(a-c), **193**(c)

Charles O'Rear/CORBIS, **168**(c-f), **169**(d)

Chateau Ste. Michelle, **176**(k), **182**(a-c)

Cintas Corporation, **36**

Ciril Hitz, **49**(b-e)

Classic Wine Imports, **176**(o, q)

Coors Brewing Company, **104**(d)

Culinary Arts Museum at Johnson & Wales University, **94**, **150**(c)

Dinker Ackerlacker, **104**(a)

Dogfish Ale Craft Brewing Company, **95**(a), **104**(f)

Dudson USA, **25**(a-v), **26**(d), **89**

Edward Korry, **95**(b), **106**(b, c) **108**(b), **110**(a-c), **113**(a), **115**(b), **150**(a), **151**(b), **153**(b), **161**(c, d), **165**(c), **167**, **169**(a), **177**, **190**(a, b), **200**(a, b)

E. & J. Gallo Winery, **152**(a-c), **167**(h), **176**(c, g, l, p), **178**(e), **184**(b), **185**(a), **186**(a), **188**, **193**(b), **196**(a), **197**(a)

Firestone Walker Brewing Company, **104**(h)

Franziskaner, **104**(b)

George Howell Coffee Company, **84**(a), **85**

George Killian's, **104** (c)

Illy USA, **48**(b), **49**(a,f), **82**(a-c), **86**, **87**(c)

Kobrand Corporation, **113**(d), **176** (d, m), **177**(t), **178**(a, b), **179**(a, b), **183**(a, b), **185**(b, c, d), **187**(c), **189**(a), **191**(a, c, d, f, g), **193**(a)

Marc DeMarchena, **9**, **11**(a, b), **12**, **14**, **20**, **22**, **33**(a), **57**(e), **84**(b), **87**(b), **108**(a), **120**(c), **125**(c), **150**(b, d), **151**(a), **153**(a), **155**, **156**, **158**, **159**, **160**(a, b), **161**(a, b, d, e), **162**(a, b), **163**(a-c), **164**, **165**(a, b, d), **166**(a-d), **169**(b-d), **171**(b), **181**, **189**(b), **194**(c)

Moët Hennessy USA, **113**(b, c), **171**(a)

Owen Franken/CORBIS, **168**(a)

P. J. Valckenberg, **169**(e),**176**(e, f), **177**(s, w), **198**(a, b), **194**(a, b), **195**

Pasternak Wine Imports, **177**(r, u, y), **178**(d), **187**(b), **191**(b, e), **197**(a)

Quady Winery, **176**(g, n)

Robert Mondavi Winery, **177**(x)

Rodney Strong Vineyards, **168**(g), **176**(i), **178**(c)

Ron Manville for Johnson & Wales University, **Front cover**

Sierra Nevada Brewing Company, **104**(g, i, j)

TransFareUSA, **83**(b)

Trinchero Family Estates, **176**(a), **177**(v), **180**, **184** (a, b, d)

United States Department of Agriculture–Agricultural Marketing Services **83**(a)